SYNTHETIC WORLDS

SYNTHETIC
WORLDS

THE BUSINESS AND CULTURE OF ONLINE GAMES

EDWARD CASTRONOVA

THE UNIVERSITY OF CHICAGO PRESS • CHICAGO AND LONDON

*Edward Castronova is associate professor of telecommunications
at Indiana University, where he specializes in the economic and social impact
of multiplayer online video games.*

The University of Chicago Press, Chicago 60637
The University of Chicago Press, Ltd., London
© 2005 by The University of Chicago
All rights reserved. Published 2005
Printed in the United States of America

14 13 12 11 10 09 08 07 06 05   1 2 3 4 5

ISBN 0-226-09626-2 (cloth)

Library of Congress Cataloging-in-Publication Data

Castronova, Edward.
  Synthetic worlds : the business and culture of online games / Edward
  Castronova.
    p. cm.
  Includes bibliographical references and index.
  ISBN 0-226-09626-2 (cloth : alk. paper)
  1. Internet games—Social aspects. 2. Internet games—Economic
  aspects. I. Title.
  GV1469.15.C43 2005
  794.8′14678—dc22

                                              2005007796

♾ The paper used in this publication meets the minimum requirements
of the American National Standard for Information Sciences—Permanence
of Paper for Printed Library Materials, ANSI z39.48-1992.

For Nina

CONTENTS

ACKNOWLEDGMENTS

The ideas in this book emerged during a stressful time in my professional and personal life; thus while it's often difficult for an author to thank everyone who has helped make a collection of ideas into a manuscript, it's impossible in my case. The conversation going on these days about our future life in cyberspace is open-ended, and occurs in blogs, gamer websites, conference hallways, newspapers, hotel elevators, wedding receptions, you name it. If you've ever shared a bit of your thoughts with me about the synthetic world, whether it was a game you were playing, a business idea you had, or a prediction about the future, I am grateful you did so. Without those conversations, this book would have been impossible to write.

I've had the fortune of working on the book in two excellent academic departments. Most of it was completed while I was working at California State University, Fullerton, where I would like to thank chairs of the Economics Department David Wong and Stewart Long, as well as the dean of the College of Business and Economics, Anil Puri. They enthusiastically supported what must have seemed, at first, quite an odd project. I'd also like to thank CSUF's lawyer, security personnel, and the internal review office for helping me deal with an early threat to the project in the form of an anonymous and threatening cease-and-desist phone call (which we traced to Sweden of all places). The manuscript was completed while I was working at Indiana University, where I would like to thank the chair of the Department of Telecommunications, Walter Gantz, as well as Herb Terry, Elena Bertozzi, and my first research assistant, Byungho Park, for making the transition as comfortable as possible under the circumstances.

Thinking of the early stages of the project, I'd like to thank the 3,619 *EverQuest* players who took my survey for their honest responses, and the site Everlore.com for publicizing the survey and the resulting working paper. It was the fanbase of *EverQuest* that first began reading the paper and passing the URL on to others, generating a hit storm that eventually got the attention of *New Scientist* and *Slashdot*. My thanks to all those who took an interest in the paper in those early hours.

I'd like to thank those outside the video game industry who took an early interest in this research, and whose queries and invitations bolstered my conviction that the subject was important. In the area of defense and security research,

I would like to thank Richard P. O'Neill, Jack Thorpe, and Mike Van Lent for early conversations. Within academia, there was no more helpful early supporter of this project than Professor Susanne Lohmann of the Department of Political Science at UCLA. The esteemed information theorist Jack Hirshleifer of the UCLA Economics Department also provided valuable moral support at an early stage. Other members of the Southern California digerati to whom I am indebted include, at UCLA: John Baldrica, Harvey Harrison, Peter Kollock, Dario Nardi, and Francis Steen; at USC: John Seely Brown and Mimi Ito; at UC Irvine: Tom Buchmueller, Celia Pearce, and Walt Scacchi; at Claremont Graduate School: Paul Zak.

When this project appeared on my plate, I had become a researcher with a quirky toolbox of skills and a great deal of freedom to explore topics outside the mainstream, which turned out to be a very fortunate and valuable positioning. For that, I owe a debt of gratitude to a number of senior colleagues, especially Robert Haveman and Gert G. Wagner. Haveman, my thesis adviser, kept encouraging my work despite its tendency to strike off in strange directions; Wagner, a long-time friend from Berlin, provided generous, open-subject research funding at several extremely critical points, enabling me to overcome thoughts of abandoning the profession entirely. Other German colleagues I'd like to thank include Hans-Werner Sinn, whose offer of research affiliate status at the CESifo institute enabled me to publish my papers through SSRN, as well as Wolfhard Dobroschke-Kohn, Joachim Frick, Richard Hauser, Bernhard Kirchgässner, and Johannes Schwarze. Former colleagues in the United States I'd like to thank for their support and advice through the years include David Austen-Smith, the late Jeff Banks, Randall Calvert, Andrew Dick, John Duggan, W. Lee Hansen, Eric Hanushek, the late Bill Riker, Timothy Smeeding, David Weimer, and Barbara Wolfe. I'd like to thank John Mueller for being always reasonable but also unafraid to speak about things other people want to keep out of the discussion.

I'm thrilled to be able to thank all of the people in the research community that is now springing up around the topic of massively multiuser spaces on the Internet. First and foremost I'd like to thank the founders of Terra Nova, Julian Dibbell, Dan Hunter, and Greg Lastowka, for working together so pleasantly and for contributing so much to my intellectual life. And I have been truly honored to be on the same blog-roll as the inventor of virtual worlds, Richard Bartle. Thanks also to the other contributors on Terra Nova: Betsy Book, Timothy Burke, Nate Combs, Cory Ondrejka, Jim Purbrick, Ren Reynolds, Dave Ricky, Constance Steinkuehler, T. L. Taylor, Nick Yee, and the dozens of commenters, tipsters, and fans who make the site and the community it has accumulated such a fun and interesting place to be, especially Angela Butler, Bridget Goldstein, and Mark Terrano.

In the wider community of scholars, writers, and pundits interested in games, I've benefited tremendously from interactions with legal scholars Jack Balkin, Jennifer Granick, Larry Lessig, Beth Simone Noveck, and Richard Salgado; Copenhagen game scholars Espen Aarseth, Jonas Heide Smith, and Jesper Juul; US game scholars Sasha Barab, Henry Jenkins, Nora Paul, and Kurt Squire; communications experts Sandra Braman, Byron Reeves, and Clay Shirky; economists Ian MacInnes and Arun Sundararajan; anthropologists Alex Golub and Thomas Malaby; tech writers Fred Hapgood and Clive Thompson; Yahoo! research scientist Gary Flake; and linguist/philosopher Peter Ludlow. Psychologist Sara Konrath suggested several sources for information on the psychological effects of video games, an area well outside my specialties.

In the game industry, I've been lucky to gain some insights into the nuts and bolts of synthetic worlds from the masters of creation, including Greg Costikyan, Randy Farmer, Robin Harper, Scott Jennings, Raph Koster, Christopher Lawrence, Alex Macris, Jessica Mulligan, Patricia Pizer, Philip Rosedale, Chris Sherman, Michael Steele, Andy Tepper, Gordon Walton, and Eric Zimmerman.

The manuscript was greatly improved through the careful editing, and substantive suggestions as well, of Russell Harper, and I'd like also to thank Alex Schwartz of the University of Chicago Press, for responding positively to what must have seemed a bizarre initial pitch.

Finally, I need to thank my family more than anyone else: Nina, my wife, and Luca, my son. We've had such a stressful time over the last few years, and my writing a book has not helped. While it is true that I wrote the book with Luca's grandchildren in mind—people who will spend so much of their time in the Secondary World whose waves are now lapping at the doorstop of our Primary World—that doesn't erase the fact that my time on the book was not time with my family. I could never have completed the manuscript, or had the travels and conversations necessary to do it properly, if Nina had not been so gracious and supporting of my work in such a difficult time. And Luca, in his infant innocence, gave me a constant reminder of the importance of the subject, as well as the importance of just getting it done and resetting my time priorities afterward. My wife and son are a great gift, precious, and I can never thank them enough for just being in my life. They have a larger share of my heart than words can express, but now that the hardest times are behind us, I can finally express my love in terms of minutes, hours, days, weeks, months, and years.

INTRODUCTION:
THE CHANGING MEANING OF PLAY

Why Are You Paging Through a Book about Games?

According to the jacket material, this book claims to take a serious look at online computer games. You are actually reading it, at least the first few lines of the introduction, and if you are a serious, hardheaded person like me, you must be feeling a bit strange. I feel a bit strange writing it. Three years ago I was an ordinary economist pursuing generally ordinary economics research. Now, however, I am pushing deeper and deeper into a realm of experience that's growing faster than I can examine it, a fantastic cosmos of dragons and rayguns and beautifully crafted human bodies. It is also a universe that hosts massive flows of real human intercourse—information, commerce, war, politics, society, and culture. I am speaking, of course, of the phenomenon known as "massively multiplayer online role-playing games" (MMORPGs), places where thousands of users interact with one another in the guise of video game characters, on a persistent basis: many hours a day, every day, all year round. As such, these places are like real cities and fairy-tale cities at the same time, and some of the numbers they are producing might surprise you:

- Users drive around in these worlds using a video game character in much the same the way we use a car to drive around the Earth. Some characters are better than others: faster, better looking. They can be bought and sold, most often on eBay. As I write this, a Jedi-type character from a fantasy world based on *Star Wars* costs over $2,000.
- Typical users spend 20–30 hours per week inside the fantasy. Power users spend every available moment. Some 20 percent of users in a recent survey (see

chapter 2) claimed that their fantasy world was their "real" place of residence; the Earth was just a place you go to get food and sleep (see chapter 2).

- This used to be a niche phenomenon. But synthetic worlds are appearing at the rate of Moore's Law (i.e., doubling every two years), and the current number of users is 10 million people, at a minimum (see chapter 2).
- Each synthetic world has a play-money currency inside to facilitate player-to-player transactions. These currencies have begun to trade against the dollar in eBay's Category 1654, Internet Games. Many of them now trade at rates higher than those of real Earth currencies, including the yen and the Korean won.
- The commerce flow generated by people buying and selling money and other virtual items (that is, magic wands, spaceships, armor) amounts to at least $30 million annually in the United States, and $100 million globally (see chapters 4 and 6).
- In Asia, people who have lost virtual items because of game-server insecurities and hacks have called the police and filed lawsuits. The police have made arrests; courts have heard cases; and plaintiffs have won (see chapters 6, 7, and 11).

It is hard to look at these developments without concluding that something quite bizarre must be going on, and perhaps something just as important as the subjects I used to work on as an ordinary economist. Thus while I have little doubt that I am just as ordinary as I was before, the subjects I write about have become quite extraordinary. Indeed, *this* subject, video games, is so extraordinary that it has attracted the attention of one such as yourself—a person who does not normally think of video games as anything more than child's play. The aim of the book is to change that view. If you had seen what I have seen in the last few years, you would sense, as I do, that the line between games and real life has become blurred. Together we might begin to understand how much this blurring will change the nature of daily life for our children and grandchildren.

The thesis of the book is that the synthetic worlds now emerging from the computer game industry, these playgrounds of the imagination, are becoming an important host of ordinary human affairs. There is much more than gaming going on there: conflict, governance, trade, love. The number of people who could be said to "live" out there in cyberspace is already numbering in the millions; it is growing; and we are already beginning to see subtle and not-so-subtle effects of this behavior at the societal level in real Earth countries. Even if you haven't paid much attention to multiplayer video game worlds up to now, soon enough, I think, you will. We all will.

Perhaps the easiest way to convince yourself that this hypothesis is, or is not, true would be to go visit one of these places yourself. Flip through the book; certain names will come up more than a few times: *Ultima Online, EverQuest, Lineage, Second Life, Dark Age of Camelot, Star Wars Galaxies.* Or visit your local game store; as this book goes to press, several hundred thousand people are exploring the brand-new *World of Warcraft.* You could find the software, pay for subscriptions, and head out into these places to see what may be seen. I predict, however, that you might find this means of discovery awfully expensive in terms of time. You would be trying to study a completely different culture, one for which we have no prior literature and no guidebooks. The natural first reaction would be bewilderment, of course. It was for me. Only after hundreds of hours of immersion did I begin to have any success understanding what is happening there and what it might mean.

Part 1 of this book attempts to shorten the process of discovery by taking the reader on a guided tour of synthetic worlds. I've found that for many audiences, mere exposure to this phenomenon as it is today is sufficient to render obvious some of the deeper consequences, for those aspects of human life and thought that the listener knows most about. Anthropologists see new cultures, entrepreneurs see new markets, lawyers see new precedents, and social and political experts see new pressures and looming crises. Part 1 attempts to deliver a basic understanding of what this technology is, how it works, how people use it, and the kinds of social institutions that arise because of it. At that point, the long-run implications—and as a corollary the merit of video games and interactive media as objects of serious study and reflection—may already be apparent. We do not have to look very far into the future to see changes looming.

As a quick test, imagine someone told you that there was a technology that could reasonably be referred to as "practical virtual reality." This technology would allow just about anyone, at a modest cost, to spend as much time as they wished in some kind of alternate reality space that was built and stored on a computer. We are not talking about a Holodeck here; this place isn't "real" by any means.[1] However, it does feel real enough to the users that they can fairly easily immerse themselves in it, for hours on end, month after month, year after year, in a sort of parallel existence. Were such a practical virtual reality possible, we can have no doubt that profit-seeking enterprises would figure out a way to make it work. They would build around certain themes and construct entertaining activities, to draw people in. How many people might be drawn into such places for hours and hours on end? Imagine there were a large number of just-good-enough fantasy worlds for people to go live in, worlds with all kinds of themes, from knights in armor to athletes to space travelers to mobsters to almost-credible lovers. How many people?

The fact is, this "just-good-enough" virtual reality technology exists today. By the time you read this, we will have already moved beyond it, to "almost-seductive." And if you didn't answer "just a few" to the question that closed the preceding paragraph, you might want to take a break here, and then at the end of part 1, and ask yourself how things might soon be changing in your area of interest.

As I argue in part 2, it is not hard to imagine that there will be major effects in many areas. The overarching idea in the second half of the book is that the emergence of these practical virtual reality spaces will have significant consequences primarily because events inside and outside them cannot be isolated from one another. It is not too shocking to imagine that the real world can affect the virtual world; when it rains on a football game, the game is changed. But we are now learning that games may become so important to some people, at some times, that events inside games have effects outside of them. Should more people become involved in practical virtual reality spaces, these external effects will become quite serious on a macro level. While one could make a case for these external effects in a number of areas, especially culture, sociality, relationships, and individual emotion, I will focus more narrowly on my own areas of interest in the social sciences: economics, politics, and security. In my opinion, major changes in these areas would be quite serious indeed, well worth contingency planning. Part 2 of the book is primarily concerned with assessing the potential for such changes.

Then in the final part of the book I draw broader conclusions for public policy. Again, imagine you had mastered a technology of practical virtual reality. What would you do with it? It quite clearly could be good or bad for humanity, depending on its usage. Given that the technology does exist, and is being driven onward by a lucrative, savvy industry, we should be aware that while we may have quite a few years to think about all this, it behooves us to start thinking right now, before the time to make important decisions arrives.

What Is a *Synthetic World*?

So far I have been referring to the technology in question as a "practical virtual reality" tool, a way to make decently immersive virtual reality spaces practically available to just about anyone on demand. For the most part, I will refer to these places as *synthetic worlds*: crafted places inside computers that are designed to accommodate large numbers of people. The specific incarnations that I will talk about in this book are places created by video game designers. Chances are, if you are under 35 years old you know exactly what that means, because you have been playing in synthetic worlds since you were a kid and you know that they have moved online. If you're not part of the video game generation, you might have trouble seeing the connection. Your kids or grandkids play video games on their TVs, on desktop computers, on little handheld devices—what does that have to do, you might ask, with "virtual reality"?

Such a question makes good sense because games and handheld video devices are not part of our standard image of what virtual reality is all about. For most people, I suspect, the first thing that comes to mind when one thinks of "virtual reality" is a laboratory filled with expensive gear. You know, the bulky vision-goggles that go over your head, the web of wires and straps for your arms and legs, the funny half-chair, half-bike apparatus that you wiggle around on, the six-sided surround-sound rooms at Disneyland that make you feel like you're standing in the Amazon jungle or on the Moon. Jennifer Lopez in *The Cell* (2000): bodies suspended on wires, wrapped in a second skin that looks somewhat like ribbed beef jerky. *That's* virtual reality, right? Well, no. At least, not entirely, not any more. At one time, virtual reality was indeed a matter of basic lab research and ingenious sensory-input devices, a scientific research program that made headlines in the early 1990s. But the virtual reality I am talking about has emerged independently of that program; it grew out of the game industry, without any influence from the scientists. Game developers had been exposed to the same basic ideas of virtual reality that everyone else had—Gibson's *Neuromancer* (1984), Vernor Vinge's *True Names* (1981), and so on—but they took them in a completely different direction. The difference was this: the science program focused on sensory-input hardware, while the gamers focused on mentally and emotionally engaging software. As you can imagine, a person can become "immersed" either way: either the sensory inputs are so good that you actually think the crafted environment you're in is genuine, or, you become so involved mentally and emotionally in the synthetic world that you stop paying attention to the fact that it is only synthetic. It turns out that the way humans are made, the software-based approach seems to have had much more success. It certainly is more popular, and also cheaper for users and developers. And so, as we head into the twenty-first century, the dominant paradigm for virtual reality is not hardware but software, and that means that any device, even a crude one, that can engage a person in the happenings it portrays, is a little virtual reality tool. When children play at their little handhelds and when executives fiddle around with the games on their smartphones, there's immersion going on, a virtual reality brought about by games rather than devices.

Now, the contrast between the scientific and the gaming approach to virtual reality is important to the intellectual placement of a book like this, but it's also something of a tangent, mostly because the interesting thing about these two fields is how little they have to do with one another. There's a man-bites-dog story here: virtual reality lost much of its status as an exciting technology over the past decade, and while it is now re-emerging with considerable force, what's strange is that it is not emerging from the ruins of the old paradigm. Rather, it is growing up in a completely different place. The story of how these development tracks emerged independently of one another is worth telling, at least for those interested in virtual reality in general and its intellectual history. However, the target audience for this book is not the virtual reality specialist but rather professionals in business, government, and education, parents, journalists, and academics, basically folks in other walks of life for whom this new and practical virtual reality represents genuine opportunities as well as threats. The members of the Army Air Corps in 1918 were not so interested in the fact that the bicycle makers who built the first airplane modeled it not on the vehicles they had been building before, but on something completely different, the automobile. That's fascinating history, but it's not necessary to an assessment of the technology's impact. No, people who are going to be affected by new machines just want to know what they are all about and what they can do.

So I won't be spending much time on the traditional virtual reality paradigm, other than to describe, as a lengthy aside (see the appendix at the end of the book), why its vision did not lead to the massively populated, yet mechanically crude, virtual reality spaces we have today. Readers interested in the contrasts between paradigms could take a pause and have a look at the appendix. Those not interested in that history could continue here without significant cost.

For those who did not grow up with video games and are not all that familiar with previous efforts to construct virtual reality, the basic idea behind the video game as a practical virtual reality tool is this: If the game is online, a user can log into it from any computer on the Earth. The screen turns into a window through which an alternative Earth, a synthetic world, can be seen. This other place (another planet, a historical domain, or any other plane of existence) can have mountains, stars, and fire in it; it can have gravity, or no gravity, or reverse gravity; it might have trees and grass, but also chickens and dragons, or chicken-headed dragons or dragon-headed chickens; it might have houses and taverns and castles, or spaceships, or tiki bars; and it might have people. Some of the people you would see might be software-controlled, but others would be controlled by real humans, such as yourself. In fact, there might be a mirror there, and if you press the right buttons and maneuver your viewscreen in the right way, you would see yourself, present, in that place. The window by which your computer is depicting the world is, in fact, the surface of somebody's eye, and that somebody is *you*.

More accurately, you have been given a synthetic body in the synthetic world, and your computer is rendering the world as it would be perceived by the ocular sensory device that your synthetic body possesses. If you see someone else in the world, and she is pointing her visual sensing device at you, well, the two of you are looking at one another through your computer screens. She may be in Hong Kong, and you may be in New York, but you are still occupying the same segment of cyberspace and you have just made eye contact. Of course, her appearance there may not match the looks of her body on Earth, but neither does yours. She may even be a he, not a she, or something else again. But she/he/it is a person, like you, and you can have a relationship with her that is just like any other relationship you might have with another person. The only difference is that this relationship is being mediated by a body that is one step removed from the Earth body, and therefore occurs in a place that is one step removed from the Earth.

I said above that synthetic worlds are becoming important because events inside them can have effects outside them. This flow of influence from inside to outside is generated by a very simple core mechanism that is easy to see in the vignette above. As soon as it goes online and begins to receive visitors, a synthetic world begins to host ordinary human affairs. However fantastical the place may be—whether visitors are represented as mobsters, dragons, or crumb cakes—it still and always is playing host to ordinary human beings, with their ordinary ways of interacting with one another. The physical environment is entirely crafted and can be anything we want it to be, but the human social environment that emerges within that physical environment is no different from any other human social environment. And because no one can permanently separate events in one sphere of their life from all the other spheres, that part of human life taking place in synthetic worlds will have effects everywhere. At the same time, the things that happen there will not be run-of-the-mill things. We will no longer be in Kansas, and many of the rules will be different. Thus not only will there be spillover effects; the effects, such as they are, will seem weird.

In short, synthetic worlds put ordinary humanity in a very strange place, producing forces that deserve hardheaded attention, in my view. All things that matter to ordinary people—their loves, their crusades, their morals, and their material assets—may now have a home in a place other than Earth. That place operates under different rules. As Lawrence Lessig (1999) describes it, the unusual thing about cyberspace is that we can be both here and there at the same time, and the place that is "there" can be constructed, essentially, however we might like. Thus, all of our interests are the same as they ever were, but the environment in which we pursue them has become untethered from the Earth environment with which we have become so comfortable.

Deep questions arise, only a few of which we will have space for. But it is easy to find a simple example of the way that the strange and ordinary features of synthetic worlds can conspire to generate phenomena worth thinking about. Consider the price of diamonds. On Earth, these items tend to be quite expensive. They are beautiful, and if crafted well, they enhance the beauty of those who wear them. Their beauty contributes to their price, of course, but so does their scarcity. Now, what if the Earth could be induced to produce as many diamonds as anyone would ever want? Such a thing is impossible here, but not in cyberspace. The coding authority who owns and controls a synthetic world could pave the streets with diamonds if it desired. The coding authority could also order the world to make gems that are more beautiful than diamonds. Or, the coding authority could make diamonds much rarer than they are on Earth, and then also purge the world of rubies, emeralds, sapphires, and every other type of gem. All of these coding decisions would affect the price of diamonds and the happiness of the people wearing them. The role of diamonds in society would be affected: Would the lover still give the beloved a glittering gem if it becomes common, or impossibly rare? How uncommon must a diamond be to serve as a love token? Or as a power symbol? Such questions are moot on Earth, because our planet is endowed with a certain availability of diamonds based on their presence in the ground and our understanding of how to get them out of the ground. In synthetic worlds, things are different. The availability of diamonds is not an endowment but a choice. Thus while the mental objects in play there (beauty, price, love, profit, scarcity, reputation, power) are nothing new, the rulebook under which they are all contested is a new thing indeed. Moreover, a love token is a love token is a love token: If the coding authority messes around with its virtual diamonds, it will affect some aspects of the love relationships between living, breathing humans. The heartaches and joys that result will not be virtual at all, nor will the behavioral reactions on Earth, which may range from new sleeping patterns to substantial purchases of alcoholic beverages. These will be genuine feelings and actual phenomena, as real as anything else under the sun.

Thus, it is the core features of synthetic worlds—the fact that they are radically manufacturable places that can be shared by many people at once—that generate their nontrivially unique inside-to-outside patterns of influence. Place a group of people in a strange place, and they will follow their usual tendencies in pursuit of their usual objectives. The outcomes will be both strange and familiar, and will radiate outward.[2]

Moreover, this combination of the bland, the fantastic, and the consequential points to the simplest answer to the question of what synthetic worlds really are: a frontier. Indeed, viewing synthetic worlds as a locus of migration is useful in coming to practical terms with their effects, and there certainly is some evidence of motion from "here" to "there." Statistics reported in this book will suggest that many people are diving into the new worlds right now, with enthusiasm. Evidently, they find the physical environments crafted by computer game designers much more attractive than Earth. Accordingly, these travelers or colonists have come to maintain a large fraction of their social, economic, and political lives there.

These migratory patterns accord with the predictions of cyber-theorists such as William Gibson (*Neuromancer*, 1984) and Neal Stephenson (*Snow Crash*, 1992), who saw no long-run limit on the amount of time people would want to spend in virtual reality environments, were they to become practical. Now indeed they seem to have become practical enough, in a rudimentary way, to serve as way stations between the late twentieth century and the future as these authors envisioned it. Furthermore: It has already been several years since perceptive people like John Walker (1988), Michael Vlahos (1998), Ray Kurzweil (1999), and Hans Moravec (1999)—none of them novelists—began to argue that that future was nearer than we might think, that humans and their machines were going to become more intimately involved with one another, and fairly quickly at that. The natural location for getting together is in cyberspace, of course, through simulated bodies in simulated spaces. Why would you type into your computer if you could talk instead? And why talk to a gray screen when you could instead have a conversation over a virtual lunch with an attractive humanoid-looking being? These kinds of interactions, which could occur most easily in a crafted, synthetic world environment, seem quite plausible to anyone thinking about the growing power of computer technology. From this point of view, synthetic worlds are simply intermediate environments: the first settlements in the vast, uncharted territory that lies between humans and their machines.

Names for a New World

Today, of course, most synthetic worlds are considered games, and the term used to describe them—prepare your tongue, this won't be easy—is *MMORPG*. This jawbreaker (I pronounce it "mor-peg") emerged from a game industry practice that refers to games like *Dungeons and Dragons* as "RPGs," for "role-playing games." Specify an RPG as an online game, and it becomes ORPG. Such a game with multiple players is a MORPG, "M" standing for "multiplayer." Around 1996, the industry acquired the technical capacity to expand the number of players from a then-ordinary number (8–16) to what was considered a very large number (3,000–4,000), and the term "massively multiplayer" was coined. MMORPG, for "massively multiplayer online role-playing game," has become the standard term of reference for all synthetic worlds—a development only the Pentagon (and some university administrators) would admire.

There are other words to use, even some that can be pronounced. The ancestors of MMORPGs were text-based multiuser domains (MUDs), commonly referred to as *virtual worlds*. The usage has now been applied to a wide variety of Internet spaces, but because of the unfortunate history of the "virtual reality" scientific research paradigm (see the appendix), the "virtual" tag has lost its meaning in many respects. Vlahos refers to the terminus of our migration as the *infosphere*, but he is talking about networked communication in general. William Gibson coined *cyberspace*, a term that has become too general, unfortunately. Neal Stephenson used the term *metaverse*, but that concept does not reflect the rendered, role-playing aesthetic that we now see is an important aspect of synthetic worlds, and by its derivation from *universe* it overlooks the fact that there are going to be many thousands of synthetic worlds to choose from, not just one.

For a more targeted term, consider *proskenion*, from ancient Greek theater. Brenda Laurel (1993) and Janet Murray (1997) propose that much of what happens in computers and online is a form of interactive storytelling or theater. Theater in Greece began as religious ritual and took place in a circular area at the foot of a hill. When ritual became drama, a small tent or hut called the *skene* was built at the back of the circular area, to facilitate costume changes and exits and entrances. Eventually, visual imagery (scenery) was painted on the *skene*, and then a raised platform was constructed on its front. This structure, the *proskenion*, is arguably the first physical space constructed by humans explicitly to serve as some *other* place, indeed, a place that exists only in our imaginations. In contemporary theater, *proscenium* is a technical term referring to the area on the stage that is outside the curtain but in front of the audience. This is apt as well. It suggests that "proskenion" serves as a term for any rendered, imaginary place, and it also reminds us, metaphorically, that the stages on which online dramas play out involve us both as actors and audience—the action occurs in a place that is not quite the stage, but not quite the seats either.[3] And once the audience becomes the players, of course, the play is no longer a play; it's ordinary life, even though it happens on a stage.

Indeed, following the theatrical metaphor, another term that might make sense is *hyperstage*. When programming allowed text to deliver radically new levels of information, text became hypertext. Similarly, MMORPGs take the concept of an ordinary stage and extend it radically. These places are theatrical locales in the sense that they are not of the Earth, and in that they allow people to take on many roles (including their true self if desired). But they are much more than that. They allow such a huge number of players, and such an unscripted plot, that the line between acting and mere living blurs and, in many cases, vanishes outright. Moreover, we can teleport from one stage to the next with the click of a button, just as hypertext takes us from page to page instantly. Foreshadowed in Shakespeare's *As You Like It*, a hyperstage is a stage of the whole, a place in which computing technology has erased the distinction between actor and audience, here and there, scenery and landscape, role and self.[4]

While there might be a number of useful new terms, I will stick primarily with the term *synthetic world*: an expansive, world-like, large-group environment made by humans, for humans, and which is maintained, recorded, and rendered by a computer.

The Consequences of New Frontiers

However we refer to these territories—virtual world, MMORPG, cyberspace, metaverse, proskenion, hyperstage, or synthetic world—the most general causes and effects of any migration into them may not be hard to predict. Human migration is a well-known and fairly well-studied phenomenon (Borjas 2001). A simplified economic story would say that those doing relatively less well in one place face the risks of change and head off into a new place. They stake claims there but retain ties with their former neighbors. If they do well, they stay; if they don't, they go back. Economists argue that as people sort themselves into different places based on their skills and preferences, everyone is better off. Those who do well by moving, move; those who do well by staying, stay; and everyone eventually finds the best possible place to be.

While this is a happy story in the long run, nonetheless, it is also a story of great change and short-run stress. Social and cultural attitudes, technology, and the distribution of wealth may all be radically altered. If the migration is rapid or accompanied by major shifts in thought paradigms, these alterations may be traumatic or lead to conflict. If we indeed experience a gradual migration of human consciousness into the synthetic universe, we will also have a growing need for economic, political, social, and cultural expertise to deal with the difficult issues that will arise. From first-hand experience, I believe there is room for both optimism and pessimism on this score. On the positive side, I've had many inquiries from graduate students and junior professionals who are eager to become experts on synthetic worlds. On the negative side, all of these junior-level thinkers, without exception, have been hampered by an (understandable) bafflement on the part of their supervisors that something really important might be happening in video games. An aspiring doctoral student forwarded me a thesis proposal in which the *main* research question was simply, "What are MMORPGs?" Since such a descriptive question seemed, to me, subpar for PhD-level work ("What are automobiles?"), I pressed for an explanation and was told that the student's major professor had required it. That kind of story tells me we have a long way to go before we will have a significant number of influential people who can make reasoned judgments about this technology. Indeed, part 1 of this book was, in one sense, written precisely to facilitate interactions between junior professionals and their superiors. Were I a graduate student, or a young journalist, or a middle-management executive, facing the inevitably crabby objections of the senior people ("Wait—what *are* these 'm-mor-pegs'?? And, why in the world would you think that anything in a video game could be that important??"), my answers would be summarized out of part 1.

But let's assume that this aspiration has been realized—that we know what synthetic worlds are—and that we also begin to observe a migration in progress. Part 2 considers some of the consequences. But I'd like to stress from the outset that there is more here than an effort to point at something on the Internet and say, "Look! It's amazing, new, and radical and will change the world!" While I do intend to talk about the conceivable broader implications of synthetic worlds, I don't intend this to be a book of hype. I'm not an eager technovisionary or an ambassador of digital hipness from the Millennial Generation. No, I am a middle-aged guy who works in Social Studies. My objective in part 2 is to discuss many of the hard economic, political, and security-related questions that synthetic worlds bring up.

Consider the questions about commerce and economics discussed in chapters 7 and 8. On the one hand, commercial activity seems to emerge automatically and with great gusto in these worlds. On the other, every world-builder and traveler knows that most synthetic worlds have what can only be termed "weird" economies at the macroeconomic level. Some say they are broken. Some say they work just fine. Some of these economies seem to function well, but they are no fun. Others function very poorly and are a blast to play in. The hard questions here are, What could the economy be, in a world where every physical object can be costlessly rendered in whatever quantities desired? And what *should* it be? Whatever the answers may be, it is apparent that nobody is waiting for them. Rather, users of these worlds are forming economic organizations left and right, some incorporated on Earth, most not. They mine items and gold from the worlds and sell them on eBay; they offer guide services; they speculate in rare quantities; and they make money. By some reports, some of them are making quite a bit of money. At the level of a few video games, this is at most mildly interesting. But what happens if these video games emerge as a parallel economy of significant proportions? By my own estimates, the collective volume of annual trade in synthetic worlds is, at this writing, almost certainly above $1 billion.[5] In other words, it already exceeds the total sales of a few real countries. What is true of sales is also true of total synthetic world production, as well as production per capita. Indeed, GDP per capita inside synthetic worlds is far higher than in the real world's poorer economies, such as those of India and China. There are clear implications for labor markets and globalization. Yet we have quite literally no formal expertise on how these economies are designed and managed.

Another hard question involves governance, discussed in chapter 9. Who owns synthetic worlds; who should own them; and how should relations between the owners and the residents/players be structured? And again, what's the objective? Should a synthetic world government be held to the same standards of performance as we apply to Earth governments? Or is the objective simply to have fun? Do all good governments, as defined by the great, and dead, political philosophers of the Western tradition, maximize the amount of fun to be had? It seems to me that this last question is a very hard question indeed, one that is intrinsic to the very act of world-building, and may be closer to the core of contemporary politics than we realize.

All of these questions raise another: Who (if anyone) should regulate transactions and relationships across the silicon border, and how? To what end? Who are the constituents of these policies and what are their rights? How are they represented? What rights do Earth governments have in regard to threatening organizations that exist only in synthetic worlds?

Finally, consider questions about war. As I discuss in chapters 10 and 11, people who play these games fight, constantly. Sometimes they fight in rooms that look like the room you're standing in. That's right. It would be easy for some computer whiz to build the bookstore or library (or trash can, I suppose) you're browsing through. He could put in all the shelves, indeed all the books in all the shelves. He could make the stairs and the counters and the doors and the locks on the doors. Using current AI technology, he could build robots that would do basically what you have been doing, wandering about pseudo-aimlessly, finding this section of books, glancing at various titles and then, as the result of some horrible cognitive catastrophe, making the mistake of sliding *this* book from among its neighbors, opening it, and flipping through its pages. Our coder could build the security cameras too, and the alarms, and he could endow the security guard's pistol with the correct range, line-of-sight, rounds per minute, and impact effects. Then he could make characters for himself and his friends, wrap sticks of dynamite to their chests, and place detonators and guns in their virtual hands. And then they could all work on their timing for the Big Event. Practice, practice, practice: since it is a virtual world, they can take all the time they need, to figure out exactly where to stand to block off your exit, where to shoot to kill the security guard who rushes down the stairs, and where to shout to get the attention of the TV crews who will accumulate outside. They could do all of this in cyberspace, using existing synthetic world technology. In fact, for all we know, they've already done it. The room you are in right now may already be part of someone's Master Plan. How would you find out? How do you stop it?

In brief, this is not a book about that wacky, wonderful Internet, wacky and wonderful though it may be, but rather about some very difficult issues that may be appearing on the horizon. It's a book that tries to apply age-old reasoning from the social sciences to some age-old problems that are resurfacing, in a new way, in a very different kind of place.

One Guy's Journey into Synthetic World Expertise

I mentioned at the beginning that, as strange as some of these possibilities may seem, it is almost as strange to be claiming expertise about them. What makes a person write a book about the serious consequences of video games? The story of my own transition into this dubious status might be illuminating, I think, because it reveals how strong synthetic world technology has already become as a force for change.

You see, to me, synthetic worlds did not seem to be anything more than fun, and perhaps funny, at first. Well before I was an economist, I was a person who played lots of games. I started with geeky board games as a teenager (*Panzerblitz*, an old Avalon Hill title, was my first) and advanced to multiplayer political games (*Kingmaker*, Avalon Hill) and fantasy games (*Dungeons and Dragons*, TSR) in college. My college years were also the golden age of arcade video games, and I spent as much time as anyone shoving quarters into slots.[6] For some reason, the powers that be at Georgetown decided that a great place for the game arcade would be directly below a classroom, and I spent many class-time hours completely distracted by the bings and beeps incessantly sounding off a few feet below me. I did manage to graduate, and I went on to higher training in the field of economics. Feeling that it was important to be as morose as the discipline I had chosen, I put the games away during graduate school. At about that time, however, personal computers became a necessity for anyone doing advanced economic research, and I saw no reason why I should not take a few moments in between statistics sessions to play a computer game or two. I mean, here was all the fun of the arcade, without spending 25 cents for each play! And no lines, either. By the end of my graduate training, I had developed a rudimentary understanding of economics but a deep mastery of the subtleties involved in stealth fighter tactics (*F-19*, Microprose), urban planning (*SimCity*, Broderbund), global domination (*Civilization*, Microprose), and the properties of odd-shaped and conditionally self-exploding blocks that fall sequentially through a low-gravity environment (*Tetris*, AcademySoft). At my first job after graduate school I remember having an uncomfortable discussion over cocktails with a very respected senior faculty member, after he revealed that he was himself a fan of the game *Civilization*. We enthusiastically traded strategies for a while, until the bemused smiles of those standing around made the whole thing feel too weird. So we went back to talking about German economic policy. It certainly occurred to no one at that party that economic policy might be happening *inside* a game within a few years.

I only discovered that in April 2001, when I started to play the game *EverQuest* (Sony Online Entertainment). This was a fantasy role-playing game, not unlike *Dungeons and Dragons*, except that it all happened online. I picked it up one evening because I thought it might be fun to act like a wizard or warrior, along with other people, in a computer game. When I first entered the game world, I was shocked at how complex the place was. Learning how to move and speak took quite a bit of time; learning my way around the huge world, with no maps, was also a challenge. Then there was the entire system of self-defense, combat, and spell-casting to be learned. Lastly, and most important, there was a rich and well-developed player society, whose language, culture, and norms were entirely foreign to me. Inside the game, there were thousands of players present at any one time, and outside of it, there were thousands of websites devoted to various aspects of gameplay. It was like no game I had ever played before. It was an intellectual challenge simply to understand *what EverQuest was*. It was a slice of practical virtual reality, as I've said, but since I had completely missed the VR hype of the previous decade, that similarity was completely lost on me. I just thought it was an incredibly interesting and deep implementation of network technology that also happened to be fun to play around in.

While having fun and trying to figure the whole thing out, however, I noticed immediately that economic transactions between players were an incredibly important part of what was happening. Within the game, in the cities, people were constantly shouting offers to buy and sell goods and services. "Want to sell Electrum Ruby Ring, only fifty platinum pieces!" "Looking for teleport to the Butcherblock Mountains, will pay." And so on. This buying and selling generated much of the sense of vitality in the place. Commerce was important outside the game as well, revealing how many people seemed immersed in this place and what they were willing to pay, in real money, to do things there. A number of fan sites listed in-game prices for items. Moreover, online auction sites hosted US dollar markets for game goods, including game currency. At these sites, people would auction off the play money of the game for real US dollars. Intrigued, I started to surf these sites from time to time and jot down the implied exchange rates. Inside the game, I took note of the items that sold for the highest prices, and I tried to explore the world to see why these items were so expensive.

As it was, the whole thing made economic sense. The prized items made a character in the game more powerful. With the right equipment, a character could cast more powerful spells, push deeper into dangerous dungeons, and travel more quickly and safely across the continents. Since these activities were fun things to do, according to the players, it made sense that items that enhanced those activities would be highly demanded. The online trade in dollars also made economic sense. Some people who had lots of dollars happened to want more *EverQuest* play money, and some people who had lots of *Ever-Quest* play money happened to want more dollars. After all, you couldn't buy super magic swords using dollars; you had to trade the dollars for *Ever-Quest* money first, and then use the *EverQuest* money to get the sword you wanted. It made sense that the people with the excess stocks of *EverQuest* play money would be willing to exchange them for dollars, and it also made sense that people with relatively large stocks of US dollars would be willing to exchange them for *EverQuest* play money.

So, here was a great big fantasy world playing host to a basically normal economy. It occurred to me to write a tongue-in-cheek paper about that. Wouldn't that be a hoot, I thought. A paper that would look like the *World Bank Economic Report for Poland*, except it would be *Castronova's Economic Report for EverQuest*. And this would not have been such a strange thing for a midcareer economist to do. There is actually a tradition of tongue-in-cheek research in economics, in which authors will write careful papers about the economics of trivial, funny things. There is a well-known paper about the economics of the American TV game show *Jeopardy!* for example (Metrick 1995). Papers like this can be quite entertaining for economists—remember that at conferences they would typically confront such a paper following a less-than-scintillating talk on "Capital Taxation in Dynamic Models with Perfect Foresight: The Case of New Zealand." After something like that, a paper about the economics of a game show can seem very interesting indeed. I felt that a paper about the economics of *EverQuest* would have a similarly pleasing effect: a joke, but an entertaining one at least. In the dismal science, it's not too hard to be a decent clown.

Tongue firmly in cheek, I began to record all the data I could lay my hands on—whatever seemed relevant to an economic report on this odd place. I got price data from in the game and from fan websites. I counted in-game populations as many ways as I could think to do it. I surveyed players and asked them about their investments of time and money into their characters. I tried to figure out how much effort it took to produce various commodities and services. I bought and played other games, to get a sense of how *EverQuest* was unique and how it was typical. And I scanned the online auctions, to try to measure the real-world money value of all these prices and production levels. I tried to get some measure of everything in this world that would matter to a Central Statistical Office or Census Bureau.

All of this took several months in the Summer of 2001, and it had to compete with teaching, my ongoing research on social policy and the welfare state, and settling in to a new apartment with my wife. However, the *EverQuest* topic steadily occupied more and more space in my mind. Those of us who do research for a living actually don't have much control over the subjects we study; thinking goes on 24 hours a day, and it seems that if a topic so desires, it can force a higher priority for itself than we want it to have. So it was with the *EverQuest* Economic Report. I kept thinking about it all the time—while commuting, on waking up, before going to sleep, sitting in church, waiting at the doctor's office. I picked up a few books about technology, computers, and the Internet. I rented science fiction films like *Brazil* (1985) and *The Matrix* (1999). I subscribed to *Wired*.

It turned out that there were dozens of synthetic world games like *EverQuest* in development at the time, and at one point I stumbled across one called *Project Entropia* that had some extremely interesting features. This game world would allow players to buy and sell items using Earth currency, and its business plan was to make the synthetic world so large that all humans—all 6 billion of them— could be in it, all the time. The world owners hoped to entice the entire human tribe to visit the game world, and then make billions by selling advertising space and virtual storefronts within it. The whole thing sounded preposterous in the moment, but it was a rather breathtaking vision of the future all the same. It led me to ask whether such a thing was even possible.

After a bit of further reading, I became convinced that it is, indeed, possible, if not now, in a generation or two. Ray Kurzweil is a brilliant and well-respected technologist, an inventor of marvelous devices ranging from sophisticated electronic music synthesizers to reading machines for the blind. In *The Age of Spiritual Machines* (1999), Kurzweil discusses the nature of computing and its prospects for growth. He makes a number of arguments about the future. Not all of them were persuasive to me at the time, but one that seemed very hard not to believe involved the raw amount of computing power that humans would come to possess. The short, simple point in Kurzweil's book is that humans are going to have *a lot* of computing power. This seems likely even if nothing especially exciting happens by way of technological innovation. As a result, the experience of every generation, for quite some time, will be that the next generation grows up with incredibly more powerful computers. My generation, those who played arcade video games as teenagers, is only the first of many to have this experience. And it follows that almost any computational problem that can be imagined by a single person right now will eventually be mastered by a computer. The way Kurzweil expressed it, at some point in the twenty-first century the standard personal computing device will have as much computing power as a single human brain. Not long after that, it will have the computing power of *all the human brains that have ever lived.*

One important use of all that power, according to Kurzweil, will be to upload brains and recreate consciousness inside silicon. I doubted that on reading it, but I was not following that line of argument very closely anyway because I was thinking about *EverQuest.* Add computing power to a game world and you get a place that's much bigger, much richer, and much more immersive. The robots running around in it, humanoid and unhumanoid, are smarter and act more and more like real people and real monsters (if there is such a thing). Add *immense* computing power to a game and you might get an incredibly realistic extension of Earth's reality itself. The place that I call "game world" today may develop into much more than a game in the near future. It may become just another place for the mind to be, a new and different Earth.

It turned out that Kurzweil was not the only one making such judgments about the potential computing power of humanity. As I mentioned earlier, a number of authors have made similarly persuasive arguments (Moravec 1999; Joy 2000). While some have argued that increases in raw processing power do not automatically convert themselves into improvements in economy and society, not too many dispute that increases will happen.[7] It's hard to see how they might not happen. Any piece of matter that can be switched between two positions can be used to store binary data and process commands on it. We know we can compute on silicon, a material whose raw computational power doubles every two years or so. But we can also compute with other materials, such as DNA or quantum particles. We have, already in place, extremely strong economic incentives to encourage researchers to discover these new computing methods. Thus, from an economic standpoint, it seems quite likely that if there are sources of computing power in the materials around us, they will be tapped. The extremely rapid growth we have observed so far—from glowing green text to immersive 3D forests in just *twenty years*—seems likely to continue, whether on silicon or something else.

The prospect of continued growth in computing power had a serious implication for my research into *EverQuest*. What was just a game world in 2001 might be a richly simulated and completely immersive mental environment in 2101. Perhaps by 2101, it would be trivial to simulate the entire scope of known human history from 10,000 BC to AD 2000 at the level of individual synapses of all the brains that lived in that period. Or perhaps worlds like that would only be possible in 2200, or 2300. And perhaps no one would want to simulate that history; perhaps we would all prefer a different history. While we are at it, why not just simulate our future instead? Those pesky stars and galaxies are so far away. Under Einstein's rules we will probably never get there. But if we simulate a space-time world that allows us to travel there in our minds, if not our bodies, we can go there right away. Whatever these simulations will be like, and at whatever pace they appear over the next few centuries, it seems clear that they will be an important host of human mental activity. How exciting, then, that early outlines of their characteristics can be seen today, right now, by looking at their ancestors: game worlds like *EverQuest*. My silly paper about a computer game thus turned into a more general study of the economic and social life just starting to develop inside this silicon shell.

Because it had to deal with such an unusual and emergent phenomenon, the paper that I eventually wrote ("Virtual Worlds: A First-Hand Account of Market and Society on the Cyberian Frontier") ended up looking nothing at all like a traditional economics paper. It had a wealth of economic and social data about the world of *EverQuest*. I found, for example, that you could work in *EverQuest* and earn something like 300 platinum pieces (*EverQuest*'s currency) an hour, on average. If you converted that into real money by selling it online, it would come to about $3.50. So you could earn a poverty-level wage, in real dollars, by "working" in the game. I also found that the ongoing exchange rate between platinum pieces and dollars was higher than that of the Japanese yen, the Korean won, and (at the time) the Italian lira. When I looked at population numbers and estimated the market value of production on an annual basis, that came to over $2,000 per person. In other words, I had found that the Gross National Product of Norrath, per capita, was about the same as Bulgaria's and four times higher than China's or India's. This game world, though small, was host to quite a bit of productive activity.

Aside from economic data, the paper was also filled with vignettes and stories about the strangeness of life in Norrath. Some kind of storytelling was essential, because the world being described was foreign to the general economist reader. This was almost more deep-immersion anthropology than economics, but, frankly, economists generally don't believe in deep-immersion research and they certainly don't care too much for "vignettes." As a result, I was not sure about the prospects for publication. I had a research affiliation at the CESifo institute at the University of Munich, however, that would allow me to place up to four draft papers annually in their working papers series. CESifo Working Papers could be downloaded through the Social Science Research Network, the main online clearinghouse for research in law, management, economics, and finance. So I decided that I could just release the paper that way. I could find out whether anyone had an interest in an unusual economics paper about an unusual thing, a thing that might be serious or might not be, depending on how you feel about the future of computing and the Internet. The paper became a CESifo Working Paper in December 2001 and was listed at SSRN.com in January 2002.

Now, at that time, economics was not the most popular thing being downloaded on the Internet, not even at SSRN. Download a finance paper, and you might learn how to make some money in stocks. Got a legal issue? Download a law paper. Downloading an economics paper was typically less likely to get you anything immediately useful. As a result, the top downloads at SSRN were all law, finance, and management papers that had been around since the inception of the site (1997) and had accumulated thousands of downloads. Comparatively, a typical SSRN paper in economics might have gotten one or two downloads in its entire lifetime; a popular paper might have had one or two a month; a paper assigned by a professor to his students might get 50 or 100 downloads. I thought "Virtual Worlds," as a quirky paper, might get 100 or so downloads. Maybe some econ grad students might use it to have something edgy to talk about over lunch.

Given these expectations, I was pretty shocked when the paper had 500 downloads the first day or so. My wife and I went out for a nice meal. When it hit 1,000 downloads a few days later, we went out for another nice meal. At 5,000 downloads a couple weeks later, we went out for still another nice meal. At 10,000 downloads, about two months later, we went out again, but agreed that our budget and waistlines couldn't handle any more nice meals. But people kept downloading the paper. By summer 2002, "Virtual Worlds" was pushing 20,000 downloads and had entered the all-time top-ten download list for SSRN, the only paper published since 1997 to have done so. It was also the all-time number one download for economics papers. Well, I couldn't avoid the conclusion that the paper had made some kind of an impact with lots of people, but, for the most part, I had no idea who these people were or why they thought the paper was worth downloading.

Then the email started pouring in, and the phone started to ring. Game companies wanted advice on developing in-game economies. Mainstream journalists wanted interviews about these insane people paying real money for magic swords. Business and tech journalists wanted to see if the numbers really added up and whether the person behind them was really an economist or just some charlatan. Entrepreneurs of various stripes wanted ideas for making fortunes. Academics in the arts and humanities wanted me to speak at conferences about digital culture. Government agencies wanted info on how synthetic worlds could be used for training and policy analysis. Intense game players wanted me to study the economy of the game *they* really thought was cool. Students at all levels wanted to know how to get gaming into their research, or how to get jobs in the gaming industry. Lawyers wondered about property issues. I learned that this exploration of a synthetic world was apparently a very serious thing indeed, to people operating in an incredibly wide spectrum of human affairs.

It was funny that the only people who did *not* call were other academic economists. Years later, I did begin to have conversations with prestigious economists that began "So *you're* Castronova! My graduate students have been citing this thing about video games and I keep wondering, who the hell *is* this guy??" But in the first months of my paper's journey around the Internet, it was clear that the profession judged it to be hype, or some kind of fad, and steered away. So, as I feared, my efforts to place "Virtual Worlds" at traditional journals were turned down. "Not the right kind of paper for our journal," one editor said. "The subject is not ripe," said another. Commenting on a later paper on the same subject, a reviewer for the prestigious *American Economic Review* opined: "Basically, these [results] tells us [*sic*] something about the distribution of tastes of a small group of individuals who play virtual reality games. Personally, I'm much less interested in the pricing of the characteristics of "virtual" things than of those that are real" (quotation marks in the original).[8]

I decided that since I had enough normal research to keep my career going, there was no need to formally publish the *EverQuest* piece. It would be fine if it remained just a Working Paper. It certainly had had more impact in that form than any journal article I had ever written.

The experience left me at a crossroads in terms of my career, however. Evidently, this was not a line of research that was going to be well received by the hierarchy of academic economists. On the other hand, it *was* a line of research that seemed to contribute something tangible to the thinking and working of a great many people. Now, according to one view of academic freedom, it is given to academics so that we can explore things that need to be explored, regardless of the consequences; that's the duty that goes along with the benefit. I never expected to be someone who actually had to rely on the academic freedom argument to make a decision about my career, but in the end, that's how it was. I had important people from many different areas urging me to pursue the study of this topic in one direction or another. My paper had raised many more questions than it answered. I decided to keep working on some of these questions, and that's why I am writing this book.

But it is important to stress the moral of the story: No one had to be persuaded that synthetic worlds were important, they made the case themselves. I just wrote down a description of what was happening inside a video game, and how the technology behind it was being considered by others for much more expansive uses. The paper was never approved by a board of editors and still has not appeared in print. It was just a document floating around the Internet, a free self-publish by an unknown economist from an obscure teaching college outside Los Angeles. But its subject was powerful enough to stir up interest in places like the *New York Times*, the Pentagon, and the grimy offices of graduate students and game coders alike. I can't possibly take credit for generating all that interest, even granting myself a megalomaniacally generous assessment of my own talent as a writer. No. The paper got passed around because many people sense that something really is happening, out there, on the other side of the screen.

An Overview of the Contents

The subject of the book is a generic "synthetic world," by which I mean any computer-generated physical space, represented graphically in three dimensions, that can be experienced by many people at once. It makes no sense to list the specific games and worlds that fit in this category at the moment; this phenomenon is moving so quickly that any list would be out of date by the time the book hit the street. To give an idea, however, I take "synthetic world" to include all the MMORPG worlds in the game industry. These are role-playing games about dragons and spaceships, and are exemplified by the game *EverQuest*. I will also include multiuser social worlds, such as *The Sims Online* (Electronic Arts), that typically do not have an explicit gaming, combat, or competitive aspect. At times, I will discuss multiplayer combat games such as *Half-Life* (Sierra), although players of these games cannot have the same kind of persistent presence as they do in MMORPGs and social worlds (for reasons to be discussed later). I will not include such things as text-based chat rooms or MUDs (Multi-User Dungeons), or online games such as online poker or online checkers; these technologies do not depend on a 3D, world-like physical interface. Of course, no single world sufficiently describes the entire universe of worlds now emerging; therefore, the book will have to focus on what seem to be generic and persistent features of all the worlds as a group.

Just what is generic and persistent about synthetic worlds, and what is not, will require some guesswork about future developments. For example, at the moment it is fairly easy in many Internet communities for users to remain anonymous, and thereby to be shielded from the consequences of their actions. I believe this is a temporary situation. Human societies rely so much on reputation for their basic functioning that online anonymity seems unlikely to persist in any significant way. Similarly, there are a number of technological issues that affect life in synthetic worlds at the moment, that are more likely to be solved rather than accepted. Right now, for example, it is hard to get a mob of 50 or so people together at one time at one place online, because the required digital video processing often becomes more than a contemporary system can handle. Nonetheless, I will not talk much about the difficulty of forming armies or markets in synthetic worlds. On the contrary, I will be assuming that armies and markets will be readily available forms of social organization; they are so important for human collectivities that the coders will undoubtedly find some kind of fix or workaround using the computation resources to come (indeed, to some extent, they already have). While assuming certain technological and social advances can be risky for a book such as this, it is warranted in some cases. A book written in 1920 about the emerging film industry might have more or less safely assumed that both sound and color would become the norm eventually.

The book has three major parts. As mentioned above, the first part is devoted to an overview of what synthetic worlds are, how they operate, and how they interact with the world of Earth. Chapter 1 gives a description, based on my own experiences in dozens of these games, of what it is like to spend time in a current-generation MMORPG. In chapter 2 I'll give an overview of the people who go to these places, their numbers, and why they make this choice. Chapter 3 sketches the technology behind these world simulations; here, I make some more or less well-grounded predictions about the near-term technological potential of these worlds. Chapter 4 describes the "institutions"—the patterns of culture and behavior—that these places induce. Chapter 5 concludes the first part by giving a brief overview of the industry that makes these worlds, its corporate structure and atmosphere, and the likely equilibrium state of the market as it evolves.

Part 2 then considers the potential effect of synthetic worlds with respect to a number of important issues. Chapter 6 describes many of the boundary-violating practices that have become common in MMORPGs, showing how fuzzy the line between the game-space and real-space has already become. Chapters 7 to 11 then discuss some of the implications of these fuzzy boundaries for economics, politics, and security.

Part 3 wraps up the book with two chapters, one an assessment of policy issues, and another that attempts to make longer-run projections about the ultimate meaning of this technology.

Indeed, what are the right policies toward these new places? This is a difficult question; we are not sure what these worlds will be, let alone what they should be. People in different positions have different opinions. Those who own worlds and want revenues from them have a certain set of goals in mind. Those who are heavily invested as users of a world will have a different set of goals. Users who have spent much time in one role in a world (as a warrior, a trader, a lover, or what have you) will not have the same idea of "ideal" policies as those who have specialized in a different role. Not to mention those who have not entered the world yet. And we can of course conceive of a common good here; there may be some policies that are commendable as is, either because they offer the best balance of conflicting interests, or because they are simply the right thing to do. While I would like to claim neutrality with respect to the various interests at play, that is going to be impossible in practice. I am going to be arguing, at various points in this book, that it's better to do things a certain way. When that happens, I will be trying to side with the common good as much as possible.

My conception of the common good is fairly simple: it's the collective well-being of the users. And by "well-being," I do not mean a strictly utilitarian conception. The mere fact that one synthetic world sells better than any other is not, in my view, conclusive evidence that it is a better world than the others. It is strong and persuasive evidence—to assert otherwise is elitist and tyrannical—but it is not conclusive evidence, and the reason it is not conclusive involves the nature of free will. Frankly, I fear the power of a simulated world to alter the mind's conception of its own desires. Many people seem to become heavily invested emotionally in the rather crude synthetic worlds we already have, and some spend almost every waking hour there. Is that the result of a rational choice, or rather of some form of chemical response treadmill similar to nicotine? Many of these worlds are designed to utterly and completely enclose the user's consciousness in an envelope of the coder's design.

What are the long-run implications of that practice? Quite a few social scientists, especially the economists who trained me, believe that tastes are fundamental. But no economist denies that, in the very long run, the social and physical environment has a significant effect on what we like and don't like. Saharan nomads don't tolerate cold weather as well as the Inuit. With synthetic worlds, we are talking about a technology that can dictate the physical environment (and to a great extent, implicitly, the social environment) within which a mind matures, for months or years or decades. The preferences that economists and other rational choice social scientists treat as fundamental and unchanging are very much changeable here. That puts them in play, and forces us to think about the Good and Bad of a world in a way that is not entirely dependent on the tastes of the people in it.

There's nothing radical in this. For decades, economists such as Nobel Laureate Gary Becker (1996) have theorized about the way preferences may change. Libertarian theorist Robert Nozick (1974) has no trouble rejecting an existence based on permanent immersion in a positive experience-producing machine: such a life would be horrible, even if the immersed person said it was wonderful. Because everything about a synthetic world can be revised by the coding authority, the world needs to be Good as well as popular. We cannot simply assume that a world that commands the reverence of its people is necessarily the best world for them.

Ideally, the synthetic worlds we revere and feel most comfortable in will also be Good worlds. We will like them, *and* they will enhance human dignity and well-being. That is my hope, anyway. The Earth is very nice, but there are experiences we can imagine in our minds that we *cannot have here*. We poor Earthlings simply cannot explore the surface of Pluto. We really cannot magically heal our best friend's sickness with a touch of our hand. We cannot cast a spell and fly away. We cannot switch from male to female and back again; we cannot become fat or thin as we wish; we cannot have the strength of a bear or the speed of a rabbit. We cannot directly observe the signing of the Magna Carta, Pickett's Charge, the remilitarization of the Rhineland, D-Day, the Defenestration of Prague, the severing of Jenkin's Ear, or the invention of Silly Putty. And certainly, we cannot cast immense fireballs that immolate things that annoy us. Much as we might want to do that, it remains, for the known future, something not possible for ordinary humans like you and me. On Earth, anyway.

Looking beyond these simple joys of immersive, interactive entertainment, however, it should be stressed that synthetic worlds may eventually make contributions to human well-being that will be judged as extraordinarily significant. We live in a mobile world, and family ties often fall victim to the locational demands of the marketplace. Synthetic worlds may become a place where families can maintain their togetherness, even though the members live thousands of miles apart. Moreover, synthetic worlds may allow us to experience human social life in an environment in which many characteristics of the body are no longer fixed endowments but have become chosen attributes. People entering a synthetic world can have, in principle, any kind of body they desire. At a stroke, this feature of synthetic worlds removes from the social calculus all the unfortunate effects that derive from the body. Imagine a world in which all aspects of our physical appearance were under our control, so that all variations in thin, heavy, tall, small, dark, and light were all voluntary. We are poorer for being still unable to experience such a world.

To sum up: synthetic worlds hold immense promise as places where humans can enhance their Earth experiences with ones drawn directly from our glorious collective history and imagination, all without bearing some of the burdens that adhere to the Earth bodies we were born with. Ensuring that the technology serves such a marvelous end, rather than a less happy one, is the real challenge for the next few decades. We will be less likely to meet that challenge the longer we treat video games as mere child's play. Multiplayer online video games—avatar-mediated communications systems, in essence—have become too fraught with heady implications to be ignored any longer.

PART I

THE SYNTHETIC WORLD:
A TOUR

IF YOU ARE NOT AN AVID PLAYER OF VIDEO GAMES AND YOU DO not spend very much time online, your first questions about these places will not be about implications but about basic features. What phenomena are being considered when someone uses the term *synthetic worlds* (or the more popular synonym, *virtual worlds*)? The chapters in part 1 attempt to describe common features of all the synthetic worlds now in existence and likely to come online in the next decade or so. Chapters 2–5 talk about the users, the technology, the behavioral pattern, and the market structures that most synthetic worlds seem to share. To begin, however, the first chapter takes the reader on a walk-through of a typical synthetic world. How is it that you "go" there? Why does it feel any different from, say, opening an email program or a game of computer solitaire? Once you are there, who else will you find and what will you do with them?

If you're already quite familiar with synthetic worlds, you could skip the walkthrough and go on to chapter 2. On the other hand, even the most experienced gamer might find it interesting to see the level at which I've chosen to describe a typical day in a MMORPG. Much that seems second nature to the experienced gamer is, in fact, a thoroughly befuddling recoding of expectations for the rest of us. It's in the interests of everyone—those who know the technology and culture inside and out as well as those who've never heard of these things before—to realize how much experiential distance separates them.

1

DAILY LIFE ON A SYNTHETIC EARTH

This chapter gives uninitiated readers an overview of how one gets into a synthetic world and what one does after arriving. These places, while being physically different from the Earth, are not socially different from it. All the standard patterns of human social, economic, and psychological functioning seem to translate directly into the new space. A glimpse of daily life in a typical synthetic world should illustrate both how strange and how normal these *proskenia* are: new stages that host age-old human dramas.

Much of the description is informed by the contemporary state of affairs, in which most synthetic worlds are produced by game companies and served to the customer from a single location. This kind of structure is not necessary to manage a world, of course. The world could also exist on a network of computers, unowned by anyone, and be served to newcomers on an ad hoc basis. From the point of view of the new user, however, the process would look about the same.

Approaching the Synthetic Divide

I suppose the first thing everyone needs to understand is that it is not exactly trivial or easy to get into a synthetic world. A user has to go through a fairly lengthy series of administrative steps before seeing anything fantastic at all. So, let's say you are wandering through the games section at the store, and you see a piece of software that claims to be a multiplayer fantasy role-playing game. The software costs about the same as any other game on the shelf: perhaps $40 or $50. The box says that using the software requires an Internet connection, a fairly high-end computer, and a credit card.

You get the software and install it. You now have a new icon on your computer screen. You click on the icon and a small box appears announcing that a "patch" of the software is overdue; your computer begins to download something from the Internet. Your computer has initiated a conversation as a "client" with some other computer, which we will call the "server." The server has informed your client that its version of the program you are trying to run is out of date; the server is now patching your client, feeding it the necessary changes. The idea is that everyone who connects is working with the same code; the patch server's job is to put all computers that connect in synch as far as the program software goes. Sometimes the patch takes only a few seconds; other times, like when you first purchase the software from the store, the patch can take hours. This is because the people who run the game tend to update the code fairly frequently. By the time you buy the software, the program version on the disk you've bought is probably much older than the current version everyone else is connecting with. You need to get your version up to date, so you've got quite a bit of code to download.

When the patch is finished, you are directed to an account-management screen. There, you might enter a piracy-prevention verification key for your software. You might also have to submit a full slate of personal information: name, address, phone number, email address. You will certainly have to enter an account name and a personal password. While some worlds—rarely—might be accessible for free, in most cases you will have to submit the number of a major credit card and authorize a monthly charge against it. The monthly fee will be at the level of a cheap meal for two, currently $10–$15. There may be some special deal; sometimes the first month is free. When your credit card or other identifying information is validated, your account is successfully created, and you are invited to enter the other world by clicking a button.

You click the button, and . . . you still don't see anything fantastic. Instead you are now prompted to enter your user name and your password, in return for which you are treated to one or more contractual agreements. If the world is owned by somebody, you will see an "End User Licensing Agreement," the EULA. Of course, we all see these things on software all the time, but we never read them. This one might be worth reading. It contains the usual language informing you that you rent rather than own the software, and that you shouldn't copy it, and so on. But one new and interesting thing in this EULA, and that you really should pay attention to, is the fact that you will be giving up your right of ownership over anything that you build and leave in the world. Moreover, if something goes wrong with the world, or if the powers that be decide to change some part of the code, and as a result you lose something important to you, you have no right to expect compensation. Indeed, the people in charge (collectively, the "coding authority") use the EULA to assert their right to change the software in any way they please, regardless of what you might think about it. Now, you have to agree to the EULA in order to go to this place at all, so of course you click "Yes, I agree."

Next, you will see a "Code of Conduct" (CoC) or "Terms of Service" (ToS) agreement (sometimes folded into the EULA). You will probably see this regardless of whether the world is owned or open-source, because this document explains that you are entering the world with other people, and that you have to control your behavior or you might be kicked out. If you call people "nigger" or pressure them for kinky sex, and you get caught, you can be banned from the world forever, with no compensation. And of course there's no doubting that you *should* be banned for these things—just because it is a synthetic world, and not the Earth, does not mean that the notion of moral choice has vanished. On the other hand, in some ToS versions, it states that you can be banned for saying bad things about the coding authority. Once again, you might want to think twice about agreeing to this infringement of your speech rights, but, no matter. You have to agree to get in, so, you click "I Agree."

The screen now fills with some opening sequences—little films about the software's subject, and credits to the developers and the publishers of the game. Then you are invited to choose a world to enter. Typically, although not always, there is more than one version of the world available. The term "shard" can be used here (it comes from one of the earliest synthetic worlds, *Ultima Online*), the idea being that a "shard" is just one of the many different locales in which the world may be experienced. Each shard is physically like all the others; each one has the same world in it and all the same physical rules. Shards differ, however, in two ways: the group of people who have avatars there, and in the rules. As for rules, the fact that some shards have different game rules is important to know, since these rules may or may not be compatible with your idea of fun. Perhaps on some shards, players can kill other players and steal everything they own, while on other shards this activity is not allowed. As for populations, this is the main reason why shards exist at all. Sharding is a way to manage overcrowding. If a given server cluster can only handle 10,000 users at once, but you have 30,000 subscribers, you will need three server clusters—the shards—to handle everyone. And if any of the shards becomes too crowded with newcomers, the developers have to make a new shard for them to inhabit. Advancing technology will probably solve the crowding problem, but the future will probably still see different shards for each game world, if only to allow for some variety in the rules of play. In any case, you choose a shard that seems uncrowded and whose playing rules best suit your personality, and click a confirming button.

Now the program brings you to a screen filled with check boxes, buttons, dials, and at least one fairly large open space depicting a body of some kind. It might be a humanoid body, or some animal, or a ship, or a machine. This is the person or thing you are going to inhabit in the world; think of it as your vehicle, your car. Clicking on different items will change it from one form to another. It might be male or female, tall or short, fat or thin. You can change skin color, facial hair, and clothing. In addition, there may be lists of attributes or skills—things like speed, strength, even intelligence—that have been given some kind of numerical rating that changes as you click around. Sometimes you have a budget of points to spend on these attributes. Not knowing what this world will be like, it's hard to know what kind of person to be. You wonder, should I increase my strength, or my intelligence, or what?

Ah. Just a moment. Something important just happened. You said *my* strength, not *its* strength. Well, actually, you didn't say it, I wrote it. But you didn't stumble over that, did you? It seemed natural enough. You were thinking of this digital body as *you*, not a representation of you. Interesting. Media researchers have argued that their studies show how quickly and easily people can "become" the objects they manipulate on computers (Reeves and Nass 1996), but perhaps you never felt that sensible people could fall prey to that level of suspended disbelief. But let's move on.[1]

You go on to click and shape and equip yourself—er, this representation of yourself—for as long as you wish to continue playing at Dr. Frankenstein. When you are satisfied with the body you've created, you have to name it. The name will be significant. It's the label everyone will know you by. If there are reputations in this world (and there are), this name is the label to which the record of your actions will be attached, for good or ill. You could use your own name, although you might be prevented from doing so. Sometimes there's only room for a first name, and something like "TheAmazingAndMagnificentEdwardCastronova" might just be too long. Or perhaps you should name yourself something that fits with the theme of the world. Let's say this is a medieval world. Well, what's a famous medieval name? How about "Arthur"? That would be fine. On the other hand, there's nothing in the software preventing a medieval knight from calling himself "SirWhacksAlot" too (I've seen worse), but there may be some social pressure against a person with that name. In some cases, the Code of Conduct will prevent it. In the end, you choose a name that suits your tastes while leaving you open to no more ridicule than you can tolerate. "Arthur" it is. Wonderful.

Being named and fully fleshed-out, you click a confirming button, accepting the body as is. A box pops up: "Character rejected. Reason: Name already taken. Please choose another name." That figures; it's a pretty well-known medieval name. And for the reputation system to work, you can't have two people with the same name, can you? Alright, enter a new name—"Lancelot"—and submit.

Shoot. Rejected, already in use.

You try Galahad. Nope.

Percival. No.

Tristan. No.

Gawaine. No.

Bedivere. No.

Darn!

Maybe the knights of the Round Table are too popular. Let's see, where else can you go for a medieval-sounding name? There's Tolkien's *Lord of the Rings* trilogy, plenty of medieval fantasy names there.

Gandalf. No.

Frodo. No.

Legolas. No.

Gimli, Bilbo, Strider, Boromir, Faramir, Sauron, Saruman, no, no, no, no, no, no, no. This is ridiculous. Enough of this fantasy stuff, just use your own name. Edward. No; taken. Joseph. No. Castronova? Hmmm. Do you really want people to know who you are in real life?

You try alternate spellings. Arrthur? No. Arthuur, Arthurr, Aarthur, Aarrthuurr. No.

You try SirWhaacksAlot. It works! (How prescient of you to guess that SirWhacksAlot—just one "a"—would be taken.) Wonderful, now you have a name. But it's a silly name, who wants to be known as SirWhaacksAlot? And, in most worlds, you cannot change the name. Ever. The only thing you can do is delete SirWhaacksAlot and start over with a new body.

You realize that the place you are going to visit, like the Earth itself, has been trammeled by many feet other than your own. There as here, names are important for record-keeping and reputation-building. Each person must have a name, and each name must be unique and unchanging. If millions of people have traversed this terrain, they now occupy millions of names and you cannot have them. You have three options. There are sites on the Internet that will suggest names that fit the kind of world you are entering. Or you can be creative and come up with something new out of root sounds that go together properly: Aralad. Gandolas. Gawur. Bedistan. Gimlamir. If you go this route, it's a good idea to keep up on pop culture slang terms, otherwise you won't know what you might be calling yourself. Your third option is to find a name source that fits the theme but is unlikely to be known to most other users of the world. For a medieval world, look at some hagiographies. Bede is also excellent. Let's see, book 2, chapter 5: *At the deaths of Ethelbert and Sabert their successors revive idolatry.* "Ethelbert" seems to connote someone bookish. "Sabert" might be read as "Saber-T" by those who think you're showing off as a sword-wielder. You decide that "Sabert" is the better option.

You rebuild the body of your dreams and submit "Sabert" as the name. It is accepted. Your new body is now stored with the server. From now on, whenever you click the icon on your computer screen, the game will patch, prompt you for account name and password, ask you to verify the EULA and ToS again, and then give you the body-selection screen. You can build a new body at that point, or use Sabert, as you wish.

You are now ready to enter the world for the first time.

Crossing Over

You highlight Sabert and click on a button that says "Enter World." There is a pause while your computer loads the elements and tools needed to run the world. Perhaps a little bar indicates that something is "Loading." Usually, the thing that's loading is information indicating the state of the synthetic world this very minute—who exactly is online, where they are, what they are doing, whether it is raining or not, and the status of things like dragons and treasures. While this is happening, the screen goes black or is replaced by a whirling vortex graphic, helping you to imagine that your computer screen is a viewing portal, a camera, whose point of perspective is now being sent magically into the head of a creature named "Sabert" who lives in an unknown place on the other side of the galaxy. When your viewpoint enters Sabert's head, he becomes your *avatar*—the representation of your physical being in that other place.[2]

The darkness fades and, finally, the screen now seems to be a window looking out into some other place.[3] If the world is a First-Person Perspective world, you will not see Sabert himself, because your camera sits on the bridge of his nose. You are seeing only what Sabert can see. If it is a Third-Person Perspective world, your camera floats above Sabert and a little behind him; you can see him, from behind, in the lower center part of the screen. That means that if you look over his head and to the front, you are seeing whatever he is seeing; with this perspective, however, you can also see some things to the side and behind that Sabert cannot see. You can probably switch perspectives from first to third and back, as you prefer. Let's say you prefer the first-person view.

Time to orient yourself; have a look at the surroundings. Looking around the screen you notice a number of controls and information sources. In a mouse-based interface, these will be buttons and clickable windows. In principle, however, the controls could be accessed by voice, or by body movement (your body, not Sabert's). Similarly, information going from the world to you is delivered in the form of information windows, but often audio effects and voices are also used.

Using motion controls, you can move Sabert's head around and, with it, the camera. As you move the view around, your screen reacts just as it would if you had a video camera sending video input to it. And this, of course, is not really different from the way our eyes see things as we move our real heads around: objects move from the corner of our vision to the center, while changes in perspective deliver information about the distance between the objects and our eyes. The objects themselves look physical, in the sense that this camera is sending images of things in a place. If Sabert happens to be an elf or a bear, the surroundings might be a forest. The camera's motion gives you a view of different rocks and flowers and walls and trees out there. If Sabert is a spaceship, of course, the surroundings are not going to be a forest, but rather a space station or planet's surface. If he is a general or a tailor, the surroundings might be a room with appropriate furnishings.

Imagine it is a forest. You see movement out there—it looks like insects or rabbits. Something strikes your eye—some glittering object not too far away. Again using motion controls, you turn Sabert to the object and then move him toward it. If you were in third-person perspective, you'd see Sabert turn and then walk forward, your camera following along behind. Either way, the object gradually gets bigger on the screen as Sabert approaches it. Now you can take a close look—it seems to be a bottle. What's inside? You find the controls for the "Take" or "Use" or "Examine" command, and apply it to the bottle. In effect, you have told Sabert to try to pick up the bottle and look at it. Your computer then supplies whatever information is available. If the object has no identity in the world's databases, nothing happens. The object is just there for looks; it can't be owned or manipulated. In essence, it is window dressing, a painting on a wall that looks like a bottle. If the object is a recognized object in the world's databases, however, accessing it will usually bring up whatever information might be relevant in the context of that world. "Brown bottle. Weight: 1.0. Contents: Special Ale. Materials: Glass." The bottle seems ordinary, but who knows, it might come in handy.

You could leave the bottle here in this place, or you could keep it. Keeping it involves accessing some kind of ownership controls, usually termed "Bag" or "Inventory" or "Backpack" or "Cargo." Accessing these functions effectively tells Sabert to put the bottle into his Bag. It is now his property and will go with him wherever he goes. If you want him to use the bottle for anything, you can access the Bag function again and have him retrieve it. If he gets too much property, its weight may prevent him from moving; eventually, Sabert will have to find a place in the world where he can store his belongings safely. For now, however, he has to use his Bag and carry all his things with him.

First Contact

Looking around a bit more, you see what seems to be another person (or ship or animal or whatever type of entity Sabert also happens to be). This person looks something like Sabert, only more dignified; he is wearing a fine robe. You move Sabert closer and apply the "Get" or "Access" command to the person. One of two things happens. If the person you see is being controlled by the computer software (otherwise known as an NPC—nonplayer character—or a "bot," short for robot), your attempt to Use or Manipulate is interpreted as some sort of Hello or Handshake gesture, and an interactive script will begin. The NPC may speak to Sabert, telling him something about the world, asking a question, offering to buy or sell something, giving instructions, or telling him to go away. These communications may appear in a text window, or they may arrive via audio feed. The robot may have interpreted Sabert's handshake as a hostile act; maybe it attacks. In any case, you (through Sabert) are now in some kind of a relationship with a robot.

If the person is *not* an NPC, be prepared for something utterly unscripted. The person you see is an avatar, and is being operated by a real human, just as you are operating Sabert. When you approach the other avatar, he or she may say something, like "Hello" or "what do u want" or "can i have ur bottle." If it is a text-based communication, you can expect that capitalization and punctuation are rare and extreme abbreviations are common; hence "u" for "you" and "ur" in place of "your." To reply to this person's message, you would have to access a chat command and type in your message (or just say it into a microphone, again, depending on technology).

At that point you can have a dialog like any two people on the Earth. You might exchange names and other info about your synthetic bodies ("I am Sabert, a Wood Elf. I have low Intelligence!"), although often there is a way to access some information about others, such as name, without asking them directly. You might explain that you just arrived and picked up a bottle; the other person might tell you what it is for ("you drink it, of course. you *do* have low intelligence, even for a wood elf."). At that point you might indicate an appropriate emotion by commanding Sabert to frown or growl or cry. If you don't like the conversation, you can just walk away. Of course, the other avatar—let's call him Ethelbert—may follow you; his owner can move him just as you can move Sabert.

Suppose Ethelbert does follow you, and his owner keeps insisting that you should drink the bottle. You open your Bag and have Sabert get out the bottle and "Use" it, that is, drink it. Something may happen to Sabert at this point. Since it is ale, perhaps some of his attributes change—his intelligence may fall even further. Perhaps it has some other qualities—it may make him stronger, or help him run faster. If it is truly magic ale, perhaps Sabert can now fly in the air like a bird. Let's say this is indeed magic ale, and Sabert goes up in the sky. Your camera perspective goes up also. Sabert can see above the trees and he can move over the ground at an extremely fast pace. You circle him about while Ethelbert runs along on the ground. In the distance you see a mountain range with what looks like a mineshaft in it; in another direction you see a village with some farms; beyond them, you see the cloud-capped towers of a city. How interesting. Then the effect of the ale wears off and you float down to the ground again. Examining the bottle, it now says only "Brown bottle. Weight: 1.0. Contents: Empty. Materials: Glass." The world's databases have changed because of what you did.[4] You have Sabert put it down on the ground.

Ethelbert picks it up. "where u get this from?" he asks. Let's see, where *were* you? Somewhere in the forest. The landscape is apparently permanent, so you can orient yourself by landmarks. Perhaps there was a small tree by a stone where the bottles were. You have Sabert lead Ethelbert into the woods and you find the spot again. There are several bottles of flying-ale there. Ethelbert starts to grab them. Flying was fun, so you want some of these bottles. "Wait," you say. "Save some for me, I want some."[5]

Ah. Pause a moment—you just expressed an interest in these bottles. That's fairly significant. They only exist in digital form. Moreover, all they do is allow your digital avatar to fly around in a world that is itself entirely digital. None of this is real. Why should it matter to you whether Ethelbert gets all the bottles? Well, it *is* fun to fly, and the city you saw looks interesting but far away. What do you mean, *far away*? "Far away" means, given the pace at which Sabert is able to traverse the ground in this place, it would take you several hours to get him from this forest to that city. These bottles will let you get him to the city by air, which is a great deal faster. And they let you get some perspective on what's in this new world. That's all worth something. Face it, digital or not, the bottles are actually pretty useful given what you want to do with this computer program. You will be a more satisfied person if Sabert can hang on to a few of these things. So, you have him ask for a share of the bottles from Ethelbert (actually, from his owner, via Ethelbert).

Ethelbert's owner agrees; you will both get half of them. Ethelbert already has all of the bottles, ten of them, so he accesses a Trade command that allows him to transfer five of the bottles to Sabert's control. He also is able to give Sabert something that seems to be money. It might be called a Gold Piece, or a Credit, or it might be some number of tiny gems or bills or any other money-like substance. Let's say it is a gold piece. "that's to help u start out," Ethelbert says.

After you spend some time examining the gold piece, it occurs to you that your share of the bottles should have been 100 percent; since you found them. You want to explain this to Ethelbert—and get some of your bottles back. He can have a few, because you want to make friends in this new place. But most should be yours. You move Sabert around, looking for Ethelbert, but now he is nowhere to be found. That fine-robed gentleman has simply absconded with these bottles, nefariously obtained by abuse of your good will! Well. You will remember the name "Ethelbert," yes you will.

Exploration

You begin to wander around in the woods, looking for things. Perhaps there are more bottles in the forest. You don't find any, but there is the occasional herb or edible berry to be collected. You put these in your Bag. After a while you no longer remember where you are; no matter, a quick sip of this ale and you can be above the trees again if you wish. The forest gets darker. Maybe it is because the foliage is more dense, but perhaps the sun (or whatever the natural light source is) may be setting. It seems that time passes in this world.

It becomes quite dark and nearly impossible to see anything. Suddenly you hear a bump from behind and you become aware, audibly or visually, that you are under attack by something. You turn Sabert around and see that some beast is evidently trying to bite him. The beast is known as a "mob," a mobile object. NPCs and moving doors and cars are mobile objects as well, but the term mob is more often applied to mobile objects that represent other beings in the world. In noncombat worlds, mobs might give users puzzles or they could become companions or pets. In worlds with fighting, mobs are things that you hunt or that hunt you.

The beast in question here is a rat, and it has evidently been hunting you. You have several options: you can run away, you can try to fight, or you can drink your ale. There's no point in running; there is really no safe place to run to. You decide to fight. So, you fumble about, trying to see if you have a weapon and can get it into Sabert's hands. Meanwhile, the rat is hurting Sabert; in most worlds, Sabert will have a number of "hit points," and those are heading toward zero as the rat does more damage.

Let's say you don't get your weapon ready in time; the rat kills Sabert. This means different things in different worlds, but usually death is associated with a teleportation and some kind of loss. The screen goes black, the computer reloads some new graphics, and you find yourself looking at a different spot. Sabert's attributes might now be lower, or perhaps he has lost some of his ale. Certainly, he has lost time, in that he will have to run a long way to get back to what he was doing before. It may take some work to retrieve a lost item, or perhaps he will have to do some training or rebuilding to restore his lost attributes. He may have to pay a doctor to get everything in shape again. In most worlds, this kind of avatar death is common, and costly, but not permanent. It interrupts whatever you are doing, and it forces you to spend some time and effort repairing the avatar.

In worlds without combat and conflict, there is no dying per se; still, it is always possible for something to go wrong for the avatar. A person can simply get lost, or accidentally drop some valued item. The point is that the environment is not entirely friendly. Rather, it poses a challenge.

In Sabert's case, the challenge was to get through the forest without being eaten by rats; he failed. No matter; let's say Sabert's death hasn't cost him any of his bottles or abilities; it just teleported him back to the point he started out in. What to do? You want to get to the mineshaft and the villages and the city; they looked interesting and, well, you want to see the things you want to see. To avoid the rats, let's say, you drink the ale and fly up, this time directing yourself right at the mineshaft. You start flying and arrive there before the ale wears off. Wonderful, you've outsmarted those rats and met the challenge they represented. It feels good.

Now you are in a new place, a mine shaft. Time to go exploring. You spend a few hours poking around down there, picking up little gems. Sometimes you run into other people, and you explore together; if there are gems, you divvy them up; if there are hostile mobs, you fight them together. Whether by picking up things, or killing monsters, or making trades, you gradually start to accumulate things and soon your Bag is quite full.

You may have noticed that some of Sabert's numerical ratings have improved. This is because in some worlds, doing activities may enhance your avatar's power. If you mine for gems, your avatar's skill at Mining goes up. If you collect roots and berries, your avatar's Foraging skill goes up. Anyone who swings an axe at a monster may get better at the Axe skill. These numerical ratings are used by the software to judge your avatar's effectiveness at various things; the higher the number, the higher the likelihood of a success. This is important. If your avatar is more skilled in this way, he can be used to do more things in the world. Perhaps a better Forager would have found more bottles when Sabert could not. An avatar good with an Axe can make his way through a rat-infested forest with no fear.

At the same time, you yourself are getting better at driving Sabert around. The commands are going from your mind into his at a more rapid pace, and you are getting better at understanding what to do, and when.

Altogether, three things are improving as you spend time in the world: Sabert is gaining possession of more things; Sabert is getting better at doing various actions; and you are getting better at telling Sabert what to do.

To Market

Very well, after an hour or so, the mine has been fully explored and your Bag is full of items. Perhaps some of them are useful; if not, perhaps they could be sold for more gold pieces. You drink a flying-ale and head to the village. Landing there, you see a few more people. It is hard to tell which are NPCs and which are avatars. You also see a number of buildings; most look like various shops and farmhouses. Like the NPC/avatar distinction, it is not clear who is behind the existence of these buildings. Some may have been put here by the computer, others may have been built by real people.

You find what looks to be a jewelry shop. You go inside and Handshake the NPC behind the counter. She is a merchant, it turns out; a buy/sell dialog begins. You offer your gems for sale and she gives you 5 silver pieces for them. Hmmm. Five silver pieces for an hour of gem-hunting. You offer to buy something—a brass ring—that has a price of 2 copper pieces. You give Ethelbert's gold piece for it, and receive 99 silver pieces and 98 copper pieces in return. After placing the ring on Sabert's finger—where it is clearly visible, by the way, to you and every-one else in the world—you query the merchant how much would she pay for a bottle of magic flying-ale. She indicates the price is 10 silver pieces.

Putting all these numbers together, we can come to the conclusion that Ethelbert was not so bad after all. It takes an hour to earn 5 silver pieces, and one gold piece is worth 100 silver pieces. So you could say his gift was worth 20 hours of gem-hunting. If you're a lawyer, that's quite a lot of billable time, isn't it? Even if your time is only worth $5 an hour, the gold piece is worth $100. If one bottle of flying-ale is worth 10 silver pieces, it's also worth 2 hours of gem-hunting, or $10.00. So Ethelbert gave you enough money for ten bottles of ale, in return for only five bottles. He gave you money that saved you two hours of work. It was actually a nice gesture. "Ethelbert" is still a name you will remember, but now as a nice person rather than a churl.

Ah. Time to pause again. Notice that you felt grateful toward Ethelbert, because you think he gave you something. Are you insane? He gave you a gold piece, but it's just play money! It's not even real, it's just a stream of ones and zeroes. How can it be worth anything? On the other hand, you did spend an hour gem-hunting, and you know what they say: Time is money.[6]

Moreover, it is evident that a gold piece can be useful here. You now recall with bitterness your encounter with the evil and fearsome Rat of the Forest. Truly, you did not come to this world to fight. However, if you can be killed while wandering innocently through the forest, it might make sense to arm yourself a bit. That costs money. It is not real Earth money, but it is the coin of this realm, certainly. And now you have some, thanks to Ethelbert. You look about the village for a shop that sells combat gear; here's a smithy. Inside, you find an NPC who offers leather armor for 5 copper pieces each. That's not very expensive, as you can judge based on the time-value of gold pieces. You buy several pieces, for your head, body, legs, and arms. You also buy a nice sword. You are now a safer wanderer.

Just to get some revenge, you go back into the forest and look for that rat. You find him and start slashing away. The rat's hit points go to zero more rapidly than yours do, and soon it falls dead. You examine the body and find some little gems, like the ones from the mine. Treasure! You also receive a statement (in a window or audibly) to the effect that you have gained 200 points of "Experience." This is different from a skill increase; when you swing the sword your slashing skill rises, but this is something else, a general increase in "Experience." If you were to continue killing rats in this forest, you would soon notice that the amount of "Experience" you have keeps going up. In the world's databases, Sabert's recorded stock of experience points keeps rising. Eventually, the stock of experience points reaches an amount that triggers a discrete change in Sabert's powers; he would go from a "level 1 avatar" to a "level 2 avatar." At level 2, he might have twice the hit points, twice the armor rating, twice the running speed, and so on. Thus, to gain experience points is to enhance your ability to negotiate the world. By level 3 or so, these forest rats would not even attack Sabert, for fear of him.

In most worlds, the primary way to gain experience is to hunt creatures. In some, it can be purchased or obtained in nonviolent ways. In most, there is a cap on the maximum level that can be attained. For a casual player, that cap can take months or years to reach. The avatar's stock of experience points, skills, and possessions is a *capital* stock, just like capital stocks on Earth. Possessions are like physical capital, and avatar skills and experience levels are like human capital. There, as here, investments in capital stock increase the power of the investing entity.

The City

You decide it is time to fly off to the city, to see what awaits there. You drink an ale and off you go. Landing, you find yourself surrounded by architecture of a truly monumental scale. Earth could not hold such wonders; physics does not allow it. Vast palaces and solemn temples are mixed in with small shops, gardens, and even slums. There are people everywhere. Evidently many are NPCs, going about some preprogrammed business. Others are avatars, going about business that has its origin in sentient thought, at least to some extent. You see people talking, trading, making things, arguing, even dueling. You notice that they all have much nicer things on their avatars than you do. Sabert is evidently poor, even with almost an entire gold piece to his name.

A short fellow walks up and asks whether he can look at your gear. You oblige him by opening your Bag. He tells you that your gear is, in a word, awful, and that you should be ashamed to walk around like that. He brags about how his equipment took many hours to acquire, and that he has a house on the other side of the river, filled with precious objects obtained in the course of difficult adventures.

Some other fellow walks up and asks you to give him some money or a piece of armor. You tell him you should be begging yourself; your looks persuade him, and he wanders off. Both of these encounters leave you feeling that everyone here knows a great deal more than you do about the functioning of this world.

You see an avatar whose looks please you; you decide to strike up a conversation by asking her whether she thinks the brass ring you bought has any special properties. After chatting for a while, you feel as though you really like her. She seems to feel the same way. At one point, she says "Hey, ur cute. Wanna cyb0r?"

You have just been propositioned. If you wish, you can find a private place now, where no one can overhear the consummation. You will then tell each other things that make the heart beat faster; you will make love with your minds. In some worlds, there are commands that, by accident or design, cause avatars to emulate certain acts of interest in such rituals.[7]

After it is over, you may see her again. You might develop a close emotional relationship over weeks, months, years. You may even have Sabert ask to marry her. If she agrees, you will have to arrange a ceremony and invite the other friend-avatars you will have by that point, especially Ethelbert, your first friend in cyberspace. Bride and groom will wear special outfits for the event, and there will be wedding cake for all, a ring, and plenty of Special Ale, too.

That, however, remains in the future. For now, you move Sabert to some quiet, secluded alley in the city and enter the Quit command. The world fades to a black screen, and once again you notice that there's an ordinary computer monitor sitting here on your ordinary desktop. All the places and people you saw in the other place are still there, even though you are not. Sabert has disappeared from there, for now, and is effectively sleeping in the database, waiting for you to fill him with life again. The skills he enhanced during the day will still be enhanced when you start the program again. He still has his bottles, berries, ring, armor, and money, and they will be there when you return. Many of the people you met will be there when you go back; perhaps even Ethelbert and your partner. If you make a regular habit of returning, you will see them fairly frequently. There are some people, usually quite a few, who seem to be in the world all the time.

The Web

You think about the experiences you just had, and a few questions remain unanswered. Does the brass ring have any properties you should know about, like the Special Ale did? Where else can you find bottles like that? Can a gold piece really be worth some amount of dollars?

You go to the Internet and open a search engine. You look up various terms relating to the world you just visited. The search calls up a huge number of sites, all run by fans and independent organizations, with the sole purpose of providing information about the world. It turns out that the brass ring is nothing special. It also turns out that Special Ale is found only in that forest, only rarely, and never in the same spot twice. The program software—which the writers on these sites seem to know to the last detail—spawns those bottles in a way that it makes no sense to hunt for them. You discover that the rats of that forest are indeed carnivorous—you knew that, actually—and are among the weakest mobs in the world. This means that you yourself are a weakling, because you had trouble with the rats. But you knew that as well, from your experiences in the city. The other avatars there had many, many things, representing the combined earnings of dozens or hundreds or even thousands of hours spent in the world. The various sites make it clear that there are some people who know what's going on, and who have quite a lot of time and experience in the world, and others who don't. Discussion forums and blogs facilitate lively discussions about the most arcane matters of the world—is the place overpopulated? What is the best hunting spot? Has anyone seen a certain mob? Why aren't wizards more powerful? Should Special Ale be made to last longer? The discussions are usually polite but often passionate, angry, even rabid. Lots of people seem to care about this world and how it operates. Some of the debate is obviously policy debate, a discussion about the rules of the game, just as on Earth.

What does this all mean? Judging from the passion of these discussions, the affairs of this synthetic world are worth something to some people. That certainly makes sense to you now, given that you've just had a romantic interlude—your first?—with someone whom you only know as a resident of that place. And you've seen that the world's items are certainly valuable in terms of gold pieces, because you observed people trading items for gold pieces in the city. What are gold pieces worth? You go to an online auction site and search for "gold pieces" and the name of the synthetic world you visited. This turns up hundreds of auctions, including many for silver pieces. It seems that silver pieces can be had in lots of 1,000 for about $500, an exchange rate of two silver for one dollar, better than many real currencies. Can this value be real? As you peruse the auctions, it seems that they function just as auctions for things in the real world, like figurines and used cars. As with those kinds of items, the buyer sends the seller some money, by check or Internet funds transfer or some other method, and then the seller delivers the item to the buyer. In the case of synthetic worlds, the delivery must happen between two avatars, online. So if you buy 1,000 silver pieces, you are expected to send the seller a check for $500, and the seller is expected to meet with you in the synthetic world, where his avatar will give Sabert the 1,000 silver pieces.

Looking further at the available auctions, you also notice that entire accounts can be sold—send the seller $800, and he will give you his account name and password. Evidently, this market allows you to buy avatar capital, for real money. In some worlds, you might be able to use your Earth monies to buy items and avatar enhancements directly from the owners of the world. In either case, the theory that time is money is here shown to be plausible. In this market, the value of time to obtain items and avatar powers is directly reflected in a higher Earthly price. And it is a robust market, with thousands of transactions every hour and millions of dollars of trade every month.

When you decide to finally end your tour of this synthetic world and the online society around it, you leave your computer and go to bed, wondering whether anything you just saw was real.

Reality Check

The little tour is over, what did we learn?

First off, the entry hurdle between Earth and the synthetic world is actually quite high, relative to some other boundaries in cyberspace. You can become a registered online user of the *New York Times* in less than a minute, and you'll never have to enter your information again. To enter the fantasy realms of cyberspace, however, you'll have to pay fees, load software, adapt to a strange user interface system, and agree to a fairly substantial sacrifice of rights.

Second, as you became immersed in the synthetic world, there were three moments worth pausing and reflecting over. The first occurred at the moment the avatar's attributes felt like they were your own personal attributes. This step appears to be psychologically natural, because the avatar is just an extension of your body into a new space. The body is the tool by which the mind receives sensation and manipulates the environment, and this avatar body does exactly and only that. And it makes sense to think of it as *your* body, just as someone with a prosthetic arm should think of it as *his* arm. Coming to own the avatar, psychologically, is so natural among those who spend time in synthetic worlds that it is barely noticed. No one ever says, "My character's strength is depleted," or, "My avatar owns a dune buggy." They say "my strength" and "my dune buggy."

The second moment to think about happened when you acquired a real emotional investment in an event in the virtual world. Ethelbert seemed to take more bottles than he should have; they were yours. Perhaps that engaged your sense of justice, and you felt robbed. Perhaps you just felt the bottles helped you get around faster and were, therefore, good things that *you* wanted. Either way, it was a sign that you were engaging emotionally in the synthetic space in about the same way you do on Earth. Your mind, when confronted with this new place, automatically developed some desires with respect to it. This gave you something of an agenda, which the bottles might have helped along. Your mind also automatically translated important functions into the new space, such as the Right and Wrong calculator and the notion of My Property, and this caused you to develop expectations for your own and others' behavior. As with the extension of the body, your emotional investment was not forced on you by the hardware or the software, rather it seemed natural and, in the end, unnoticed. Those who spend time in synthetic worlds never say, "Sabert believes those bottles belong to him, and, if he existed, he would be mad at you now. Of course, I am not mad myself. This is just a fantasy world." They say, "I am mad that you took my bottle." On the other hand, it is fairly common for some users to assert that this place isn't real and that no one should be upset about what happens there. Invariably, this comment is made when something bad happens to *someone else*. When it happens to *them*, they invariably splutter, "Hey! You took my bottle!"

The third point of reflection happened when you were grateful to Ethelbert for giving you a gold piece. It is one thing to say that someone has an emotional investment in the events of a playland, but what about a financial investment? The gold piece doesn't help you fly the way the bottles did. Yet you thought it was a valuable thing, just like real money. And that seems crazy. Is it not insane to think that fantasy gold pieces are worth anything?

If you do think they are worthless, you have fallen into the diamond-water paradox, an old brain-teaser in economics. Why is it, the paradox goes, that diamonds, which are generally useless, command such high prices, while water, which is necessary for life, is so cheap? The resolution lies in an understanding of supply and demand: water is inexpensive because it is abundantly supplied relative to its demand, while diamonds are expensive because they are poorly supplied relative to their demand. But what are supply and demand? Supply tells us how much people have to sacrifice to bring goods to a marketplace for sale. Demand tells us how much people are willing to sacrifice to have the goods so they can use them. Think of it in terms of time: Diamonds are expensive because it takes quite a lot of time to get them discovered, mined, cut, and set. As a result, people have to be willing to work many, many hours to earn enough money to buy them, but as it turns out, lots of people are willing to do just that. Water is cheap because it doesn't take very many person-hours to provide an amount that satisfies the needs of a typical household. As a result, no one has to work very many hours to earn enough money to get quite a bit of water. So no one offers very much for water because they can get all they want for only a little bit of work time. Thus the resolution of the diamond-water paradox forces us to reflect on the costs and benefits of engaging in transactions, by all parties, as expressed in terms of time.

Note that this market-based translation of time into value is an entirely normal and accepted practice among economists and public policy analysts (see Boardman et al. 1996, chapter 10, and also pages 386–87). A standard assumption in all benefit-cost analyses is that anything of value can be denominated in terms of Earth money, as in "an hour of gem-hunting is worth so many dollars." Applying this reasoning more broadly to the case of digital items in synthetic worlds, it is obvious that these things do have value that can be counted in terms of dollars. They take time to acquire—the cost—but they help you do things you might want to do—the benefit. This means that in the normal case, there will indeed be a market-clearing price for these goods. And in all other circumstances, economists are quite content to say that this price is the social value of the item. Just as one cannot conclude that diamonds are worthless because they are said to "have no valuable uses," one also cannot conclude that the items in synthetic worlds are useless because "they are only virtual." Price indicates social value; virtual items have a price; therefore virtual items do have social value. Far-seeing legal scholars have already made this point explicitly (Lastowka and Hunter 2004), and courts will probably not be far behind.[8]

Now suppose you disagree with the teaching of the diamond-water paradox. As an aesthetic or moral judgment, you wish to assert that diamonds are, in fact, valueless, whatever price they may command on the market. Similarly, the existence of a positive price for these digital things also means nothing to you; they are intangible play toys and have no value at all. You may make these assertions, but you should realize that no such claim can ever be socially or politically or commercially accredited. You are free as an individual to decide whether any particular thing has value *for you*, but it is not up to you to decide what value these things have for society. Society decides that. Society consists of thousands or millions of people in decentralized relationships, quietly expressing their interests; the aggregate effect of their activity is to create an anonymous force that dictates the price of things. Once this force has determined that a certain diamond or digital bottle is worth $50, that is the end of the story. Its value is $50. And you would be wise to accept that judgment yourself.

Again, you don't have to; you could hold the Hope Diamond in your hand and boldly announce, "I owe no fealty to the crass marketplace of consumerist lust! This is a worthless crystal!" I am sure someone would step forward to relieve you of the worthless, all-too-heavy thing. I would be first in line, in fact. And that's even though I actually agree with you, in a sense. The Hope Diamond is not worth anything to me. But it *is* worth something to others, and that means I can trade the diamond for something *I* want. Indirectly, then, all things that the market values do have a value, for everyone. If the price of a thing is $500, it is worth $500 to everyone, either in use or in trade. Thus, even if you persuade yourself that Sabert's gems and silver pieces are worthless digital objects, the mere fact that *others* find them valuable, and are in principle willing to give you something that you *do* value in exchange for them, forces you accept their value.

In the synthetic world, therefore, it was proper that you were grateful to Ethelbert. He gave you something that has value to people; if it had no value to you in particular, you could have exchanged it for something that does, either in the world or out of it.

One might wonder what, if anything, would justify spending so much time here on an overlong disquisition about the "real" nature of "virtual" value, but the point is actually quite critical. This book claims that synthetic worlds have become important in some sense, that they are now well worth study, even if they are, at the moment, little more than souped-up video games. Once one recognizes that a silver piece in Sabert's world can have value just like a US dollar, one also must realize that the silver piece is not merely *like* money, it *is* money. Genuine, actual money, defined as "any commodity or token that is generally accepted as means of payment." Within Sabert's world, the silver piece is indeed generally accepted as a means of payment, and the fact that it bears a value in exchange against the US dollar indicates that this function is not a trivial one. As a result, one observes here a blurring in the distinction between virtual and real, fantastic and genuine, game and life. Indeed, all three points of reflection were moments that blurred the distinction between this world and the synthetic world, physically, emotionally, and financially. And this blurring happens on a personal level, to everyone who crosses over. While the boundaries can be firmed up in some places by an act of individual will—one may insist that the avatar's body is not *my* body—in many places they cannot be, because it is society, and not the individual, that has been breaking them down. This was the case with prices and values. The market decided that silver pieces were real money. No one (at least no one who remains socially active) can turn them into un-money just by imagining it to be so. The fading of lines has started to happen at the societal level, largely beyond anyone's control. As a result, video games are melding into daily life, and vice versa. And that is, in fact, a fairly significant development.

The fading of boundaries between our world and the synthetic worlds of cyberspace is what justifies serious inquiry, in my view. As the lines disappear, we move toward a state in which there really is no barrier to a complete translation of every interpersonal human phenomenon on Earth into the digital space. The interactions between Sabert and Ethelbert, his fellow spelunkers, the citizens, and his romantic partner, were all real human interactions. True, their subject matter was different from what we are accustomed to on the Earth—bottles of flying-ale, digital gems, gold pieces, verbal sex. Yet this apparent hyperreality of the objects has no implications whatsoever for the subjective import of these events. The object-world of Shakespeare's plays is also quite different from what we are accustomed to: falchions and codpieces are not common pieces of personal apparel anymore (excepting Renaissance Faires, Mardi Gras, and certain neighborhoods in Los Angeles). These object-level differences have done absolutely nothing to diminish the emotional and psychological impact of Shakespeare's plays, because these plays involve the stories of credibly human characters. Similarly, synthetic worlds involve the stories of credibly human characters, avatars whose every behavior is motivated by the decision of an actual human mind. Everything that happens in a synthetic world is the consequence of the interaction of human minds, and our minds have things like Love, Property, Justice, Profit, War, and Exploration hard-wired into them. We could not create a world and put people in it without also enabling sex, trade, and battle. Whatever physical environment and object-set we create, once populated, will be forced to play host to a full spectrum of personal emotions and interpersonal relations.

Such places may be physically strange, but they *must be* human. And all things human may be admitted as candidates for serious study and reflection.

Perhaps we can take this argument for significance further. Synthetic worlds may indeed play host to human dramas, making them potentially worth studying, but does anything make them *necessary* to study?

Consider this: We saw through Sabert that the human story can play itself out in a synthetic world, at the micro level. However, once we recognize that this is true for Sabert and his owner, we must also realize that it is true for everyone else who visits the place. The human story always plays out at a macro level too. And macro-level effects are significant at a macro level, which means: to us all.

Focusing on economics for a moment, note that Sabert found gems in the environment and he sold them for money. That looks like individual labor supply to me, and individual money demand. In economics, there's no magic involved in going from individual supply and demand to market supply and demand: you simply add up the individual supplies and demands of all the people. As a result, Sabert's world definitely hosts an aggregate labor supply and an aggregate money demand. It therefore has a nominal wage rate and price level. That means it has a real wage rate and a real gross domestic product. In fact, Sabert's world can potentially be measured by every macroeconomic indicator that can be applied to Earth countries. Even the online auction trade is a fairly typical form of trade on Earth; people in countries with unreliable currencies often conduct trade in US dollars. Therefore, in all aspects, the synthetic world is a genuine place of macroeconomic activity. And that means something significant: a synthetic world can, in principle, affect macroeconomic conditions on Earth.

This again is an effect of the blurring boundaries, but this time on a larger scale. If large numbers of German laborers decide to work in France, the GDP of both France and Germany changes significantly. Similarly, if large numbers of Earth laborers decide work in cyberspace—by which I mean, spend their time creating digital goods rather than ones made of metal and plastic and cloth—the GDP of both the synthetic world and the Earth must change, significantly.

The same argument carries through for any social science. Sociology: relationships form at the micro level in a cyberspace territory; relationships become social groups at the macro level; the same kinds of group differentiation that we see on Earth happen in cyberspace; the cyberspace groups can, in principle, have interactions with Earth-only groups, creating a macro-level spillover effect. Political science: people negotiate mutual agreements in a synthetic world; at a macro level, these form into organizations like clans and guilds with power hierarchies; these institutions develop modes of succession to office exactly like those we see on Earth; these officers can, in principle, negotiate agreements with the officers of Earth organizations, creating a macro-level spillover effect. Anthropology: people imbue certain digital objects with meaning; those meanings become shared, making the objects symbolic on a macro level; people begin to manipulate the symbols and meanings just as they do on Earth; in principle, the symbol structure can extend into or interact with the Earth's symbol structure, another macro spillover. And so on.[9]

In principle, then, events in synthetic worlds claim serious attention not just because they are human, but also because they may have effects that radiate outward into the ordinary world of Earth. Synthetic worlds may affect the daily lives of people who have no idea what the Internet is. And this is not necessarily a matter of scale. Jamaica is a country of some two million people, but on the basis of cultural impact, if nothing else, it cannot reasonably be argued that Jamaica is a trivial place that should be ignored. As we will see in the next chapter, synthetic worlds already host populations many times that of the island nation that gave the world reggae. They are also growing much more rapidly. As the synthetic country that Sabert visited becomes more populous, even in the near term if not over a longer time frame, the ripples of outward influence that we first observed through his eyes will begin to loom larger.

2

THE USER

The introduction claimed that games, especially virtual world games, were becoming serious business. Chapter 1 then offered a tour of a typical virtual world of today. Some effort was made to show how easy it is for a user to become immersed in the virtual space, with feelings closer to "I am there" as opposed to "my character is in the game." That transference of identity and place is not exactly remarkable, however, now that the Internet has been around for a decade or two. Ever since text-based chat rooms began cropping up in the 1970s and 1980s, many writers have described how virtuality works, how it affects identity and presence, and how experiences online can be so meaningful for those who pursue them. The literature on cyberspace in general is in fact very large and it would be distracting to get into it too deeply. The point is that many a hardheaded and experienced reader would react to chapter 1 with a healthy "So what? It's been done." The mere fact that practical virtual reality has moved from glowing green text to a graphical, games-based interface does not necessarily imply that anything important has happened. I would argue, on the contrary, that these changes make virtual worlds much more immersive and, by deepening the level of social realism, much more like real life, a factor which is in my view quite significant. But let's accept the point: Someone made a cool Internet video game; so what?

Here's where significance really starts: the users. This chapter will discuss the scope and practice of synthetic worlds usage as we observe it at the start of the twenty-first century. The basic message is that there are many more users than you might imagine; their numbers are growing rapidly; they are located in places you'd never suspect; they are not the people you thought they would be; and their motives seem to be both sensible and loaded with heavy implications. In other words, you might think that once a fantasy world appeared, there would be a few rather nerdy people who would use it; they'd probably be high school kids from places like San Francisco; and they'd be playing because they like to hang out in dark basements and shoot orcs. All of these impressions are wrong. The people who immerse themselves in virtual worlds are much more like the target reader of this book (a reasonable, professional, serious adult person) than one might have thought. The margin of society is not likely to be the permanent home for the people and practices involved with virtual worlds. Most near-term projections indicate, in fact, that the lifestyle described in chapter 1 will be part of ordinary life for a rapidly growing fraction of the Earth's population. And while long-run projections are more tentative (and will be left to the final chapter of the book), it seems that, unlike gory shooter video games, skateboards, and punk music, there is no obvious limit to this growth, no point at which one can say, "Even the truest fan will give this up and start living like the rest of us." In other words, the arguments and data here suggest that synthetic worlds may well be like cars, radio, and TV in the long run, gradually becoming something that everyone uses without thinking about it. Whether things will develop that way is too hard to predict, though, so for now we will keep the focus on near-term projections, which, as I said, indicate substantial growth.

The Lay of the Synthetic Land

Before getting into the possibilities of growth, let's first consider some data about the state of affairs today. At the time of this writing, synthetic worlds constitute a small subset of the Internet. Table 1 lists all of the known worlds with more than 100,000 paying subscribers as of late 2004.

The first thing that leaps out of the table are the raw numbers. There are over 15 virtual worlds that meet the 100,000 subscriber criterion, despite the fact that Internet access costs and game subscription fees are not insignificant anywhere. In the United States, the game software for a virtual world typically costs as much as $50, subscription fees are $10–$15 monthly, and the required high-speed network setup requires a fairly high-end computer ($1,500) and a cable or DSL subscription ($30–$50 monthly). Elsewhere, some components might be cheaper (game subscriptions in China, for example) but others more expensive (Internet access in China), so that one cannot explain variations in the numbers on the basis of overall cost. Rather, culture and net access seem to be the determining factors.

The largest subscription figures are for Asian games such as *Lineage*, *Legend of Mir*, and *Mu*; in fact, all of the worlds with more than one million subscribers are in Asia. The reports from which these data were drawn also indicate that China already appears to have the single largest number of users, while Korea seems to

Table 1   Subscription-based synthetic worlds (December 2004; minimum subscription level 100,000)

World	Release date	Subscriptions*	Subject	Headquarters
Ultima Online	1997	220,000	Medieval	US
Lineage	1998	2,500,000	Medieval	Asia
EverQuest	1999	420,000	Medieval	US
Dark Age of Camelot	2001	250,000	Medieval	US
Legend of Mir II	2001	2,000,000	Medieval	Asia
Runescape	2002	100,000	Medieval	Europe
Final Fantasy XI	2002	500,000	Medieval	Asia
Ragnarok Online	2002	300,000	Medieval	Asia
Westward Journey II	2002	1,500,000	Medieval	Asia
Mu	2002	1,500,000	Medieval	Asia
Cross Gate	2002	1,000,000	Medieval	Asia
Star Wars Galaxies	2003	300,000	Space	US
Lineage II	2003	1,500,000	Medieval	Asia
World of Legend	2003	1,000,000	Medieval	Asia
Toontown	2003	150,000	Children	US
Legend of Mir III	2003	1,000,000	Medieval	Asia
City of Heroes	2004	175,000	Superheroes	US
EverQuest II	2004	200,000	Medieval	US
World of Warcraft	2004	500,000	Medieval	US

*Subscriptions: number of paying subscribers. Data are approximate, as there is no centralized reporting source. Industry analyst Bruce Sterling Woodcock summarizes population levels drawn from insider reports and press releases at http://pw1.netcom.com/~sirbruce/Subscriptions.html. Consultant Betsy Book maintains an updated review of social virtual worlds at http://www.virtualworldsreview.com/. Figures for Asian virtual worlds rely on "China Internet Sector," a report by JP Morgan Asia Pacific Equity Research (May 2004).

have the highest density of users per capita (Herz 2002). The figures for China are especially worth noting, given that Internet penetration in that country remains very low, less than 6 percent of the urban population as of 2004 (JP Morgan 2004). We can expect Chinese participation to grow even more, since the track record for growth in this sector has suggested that high-speed Internet access is a major predictor of virtual world size: as DSL and cable expand in a country, the number of subscribers rises.

The United States and Europe, meanwhile, have smaller numbers but more product innovation, with worlds deviating from the Medieval Fantasy norm by going into such areas as Space/Science Fiction, Children's Adventure, and Superheroes.

Overall, the figures in table 1 suggest that virtual worlds are significant, just based on populations. The worlds listed there together have almost 13 million subscribers. While this almost certainly does not amount to 13 million separate individuals (players are known to buy two accounts in the same game, or hold accounts in several games at once), it very probably does exceed 10 million people—for reference sake, that's the size of the city of New York.

And there are many more worlds that are not listed in table 1:

- There are dozens of places that are modeled as subscription services but have fewer than 100,000 subscribers.
- There is a growing number of synthetic worlds that do not follow the monthly subscription model. For example: Playdo is a Swedish virtual chat space, mostly for teens but not restricted to them. It's free to register, and members can walk around in a 2D virtual space and talk to friends and so on. The service has more than 300,000 members. If it's free, then where does the revenue come from? Consider the business model for Habbo Hotel, a similar UK site. Registering for Habbo is free, but to gain access to in-world activities (swimming pools) and items ("furni"—furniture) you have to buy in-world currency—using real money. Beyond this, the opportunities for product placement are obvious. Coke maintains a virtual world called "Coke Studios" at http://www.cokemusic.com/, where users can hang out, wander, chat, and be immersed in the idea that drinking Coke is a cool thing. Project Entropia, with more than 150,000 downloads of its free software, charges no fee but rather sells its currency for real-world cash.
- Even simple instant-messaging systems are acquiring a virtual reality backdrop of sorts. If you use Yahoo! Instant Messaging, you can make an avatar that will appear whenever your messages arrive, and, well, you don't want your avatar looking stupid like the free ones they offer, do you? Of course not. Nice faces, outfits, backgrounds, and more can be purchased for a modest fee. It is evident that well outside the realm of fantasy game worlds, the virtual world experience is beginning to take root as a common feature of human communication.
- Many people are becoming familiar with online gaming in general. As I write this, on an ordinary Thursday afternoon, 178,000 people are playing games with one another at Yahoo! Games, and a further 148,000 are at MSN's gaming site Zone.com. Studies have suggested that these casual gamers tend to be older than synthetic world gamers, many in their 30s and 40s, and are also more likely to be female. It would be a small step to embed these casual games (card

games, puzzles, and so on) in an environment, with an avatar interface; one recent game/world, *Yohoho! Puzzle Pirates*, has done exactly that, growing rapidly to more than 10,000 paying subscribers. Casual online gaming is even more widespread in Asia. In a press release dated September 2004, Chinese gaming industry partners Shanda and Nexon announced a world record for simultaneous online play of a single game, with over 700,000 Chinese gamers playing a game called *BNB*. It's a game where families play as a team against other families, and it's just the latest example of the immense numbers coming from the Asian gaming market.

As the phenomenon of practical virtual reality spreads beyond the model of subscription payments for access to a terrain, it becomes harder to measure, forcing a reliance on (still too rare) surveys and reports as another way to estimate these numbers. Perhaps the most likely to be accurate is the annual survey of the Interactive Digital Software Association, taken from a representative sample of the US population. The survey suggests that of the 145 million people who play games in the United States, 7 percent are involved in persistent world gameplay.[1] This would make the synthetic world population 10 million people, and that is in the United States alone. A more global estimate comes from a report by DFC Intelligence, a reputable game industry analysis firm, which counted 73 million online gamers worldwide in 2003 (DFC Intelligence 2003). Of these, 38 percent are "hard-core," intense users. Since synthetic worlds tend to be *the* example of hard-core use of online games, assigning the 38 percent hard-core users to synthetic worlds would place the number of these gamers at 27 million.

We really have no idea how many people are currently quite comfortable putting on an avatar and going "somewhere else." An absolute minimum figure would be 10 million. My guess is that it is perhaps 20 or 30 million.

At this size, the phenomenon of synthetic worlds seems to have become something more than a niche activity. Indeed, the activity in these places is orders of magnitude larger than in their ancestors, text-based adventure games and chat rooms.[2] Yet the road from simple text to immersive worlds is basically linear, and many of the practices and usage patterns we see today have been in place for quite a while. Text-based multiuser spaces first appeared in the late 1970s, and the first graphical chat world—a world with visible characters rather than just typed sentences—was developed in the 1980s by LucasArts (Morningstar and Farmer 1990). Over the next decade, this basic visual chat concept was expanded to include immersive gaming systems and richer graphics. When first-person graphics were developed (Kushner 2003), they quickly made their way into the graphical chat arena, and the first visually immersive synthetic world was released as *Meridian*

59 in 1996. *Meridian 59* was not extremely successful, but several games in its wake were. *Ultima Online*, released in 1997 (Electronic Arts), acquired a population of over 200,000 people. *Lineage*, released in September 1998 (NCSoft) quickly had over one million. *EverQuest*, released in 1999 (Sony Online Entertainment), grew to 450,000. After these successes, new worlds then began to appear at a rapid rate. By my own calculations, the rate at which new worlds now appear is an almost exact match of Moore's Law: like the amount of processor power on a chip, the number of virtual worlds has been doubling every two years or so. The phenomenon that was first discovered in online text messages has continued to grow exponentially for some 20 years now.

Perhaps most interesting about these developments is the fact that most of the worlds never go away. With few exceptions, worlds do not close once they are opened. This is absolutely astonishing in the context of games, where an industry rule of thumb holds that approximately 95 percent of titles will fail and disappear from the shelves after six weeks.[3] By contrast, the seven-year-old world of *Ultima Online* still has more than 150,000 actively paying subscribers, at more than $10 a head. Indeed, all of the oldest games have amazingly robust population counts. Synthetic worlds, it seems, almost never die.

Thus in terms of raw numbers, growth, and sheer persistence, synthetic worlds have made themselves worthy of note, especially given the unusual nature of life inside them.

The Connection to Video Games

Some of the success of synthetic worlds derives from the general increase in online video-gaming as a social phenomenon, whose development has been described by Brad King and John Borland (2003) among others.[4] When technology first provided games on video consoles in the late 1970s and early 1980s, there was an explosion of arcade gaming that collapsed fairly quickly. We now know that the collapse did not occur because people tired of games and went back to watching TV; it happened because the personal computer arrived and, with it, the ability to play games in your own room at drastically lower prices. More and more households bought computers, and they also bought computing devices that did nothing but play games. Within just a decade, the introduction of the computer and the game console as standard home entertainment gear induced a radical change in the nature of a typical childhood in the United States, Japan, and Europe (Rushkoff 1996). By the year 1995 or so, the typical child grew up playing video games at home. And it seems he did not stop playing video games once he left

home: The Pew Internet and American Life Project reported in 2003 that 70 percent of college students played video games at least once in a while (Pew 2003).
Each year saw another increase in the average age of a game player. By 2004, the
IDSA's annual consumer survey revealed the following general statistics about
the state of game-playing in the United States:

- Those people who play video games or computer games now represent more
  than 50 percent of the population over age 6.
- The average game player is 29 years old.
- 43 percent of game players are women.
- 97 percent of games are purchased by adults over age 18.
- 60 percent of parents play games with their children at least once a month.[5]

The people who played games as kids in the 1980s and early 1990s became game-
playing adults after the turn of the century. And apparently many of them—20
million or so—began to play massively multiplayer online games.

As this growth continued, games began to garner more attention from scholars. In the humanities, a new field of "Ludology" has appeared which claims that
games are a unique form of cultural expression; opponents of this new school
argue that games are an extension of existing artistic forms (Aarseth 1997; Juul
2001; Murray 1997). In other words, scholars in the humanities tend to view games
as special books, or as something more powerful than books; either way, games
have become important. Meanwhile, education scholars now point to the interactivity of games as a feature that makes them excellent teaching and training
tools (Prensky 2000; Pesce 2000; Berger 2002; Gee 2003; Williams 2003; Squire
and Jenkins 2004; Steinkuehler 2004). And as soon as games began to acquire
a strong multiplayer component, social scientists began to take notice. The early
text-based virtual worlds were subjected to incisive ethical and legal analysis
(Dibbell 1999; Mnookin 2001), and the best paper on the social scientific meaning of the much more populous contemporary virtual worlds has been written
by two lawyers, F. Greg Lastowka and Dan Hunter (2004). Contemporary synthetic worlds have also caught the attention of sociologists (Jakobsson and Taylor
2003), economists (Castronova 2001), historians (Burke 2004), and social network analysts (Ducheneaut and Moore 2004). I am certain that by the time this
book goes to press, there will be many more articles to cite here, from a wide variety of disciplines. And as scholarly activity increases, we see the foundation of
new journals, research centers, and Game Design and Game Studies certificate
programs at universities around the world.[6] As games have grown in social salience,
the attention scholars give to them has increased likewise.[7]

All of these signs suggest that video games have become an important force in contemporary culture. Within the category of video games in general, we now see that the massively populated online variety is gathering steam, growing to occupy the time of perhaps 10 to 20 million people, as noted above. With all of the scholarly work now emerging, we can take a closer look at who these people are.

User Characteristics

So: who are the people who spend time in synthetic worlds? Based on the way history unfolded, with video games effectively acting as a spawn-bed for synthetic worlds, it would be tempting to assume that people in synthetic worlds are just like video gamers in general. That would be a mistake, however. I've noted already that the game industry is only the easiest place to observe the virtual world phenomenon; the phenomenon itself now extends beyond games and into human communication as a whole. Surveys of general game-player characteristics are therefore going to be less relevant than direct surveys of people who participate in virtual worlds of some kind.

We are fortunate to have a number of these direct surveys which, for mostly accidental reasons, have focused on the most popular synthetic world in the United States, *EverQuest*. The first person to collect systematic data there was a then undergraduate Haverford College psychology student named Nicholas Yee. Yee's project was called "The Norrathian Scrolls," "Norrath" being the name of *EverQuest*'s world (Yee 2001). In his initial study Yee posted surveys at his website and then invited *EverQuest* players to take them, collecting reliable demographic and psychological data from about 2,448 players. To date, Yee's website (www.nickyee.com) remains one of the best online sources of information about this phenomenon. Yee found that while the vast majority of his respondents were male (84 percent), their average age was 25.7 years. Two-thirds were working, only one-third were students. One-third of the men and 60 percent of the women were married. Twenty percent of the respondents had at least one child. A quarter of the respondents played with a sibling or a child or a parent. These figures certainly do not cohere with the vision most of us have about online fantasy game players: we expect to see unmarried teenagers, students, with no children, playing alone; we find older people, who are more connected than we would expect.

These impressions are confirmed by a second study, namely my own, conducted in summer 2001. Once again *EverQuest* players were the target. Like Yee's, my data were drawn from a sample of fan-site browsers who were invited to answer a questionnaire. I recognized that this would bias the results toward hard-core players, so I used data from direct observations within the game world to construct weights that would improve the representativeness of the survey data.[8] In any case, tables 2–4 present weighted characteristics from my sample of 3,916 respondents (for more detail on the survey, see Castronova 2001).

My first concern in the survey was to determine how immersed a typical user felt himself to be. I posed a series of questions asking how the respondent felt about Norrath. Table 2 gives the responses. They show that a significant number of people think of Norrath as their main place of residence; large numbers would spend all of their time there if they could. Roughly speaking, we can characterize about one-fifth of Norrath's users as more or less fully immersed; they treat the game world as their life world. Moreover, a clear majority wishes to spend more time in Norrath than is now possible. These attitudes mesh well with my personal impression when visiting the place: most people wish they could spend more time there, and a smaller but still significant number devotes all thought to the world.

The next question I posed was whether these self-styled "residents" of Norrath, those who viewed it as their principal home, were much like the stereotype that we apply to video gamers: disaffected, isolated, socially awkward, youths. Data presented in table 3 argue against that view. The table lists the demographic and

Table 2   Participation in Norrath and Earth society

Statement	Agree or strongly agree	Disagree or strongly disagree	Don't know/not applicable
I live outside Norrath but I travel there regularly.	84	12	4
I live in Norrath but I travel outside of it regularly.	20	74	6
I wish I could spend more time in Norrath than I do now.	58	34	8
If I could make enough money selling things from Norrath, I would quit my current job or school and make my money there instead.	39	57	4
If I could, I would spend all of my time in Norrath.	22	74	4

Source: Norrath Economic Survey 2001. N = 3,353 to 3,365. The data are weighted so that the distribution of avatar levels in the data is comparable to the distribution of avatar levels in Norrath.

employment characteristics of self-reported "residents" and self-reported "non-residents." It appears that there are few differences between the fully immersed and the less immersed. The residents are somewhat less likely to be married or caring for children, but not dramatically so. Both groups are above college age. Both consist primarily of workers, not students. Both earn reasonable monthly incomes. Both groups are overwhelmingly male.

Table 3   Characteristics of *EverQuest* players

Characteristics	All respondents	Residents*	Visitors*
Age (years)	24.3	22.4	24.8
Female (%)	7.8	10.1	7.2
Region: United States (%)	81.3	82.4	81.1
Region: Canada (%)	6.6	7.5	6.4
Region: Western/Southern Europe (%)	8.9	7.1	9.4
Number of adults in household	2.1	2.1	2.1
Married or cohabiting (%)	22.8	15.9	24.5
Single (%)	60.0	68.0	58.1
Have children to care for daily (%)	15.0	11.4	15.9
Education: less than high school (%)	12.4	19.4	10.6
Education: high school degree only (%)	35.6	41.7	34.1
Education: college degree or more (%)	31.0	18.6	34.1
Employment status: working full-time (%)	53.4	41.5	56.4
Employment status: student, working (%)	19.4	22.3	18.6
Employment status: student, not working (%)	15.6	21.1	14.3
Weekly work hours[†]	39.0	36.5	39.5
Monthly earnings ($)[†]	3,154.12	2,621.85	3,268.96
Hourly wage ($)[‡]	20.74	17.57	21.42

Source: Norrath Economic Survey 2001. $N = 3,619$. The smallest cell count is 401, for resident hourly wage. The data are weighted so that the distribution of avatar levels in the data is comparable to the distribution of avatar levels in Norrath.
*Residents agree or strongly agree that they "live in Norrath and travel outside of it regularly"—see table 2. Visitors are all others.
[†]Work hours less than 5 per week were set to "missing." Earnings less than $5 per month or more than $100,000 per month were also set to "missing." Thus, these are averages among those who work for pay, excluding those earning more than $1.2 million per year. Monthly earnings are after tax ("take-home pay"). Non-US respondents converted earnings to US$ using prevalent exchange rates. Many respondents refused to answer the income question on grounds of privacy. Still, there were 2,853 valid responses to the question, a 79 percent response rate.
[‡]The hourly wage divides monthly earnings by four times weekly hours.

In terms of their use of the game world, residents and nonresidents also appear to be similar. Table 4 gives the hourly time investment of a typical player, and shows that while fully immersed people do spend more time in Norrath, it is not dramatically more time. Both groups spend more than 4 hours daily and more than 24 hours weekly in the world. In terms of time investment, both groups seem to be heavily immersed in Norrath.

How much time is this really? Figure 1 presents the distribution of typical weekly hours in Norrath among survey respondents. The vast majority of players seem to play less than 30 hours weekly. Data from Nielsen Media Research, also indicated on the figure, show that this is less than the average weekly TV viewing hours of adult men and women, and comparable to that of children and teens. If we note that this sample of *EverQuest* players is biased toward hard-core, intense players—these are people who surfed a fan site and then chose voluntarily to answer a lengthy survey about the game—the data suggest that *EverQuest* is just another form of media entertainment for most people. Even hard-core players seem less invested in *EverQuest* than the average adult is invested in television.

More recently there have been two new statistical studies of *EverQuest* players, by UK psychologists Griffiths, Davies, and Chappell (2003, 2004). In one study, the psychologists gathered data from the polls that are posted occasionally at fan sites by the site administrators. As in previous studies, about 85 percent of the respondents were male, but the vast majority were above age 18. Only about one-third were in school. In a follow-up web-based survey study, Griffiths et al. found that of the 541 respondents, 81 percent were male, and the average age was 28. Some 40 percent were married or cohabiting. Eighty percent reported an occupation other than "student." Over 75 percent played *EverQuest* with friends; 25 percent reported playing *EverQuest* with their romantic partner. The average weekly time in the

Table 4   Norrath characteristics

Norrath characteristics	All respondents	Residents[*]	Visitors[*]
Hours in Norrath over the past 24 hours	4.5	5.4	4.24
Hours in Norrath in a typical 24-hour period	4.7	6.0	4.43
Hours in Norrath in the past 7 days	26.3	32.5	24.8
Hours in Norrath in a typical 7-day period	28.9	36.1	27.1

Source: Norrath Economic Survey 2001. $N = 3,467$. The data are weighted so that the distribution of avatar levels in the data is comparable to the distribution of avatar levels in Norrath.
[*]Residents agree or strongly agree that they "live in Norrath and travel outside of it regularly"—see table 2. Visitors are all others.

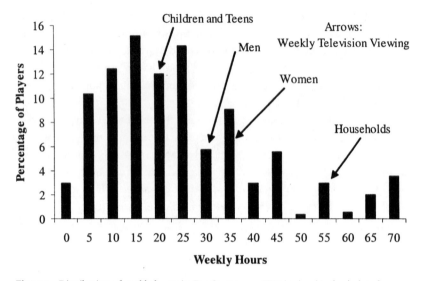

Figure 1   Distribution of weekly hours in *EverQuest* versus TV viewing (Author's data from the "Norrath Economic Survey," 2001, and Nielsen Media Research, obtained June 22, 2003, from http://www.tvb.org/)

world was about 25 hours. As for what they liked most about the game, the top three responses all related to social roles: "It's a social game," "You can group with others to have adventures," and "You can join a guild [an in-game player club]." Again, the data resist interpretation along the expected lines; we would not conclude from this that the synthetic world phenomenon is mostly about teens, mostly about outcasts, mostly about shooting orcs and demons. It rather seems social, even communal, and no more intense time-wise than watching TV.

This actually accords well with my own anecdotal impressions from touring and traveling in a great many synthetic worlds. *EverQuest* is not special in this regard. Indeed, if anything, the *EverQuest* players ought to have more in common with the stereotypical teenage video game junkie, since it is a fairly intense fantasy-based game, far more than a dressed-up chat room. And indeed, *EverQuest* players share some similarities with video gamers in general; they are predominantly male, for example. And yet my feeling, backed up by my own surveys and those of others, is that the comparison between video gamers in general and the typical synthetic world user is not helpful. These folks are not so much game players as travelers or explorers. They are generally mature, well-spoken, and responsible. They are usually in close connection with family members (including both parents and children), whether those family members play or not. It is common, for example, to be traveling in a party and have one member say that he'll have to take a break for the night because his child is now home. Synthetic world users are avidly social, always looking for ways to team up with others to go pursue some activity or another. Like most game players, they came of age in the late 1980s and early 1990s, when computer and console gaming had become normal. And while they are now older and holding down jobs, they are still playing video games, albeit much more sophisticated ones. Like most game players, the synthetic world visitors spend quite a lot of time playing, and they do so with family and friends. But unlike regular gamers, those in the synthetic world seem to maintain a great deal of their social connections exclusively online, which accounts for the large number of hours spent there (as well as some of the more medieval-like social structures that emerge; see Jakobsson and Taylor 2003). And yet the motive for pursuing their sociality in cyberspace rather than the real world remains obscure.

Effects of Games

Searching for motives, we might consider more deeply the effects that games have. What is the experience unique to synthetic worlds that is so attractive for so many?

Unfortunately, there is much more research into the effects of video games in general than on the specific effects of massively multiplayer virtual world games. And it would take us astray to delve too deeply into the video game effects literature. (For a comprehensive review, see Kwan-Min and Peng 2004.) The games in this literature are, in many ways, so completely unlike the typical synthetic world experience as to make any findings about their effects of only doubtful relevance. For example, a typical study places a subject in a first-person, single-player shooter-type game, and then observes how physiological or cognitive metrics respond to various in-game events, or how attitudes change before and after the experience. Unfortunately, the core features of this kind of game (raw violence, rapid-fire action, and the lone-wolf, kill-or-be-killed mentality) are almost never observed in synthetic worlds. First, a large number of those worlds are really only about chatting; there's no fighting at all. Second, very little happens individually; the whole point of a social world is to be social, to work in teams. Third, in those worlds where fighting happens, network latency prevents any kind of rapid-fire combat action.[9] By far the most frequent combat move is to wait until the time is right, and then hit one button: Attack, Heal, Cast Spell, etc., depending on the role you occupy in your group. Therefore, studies of single players, playing games with rapid eye-hand coordination and a flow of gory moments, are really not relevant.

Since there do not seem to be any studies that focus specifically on the physio-logical or attitudinal effects of synthetic world experiences, however, the ordinary video game research is the only evidence we have. Video games have been shown to have some positive impacts; kids who play them have better eye-hand coordination, for example (McSwegin, Pemberton, and O'Banion 1988; Green and Bavelier 2003). Nonetheless, most research focuses on the negative. Indeed the dominant issue in the literature has been the question of whether violence in games makes kids vio-lent in real life.[10] On the basis of this literature, and with the support of anecdotal evidence from parents and teachers, legislatures in the United States have on occa-sion sought to ban violent video game sales to minors. These laws have regularly been overturned by courts as violations of free speech rights. Still, from the tenor of the outrage expressed, it is hard not to conclude that video games are just the latest in a series of bugbears of parents who have become frustrated and frightened about how violent American society has become. In sympathy with those parents, I truly wish that video games, TV, rock n' roll, the nickelodeon, and wireless radio receivers were at fault, because then we could just have banned these things in sequence and our problems would have been solved long ago. Unfortunately, one suspects that violence in youth media is rather more of a tonic against violence in daily life than an incitement to it. The preeminent scholar of fairy tales, Bruno Bettelheim (1976/1985), reminds us that make-believe violence is very helpful for childhood psychological development. There are violent fairy tales that are good, and peaceful ones that are awful; the same is probably true of video games. The ethical analysis of playing and designing is still in its infancy (Reynolds 2002). Still, the implicit message here is that we ought to be thinking very seriously about the quality of the games that occupy the time of our children.[11]

And when it comes to issues of time, here we have a clear point of overlap between video game research and synthetic world user effects: the prospect of addiction. According to Yee's surveys (2002), many *EverQuest* users consider them-selves addicted to the game. In 2003 there were reports, perhaps apocryphal, that a Korean player had died of exhaustion after spending 80 continuous hours in *Lineage* without a break. An *EverQuest* user who committed suicide was said to have done so out of desperation at events within the game world. Indeed, Yee is able to identify a smoking gun: he finds that the reward structures in *EverQuest* are designed as a classic randomized reinforcement mechanism that is known to induce process-based addictions.[12] And in this potential for addiction, synthetic worlds are quite similar to ordinary video games, and even computers in general. There are doctors who focus exclusively on Internet and computer addiction as a behavioral pathology (Young 1998; Greenfield 1999). According to Dr. Maressa Hecht Orzack, of the Harvard Medical School, the dangers are apparent:

She [Dr. Orzack] has studied recreational drug use and thinks that inappropriate computer use is similar. Her sense is that we are just seeing the tip of the iceberg. Our society is becoming more and more computer dependent not only for information, but for fun and entertainment. This trend is a potential problem affecting all ages, starting with computer games for kids to chats for the unwary or vulnerable adult. ("Computer Addiction Services" website, http://www. computeraddiction.com/)

When people spend dozens of hours weekly at their computers, or on the Internet, or playing video games, it is almost certain that some other activities will suffer. The question is, when does this behavior warrant the label "addiction"? Addiction is a strong word, calling for both renunciation on the part of the subject and forceful intervention by others. For some behaviors, it is the right word. My mother was addicted to alcohol; it added no joy to her life but rather interfered severely with all of her relationships; she should indeed have turned her back on it, and others ought to have taken some responsibility. Now suppose she instead had been addicted to *EverQuest*. To me, that sentence, in comparison to alcohol addiction, sounds like someone suggesting, "What if your mother was addicted to France instead of alcohol?" I would reply, "Fine! She likes France. Let's move to France. End of problem." The point is, a behavior becomes problematic when, and only when, it degrades other important things in life. A 60-hour-a-week compulsive *EverQuest* user who fails to speak to his own children when they come home from school is engaging in a problematic behavior. But consider the same user, living alone, with all his friends being online and in the game—is his devotion of time to cyberspace problematic? In the end, we can only judge whether presence in a virtual world is good or bad by reference to the ordinary daily life of the person making the choice to go there. For some people, Earth is where they really ought to spend their time. For others, perhaps the fantasy world *is the only decent place available*. Unfortunately, we have no studies that go into any detail about the daily lives of synthetic world users, so we cannot really tell whether they are addicted, or just making an understandable choice.

Prospects for Growth: Basic Projections

Having been unable to make solid statements about the motivations behind the choice to enter a synthetic world, then, we now face a certain degree of difficulty in answering an important question: Will this behavior become more common or less? Or will it level off at some point?

The question demands some attention primarily because social scientists have begun to raise it. A game world like *EverQuest* is not so interesting necessarily for what it is; it bears interest because of what it may become, and more than a few analysts have pointed out that a widespread growth of synthetic worlds would have fairly serious implications for daily life. Certainly the behavior patterns, time use, and even cognitive functioning of countless individual people would change. For society as a whole, however, the effects on relationships, law, economics, and even government would be too large to predict with any accuracy. Suffice it to say that the decampment of hundreds of millions of people into computer-generated fantasy worlds would be noticeable in many spheres of life.

Strong growth is certainly the shared projection of market analysts, such as the Asian Equity Research wings of firms like JP Morgan and Bear Stearns. In 2004, both groups issued "buy" recommendations for a number of Korean and Chinese firms based on an anticipated growth in online gaming (JP Morgan 2004; Bear Stearns 2004). Their growth predictions do not consider user motivations directly; rather they simply note that high-speed Internet access and age cohort have been the most reliable historical indicators of growth, and both are trending upward. The Internet access effect is easy to understand; online games are better to play and easier to get involved in when the Internet is an always-on, always-fast service in the home. As for the age cohort, data indicate that even after Korea was broadband-saturated right around the turn of the century, its online gaming activity continued to increase. Apparently, once an age group becomes familiar with the act of visiting a virtual world, its members never quite give it up completely. Thus as the net-savvy age cohort makes its way upward in Korea's age distribution, the fraction of Koreans who are interested in virtual worlds continues to rise. A similar phenomenon is observable in the United States, as the general popularity of video games keeps rising along with the average age of a video gamer (now 29). Both the age cohort effects and the penetration rate of broadband in China have led analysts to predict strong growth for games and large profits for Asian game developers.

Spreading Internet access and aging are processes that are not confined to Asia, of course, and this has led analysts in the United States to predict strong growth here. Only 4 million US homes had high-speed Internet in the year 2000, but about 14 million had it by 2002. According to an August 2004 report by DFC Intelligence (2004b), a well-reputed US consulting firm that specializes in video game markets, this figure had risen to 26 million by the end in 2003. DFC compares this figure to about 20 million networked homes in Europe and 36 million in Asia, concluding that there is much growth potential for high-speed Internet around the world. DFC therefore expects global revenues from online gaming to follow that growth, rising over 500 percent (!) from 2003 to 2009, reaching almost $10 billion by that point. In April 2003, DFC also predicted that total game industry revenues (including both online and offline games) would rise from $20 billion to $30 billion between 2002 and 2007, an annual growth rate of 8.4 percent.[13] In June 2003, PricewaterhouseCoopers predicted an annual growth rate of game industry revenues of 24.6 percent for the same period.[14] In July 2003, DFC estimated that the number of *online* gamers would grow from 73 million in 2003 to 198 million in 2008, a growth rate of 22 percent annually. As to whether or not these figures are at all reliable, a June 2004 DFC report (2004a) noted, meekly, that its growth predictions had consistently been on the low side during this period of rapid growth. We all know that prediction is a tricky business ("especially when it involves the future," said Niels Bohr). And yet it is hard to walk away from this stack of reports by well-known and reputable consulting firms without believing that there will be many more people in synthetic worlds in years to come.

Let's examine what the growth rates reported above might mean for the population of synthetic worlds. Assume that the global virtual world population is at the low end of conceivable estimates, at 10 million people, and that it will grow only as fast as the most moderate game industry growth projections given above (8.4 percent annually). Under these assumptions, the population of synthetic worlds would grow to over 40 million people by 2020 and almost 100 million by 2030. I hesitate to project much farther than that, but it seems that the base is significant enough that even a moderate growth rate, over just the course of the next generation, would transform synthetic worlds into a broadly significant phenomenon. And this also raises the possibility that, from that point forward, their impact may end up being comparable to the media innovations of the twentieth century—radio, film, television. The only way to argue against this conclusion requires a story in which high-speed Internet (which will only get faster) and the maturation of the population, for some reason, no longer induce more online gaming as they have done in the past. I think that this would be a hard story to sell, certainly harder than the story of growth told by these consulting firms. And for that reason I am fairly well persuaded that synthetic worlds will become more and more important at least for the next decade or so and perhaps beyond.

The Open Question: Why Will They Grow?

So far in this chapter, we've analyzed the current population figures of synthetic worlds and then attempted to discover, through the existing research on synthetic worlds in particular and video games more generally, a set of user motivations that would allow us to predict the near-term course of this technology. Unfortunately, the existing scholarly research does not shed much direct light on user motivations in the case of synthetic worlds, so our only real source of basic projections has been the game consultant industry. The projections they make are quite strong. They are also mechanistic, relying entirely on a historical connection between broadband penetration, population aging, and online gaming. And while I find those predictions persuasive, they are also unsatisfying. To say that Timmy Jones now spends 30 hours a week enacting a second life as a pirate in a virtual world, and that he does that because his family just got a cable modem, does not really explain why Timmy has the latent desire to be a pirate rather than just plain Timmy Jones. Similarly, to say that more Canadians are pretending to be wizards and warriors these days because people born after 1980 are quite likely to do that, and there are more and more of them every year, does not explain why people born after 1980 like to be wizards and warriors in the first place. What's wrong with just being Canadian? In the end, then, even though we ought to be very confident that synthetic worlds will grow, we still haven't understood why.

Asking "why cyberspace—why not Earth" is, of course, asking the most important question, fraught with implication. Since we have no direct research on it, we will have to paste together what conjectures and evidence we can. Largely, this is a move from data analysis to cultural theory, and thus more open to critical assessment on the part of the reader. But the move is necessary, at least at a speculative level; we really do need to ask why, and to try to grasp for an answer.

One avenue of attack might focus on synthetic worlds primarily as games, and then assume that, since games are fun, an increase in access will result in more game-playing. While this is easy, it is too simple. Synthetic worlds are more than a game, or, if they are a game, they are such a unique game that assuming they are "fun" does not really help. We would still need to ask why they are fun, for whom.

Now let's take the other extreme and assume that synthetic worlds are not games at all but rather forums for communication. This requires a somewhat more complex answer to the question of growth. Under this view, growth will depend on whether avatar-mediated communication is better than its competitors at facilitating the interactions that humans want to have. This, certainly, was the argument put forth long ago by the early advocates of virtual reality in the workplace, such as John Walker (1988). To define what we mean by "better," imagine an economic theory of communications technology, which says that of two technologies with the same communicative quality, we should expect the cheaper one to dominate. Another way of saying the same thing is this: of two technologies with the same cost, the one that delivers communications of better quality will dominate. Synthetic worlds are a form of word-communication (through text and, lately, voice) that also enables a kind of physical bodily communication, through the gestures and position of the avatar. They thus offer a higher-quality forum of interaction than the chat room or the telephone, neither of which gives any scope to the body. And while video conferencing gives both body and voice, it does not do so in a way that allows people to mingle with one another in a world-like space; it is very expensive, bandwidth-wise; and avatar voice conferencing is a pretty close substitute that costs much less. Thus, relative to these other communications tools, synthetic worlds do seem very competitive on grounds of either service or cost or both. By this reasoning, we would once again expect synthetic worlds to grow in time, because they are a lower-cost, higher-quality communication tool than any of their competitors.

What about an in-between view, that what happens in these places is not just play, and not just communication. It is a complex thing, a combination of real interaction and a play-like context. That complexity may be easy enough to perceive, since we are talking about a fantasy world here; it really does seem odd to think that people can quite comfortably chat about their affairs when one looks like a wizard, the other looks like an orc, and the things they talk about include the killing of dragons. The mixing of play and not-play there is almost tangible. Where things get stranger still, and become harder to handle, is when we realize that we only understand this mixing of play and nonplay because we are actually involved in it every day, here on Earth. No, not as conversations between wizards and orcs, but as conversations between professors and athletes, judges and truck drivers, presidents and fruit pickers. If I were to say that the primary distinction within these pairs is, mostly, the powers and especially the costume given to them by the "Game of Life," I would not be the first to do so (see, for example, Baudrillard 1981/1994). It's actually an old and respected way to view human society. And thus we can say equally of our daily lives and of synthetic worlds, that "all the world's a stage, and all the men and women merely players."

We might well wonder why the real world has developed into what seems to be a game at times. Two writers in particular can shed some light on that. Specifically, the works of play theorist Johan Huizinga (*Homo Ludens*, 1938/1950) and child development expert Jean Piaget (*Play, Dreams, and Imitation in Childhood*, 1945/1962) clue us in to just how complex the interaction of play and society may be. Taking Piaget first, he could be said to argue that playing is an integral component of our development. We seem to have intrinsic motives to engage in pretense and fantasy, both as a way to learn about the world as well as to build our own skills. Play brings us joy, intrinsically, and evolution has specifically made play a joyful activity because that joy motivates us, especially when very young, to learn and train and grow in ways that will help us survive.[15] Now considering Huizinga, he could be said to argue that play is a cultural practice that has existed both in its own, separate sphere (for example, as sport), but it has also appeared as an integral part of ordinary life (for example, as ritual).[16] Thus the game-like character of life may come from a deep-seated motive to play: how do we know that the activities we engage in out of a self-expressed joy (buying and selling stocks for thrill rather than profit, for example) are *not* moments of play? And it may also stem from the insertion of play institutions into ordinary life: how do we know that a given social institution (the stock market, for example) is *not* a game?[17] Thus for both cultural and developmental reasons, it makes sense that any given activity may be play or not-play, depending on the judgments of both the players/users and the broader culture. And this in turn shows why aspects of daily life can often be compared to a game.[18]

Taking this comparison to the macro level, when we think of the Institution of the Whole, of all our society at once, our minds can use Piaget and Huizinga to conceive of a "Game of Life," a game that is, in fact, everything, and is played by everyone. This is exactly the situation described by the Argentine writer Jorge Luis Borges in his short story "The Lottery in Babylon": a society with a game turns into a game with a society. From this perspective, there really does not seem to be an essential difference between the synthetic world and our world. If our world can be said to be a game of the whole, then surely a synthetic world is no more and no less than that.

And in the recognition of essential similarity between our world and the synthetic world, I believe, is where we get some solid answers to the question of growth. When Huizinga and Piaget (and for that matter, Shakespeare) wrote that real life is something of a game, they were writing at a time when real life was the *only* game.

That is no longer the case.

This realization truly deserves emphasis:

- For the first time, humanity has not one but many worlds in which to live.
- We are no longer stuck with the Game of Life as we receive it from our ancestors. We can make a new one, almost however we like.
- The human systems on old Earth are comparable to the human systems emerging on terrains created inside machines.

These are but different ways of saying the same thing, and they all have the same implication for our predictions of the future: the new worlds being built will grow in popularity if, and only if, they provide a better life experience than the world we were born into. A competition is afoot. As with any competition, the outcome depends on the characteristics of all participants. Whether the synthetic world grows does depend on the nature of experience within it, but, critically, it also depends on the nature of experience here on Earth. People will go where things are best for them. It is an issue of migration.

A theory of growth, then, boils down to this: Synthetic worlds, being much like our world in their essence, will grow in popularity if they seem to be better places to spend time. There's already some evidence on this score, in that whenever synthetic worlds have become better, more people have begun to use them. It is a fact of history that when the linking of computers in networks first became common in the late 1970s, text-based online multiplayer virtual worlds were among the first applications to emerge immediately (Bartle 2003), almost as if that was the one function that humans most desperately wanted networks to perform. The worlds that were created then were not simple gaming worlds; rather, they quickly became hosts to very intricate and very real social dynamics (Dibbell 1999; Curtis 1997). Then when networks became able to transmit enough data to render 2D environments, graphical chat worlds appeared, again, immediately, as if that deeper level of virtual interaction were, as before, the one thing people wanted from the new technology. And a third time, when immersive 3D environments became available in the mid-1990s, the first virtual world employing that technology appeared—again—*immediately*, and again as if that were the principal thing people wanted from their 3D technology. At each step, the number of people living virtually has increased, from hundreds to thousands and now many millions. None of this was strictly necessary. It could have been the case that the move from 2D to 3D rendering had no effect on the number of people who like to spend time in an alternative life. On the contrary, though, this history gives one the impression that there is a huge throng of people just waiting at their terminals for a fantasy world to come along, one that is just immersive enough, under the technology they can afford, to induce them to take the plunge and head off into the frontier forever.

Perhaps we can find further evidence by asking whether life in a synthetic world, on its face, seems to have characteristics that might make it a better place, at least for some people. Consider *Ultima Online*, released in 1997, which became one of the more popular 2D worlds. Here you have a world that looks like our world, only better: it has trees and buildings, but they are ideal trees and ideal buildings, and there's no smog or traffic. The social world of *UO* also functions in a very pleasing way: The trees can be chopped for wood, the wood can be carved into axes, the axes can be used to chop trees. Players can become miners, smiths, musicians, hunters, tailors, or inhabit any of a wide variety of legitimate economic, social, political, and military roles, all of their own choosing. All of these roles are actually useful in society: Loggers are needed because house-builders and ship-builders need wood. Miners are needed because smiths need ore. Smiths are needed because adventurers need armor. And the more time one spends being a smith or a logger or a miner, the better one's avatar's skills become. As skills improve, so does social standing; it is possible to become a very important person, just by devoting time to the development of your avatar's human capital.

How does all this compare to Earth? On Earth, as noted, we have trees and buildings but they are not always designed to please the eye. And we certainly cannot be whatever we want to be; much depends on our endowment of abilities and dumb luck. Plenty of roles that people want to play seem to have no use at all (blacksmith) or are currently over-occupied (aspiring artist). Devoting more time—the most equally distributed resource on the planet—to the development of a skill will not guarantee that you will get better at it. On the whole, were I the proprietor of "Earth Incorporated, the Fantasy World," I might very well be concerned about the long-run viability of my enterprise once places like *Ultima Online* began to appear.

In contrasting the virtual world and the real world in terms of available experiences, we should consider what game designers know about the attractions of synthetic worlds to their users. Richard A. Bartle, who co-wrote the first text-based multiuser world in 1979, is a recognized authority on the motivations of the users (see Bartle 2003, p. 130), and he divides them into four types:

1. Explorers: People who come to see what is there and to map it for others. They are happiest with challenges that involve the gradual revelation of the world. They want the world to be very big, and filled with hidden beauty that can only be unlocked through persistence and creativity.

2. Socializers: People who come to be with others. They are happiest with challenges that involve forming groups with others to accomplish shared objectives. They want the world to have extensive social infrastructure and shared activities: towns, clubs, arenas, weddings, hunting parties.

3. Achievers: People who come to build. They are happiest with challenges that involve the gradual accumulation of things worthy of social respect. They want the world that allows all kinds of capital accumulation and reputation-building. They want the ability to increase the power of their avatar, to build new structures, to hoard wealth, and to change the world itself.

4. Controllers: People who come to dominate other people. They are happiest with challenges that involve competing with others and defeating them. Also described as "griefers," they want worlds that allow users to intervene in the

activities of other users, so that a record of domination and control can be established. To them, it is all sport.

Of course, one's motives can be a mix of these, but the basic idea is that these types can help us think about the likelihood that synthetic world use will grow. They point to areas of ordinary life where something might be missing. Ask yourself: How many people do I know who have a frustrated desire to go exploring in a new frontier? How many wish they could find a different social circle? How many find themselves dying on the vine of some corporate or academic achievement system? How many just want to exert their force on others but cannot? Bartle claims, credibly, that it is possible to build virtual worlds that satisfy all of these impulses. The number who might find them attractive on these grounds may indeed be substantial.

What about the reality factor? Even if a synthetic world might provide some better experiences, that does not mean that many people will find those experiences credible. For example, perhaps not everyone can master the suspension of disbelief required to live an alternate existence. On the other hand, we noted in chapter 1 the inherent tendency of people to assign realness and emotion to things they see on computer screens (Reeves and Nass 1996). This point can be taken further. Our apparatus for sensing the environment is adapted to the environment in which humans evolved. That environment did not have media in it. If your eye sees a roaring tiger lumbering in its direction, your brain concludes, at least initially, that there is indeed a tiger on the attack. Then, within milliseconds, the lower-order reaction system (the "old brain" that evolved prior to consciousness and reason) sets off a number of processes, pumping out hormones and generating twitches and startles (Lang 2004). Eventually, your higher-level functioning may kick in, reminding the lower-level systems that the image of a tiger is only a picture on a movie screen. But that in itself requires effort; the default and unconscious assumption of the brain is that everything seen is absolutely real. In the context of immersive computer-generated games, the old brain becomes insistent: everything perceived is acting in a way that is tremendously close to the jungles we grew up in: threats are moving around out there, often barring the way between our perceived self and the resources that will help the self thrive. The new brain must either engage in a constant stream of "it's not real" reminders, or just give up and take the experience as is. In an environment populated by other people going through the same thing, the new brain is further discouraged from resisting by social forces that define Reality and Truth: if everyone pretends the dragon is real, and reacts as though the dragon is real, then for that society it *is* real, just as real as the value of a dollar. Thus as a result of both internal and external costs, it becomes more mentally and socially expensive to *disbelieve* the dragon than to believe it. The act that requires consciousness and will is suspension of *belief*, not disbelief. The default assumption of your mind, unless you fight against it, is that everything in an immersive game world is completely real.

In an older paper, Brickman (1978) explains the apparent reality of unreal things in a different way. He argues that the psychological keys to the sense of realness are internal and external correspondence. A case can fairly easily be made that synthetic worlds establish these correspondences more securely than the real world does. Internal correspondence increases as a person's behaviors become more consistent with their own emotions; they do things because, and only because, they really do care about the consequences. External correspondence increases as the actor becomes aware that her specific actions are generating specific consequences in the world. From these definitions, one might understand how even a single-player game could become real; a person can certainly see that her actions are changing the game world (interactivity is what defines a game, after all), and she may also come to care about it as well. A multiplayer persistent world game like *UO* has even higher degrees of external and internal correspondence. Externally, there is a huge world with a large number of open-ended paths to follow, all of which have logical and visible consequences. Apply axe to tree, and you get logs. Apply pick to stone, and you get ore. Apply sword to head, and you get death. Internally, the presence of other players makes an emotional investment almost unavoidable. Even if I don't care that the Dragon of Zorg has been killed, the fact that everyone else is excited makes me excited; hence we are all excited.

It is surprisingly easy to make the case that these coherences are actually less often realized on Earth than in the synthetic world. As far as external coherence, the underlying rules of Nature, viewed as a game system, are incredibly complex; we have an entire field of endeavor, Science, devoted solely to discovering cause and effect. Internal coherence is also often blocked by the simple fact that we've been placed in roles that we do not want, yet can't escape. Compare this to fantasy game worlds, which provide free role-playing and comparatively simple cause-and-effect rule systems. They may be providing a mental experience that is pleasantly unfractured, and hence more real-seeming rather than less, in comparison to that available on Earth.

The idea of virtual worlds as a competitor with daily life clearly cannot be rejected out of hand. They may well have characteristics that make them seem just as real, or even more so, than Earth; they may satisfy desires that Earth cannot; and their brief history indicates that improvements in the immersion technology have consistently led to increases in population. To think about the future, then, we need to predict how the comparison between the synthetic world and the real world will evolve.

Looking first at the synthetic side of the competition of the worlds, we have to recognize that virtual worlds are malleable enough that almost anything could be built there. Given time and technology, in other words, we can assume that any-one who wants a certain kind of fantasy world will probably find it being pro-vided sooner or later; in chapter 3 we will directly address the validity of this assertion. Until then, let's assume that the options for exit into fantasy will only become more varied, more intricate, more specialized as time goes on.

While virtual worlds are improving and specializing, what will be happening to our world? This is perhaps the real key to whether a mass exodus will occur, and the picture may not be so bright. Let us consider the Earth as a synthetic world itself and ask, Will this always be a fun game to play? Or, more accurately, what are the conditions under which daily life would be the best game to play, better than any computer-generated fantasy, and for how many people will these conditions apply going into the future?

These questions have only troubling answers; not many cultural theorists des-cribe daily life in the modern era as wonderful, uplifting, exciting. Huizinga, for example, lamented the fact that modernity was gradually destroying the institu-tions of play in daily life: "More and more the sad conclusion forces itself upon us that the play-element in culture has been on the wane ever since the 18th cen-tury, when it was in full flower. Civilization today is no longer played, and even where it still seems to play it is false play" (Huizinga 1938/1950, p. 206). As Piaget reminds us, play has given us joy from our earliest moments of life; if it is being eroded from our daily routines, as Huizinga feared, we must be less happy as a result. Another play theorist, Roger Caillois, makes a similar point (1961/2001, p. 122). He says that things like hobbies and games, now so popular in the con-temporary world, have emerged partly as distraction from the "dull, monoto-nous, and tiresome existence" that users otherwise would face. Ordinary life, without play, seems to be emotionally unsatisfying.

According to game developer David Rickey (whose credits include the impor-tant games *EverQuest*, *Dark Age of Camelot*, and *Wish*):

> At the most fundamental level, these games are about empowerment and achievement, providing a never-ending sense of increasing importance and power to the player in the form of ever larger and more important-sounding skills, items, numbers, and achievements for their character . . . At this very fun-damental level, MMOs [massively multiplayer online games] . . . provide a vaca-tion from the pointlessness of life's rat race, where no amount of effort can ensure you do more than tread water, because in the end, only a few people can be the big winners in the Game of Life.[19]

In other words, people go to the synthetic world because it offers emotional joys that the Game of Life does not. The Game of Life, on Earth it seems, is not a very good game at all, at least not for some people.

There is also ample social science research in the study of human happiness to support the preceding conjectures about the Game of Life. Social psychologists remind us that the need to connect is fundamental, and our increasingly mobile society may well be leaving many people isolated (Baumeister and Leary 1995). Clinical psychologist Jordan Peterson (1999) argues that a sense of the *significance* of acts is absolutely critical to basic mental functioning, and our daily life, which is now bereft of any overarching shared mythos, must inevitably suffer from the loss of meaning. Economist Richard Easterlin (2001) has shown that the incomes that many people pursue so zealously, at great personal and emotional cost to themselves and members of their family, have surprisingly little long-run impact on human happiness. Similarly, psychologists Ed Diener and Robert Biswas-Diener (2002) note that income and subjective well-being are not at all correlated. Brickman, Coates, and Janoff-Bulman (1978) discovered that people who win lotteries are not much happier after the fact than before. It seems that the moment of obtaining income is a happy one, but that the happiness does not last. From the perspective of play theory, the treadmill of income acquisition in ordinary life does not provide a good game; there are not enough moments of success, and new rewards appear only infrequently and for too few people. As a result, very many us come to feel like we are getting nowhere at all. Behavioral psychologist Tibor Scitovsky (1976) put it bluntly: Our economy is joyless.

Is it possible that the fantasy worlds built by developers might really be better than Earth, over the long haul? In fairness, we should note that an experienced reviewer of these game worlds once tasked himself, tongue firmly in cheek, with the job of reviewing the game of Real Life. He gave it a score of 9.6 out of 10, quite high, praising especially the physical sensations and visceral thrills it provides.[20] But in even posing the question, this reviewer (Greg Kasavin) raises an important point: not everyone would give such a high rating to *Real Life: The Game.*

And for those for whom *Real Life: The Game* is indeed joyless, the synthetic world evidently represents a game that has many of the same features but is more fun to play. Its use therefore represents a choice, a completely rational one in fact. The reasonableness of this choice deserves to be stressed. If a person rejects a bad game in favor of a good one, who can blame her? J. R. R. Tolkien, creator of the fantasy world of Middle-Earth, once asked, "Why should a man be scorned if, finding himself in prison, he tries to get out and go home?" (1939).[21] Going to a synthetic world may not necessarily be an exit from prison, but it is certainly an exit, and all exits are inherently political statements, according to political scientist

A. O. Hirschman (1970). Using a synthetic world can therefore be construed as a rebellious act, an exit from ordinary life, a rejection of the world that has been built on Earth. Again, Caillois (1961/2001, p. 157): "Simulation [is] in principle and by nature in rebellion against every type of code, rule, and organization."

In viewing these journeys into cyberspace as acts of rejection, I believe, we can locate the theoretical forces that will predict whether synthetic worlds will indeed grow as much as the business analysts say they will. When people choose synthetic worlds, they do so simply because, for them, ordinary life does not meet their needs. The question of whether synthetic worlds will grow is therefore ultimately a question of how many ordinary human lives exhibit that level of cultural and emotional emptiness. If critics from Charlie Chaplin to Michel Foucault are to be believed, the number of people who fit this criterion is very, very large.

While it seems likely (to me, at least) that a fairly substantial exodus may loom in the distance, I believe that there is no way to make such a prediction firm. It rests on the charge that contemporary culture leaves people feeling isolated, aimless, and bored. This may be anecdotally persuasive to some and religiously adhered to by many bright people (e.g., Putnam 1995), but it is too broad to be resolved conclusively by any evidence I can imagine. While I will return to the question of longer-run developments in the final chapter of the book, for now, we will just have to wait and see.

To sum up, we began this chapter by recognizing that the activities of a few ordinary people, no matter how odd or interesting those activities might be, do not necessarily deserve all that much attention (unless you are one of those people or related to them in some way). Thus if they are only a niche phenomenon, synthetic worlds would not seem to warrant a study like this. Participation figures show, however, that a conservative estimate puts some 10 million people or more in synthetic worlds as of 2004. This level of participation, which is comparable to the population of a great city, might already be enough to seem significant to some. Even so, an examination of market forecasts and user motivation data and theories suggests that this may only be the beginning. In the near term, if market analysts are to be believed, we can expect rapid growth. But we do not know how long that growth will last. I've assumed throughout that virtual worlds may become almost anything we want them to be, an assertion that needs to be examined more thoroughly. But I've also taken some effort to compare synthetic worlds to our world, in an attempt to understand just how many people may end up spending time "out there." It has not been hard to make the case that for some people, the synthetic world just might be a better place, and therefore any decision to spend time there might seem quite sensible. Those who feel alone or discriminated against *here* may feel connected and accepted *there*. The social roles that we cannot have here may be possible there. Whatever you may not like about your body here, it can be undone in the building of a new body there. If you despair at your physical weakness here, you can play the role of a strong person there. If you feel ignorant here, you can play the role of a wise wizard there. If you feel frustrated at your limitations here, you may make great things happen there. And all of these experiences can occur in a way that is not mere fantasy; hundreds of thousands of other people are in that other place to validate your feelings and achievements as genuine. For indeed, everyone there will treat the place as genuine—as a place, not a fantasy. These positive experiences, available only in the synthetic world, may eventually attract large numbers of people. In that case, the phenomenon of virtual worlds might not remain in the margins of society, but rather become quite normal.

Thus, synthetic worlds may find their significance, not in being radically different from the world of ordinary life, but in being so similar to it as to present a comparable option, one that in some cases may be the better of the two. Synthetic worlds are significant not just because of the unusual things that happen there, but also because of the likelihood that within the next few decades, many more millions of people may eventually desire a life full of those unusual things, and may indeed prefer that kind of life to the life they lead now. Whether technology will be capable of fulfilling so many desires remains an open question, however, and is the subject of the next chapter.

3

THE MECHANICS
OF WORLD-MAKING

This book has thus far made the case that something new and of more than passing interest is happening in the area of video games. The bizarre behaviors and experiences that have become typical within online games are somewhat worthy of note, but they seem to deserve more serious attention when we realize that, by 2004, they've become part of the normal lives of at least 10 million people around the world. Analysts expect that number to rise rapidly for at least the next few years, and it may go on growing after that. One possible limitation on growth might be that the demand for these spaces might dry up at some point. But what if, as discussed toward the end of the last chapter, the synthetic world can really be seen as a substitute for the real world, one that might well have superior features, in some cases, and for some people? We don't know how many people might find the synthetic world to be better, but it might be quite a few; the historical pattern has been that each new innovation in immersive quality has led to a leap in its population. And so we cannot rely with any confidence on a prediction of slackening demand. Put simply, if we could all live in a world that came closer to our fantasies than this world, how many would resist the temptation to do it?

The last chapter also assumed that those worlds of fantasy would eventually come online, brought to us by the new technologies that are the subject of this chapter. That claim needs to be examined very carefully. It seems likely in the short term that the makers of virtual worlds will become established as a substantial global industry. And that industry will certainly attempt to meet whatever the demand may be for more and different and better worlds. Whatever is the palette of experiences that people request, one can be fairly confident that a competitive industry will be able to provide it. One might conclude from this that making virtual worlds is easy. It is not. Virtual worlds have consistently demanded every resource from the absolute bleeding edge of technology. Before jumping to any conclusions about how many people may decamp for cyberspace, we should ask whether there are any technological barriers ahead.

In the case of world-rendering, four branches of technological innovation deserve some examination: the technology of Place, the technology of Immersion, the technology of Migration, and Artificial Intelligence (AI). Place technology determines the conditions under which people can share knowledge about the state of a synthetic world. Immersion technology involves their interface with the world. Migration technology dictates the rules under which they may make transitions into and out of worlds. AI determines how the world reacts to the users. In all four areas, it is fairly safe to say, there are no obvious barriers in sight. Rather, we can already see some innovations that will dramatically improve the immersive quality of synthetic worlds.

This chapter briefly discusses the state of the art in these four areas of technology and makes some conservative guesses about how their evolution will influence the development of synthetic worlds.[1]

Technology of Place

If synthetic worlds are to be treated by their users as places rather than games or chat rooms, they need to resemble the Earth to some extent. The Earth, after all, is

Persistent. If I go to sleep, when I wake up, the Earth is still there where I left it. In Los Angeles, the San Gabriel Mountains still gaze placidly over the palmy, circuited basin. The moon is not visible, but it is still there, doing what it always does. My car is still in the garage, and it is still mine. I look about the same too, maybe a little older.

Physical. The Earth imposes certain laws of motion on us humans and every other object here. We can't walk through walls, we can't breathe under water, we can't fly. Of course, we *can*, in fact, do all of those things, but only if we have some magical equipment—doors, scuba gear, airplanes. We can bend the rules, but the point is, there *are* rules.

Interactive. If I sweep the dust off my balcony, it settles down below. If I play loud music, it travels to the ears of my neighbor. If he plays loud music, it travels to my ear. We both can affect the world in ways that we both can perceive.

The first of these is perhaps the most innovative feature of synthetic worlds. Among the programming savvy, synthetic worlds are known as "persistent state worlds" to distinguish them from other kinds of worlds that programmers can make. An ordinary computer game for one or several players can have both physicality and interactivity. For physicality, one renders a 3D environment and imposes rules of motion on it: gravity, solid walls, line-of-sight, and so on. For interactivity, one creates a series of commands that the player or players can execute on the environment. The command "Equip Weapon" gives the player's avatar a weapon, which means, access to further commands. "Pull trigger" sends a projectile from the weapon, and various consequences ensue. Making the consequences persistent, however, moves the exercise to a different level. A persistent world continues to exist and execute its rules whether or not anyone is there to be in it.

It is a significant step because it requires that the world be alienated from any one user's control; since many users must be able to experience the same state of the world at the same time, no single user can be allowed to arbitrarily alter that state. In a single-player game on my home computer, suppose I destroy a bridge that I later wish had not been destroyed. I can simply go into the program and restore the bridge if I so choose. The most common method of doing that is to save the state of the world at various time points, and, if I don't like how things are turning out, I can simply roll back the state to some earlier point in time and start again. Or I can directly hack the program and reset the bridge status from "destroyed" to "OK." While this works in a world that exists just for me, it is a problem in a shared world. If my enemy is relying on the bridge's destruction as part of her defensive strategy, she would be surprised to discover I had rolled back the world to a time when the bridge still existed. She would certainly be annoyed if I restored the bridge by hacking the world, which, after all, is shared property.

The shared nature of synthetic worlds is a critical part of the technology of place, because perceptions of how things are have to be shared and agreed upon by many people before they acquire the flavor of Reality. This is true of things in the world—the virtual tree that I see on my computer is the tree you see on your computer, and it is the same tree we both saw yesterday, which makes it seem a lot like the trees I see here on Earth. It is also true of the rules by which the world operates—I cannot walk through that wall, you cannot walk through that wall, and neither of us could walk through it yesterday either, so the wall has a persistent property of solidness which makes it seem much like the walls here on Earth. The walls and trees all follow rules of existence, appearance, and behavior that are perceived in the same way by all users, and that persist no matter how many users are there or what those users do. The synthetic world has its own separate terms of existence, which no one user can affect.

In practice, there are many ways to create a world that is alienated from the users' control. The most common technology of place currently is the client-server approach. The world exists on a server computer, and users access the world from client computers. The server maintains the state of the world, while the clients do nothing but render the world and send messages back and forth to the server. Users can only affect their local client; they have no access to anything on the server. The client-server relationship determines how messages from the client affect the world. The command "Sabert drinks bottle of ale" can be sent from the client to the server, but it will be executed on the server only if Sabert actually has a bottle of ale and is, according to the server's records, in a position to drink it. Moreover, the server determines what information the client may give to the user, which in turn determines the commands that the user might conceive of sending. If I do not see the orc behind the tree, I will not know it is there, so I will not try to cast my Magic Missile at it.[2]

The process by which many users can interact in one world is simple in concept. Castronova and Smith are sitting at their computers, manipulating Sabert and Ethelbert in a synthetic world. Castronova hits the up arrow on his keyboard, which sends the command "Sabert goes forward" to the server. The server checks the command against the rules. Is Sabert facing a wall? Has he been paralyzed? Is he so drunk that the command's effects have to be modified to "Sabert falls down"? If the command is okay, the server executes it and writes the consequences to the world's databases. Specifically, Sabert's position has now changed, so the server updates the state of the world by changing where Sabert is. The server sends that information back to Castronova's client computer. The client grabs the graphics files on Castronova's computer and renders the movement from Sabert's point of view. Meanwhile, the server also sends the information on Sabert's action to Smith's client computer. That client also accesses the graphics files, on its own hard drive, that render Sabert in his environment; these are just copies of the files on Castronova's machine. Now, taking Ethelbert's position into account, Smith's client renders Sabert's movement. Smith, watching all this on his computer screen, sees Sabert step forward or fall down or whatever.

This all happens so quickly that it seems as though both Sabert and Ethelbert are moving and doing things at the same time, while the world and other users are all doing things as well. Each client is continuously sending commands up to the server; the server is validating the commands, executing them, and updating the databases that maintain the state of the world; the new states are streamed out to all users; the clients take the new state information and render it from the point of view of the client's avatar, using graphics files stored on the client machine. The process happens so quickly that the visual effects of the changing world state can be rendered continuously, smoothly, and in real time. It looks like live action.

It might seem impossible that so much information can be transmitted so rapidly. Note, however, that the information packets being sent here are quite small. When the fireball blows up the building, the server does not have to send a new graphics image of an exploding building to all the clients. The clients already have those graphics files. The server only needs to tell them to *use* the files. Moreover, if a building blows up outside of the visual range of Sabert, the server does not need to send him that information right now. Later on, if Sabert walks by the wrecked building, the server will say to the client, "Your guy is walking up to something that got blown up yesterday; replace the ordinary building graphics files with the wrecked ones."

The critical achievement of the system is that all the clients persistently agree on the state of a certain database.[3] How this is accomplished is easiest to see with the server-client model just described, but there are other models that can establish the same kind of persistent state coordination. In a peer-to-peer system, the work of storing the database, checking it, and validating client commands would be distributed among all clients. An intermediate version would be an ad hoc trusted-peer system, in which certain clients, with a reputation for speed and reliability, would act as temporary servers to other clients as needed.

Things can go wrong. If the world changes too rapidly, the system can break down completely; the user's screen suddenly goes black. Less dramatic problems include lag, rubber-banding, warping, and slideshows. Lag is the effect a user perceives when there are long delays between the time a command is executed and the time its effects appear. Rubber-banding and warping happen when the client is forced into a default or as-if mode while waiting for information from the network. When the information arrives, objects and people can be out of place. If so, they have to be yanked to the proper place (rubber-banding), or they simply disappear and pop up again instantly somewhere else (warping). Slideshows are the effect of overloaded graphics cards on the client; when the information the card is forced to process becomes too much, it renders new screens at a very slow rate. The user no longer sees a movie, but a frame by frame slide show. Sometimes after lag or graphics-board overload stops the action, the logjam breaks all at once and a brief catch-up period ensues in which everything seems to happen at triple-time, the effect of which is quite humorous. But fairly often the net result of any of these overloads is that the connection between client and server is simply closed down for a period. For that player, the game is over until he can re-establish a connection.

Even though these systems are parsimonious, the information-pumping that they require becomes especially heavy at certain times. If human beings usually enjoyed congregating in pairs only, there would be few problems. In pairs, the number of clients that need to be kept mutually informed of one another's status is only two: *A* needs to be updated regarding *B*, and *B* needs to be updated regarding *A*. If you add a third person, however, the load goes from two to six: *A* must be informed about *B* and *C*, *B* needs to know about *A* and *C*, and *C* needs information on *A* and *B*. Add a fourth person, and the load is now 12. For five people, it is 20. In general, the number of simultaneous message streams that need to be monitored is equal to $N \times (N - 1)$, where N is the number of clients involved. This figure is dominated by the fact that it contains a squared term in N. That means that while small groups are fine, crowds are a problem. If you wanted King Harold's 7,000 housecarls to engage William the Great's 7,000 Norman knights at Hastings, you'd have to keep 200 million relationships up to date, second by second.

This can create bottlenecks on three levels. First, interacting with the database can be a problem when the database has to store and reveal the information of thousands of people. Second, updating clients in real time can be a problem when many of these people want to have direct interactions with one another. Third, the amount of information can be restricted by the size of the pipeline. People connecting from home on an old modem may have problems. The typical consequences of these bottlenecks have been, first, that the number of people who have access to a world has been limited to about 2,000–4,000 people. The shards mentioned in chapter 1 are one way to accomplish this: the world is broken down into multiple copies of itself, and then users are encouraged to sort themselves among them. If the shards get too many people, set up a new shard. The second consequence has been that the number of people who can be in one spot in the world at one time is limited to perhaps 50 or 100. When larger crowds gather—as with large battles and popular markets—the world's technical performance plummets.

There are fixes to these congestion-related problems. The loads can be distributed dynamically according to rules that sort information according to its importance. If I am standing in the middle of the Battle of Hastings, I do not need to know that, on the other side of the battlefield, Edwin the Erstwhile Tailor has just struck down the horse of Duke William's second page. I *do* need to know that Edwin's second cousin Fridwulf is now standing close enough to me to examine my retinas and is about to lop off my head. My focus is here, and here alone, and this should allow the system to reduce the amount of information it needs to send. In fact, by distributing the database work properly, it is possible to build worlds that can be accessed by thousands or even millions of people at once. At this writing, a number of worlds with apparently unlimited populations are in place, although none has grown above the 100,000 subscriber mark. Another approach is simply to limit drastically the amount of information being sent, which is the strategy of extremely low-tech, cartoonish chat rooms. However, there is, as they say, quite a bit of "dark fiber" out there, bandwidth constructed during the early boom years of the Internet that has been waiting for a truly massive data-intensive application to come along. It has. As the "massive" component in the MMORPG arena grows, it is unlikely that bandwidth limits will provide a long-run barrier. We may one day see something much more than a MMORPG, an UHIMIJLAEMORPG (Unbelievably Huge Incredibly Massive It's Just Like Another Earth Multiplayer Online Role-Playing Game).

There are benefits and costs to running the worlds on different structures, of course. A server-client system keeps all of the data in a central location, which makes it easier to secure. On the other hand, the central server can be a significant bottleneck: it has to do all of the work. Peer-to-peer systems might be faster and more reliable, but less secure. Security is a critical issue (see chapter 11); in a persistent world there are obvious incentives to hacking. Some of these are minor, such as sniffing the information that the network sends to the client and making use of data that the client has been ordered to conceal. For example, in worlds where clients might be involved in hide-and-seek games, the locations of other users and mobile objects in the world are important pieces of information. If the system sends this information to the client under rules involving line of sight, a data sniffer can effectively override the rules. "The orc is behind the tree," says the server; "don't tell the user he is there." The data-sniffer finds the orc, however, and alerts the user anyway. This kind of hack significantly changes player-versus-player combat; if one player is using the ordinary client while the other has a form of radar, in effect, we know who will win. More serious hacks include directly altering the world database to increase the assets or powers of one user's avatars or to decrease those of another user. All of these hacks, and others, have been known to occur on the most centralized server-client systems. The issue is ultimately whether trust can be established among the nodes of a mechanical network—a question that applies not just to synthetic worlds but to the entire global information system.

Given a level of trust among the clients and users, developments in the technology of place may allow the development of the worlds as open-source projects. With current technology, users could conceivably build subsections of a world and host them on their own clients.[4] Users could teleport from one region to the next at will, so that the network of mini-spaces became a single large space. This opens the possibility of peer-to-peer open-source worlds that grow of their own accord, as a kind of alternative Earth beyond anyone's control. Such a prospect is exciting to some, frightening to others.

Overall, developments in the technology of place suggest, at the moment, that there are no immediate barriers to an expansion in the scale of synthetic worlds. Broadband usage continues to increase across the globe, implying that whatever bottlenecks there may be, they will become looser as time goes on. Meanwhile, new higher-speed network protocols (Internet II) are being developed. And as noted, there is all that dark fiber. The technology of place has advanced to the point that spaces larger than the Earth can be simulated in digital form, and fairly soon the number of people who could visit such a place at the same time will number in the millions or hundreds of millions.[5] In other words, we are on the verge of being able not only to create a new Earth in cyberspace, but also to teleport every living human into it at the same time.

The Technology of Immersion

There seem to be no pending limits to the raw communication functions of synthetic worlds; what about their internal qualities? At the moment most synthetic worlds are rather cartoonish places with a steep learning curve. One might be tempted to think that advances in immersion technology will make the new places less cartoonish and more accessible, but current trends suggest that only one of these two will happen. Accessibility will almost certainly improve, but, while it would probably not be much of a challenge to render the world in a way that looks exactly like the Earth, it is not clear that users *want* the world to be rendered that way.[6]

As far as access is concerned, while it is important not to fall too easily into the assumptions that imposed too-heavy expectations on earlier virtual reality research, it seems fairly clear that a number of emerging technologies will make synthetic worlds almost ubiquitous, and easier to use. Wireless technology makes every conceivable interface device portable and mobile. The miniaturization movement points to wearable devices. Advances in controllers suggest that voice and body motion will eventually be used to send commands. Feedback systems are being improved, presenting the possibility of experiential data being sent by various means to the brain. Real-time voice communications over the Internet are here.[7] As I type this out, most synthetic worlds are accessed by looking at a screen and key-punching or clicking commands. By the time my toddler's children are teenagers, we may well be jacking in from our armchairs, seeing the rendered place on wall- or head-mounted displays, and moving our avatars with our fingers. "Computer: Take us to Gondor!" or some such place. And off we would go.

Rendering is a different story; in my opinion, there is very little reason to advance technology at all, because the state of visual craft in these worlds is already at a level sufficient to make every user feel as though it is a real place. True, everything looks drawn rather than photographed. Colors are rather vibrant and cartoonish compared to Earth colors, and lots of detail seems to be missing. If you walk your avatar directly up to a wall, you do not see little specks of dust and small ants crawling about, you see a blurry gray field. None of this seems to affect anyone's attitude toward the place. One reason, I suspect, is because accurate detail is not the ultimate objective of any work of art (any good one, at least). Shakespeare's Veronese and Danes and Celts are certainly not accurate depictions of members of those historical culture groups, but it does not matter. We don't watch Shakespeare to learn about those folk, we do it to learn about ourselves. A certain amount of sophistication in stage design is, of course, necessary to enable us to immerse ourselves in the drama's image-world. It seems that the sophistication of current computer graphics is already sufficient to enable full unconscious immersion in synthetic worlds.[8]

Nonetheless, there are advances in rendering on the way, perhaps unintention- ally driven by the protocols of deal-making in the game industry. There seems to be a general bias in favor of graphical sophistication, driven by the fact that a game under review will, at first, be judged by how it looks.[9] When I tour the floor of the massive Electronics Entertainment Expo, I stop by the booths of up to a dozen or so gaming companies to see what sort of synthetic worlds they are cre- ating. The amount of time I have at each one prevents me from learning much about the way the game is played, the kinds of social structures being encouraged, or the way markets and governments are being structured. I can, however, look at the screen and see what kind of world the avatars run around in. At most booths I am subjected to something that I have come to call "The Test of the Water," in which the person giving me the world tour has the avatar jump into a lake or river or ocean and swim around. I sit there and wonder why we always go swimming. Swimming is not really an integral part of gameplay in most worlds. Then I learned that rendering water is a very hard thing to do, technically speaking. The world-builders apparently show off to one another by flexing their digital muscle in the aquatic competition. Visuals like this seem to be the critical element in landing publishing contracts; closing deals seems to be all about pushing poly- gons to the screen.

As a result, with each year the worlds become more breathtaking. Where the sun was once a flat yellow circle in the sky, it has become a glowing orb that peeks at you through the branches of nearby trees. The branches are new too—they used to be collapsed into two-dimensional boards, but now they swing about individually in the breeze. Oh yes, breeze too—the weather that used to consist of the occasional rainfall now provides wind, rain, and snow, with levels of intensity ranging from mild to horrendous. Climb up on a roof and now you can see gray, misty mountain ranges dozens of miles away. Go into the temple and gasp at the towering pillars and impossible flying arches. Look at other people too. It used to be that everyone was one of a dozen or so types, and each type looked rather like a mannequin. Now, no two avatars look alike, and each avatar makes use of a wide range of natural motions—yawning, stretching, glancing about.

While all of this is beautiful and wonderful, after a day or so it no longer seems to matter. The real miracle has happened: like the guy selling sausages in the Domhof zu Köln, you don't even notice the glory of the cathedral behind you. You have begun to take it for granted. You become immersed in it. And that is just fine, because that's what all this rendering is supposed to help you do. However, it is worth recalling that this immersion effect first became possible for a large number of people with the mid-1990s graphics engines of *Ultima Online* and *Lineage*, which, by any account, are not very whiz-bang engines at all. They are third-person perspective, which means you are looking down at a map of the world rather than being in the world. The figures and buildings are tiny and rendered with little detail. The landscapes are absolutely blah by current standards. Yet both games continue to enjoy hundreds of thousands of subscriptions. Great graphics are neither necessary nor sufficient for a successful synthetic world.

All of this is just a specific example of the general point that the ultimate objective of the rendering profession is not virtual reality but "selective fidelity," a term coined by Jack Thorpe in the 1980s. Thorpe was then a colonel trying to build a tank simulation game for the US Department of Defense. He wanted to put tank crews inside of simulated tanks and have a computer network synchronize each tank's simulation. The network, called Simnet, did exactly what MMOG networks do: it sent information about Tank A's movements and fires to Tanks B, C, and D. What it did *not* do was render photo-accurate visuals of the other tanks in Tank A's mock windows. Instead, it depicted green tank outlines. And that was enough. The simulation had to render only the things that mattered for the exercise in question. Realism was only needed for certain things—for example, the round green thing is a tank and the long thing sticking out the front of it is the barrel; if it points at you before you point at it, you are going to die. The simulation's fidelity was selective. If the designer makes the right choices, the simulation will render all it needs to.

In the case of synthetic places, the selective fidelity criterion says "you don't really have to render much at all." When it comes to European medieval life or conditions on other planets, too much reality can be a very bad thing indeed.

I once spent some time acting in Renaissance Faires, those weekend camps where people go to pretend to be kings or paupers for a day or two. I was in a Shakespeare troupe—actors portraying actors. After a trip to the public restrooms—which, mind you, were never maintained at even early twentieth-century standards—I was quite glad that the Faire had not tried to recreate realistic sixteenth-century sewage conditions on site. I was also glad our troupe did not have to subsist on cabbages and rat soup. Similarly, synthetic medieval worlds thankfully omit many of the more disgusting visuals that should accompany a truly preindustrial experience. It suffices that the palace looks like a palace, both inside and out, and that smoke wafts from the chimneys of the little cottages.

All in all, the synthetic environment looks rather like a very nice painting. Even a dull painting would have been sufficient, but nevertheless, the painting is getting better and better every year.

One aspect of immersion technology that seems likely to remain a problem for some time is in the area of player-to-player communication. At this writing, chat has been the nearly universal mode of communication inside these worlds for many years. Before there were visuals, chat was also how the worlds were rendered: "You are sitting in a cramped office. There is a desk with a computer and a phone on it." When visuals came along, additional messages could be sent through avatar body language, but the task of directly telling someone something still involves typing it out on a keyboard and hitting "enter." As mentioned, technology already exists that would allow users to talk to one another by voice, and for some synthetic spaces, implementing a voice communications feature will be a natural tech upgrade. Other worlds will have considerable difficulty with voice, but for reasons of gameplay, not technology per se. Right now, much of the immersive effect of the world occurs because everything you see and *hear* in the worlds conforms to the designer's theme. If it is a medieval world, all the buildings look medieval, the music is medieval-sounding, the animals and trees look like they were taken from fourteenth-century France. Even the other avatars look medieval—the fighters look like knights, the thieves look like street urchins, the merchants look like cobblers and tailors. And down in a little window, you see a text chat scrolling by, with statements like "shout out to all my homies over on tha westside! ya babieeeee!!" and "d00d, ur sword is teh suxx00rs." Not very medieval, really, but not all that obtrusive either. The failure of user communication to conform to the world's atmosphere is not much of a problem when it is confined to a small chat box. With a voice system, however, everyone will hear the modern-day babbling of others all the time, with a much more powerfully negative effect on the atmosphere. Forcing voice into role-play mode is hard. It is one thing to mediate a contemporary person's body through a constructed, medieval-like avatar; it is another thing to mediate his voice communications through some kind of constructed, medieval-sounding speaker. The sentiment of "Hey man there's this big-a$$ dragon right behind you, get moving" must be understood and then re-rendered as "Hail, friend! The fire-breathing beast approacheth! Avaunt!" AI would have to recognize the content of the communication and then render it audibly in a theme-appropriate way, all in real time. No such system seems to be on the horizon.[10]

Thus with the exception of voice communications, it appears that the technology of immersion is proceeding rapidly. The visual impact of synthetic worlds is improving, and the tools by which we use them are becoming handier.

The Technology of Migration

The transition into and out of virtual worlds seems to be getting smoother. This is partly because the procedures involved are becoming second-hand to world-owners and many users, but also because of innovations in hardware and software that are blurring the distinction between the computer-generated part of our experiences and the Earth-generated part.

To begin with the latter, technologies are emerging that will increasingly blend the synthetic with the natural. Most synthetic worlds work with maps no more complex than the map of Earth itself; it is a small step to use the Earth as a map and play games in it. This realm of research is called "augmented reality"—one takes the real world as it is, but adds something virtual to it. For example, scientists at University of Lancaster, UK, have developed toy guns with video screens that link up to central computers. The computer generates a monster and places it somewhere on the Earth; the user can find the monster's location on his screen, and, if he runs to that spot on the real Earth, he can target the nonvisible, yet virtually present, monster in that spot and shoot it (Mitchell et al. 2003). At Singapore National University, another group of scientists has developed a technology to render computer-generated graphics on a head-mounted screen, so as to play human Pac-Man games in real space. Users who wander about the real Earth wearing this gear will primarily see Earth, but they will also see things that the computer has added, such as treasures and monsters (Cheok et al. 2003). One can perceive in this a future in which most of the things in our visual and auditory range will still be from the Earth, but some will be synthetic. Imagine two apples side by side. The one on the left can actually be eaten and makes the user feel less hungry. The other can be "eaten" by entering the commands "Take Apple" and "Eat Apple." The virtual apple, like the real one, disappears, but its effects will depend on the rules of the world that generated it.

The trend here is related to the broader trend in information technology toward a world of ubiquitous computing. Processors are multiplying and crawling all over the Earth. We have learned that whenever humans interact with processors, it seems the very first thing they want to do is play games. It follows that ubiquitous computing will also be ubiquitous gaming. The synthetic amusement parks that are currently confined to little boxes on the floor at home will soon be accessible everywhere—through the phone, at work, on a plane. The synthetic world is emerging outward into daily life.

In the other direction, there is a trend toward bringing Earth elements into synthetic worlds. At least one virtual world (*There*) provides a web browser directly from the game world. Others already have content derived from Earth actualities, such as hamburgers by McDonald's, pants by Levi's, and computer chips by Intel. Direct in-world advertising has already begun in video games and seems right around the corner in multiplayer online games (Book 2004). *EverQuest* has developed an instant-messaging system that allows users to communicate with others users even when neither party is actually in the game. This stems from out-of-world communication practices that developed endogenously among players; it has become common for users to IM or VOIP one another while playing, using outside services.

These practices can be encouraged or discouraged by the world-builders, and there is much controversy about it. User discussion boards often host debates about whether the worlds should be offered in a windowed mode or not. If one allows windowing, it is easy for a user to run out-of-world programs. For some users, it might help them stay in touch with things from ordinary life that need to be watched, such as email. For others, it allows access to other communications channels and information about game, that is, from fan sites. For still others, however, it allows management of hacking programs and access to cheating information. Those worlds that do not allow windowing or browsing or outside messaging typically find that the community develops and distributes shareware workarounds. At first, *EverQuest* could not be windowed. Then someone developed "EQWindows," a free, easy-to-install modification. Bowing to inevitability, *EverQuest* now offers a windowed mode.

As transitions from synthetic spaces to the Earth and back get easier, will transitions among different synthetic spaces become easier as well? Probably not. While it would technologically be trivial to implement a teleporting technology that allowed someone in *Ultima Online* to vanish there and reappear with comparable powers somewhere in *EverQuest,* no such technology has been implemented. The barriers here are economic, not technical. The locations of the users determine who can charge access fees to which credit cards and for how much. Letting users move about freely would require financial contracts among world-builders, something that the industry does not seem to have considered thus far. A few new firms have moved to fill this vacuum by establishing themselves as brokers and offering to convert assets in one world into comparable assets in others.

If the various worlds (including the Earth) are eventually to blend together, more than just the technology of migration must change; rules and protocols governing the transitions will have to be developed. Their emergence will probably be similar to the evolution of migration policy on Earth. One common impulse of the controlling authorities on Earth has been to prevent all out-migration while encouraging all in-migration, on the theory that population is good. A competing theory, that migrants are always competitors, results in policies that prevent all in-migration. More sophisticated policies attempt to encourage some designated "desirable" groups to immigrate while encouraging undesirables to emigrate. The most sophisticated policy, and the one that seems to make everyone happiest and richest in the long run, allows people and goods to move freely across political boundaries. The historical tendency has generally been in this direction, and it seems likely that cross-world transitions in cyberspace will become increasingly liberal in the future.

If people are eventually to move freely among worlds, there will be a demand for portable identities and reputations. One barrier to movement right now is that a user who appears in a synthetic world for the first time is a completely unknown quantity to those who are already there. She may happen to be one of the most powerful and proficient wizards in the history of Britannia, but in Norrath, she is a nobody. Or, she may be a mature, kind, well-spoken professor on Earth, but in Norrath no one knows that and she must develop her kindly reputation again from scratch. In some ways, this is liberating; it allows people with bad reputations in one world to wipe them clean and start over in another. Unfortunately, there is at the moment no technology that allows those with good reputations *not* to wipe them clean when moving between worlds. Innovations in the way personal identification data are validated by worlds would make a difference here. It should be possible to build and store reputational identities that are accessible, on a voluntary basis, in different world platforms. Those who have good reputations can make use of them in many places. Those who do not can still start over. Portable reputations would also settle a number of security concerns; see chapter 11.

AI

Of all the technological frontiers in world-building, artificial intelligence (AI) holds the most promise of change. Textbooks think of AI research as the study of machines that sense the environment and then act on it (e.g., Russell and Norvig 2003). The objectives of game AI are not so general but, in a sense, much more lofty. Game AI is a feature of the software, not the machines that run it, and it operates not in our world but in a world of our creation. This makes it much easier for the AI to sense the environment and do things there. On the other hand, merely sensing some object in the environment and talking to it or shooting it is not enough. Game AI has to do things that make users happy. The Honda Corporation's robot program has produced Asimo, a child-sized robot that can walk up stairs. Is that a great achievement? Robots I have met in synthetic worlds can not only climb stairs, they can fly, shoot arrows, and cast spells. More important, they can develop something of a relationship with me, whether it be commercial, collegial, or deadly. Sometimes they perform so well in these relationships that I actually feel better, emotionally, for having had them in my life. At other times, they drive me insane with frustration. Computer scientists John Laird and Michael Van Lent (2000) have argued that games are *the* place in which general concepts of artificial intelligence should be developed and tested. Improvements in game AI allow the computer-driven entities we encounter in synthetic worlds to get better at meeting our emotional needs. It seems likely indeed that it is in game worlds that AI will have its first and greatest impact on human life.[11]

What kinds of AI does one encounter in synthetic worlds? At the simplest level are the armies of robots, or "bots," that move through the world according to set programs. Some of the bots are known as mobs, an abbreviation that originally referred to all mobile objects, but now is taken to mean monsters. A mob's programming tells it to kill human avatars on sight. The role of a mob is to provide hunting adventures for players; when a mob sees you, it's kill or be killed. Mobs introduce danger and risk to the world, effectively preventing you from doing certain things in the game by keeping you from traveling about freely. They provide a very rich and complex set of puzzles to negotiate. Only when you have become powerful enough to handle the local mobs can you get safely through the areas they dominate.

Other bots are the nonplayer characters (NPCs) that do not seek to kill you automatically but rather seek some kind of relationship with you. One common NPC form is the merchant; you take your wares to the merchant NPC and she haggles with you (or not) about what she will pay. She also offers things for you to buy. Other NPCs provide similar services—fixing items for you, teleporting you around the world, or providing training. Many synthetic worlds impose a higher-level AI to regulate attitudes of various NPCs toward your avatar. This is known as a "faction system," wherein each NPC belongs to a faction and your actions determine how members of a certain faction feel toward you. If you kill this merchant NPC, and she is a member of the Merchants of Stormwind faction, then you can expect every other Merchant of Stormwind to attack you on sight. The faction AI might allow you to do other actions to atone for killing the Stormwind merchant; perhaps if you kill some enemies of the Merchants of Stormwind faction, the merchants will begin to like you again. Faction systems immerse the users in a network of complex relationships with the world's bots; managing those relationships is not unlike managing relationships with other people.

AI appears in a third way when bots come under your control. Many synthetic worlds offer users the ability to charm existing bots or conjure new ones. Either way, the newly controlled bot is now known as the user's "pet." You can give commands to your pet, such as "Attack the Stormwind Merchant." As AI has advanced, the level of pet control and sophistication has risen with it. Where initially it was common for players to have access to perhaps one pet at a time, at this writing there are several worlds in which users can manipulate whole teams of pets, including teams where a leader pet commands a number of follower pets.

A fourth use of AI involves mentoring. Certain NPCs are programmed to lead the user into the world and then spur them to activity. Often the first instruction a user receives when entering the world for the first time is to go visit some kind of mentor bot ("Young Wizard, seek out Balicus, Arch-Mage, to receive your training!"). The mentor bot gives tutorials on the interface and then sends the user out on missions, known as quests. "Orcs have overrun the Forest! Go to the evil Dungeon of Blasmorg, kill the Orc Captain there, and bring me his head!" Simpler, more peaceful quests involve taking items from one place to another, or finding the components for a potion that will cure an NPC child of some disease.

Not all worlds have mentor bots; their presence or absence is, in my opinion, a major distinction among worlds. Worlds with mentor bots and quests are attempting to provide a sense of mission to the user; they are trying to make the user's actions seem meaningful in some larger story. Worlds without mentor bots rely on other users to do the mentoring, and the meaning and import (if any) of the user's presence is expected to be generated entirely from within the society of users. Put more bluntly, worlds with mentor bots explicitly tell users they need to go *do* something. Worlds without mentor bots are agnostic about whether anything needs to be done. If the users want to do things, they can. Or not. If no players care about something, there is no bot there to care about it for them. The reason this is significant, it seems to me, is that a sense of mission and personal meaning is perhaps the most apparent void in contemporary life. If synthetic worlds grow larger, it may be because they make life feel more meaningful than our world does.

A fifth type of AI presence, which might arguably be considered something besides AI, appears in nonperson form. A door that opens when you command "door open" and closes a moment later is a bot, technically speaking. It senses your virtual hand on its doorknob and it interacts accordingly. Similarly, the bottle that breaks when you throw it and the paintball that explodes and colors your friend's avatar are also bots. They are objects that sense things in the world and interact with other things as events dictate. In some worlds (boring ones, in my opinion), these are typically the only bots around. Every service you need from the world comes from a nonperson bot, usually depicted as some kind of machine in the synthetic space. Want some new clothes? Go to the fashion store, shop, then click on the cash register to make purchases.

Are nonperson bots being run by AI, or are they just an element of the code? If they are considered AI, then the entire physical world is also an AI. This would not be an unprecedented conclusion but rather connects nicely to some notions in the social science field of game theory. There, it has become conventional to treat anything random not as *true* randomness but rather as a move by a player known as "Nature." For example, suppose I am trying to guess the flip of a coin. One way to think of this is as a single player game with a random component; that is, I choose a move "Heads" or "Tails," and then the true state is determined by a random process that determines how the coin falls. But you could also consider this a two-person game between me and Nature, in which we both simultaneously choose either "Heads" or "Tails." If we both choose the same option, I win. If we don't, I lose. Applied to synthetic worlds, the idea is that the entire physical environment is being operated by a player called Nature.

In all of the areas just listed, AI clearly has a dramatic effect on user experience and is therefore a critical element of design. If we take it for granted that nonperson bots (doors that open) are not really AI, then a world consisting only of terrain and nonperson bots is a world devoid of AI. If there is any conscious life there, it has to come from the users. This can be a problem when one visits at a time when there are not many users around. The world can feel empty.

On the other hand, worlds with substantial numbers of mobs, pets, NPCs, and mentors rarely feel empty. Of course, it remains important for user sensibilities that the AI that runs these bots is crafted well. There is the danger that poorly programmed bots can make a world feel decidedly so un-world-like that it would have been more immersive with no AI at all. And here there seem to be certain limitations. Under current technology, there is not much room to flesh out the AI of NPCs and mobs, especially if they move.[12] Movement AI is also called "pathing," the code that tells bots where to go. Poor pathing algorithms can make bots walk into walls or turn only at 90-degree angles. Often these odd movement patterns can be exploited. So, perhaps a powerful mob can be drawn behind this boulder, where it gets trapped; even the weakest of users can then stab it slowly to death by poking its foot from the other side of the boulder. While it is often the case that, at first, new users can be fooled into thinking that an NPC is not a bot but an actual avatar, bad AI will eventually make NPCs reveal how very bot-like they are. If they stand for hours staring straight ahead, endlessly repeat the same conversations, or walk back and forth between two spots from now to eternity, the "artificial" part begins to overwhelm the "intelligence" part, to the detriment of the user's immersion experience.

In worlds that do have an AI component, the AI has a direct effect on each avatar in the world, and therefore a dramatic impact on macro-level features in avatar society. If NPC merchants are told to change their prices, the availability of goods will change and, with it, prices of objects transacted between users. Complex faction systems can put players in conflict with one another; one wants a certain NPC to live, the other wants it to die. The realness of the AI in pathing and con-versations affects each user's sense of immersion, and thereby it affects the global level of emotional investment in the events of the world. The tone of AI language, and the lore it delivers, reinforces the fantasy atmosphere for everyone. (There's nothing more disappointing than bad spelling, bad grammar, and poor story-telling from a mentor NPC who is supposed to be a wise elderly wizard). Simply put, AI is a critical element in the paradigm shift from game to place.

Recent developments suggest that the trend in game AI is toward ongoing improvement. Developers seem eager to deploy any and all AI improvements that they can. After the Water Test, one of the things that the exhibitors of synthetic worlds often demonstrate is the way that NPCs act, walk, and talk. Some of that is game design (interesting quests and an overall sense of High Mission), some of it is rendering (the face looks like a very nice, or very scary, face), but much of it is AI. The standard thing for AI to do, today, is stand in one spot and repeat a styl-ized conversation when prompted. How startling it was for me when, in May 2003, while touring a major city in the then unfinished game *World of Warcraft*, I observed a schoolmarm shepherding a group of children through the streets, not all of whom seemed to be behaving properly. In a moment, life in that city came to seem quite real. It made me wonder what is to come.

Indeed, the example of the schoolmarm and her eerily wayward charges sug-gests that small improvements in game AI should be taken fairly seriously in a more general sense. Chapter 2 emphasized that people come to these worlds for the experiences, many of which are hard to find on Earth. Are AI bots an integral part of the attraction? In other words, it is conceivable that the main reason people are interested in synthetic worlds is because there are synthetic people there. While this point could be made about video games as whole, it acquires a some nuance when applied to games with many other human players. These games allow users to interact with *both* humans and robots. What does a mix of humans and robots in the social milieu offer that a world of only robots or only humans does not? Robot/human diversity in the social environment can provide truly extraordinary enhancements to our emotional experiences, even to a point that there may be breathtaking consequences for human emotional and social development; more on this in chapter 6.

For now, consider an example that demonstrates the way AI technology and human sociality interact. One shard of *EverQuest* allows players to enter into combat with other players. As a result, all players have incentives to hide from other players, especially when those players seem to be powerful and hostile. When playing on this shard, I often took to wooded areas, since the lines of sight there are quite restricted. It is easy to hide behind trees and no one can see you from any distance anyway. They can, however, hear you. When you run in Norrath, the code generates footfalls and broadcasts them to nearby players and mobs, with a volume related properly to distance. Now, as it happens, mobs are programmed to walk to most places they go. Players, on the other hand, choose to run. In the forests of Norrath, then, you can tell whether a player or a mob is nearby by listening to the speed of the footfalls: if fast, player; if slow, mob. In a situation where players are hunting one another rather than the petty mobs in the area, it makes sense to act like a mob. I found myself walking instead of running, to emulate the sound of local orcs and therefore be ignored by the players. In other words, the social world of the players created incentives for me, and all players, to conform to the behavioral patterns of the AI. The humans matched the AI, not the other way around. Now, the famous Turing test requires that a human will not be able to distinguish an AI conversation from a human conversation. If humans and robots spend many hours together under circumstances that encourage them to act in similar ways, the Turing test may well be passed not because someone has written a great AI program, but because humans have begun to think and act the way AI does.

Sketching a Steady-State Synthetic World

Technology changes so rapidly that it would be foolish to try to list innovations now emerging in particular synthetic worlds. What is an innovation today may be old hat in a few years, and the world may not even exist anymore. It's equally dangerous to assume that developments will happen, when of course they might well not. Economists who study dynamic processes typically avoid describing the state of some system when the system is in major flux. Rather, they attempt to analyze the steady states of the system. The steady states are those states which, once achieved, tend to be maintained by the reigning dynamic. In the context of synthetic worlds, we can think of the steady-state technology as the one that will best meet the desires of the users, with tools that may or may not be available right now but that are vaguely foreseeable in the near term (15–20 years). Using current development paths in technologies of place, immersion, migration, and AI, we should be able to get a rough idea of what synthetic worlds are about to become.

The steady-state synthetic world of the near-term future is very large in geographic terms and can hold more than a million users at the same time. Its workload is handled in a distributed fashion by a network of servers that may or may not be ad hoc. The users have created a significant fraction (though probably nowhere near 50 percent) of everything that is there, using designer-created tools on open-source world-building software. Users perform actions and enter commands using intuitive voice and hand motions, and they communicate with one another by voice or some computer-aided speaking system. The equipment they need to do this does not weigh much; it is wireless and may be wearable. Entry portals are ubiquitous; users can access the synthetic world from anywhere. The worlds they see in there do not look exactly like the Earth they live in; they look much more pleasant than that. Elements of the one are often found in the other, and vice versa. While visiting the synthetic world, they can send and receive email, talk to other people, delve Earth-bound information sources, and browse the descendant of the World Wide Web. If they choose, they can make themselves almost entirely immersed in the synthetic space, and build intimate relationships with other humans there. They can also spend a great deal of time interacting with AI bots of one kind or another, each one providing the user with an experience that is designed to make him feel happy or satisfied or validated in some way. Integrated in the emotions and daily routines of ordinary people, synthetic worlds have become a valuable enrichment of life on Earth.

Synthetic worlds also have become host to significant numbers of people, and to a substantial fraction of their time. As noted in chapter 2, if these numbers become truly large, the integration of the synthetic world experience in ordinary life may have large implications for everyone, regardless of who is going to the synthetic world and what motivates them. Those implications are mostly the province of the later chapters of this book, but there is no indication that the state of technology will prevent them from occurring. Technology in this sector continues to advance fairly rapidly. And we are already beginning to see changes in the "outside" world as a result. These changes are the subject of the next two chapters.

4

EMERGENT CULTURE: INSTITUTIONS
WITHIN SYNTHETIC REALITY

It is perhaps shocking to think that, even at their comparatively small size of a dozen million or so participants, synthetic worlds are already beginning to affect the "outside" world, by which I mean the ordinary institutions of human connection: marriages, the web, markets, companies.[1] Yet it is so; it seems that the patterns of behavior spawned by synthetic worlds are not completely contained within them, so that the way people act in other contexts is affected. The most obvious case (though thoroughly anecdotal, in that there have been no studies on this) involves marriages and other close relationships. People who spend all their time pursuing friendships and romance online are choosing to let their offline relationships wither. The institution of online friendship takes away time from the institution of offline friendship. This interaction of institutions, cultures, and the "rules of the game" happens because no one can actually spend every moment inside a virtual world. Even those who try to build a life in cyberspace do come out from time to time, and even if they did not, their absence would make a difference. And so there are already observable phenomena in the real world that have only happened because of the emergence of the synthetic world. But before we can outline some of these external changes (the subject of part 2), we need to describe, in this chapter, the kinds of macro-level behavior we typically see inside the worlds.

In describing behavior, I will treat the terms "institutions," "culture," "behavior patterns," and "rules of the game" as more or less interchangeable. This usage, which I've found extraordinarily helpful in the analysis of macro-level evolution of human society, derives from the notion of *institutions* as developed by scholars operating in the borderlands between economics, political science, and mathematical game theory. Institutional theory tends to be different things to different people, but in its most persuasive expression it holds that human institutions are the rules of some game, rules that all the players adhere to out of self-interest, and yet which have a powerful structural influence on what they do (Baron and Ferejohn 1989; Calvert 1995). A typical example holds that the US Constitution is an institution that defines the rules of the game involving elections, the branches of government, executive authority, individual rights, and so on. Whenever strategic conflicts emerge over these issues, the Constitution is considered the final arbiter of which moves are allowed and which are illegal. It also dictates what happens after a series of moves by the players. In referring to these rules as "institutions" rather than "laws" or "natural orders" or "history," scholars are able to emphasize the fact that the institutions themselves have emerged from gameplay at a higher order. The US Constitution itself emerged from a struggle, and that struggle itself was part of a game. Its predecessor, the institution of the British Monarchy, is also a series of rules dictated by the play of some distant and, importantly, *long-forgotten* game. This is never more evident than during a coronation ceremony, when it is obvious that the Queen herself cannot choose where to go or what to do; she must abide by the formal rules that dictate her every position, gesture, and mood. A web of rules like this is also a way to understand what is meant by the term "culture." If we understand culture as a set of shared symbolic meanings, we can get the same understanding by viewing it as a series of rules that tell people how a symbol translates into a meaning. Constitutions, coronation ceremonies, languages, and rituals: these are all regular behavior and signification patterns that result from the choices and understandings of participants, under some set of rules.

In the current context, the institutional way of looking at the world delivers an important insight: patterns of behavior are emergent. The rules of the game today evolved from some prior set of rules, which dictated not only play but meta-play, the play of the game that's intended to change what the rules are. While it may be comforting, in the real world, to take some of the rules as stable and unchanging (such as the US Constitution), the actual and maddening fluidity of rules has become part of the daily life of those who design and operate synthetic worlds. Every rule they declare, even ones they code into the world as part of its physics, induces reactions by the user community that may subvert or amplify the rule's effect. Designers and the user community are in an endless tug of war about what the rules actually are.

As an example of this tug of war between the coding authority and the users, consider the common practice of assigning combat roles to different character types. In many games, the coding authority defines a character class known as "healers" of some kind (doctors, clerics, medics, druids, and such). Because of their intended role, these characters are given access to abilities that will heal other users of various kinds of damages, poisons, and wounds. But it is also quite normal for the coding authority to give these characters many other abilities, to do damage and engage in combat, for example. However, the collective will of the users may impose a much more restricted set of abilities on such characters. It is not uncommon, in my experience, for healing characters to be literally forced to use only their healing abilities when teamed up with other players. Healing is much desired and in very short supply (it is an altruistic thing, in a sense), so healers who attempt to do anything but heal are often subject to stigma and outright verbal abuse. If you even reach for your mace, the warrior shouts "DON'T FIGHT. JUST HEAL." Thus, while healers may have guns and fireball spells, they can't use them, because of the stigma that attaches. And none of this is in the official rules of the game. It is a social convention, an institution. Thus the rules of the game involving what a character labeled "healer" can and cannot do are not determined only by the code of the world, but also by the norms of the users. And this is no surprise; game players are humans, and humans always extend the set of formal laws with a set of equally powerful informal norms.

The institutions of synthetic worlds, their culture of play, are really no different in their essence from the culture of play in our world, and thus it is apparent why their effects cannot be contained in cyberspace: institutions always affect one another, and these effects can cross the synthetic divide as long as people do. Of course you could argue that the whole point is ridiculous, that because the synthetic world is a fantasy world, a game, no norms or laws can exist there. Yet we have seen in chapter 2 that these places are considered quite real by the people who go there, and that these people are not children by any means. Perhaps the synthetic world is a game; but then, our world is a game too. There's really no difference. If everyone thinks a certain piece of money has value, they will treat it as a valuable thing, and therefore it will have value. When I hand someone a worthless old scrap of paper that says "$1," she will give me something valuable—a Coke—in return, because of the institution of money. And it is the institution, the patterns of behavior, that actually gives the dollar bill its value; the government has little to do with it. The very same institution gives gold pieces value inside synthetic worlds: when someone gives Sabert a gold piece, he knows he has received something of value. Similarly, the same institutions that make norms effective in the real world make them effective in the synthetic world. In general, the forces that create and evolve institutions are human social forces, and they will operate the same way whether the humans find themselves on Earth or on some cybernetic version of Pluto.

A Taxonomy of Worlds

The first thing to notice about the institutions that have evolved inside synthetic worlds is that they are many and richly varied, perhaps enough to constitute a legitimate culture of their own. Living in a synthetic world takes some getting used to; everything from language to the courtship ritual is different. In order to summarize this institutional pattern efficiently, it would be useful to give an overview of world types.

One dimension is the size of the user base. Some synthetic worlds have few players (8–12), while some have "massively" many (in the millions). On a second dimension we have the question of what the players do; some worlds are about role-playing games, others are about shooting, still others are about peaceful social interaction. The game industry has terminology for all of these categories: for example, in addition to MMORPGs, there are FPSs, or first-person shooting games; and there are other worlds without role-playing or combat that could be referred to as "social games." A third dimension involves the presence of AI; some synthetic worlds have no AI, others have many mobs (monsters) and nonplayer characters (NPCs).

A world can score high or low on any of these dimensions; the last two, especially, impose significant costs on the developers. For example, purely social worlds typically consist of beautiful landscape and lovely avatars, and they give users the ability to manage their in-world communications and contacts in a number of ways. There is little content and usually no AI, however. The users must entertain themselves with whatever activities, conversations, and toys they can come up with. Often, such a world gives users the ability to expend their own time to make new things, meaning that content appears in the world but only because it is generated by the users, not the developers.

Add content and AI to a social world and you have MMORPGs. The content is in the form of buildings, quests, puzzles, challenges, and interaction structures (clubs, battles, markets, and so on). Much of the content is regulated by AI, in the form of monsters, merchants, and quest-givers. Some MMORPGs are heavy on content while light on AI; there is a big world to explore, but only a few bots to contest it. Others are heavy on AI and light on content; there are many critters but the world is small and players are expected to entertain themselves primarily by fighting one another endlessly.

At the other end of the spectrum are FPS worlds, which typically have few players (8–30) with little persistence in population across time. Players enter the world and fight a quick, decisive battle. The playfield is small (the size of an office building) and it remains the same, but the players change with each new game. There is no AI and very little content in these worlds, besides the playing area itself.

In what follows, these three canonical game types (large role-playing, large social, small shooter) will dominate the discussion. First, in the section that follows, I will discuss the kinds of institutions that have emerged within the different kinds of worlds, and then, in the section after that, I'll describe how these institutions blend into real life. The chapter will conclude with an effort to predict how institutions may change as the industry matures.

Crafting the Social World

Although the people who design synthetic worlds—the usual term in the industry is "game designer," but not all virtual worlds have games in them—have a great deal of power to structure the institutions that emerge within their worlds, that power is not unlimited. On the other hand, the coding authority certainly has more power than Earth's governments do. It has tools at both the micro level to affect choices and at the macro level to induce institutions.

Let's explore some of the tools that developers have discovered for creating their new societies. Beginning with the simplest worlds, small-population shooters, all that a developer has to do is create a combat system within a set of physical rules. They typically also design a set of standard maps with terrain to fight over, but commonly the terrain-building code is released and third parties also design maps. The net result is that the FPS worlds have very little content and no AI. The society that emerges is correspondingly bare-bones. Friendships might develop if the same players go to the same map for repeated games, but there are no persistent assets that a player can leave in the world and nothing to do there except shoot at other avatars.

Social worlds are a significant step up in complexity. Here the developers provide a persistent terrain and rules governing the creation and maintenance of assets. They design an avatar-based communication system that allows people to send all kinds of messages to one another. The developers then step back and let the people who gather there provide the rest of the entertainment. Social worlds are usually built to a large scale and the emphasis is exactly the opposite of the small-scale FPS worlds: rather than join the world, fight, die, and join again, in social worlds the pattern is to join the world and just hang out. Players might spend their time building new things—a house, some object—or in more or less peaceful pursuits, like racing a car or exploring the terrain. Primarily, however, the world exists as a place for people to meet other people and talk to them.

I've heard social worlds described as "chat rooms on steroids," and the description is not far off. With no danger, no lore, and no missions or objectives, social worlds don't seem to have any game elements at all, unless users make them. Indeed, the most forward-thinking social world, *Second Life* by Linden Lab, enables a scripting system that allows users to make any object desired. Some build homes, flowers, or motorcycles; others build games. In principle one could build an entire *EverQuest* style game within Second Life (and prototypes of such games have actually been completed). Social worlds do generate complex relationships, and they allow assets to persist, especially reputation. However, the developers, by design, leave the evolution of society almost entirely to the players, as with FPS games.

The highest level of structured social complexity occurs within the MMORPGs, places where danger, lore, and missions have been coded into the world from the start. MMORPGs rely heavily on content and AI to shape the society that emerges. And it is in MMORPGs that we see virtually all of the interesting social-shaping tools that developers have imagined. These tools try to address all the motivations that users might have for coming to these places. Returning to Bartle's player types of chapter 2: where FPS games satisfy the motives of Controller types, and social worlds satisfy the Socializers directly and the Explorers and Achievers to a lesser extent, MMORPGs seek to satisfy them all.

The ability of MMORPG content and AI to structure behavior and society can be demonstrated in a simple example. Suppose you are an explorer type; you like to look at new terrain. If you join an FPS world, you would be able to explore the available map area in a matter of moments, because it isn't very big. It still may take some time to explore—remember your avatar is constantly under fire because that is the entire purpose of the world. Take a few steps, die, re-enter the world, take a few steps, die, re-enter the world, die, rinse and repeat. Other than this, there's not much for an explorer to do in an FPS.

If you join a social world, there is usually lots of land to explore. Perhaps you start in a small village, where there are five people standing about. You chat for a while, then you go exploring; you climb the nearest mountain. There's no monster to bar your way, and, of course, there are no people up there; everyone's down in the valley, chatting. From that mountain, you see another mountain; you go to climb it, once again meeting no sentient beings, AI-driven or otherwise, on the way. And then you climb the next mountain, again seeing no sentients. And then you climb the next mountain, and the next, and the next. Lonely! See, since the social world is mostly about other people, the developers have not bothered to place NPCs or mobs or anything out in the wilderness to entertain you. It's just empty. For entertainment, you'll have to head to wherever the people are. So, tiring of your solitude, you teleport yourself back to the village. You were able to tele-port rather than run, because social worlds typically allow instant transporta-tion—distance being a tremendous inconvenience when social interaction is the main idea. But when you get back to the village and start chatting, somehow you don't feel like you really explored anything. You can tell people that there are five mountains over yonder, but there really isn't any social use for that knowledge. None of you need anything from over there; the world is about chatting, and here you are in the village, chatting. Anyway, everyone could just teleport out there and back if they wanted to. And thus while there is more exploring to do here than in an FPS, it doesn't give the emotional high of real exploration. Nothing was discovered. All of the significant terrain is where people are, and once people are there, well, it's all been discovered.

Now let's say you join a MMORPG and try to explore. You start your character, and when it comes time to choose an occupation, you pick "scout." You enter the world in a village and chat for a while, then head off looking for mountains. Five steps beyond the village gate, some AI-driven animal devours you. You re-enter the world, return to the village, and find an NPC to help you. This is typically a mentor figure, a "Captain of the Royal Scouts," whose band you are said to have joined. This fellow gives you a quest, a job really, so you can earn some funds to buy armor or weapons. Having accomplished that, you leave the village again and, being more powerful, you protect yourself against the animal that ate you before. You get to the mountain this time, and there you find a secret cave filled with things of wonder. You head back to town—no teleporting here, you have to hoof it—and show some people what can be found in the cave on the mountain. They might be impressed; they might say, "We want some of that too! Let's go find that cave on the mountain!" And so you lead them there. Deciding to move on, you head for the next mountain and—a monster, one more powerful than the one before, comes by and eats you up again. To get to the second mountain, it seems, you'll have to become more powerful. To gain more freedom of movement in the world, you'll need to perhaps sell off some of the treasures from the first cave (per-haps that's why your colleagues were so interested). Thus, in a MMORPG, explor-ing is not just seeing new things; it involves managing resources to overcome challenges, for which the rewards are the new vistas. The MMORPG utilizes AI in heavy doses to make the satisfaction of the exploration motive, and any other motive, really, into a serious challenge. As a result, the exploring one does in a MMORPG comes the closest of any of the game types to satisfying our legitimate urge to explore new and exciting territories.

This example shows how MMORPG designers create a fun and challenging way for people to satisfy their exploration motive. It can be generalized. In brief, the formula goes like this: Define a series of *roles* (such as "scout") for players to assume and use game mechanics (a set of options and consequences) and AI to get people into them. Establish an *advancement system* to reward certain behaviors (treasures in the cave that allow you to buy better armor). Generate *status* inequality so that the rewards matter (most villagers don't have treasure). Make sure the physical world has *risk and danger* (scout-eating monsters) so that the act of achieving is also challenging. Use scarcity and game mechanics to induce *conflict and cooperation* among players (scouts can buy armor from others, or steal it). Embed more subtle incentives through implicit *messaging* (the mountain looks beautiful). And finally, *personalize* the world so that it provides the right kinds of incentives to the right people (the world needs good exploring by people who are inclined to do that).

These tools did not spring out of the ground whole-cloth with *Ultima Online* in 1997; they are the product of gradual innovations in game design that date back to the early 1970s.[2] And they work. The combination of these effects produces a society with Earth-like richness and complexity, even though the objects about which this society dances are completely fantastical. Each will be described briefly below.

ROLES

Perhaps the most critical incentive structure comes from the "RP" in MMORPG, the role-playing aspect. The term refers to a class of pencil-and-paper games from the early 1970s, most notably *Dungeons and Dragons*. In these face-to-face role-playing games, each player around the table brings a well-developed alternate persona to all interactions with other players; it is, in essence, improvisational theater. I am not Castronova the Economist, I am Simpel, the powerful but absent-minded Wizard, whose spells sometimes go off in unexpected directions. Now, not everyone is a skilled extemporaneous thespian, of course, so this genre of games developed templates for people to follow. The attitudes, history, and typical choices of a Dwarven Warrior could be studied in books so that a player basically knew what to do when a moment of choice arrived. For dwarven warriors, tradition suggested that the right choice is usually "try to wallop whatever it is we are talking about." Aside from these general notions, role-playing games developed specific rules and game mechanisms to bend player choices toward in-character actions rather than out-of-character ones. Dwarves might be defined as inherently not bright and therefore capable of doing little but fighting, meaning, in most situations, that there is little else a dwarf can do for effect besides wallop the object in question. Once dwarves are defined in this manner, any player choosing a new character takes into account the fact that playing a dwarf means you will not be casting spells, nor persuading opponents to surrender, nor charming them into friendship—you will be whacking them on the head. Moreover, in a computer game context, a dwarven warrior would be surrounded by AI that validates the warrior role. The in-game home of the character is a fighter's guild where courage and mead are both in more abundant supply than reason or subtlety. The warrior's mentors give quests that involve face-to-face combat. The warrior's companions tend to be not good at walloping, generating a need for his prowess at that act. The key effect of all of this walloping, glorification of walloping, and remuneration of walloping, is that dwarven warriors will tend to be played by people who feel comfortable walloping. In essence, the game mechanics utilize processes of self-selection to encourage players to take roles that suit them emotionally. The great joy in inhabiting such roles comes from the fact that almost all of us are playing a role right now that simply does not allow us to express many of the emotional roles we would like to. In my daily life I have to be a reasonable, subtle professor, but perhaps I, like you, may also have a side of me that gets a kick out of just walloping things. That makes dwarven warriors fun for me to play. Thus, even a group of amateurish actors can drive an interesting and enjoyable narrative; in tabletop role-playing, everyone gets to perform a role (if badly) that is fun for him or her.

When we move from tabletop role-playing to synthetic worlds, the palette of available roles expands dramatically. There are dwarven warriors, yes, but also various other kinds of fighters—thieves, rangers, beastmasters, archers, paladins, and so on. There are umpteen classes of wizards—enchanters, sorcerers, cabalists, magicians, summoners. There are roles for virtually any longing that a person can have. Want to be a musician? There are bards and entertainers of all kinds. How about a merchant? There are extensive opportunities for industry and trade; you can be an armor-crafter, a fletcher, an engineer, an architect, a jeweler, or a simple go-between. Missed your religious calling? Why not try being a priest, a cleric, a shaman, a druid, a prelate, or a confessor? No, you always wanted to be a surgeon—so try being a medic, a doctor, or a healer. And on and on. And this is just in high fantasy worlds. In other worlds, with other themes, there may be thousands of other roles to play: sniper, sous chef, gambler, samurai, suffragette, spaceship captain, terrorist, Emily Dickinson, octopus, cloud, trapezoid, borscht, you name it. Even "economist," although I imagine few people daydream about that one. Considering all the games that are or may be, there seem to be roles for almost any kind of play-acting imaginable.

In each role and each game, things have been engineered to encourage self-selection into comfortable roles. If you want to be a cleric, you'd better be happy helping others; you might be able to swing a sword or cast a fireball, but the mechanics of social interaction guarantee you won't be asked to do either. If you are a wizard, don't expect to be doing much hand-to-hand combat— you're designed to be old and frail, and you'll find yourself in trouble if something gets too close. The games have been coded such that the clerics one encounters tend to be helpful people and the wizards tend to be aloof, especially from anything messy.

While this role-playing mechanism was invented to assist little narratives in basement games, in MMORPGs it has an important immersive effect. A world of warriors and wizards and clerics who really act like warriors and wizards and clerics easily begins to feel like a world of, well, warriors and wizards and clerics. The warrior, wizard, and cleric go traveling together; a monster is encountered; the warrior attacks it, while the wizard defangs it with a spell; afterward, the cleric heals the warrior's wounds. The challenge is overcome through actions that are perfectly consistent with the roles that the players have assumed. And at some point, a person who repeatedly commits warrior-like acts becomes a warrior, in his own eyes and in the eyes of everyone he encounters. Thus, the mechanics of role-playing allow an entire community to mutually validate itself as a society of people who serve the functions defined by the game, even though, from an outside perspective, those functions seem fantastic.

But perhaps the most important effect of these synthetic roles is their influence on your own self-development. Richard Bartle argues in his book *Designing Virtual Worlds* that their core effect on a person is to aid in a journey of self-discovery. The steps in the journey are revealed by the roles you play. Perhaps you, a man, began playing as a male avatar. Then you switched to a female avatar, just to see. Then back to male. In the real world, nothing seems different. But you learned something, about the world, about yourself. Indeed, cross-gendering is incredibly common, and I can say from personal experience that it can dramatically affect one's perception of the game of gender as we play it here on Earth. If you're skeptical, buy a game and try it. You might be surprised how your thinking changes when your role is different.

Indeed, I've begun to wonder whether long-run changes in my avatar types reveal something about changes in my core personality. I have changed from playing healers and religious figures, to wizards, to scouts, and lately back to priests. I wonder what that should tell me about myself? Though there's clearly something Jungian going on, there are no therapists who know the answer, today; I doubt that many scholars of the mind are even aware that this psychologically powerful tool, the role-playing element in the MMORPG formula, has emerged.

ADVANCEMENT

The second socially significant part of the MMORPG formula is advancement. An avatar is usually born weak and poor. Through achievements, the avatar gradually accumulates powers, either through wealth, an increase in skills, an increase in attributes, or an increase in general experience. The accumulation is done by a simple numerical rating system: my skill at Swimming starts at (1) and goes up to (2) or (3) or (300) after I swim for a while. The higher my Swimming skill rating, the faster my avatar swims. The MMORPG keeps a database entry for each avatar that stores numbers reflecting her wealth (gold pieces, equipment, buildings), her skills (Archery, Two-Handed Swords, Pottery), her attributes (Strength, Dexterity, Health), and an abstract concept called "experience points." Experience points are earned for accomplishments in the world, say, killing a monster or completing a quest. Kill the monster, and you receive 27 experience points. Retrieve the secret message from the spy and return it to your mentor NPC, and you receive 2,000 experience points. And so on. Once sufficient experience points are accumulated, the avatar will attain a new experience "level." The game mechanics reward players who attain a new level by enhancing their powers in some way—increased damage from spells, faster running, and so on.

To get above these details, however, advancement systems involve the enhancement of the avatar's physical or nonphysical capital as a consequence of specific actions. Physical capital includes things like money and armor. Nonphysical capital would be the experience points and skill ratings and attribute enhancements. The analog is to the economic concept of *human capital*, which refers to things like education and on-the-job experience that enhance earning power but are intangible and inalienable. Avatars aren't humans, of course, so we might call the accumulated experience points and skills and attributes *avatar capital*. Seen this way, advancement systems reward specific actions with increases in physical and avatar capital. They are a set of rules that allow people to make investments, investments whose returns are in the form of increases in their ability to see and do things in the world.

These rules and rewards are incredibly powerful tools for shaping behavior. Once players become emotionally committed to a synthetic world, their entire community will become focused on conquering the challenges that have been presented. Any object that assists in this effort becomes valuable in that society. If it is made powerful and rare, it will be a great treasure. This is how value is acquired by things like gold pieces and magic spells, which are nothing but bits of code that unlock abilities. Thus if we want society to value something, such as the plays of William Shakespeare, we should just build a synthetic world with exciting challenges, and make it so that a mastery of Shakespeare is required to meet them. A world built on that premise could produce hundreds of thousands of new Shakespeare cognoscenti in the course of a few years. The advancement system can be used to induce a player's emotional investment in all kinds of actions. It can endow seemingly trivial and inconsequential acts—the slaying of a digital dragon—with significant personal and social consequences. Prestige shifts; alliances change; power and wealth flow in new channels; and, most important of all, people feel happier. In the historical record of MMORPGs, the willingness of people to acquire vast storehouses of truly arcane knowledge (the casting times of hundreds of spells; the order of birth of various gods; the number of iron ingots required to make a medium-quality dwarven hammer) has been demonstrated over and over. Advancement mechanisms turn the synthetic world into a place where value can be assigned to anything, and behavior directed accordingly.

In a typical MMORPG, the advancement system is designed so that each enhancement of the avatar brings that avatar to a new, tougher challenge. Climbing the first mountain generates experience points and treasure; the avatar rises from level 1 to level 2 and can buy some better armor. On returning to the first mountain, the avatar finds that the treasure is no longer there, and no experience points are awarded for climbing the same mountain twice. Therefore, it's off to the next mountain, which, as it happens, is higher, farther away, and surrounded by slightly more difficult dangers. After that mountain is a third one that is still a bit tougher. After that, a fourth, and a fifth. And so on. The vast scope of MMORPGs allows them to provide an incredibly long sequence of challenges; it is possible for a player to spend literally thousands of hours repeatedly overcoming tests and thereby being admitted to new ones.

The process is often described as a "treadmill," but in my view it is not as Sisyphean as that. Sisyphus, in the myth, is fated to forever struggle to roll a huge boulder over a mountain, yet each time, as he nears the top, the stone overcomes him and rolls back down into the valley. But in a MMORPG, the huge stone does not roll back down the mountain. No! The Sisyphus in a MMORPG gets the stone to the top and rolls it right over! Hurrah! But the stone does then roll down into the next valley, where it comes to rest at the base of a still taller mountain. As he walks to the stone's new location, Sisyphus notices that he's become stronger. And indeed, after great efforts, he is again able to roll the stone over this new, higher mountain. Hurrah again! And while the stone now lies at the base of a mountain taller still than the first two, Sisyphus again feels stronger. He can defeat the third challenge as he did the first and second, and will go on to defeat the fourth and the fifth and the sixth. With some perspective of course, it's clear

that Sisyphus isn't getting anywhere at all. And yet, this task is much more rewarding than his original one. There are moments of great achievement. Indeed,
they repeat themselves at regular intervals. Sisyphus can see himself advancing in
power, mountain by mountain. There's progress, a sense that he is actually getting
something done, and flow, a sense that he is in control of a process whose outcome is not certain. Both sensations are quite pleasurable. If they were reinforced
by roles and AI that help Sisyphus believe that the job is important and meaningful, he might approach a state of genuine happiness.

Indeed, MMORPG advancement systems are especially suited to restoring
meaning to our activities, because they place our struggles in a context marked
by the presence of other people. All players in a synthetic world will generally
share some notions of what is important there, and will therefore deeply validate
the emotions that result from the actions one takes. If I am a powerful character
and I see someone struggling up the first mountain, I will recall with pride my
own efforts there when I first started out. That new person may look at my shiny
armor with envy, recognizing that I am a person who has been over this mountain and many others. Neither one of us has an incentive to invalidate the entire
effort. Rather, given that we are both there climbing mountains, we will interact
with one another on the basis of a shred understanding that climbing mountains
is a valuable thing to do.

Yes, if one disbelieves the fantasy, the whole process may seem to be a meaningless treadmill, with no more of an outcome than that offered by a life of dull
work on Earth. But what are the alternatives? The task as described in the original myth of Sisyphus is terribly frustrating. It would be almost as frustrating,
horrifying even, to have the rock roll over the hill into an endless valley, where
there were no more mountains to conquer. Game over—and nothing to do for
the rest of eternity. A sequence of never-ending, ever-increasing challenges means
a sequence of never-ending conquests and never-ending improvements, which
may well be the sublime state even if there is no fantasy to make it seem meaningful. But why disbelieve the fantasy? If enjoying the Quest of the Rock requires
a bit of mental effort, a bit of disbelief suspension, it is worth doing. It is especially sensible to do if the alternative is to labor endlessly on the demystified
Earth, knowing that one is achieving nothing at all, never experiencing that
moment when the stone rolls down the other side, never feeling one's muscles
bulging with new strength. Between these alternatives, the choice is clear and sensible. In short, my guess is that Sisyphus would have gladly abandoned his traditional fate to advance himself in a MMORPG. The implications of this choice,
which I'll take up in the last chapter, are potentially quite far-reaching.

It seems fantastic that a whole community of people would invest their emotions in such things. On the other hand, who would deny that the bouncing of little round balls on Earth can often make millions of people gasp, shriek, or break down in tears? Those little balls also affect finances and even health. You are perfectly free to declare that the World Cup is a silly game and does not matter, but if you do not have good insurance, I would advise you not to make such a declaration in a pub or kneipe during an England-Germany match.

STATUS

A third element in the MMORPG formula involves the distribution of status. In MMORPGs, people are not merely encouraged to be different—the role-playing system handles that—they are forced to be better and worse along a number of dimensions. The avatars all look different, but if you make yourself a dwarf, you're not going to be all that beautiful. Make yourself an elf, however, and you can have a truly stunning figure, and this may indeed affect your ability to find romantic partners. Similarly, if you accumulate piles and piles of money, the developers will make sure you have the opportunity to let others know. You can buy expensive things—houses, vehicles, shiny clothes. If you have power, say by becoming the leader of an important guild, you will be heeded by large numbers of other players, and you can literally lord it over anyone you like. In player-versus-player combat worlds, you can have weaker beings killed on sight. Even in peaceful worlds, you might order that no one from guild X shall have access to resource Y, and it would be so simply because of the influence you wield. Status inequality is hard to avoid in human systems in general, but in MMORPGs it is glorified.

The status distinctions found in synthetic worlds engage emotions that correspond to ones we have on Earth. There is plenty of saluting, groveling, and moaning going on. One is spurred to complete tasks of advancement not merely for their own sake, but because it will enhance one's social prowess. The effects on the psyche are much the same as they are when such things are accomplished in ordinary life: a sexual conquest, the receipt of new riches, and the thrill of crushing an opponent all can provide emotional highs. The critical point is that these status effects are in the world as an explicit factor of design; one could have made a world of androgynes, but having men and women who act like men and women is more fun—even if (perhaps especially because) the person and the avatar do not necessarily walk the same way. One could make a world of equal economic outcomes, but then what fun would there be in finding a bargain? What *is* a bargain, anyway, except a deal that is better than a deal that someone else got? In the end, MMORPGs (like all video games) seek to create a stream of pleasant moments, and inequalities are apparently an inherent element of that. Humans seem to prefer the challenge that inequality represents rather than the security that equality affords—with one very important proviso: everyone's status at the start of the game must be equal. If (and only if) everyone starts with the same opportunities, the same amount of money (usually none), the same ability to choose roles and character types, then the resulting inequality is not taken to be unfair. Rather, status inequality happens because of the choices people make, and so long as everyone starts out with the same opportunities, the inequalities that choices create acquire the character of a fun game rather than a crushing of the spirit.

RISK AND DANGER

A fourth element of the MMORPG institutional system is risk. Violence plays a role in FPS games, but there is really no risk involved at all: if you die, you simply reappear moments later with nothing lost. In social worlds, there's no violence, no loss, no threats whatsoever. In MMORPGs, by contrast, almost anything one acquires can be lost: money, items, even avatar capital. Most MMORPGs have the concept of avatar death, with an associated death penalty. Usually death is not permanent—the avatar reappears at some other place, with fewer experience points, or lower skills, or a loss of capital. All of these things will take time to restore. It is as if the death robs the user of some of her precious time. The death indicates failure of the expedition, quest, or hunt; the Stone of Sisyphus has rolled back down into the first valley, and has to be rolled up again. The presence of these risks certainly intensifies the effect of the other incentive structures. When undertaking some venture, the player knows that failure may cause the loss of previously accumulated advancement or status. A player who has accumulated much has done so in the face of repeated risks of loss. The presence of danger further validates the accomplishment.

There are other forms of risk besides the mechanism of avatar death. Items may be lost or stolen. Assets may plummet in value, even avatar capital. If a new and better sword becomes available, the old sword that I have is not worth much on player markets. If the player community decides that a certain activity needs to be done with a certain set of avatar roles, and your avatar does not inhabit one of those roles, whatever skills she has may become worthless. "We need five warriors, one cleric, and no wizards for this job" means that wizards go unemployed and the rate of return to wizard skills is zero.

Risk and danger are effective in another sense: they are necessary as a way to validate players' resources and skills other than time. These are persistent worlds, remember. If challenges imposed no risk of loss, even the most incompetent player could accumulate high status just by devoting immense amounts of time to the world. If buildings could not collapse, even the most careless architect could build the tallest building just by piling objects on top of one another for a very, very, very long time. Having a mechanics of loss guarantees that the mere investment of time is not sufficient to advance; doing a silly thing over and over will destroy rather than enhance the value of your avatar.

Risk also increases the immersion effect of the world, since one quickly and clearly perceives the (painful) consequence of some mistake. Worlds without risks, many players might say, are simply not real and not fun. But the deeper message is that risk strengthens the formation of other institutions within the synthetic world, making status and advancement and roles much more emotionally compelling.

SCARCITY AND FORCED COOPERATION

The fifth element of MMORPG institutions is scarcity, which is similar to risk. While one could make all activities and resources equally available to everyone, this would surrender an important source of player incentives. By making sure that content and activities are scarce, developers can guarantee that the players must either cooperate or come into conflict over them. In Eden, Adam and Eve can get along or ignore one another as they wish; they have no reason to *hate* one another, but they don't *need* each other either. Outside of Eden, everything is different. There, humanity's love-hate relationship with itself can truly blossom. A MMORPG could be built on the basis of Eden, but there would be little in such a place (aside from mutual attraction) to bring the sons and daughters of Adam and Eve together: if everything is free, why bother interacting with anyone at all?

MMORPGs use scarcity of resources and game mechanics to replicate an out-of-Eden experience, a place where love-hate relationships among players are born. Resources are usually made available to anyone who has advanced sufficiently, but that can mean that there are hundreds of people competing for them. Eligible players can either cooperate and share a resource, or fight over it.

Social institutions, some of them explicitly designed by the coding authority, tend to support player cooperation rather than conflict, on numerous levels. Players can typically form themselves into guilds, and guild-level negotiations often determine who gets a resource and when. While guilds have 50–200 members, smaller associations are also possible. Most games have group-hunting mechanisms that allow 5–10 players to form ad hoc adventuring parties. Above the guild level, large raiding parties and armies may form to achieve one objective; again, there are often game mechanics that allow army leaders to exercise command and control over the group.

Most MMORPGs give players strong incentives to adapt to these grouping structures to some degree. At the level of the individual adventuring party, the roles of the avatars may be designed so that no one player can accomplish things alone. Warriors may need wizards and vice versa. At higher levels, certain resources may not be accessible unless one has the help of an army. Outside the realm of combat and adventure, group structures give players access to markets and opportunities to socialize.

What if a player does not like the available groups? The game mechanics tend to ensure that players who don't get along also never achieve much in the world. This, like risk, is another way to ensure that mere time is insufficient to succeed at the game; you must also be able to integrate yourself socially.

And that, in turn, generates perhaps the most important effect of scarcity: reputational capital. Since everything is not free, and since you need other people to get the things you want, you had better behave.[3] If you don't, none of the other users will help you get what you want. It is interesting that MMORPGs are filled with various grouping mechanisms but have no explicit justice systems or governmental structures. A state of anarchy seems to be preserved as a conscious choice of the developers, so as to give maximum possible scope to reputation systems and the informal norms they support. Much research in political science validates this strategy (Ostrom, Gardner, and Walker 1994; Kollock 1996): reputation and norms are often more powerful than law. What law there is, is in the form of customer service representatives, whose unhappy job it is to intervene in particularly bitter fights among players. Truly nasty players can be banned from the world, but this seems comparatively rare. Indeed, customer service representatives are pretty rare. Labor is expensive; most developers would prefer that the player community regulate its own conflicts.

As a result of this decision, players in MMORPGs are thrown into a social environment with a truly unprecedented level of cooperation, with attendant effects on their behavior (Kollock 1999a). Anyone who wants to do anything usually has to learn how to cooperate. Think for a moment how different this is from social life in contemporary postindustrial communities. For the most part, we sit in our homes and watch TV. At work and school, we complete individualized tasks to receive an individualized compensation. We change residences and jobs and even families with such frequency that there is little point in maintaining a reputation, and doing things with other people in groups is becoming more and more rare (Putnam 1995). True, there are many situations in which teamwork is necessary, but these situations used to dominate social life only a few decades ago. At the start of the twenty-first century, the town square is empty, and barn-raising is a do-it-yourself affair. In the face of this extreme level of social isolation, some people now congregate in online worlds, where Society matters once again. There, people are thrust into countless cooperative ventures and find themselves unable to perform the most rudimentary tasks without the help of others. All of this is *by design*; the worlds are this way because people want them to be this way; they enjoy working with others.

MESSAGING

A sixth form of social institution in MMORPG design praxis is more subtle, involving the implicit messages that design decisions send. In the time-tested tradition of advertising, it is possible to embed messages in the very structure of the world, messages that are not really seen or heard but that become implicit in the way things are. Consider, for example, the fact that most MMORPGs code male and female avatars to be different in appearance only. Typically there are no differences whatsoever in what male and female avatars can do. On the other hand, female avatars are often depicted as much more sexualized beings than males, with costumes that exaggerate the stereotypical features of female eroticism. Similarly, avatars who are said to be wise are usually not depicted as being robust, whereas the warrior-like and courageous types typically do not wear markers of sensitivity. The designers are saying something—something fairly obvious in the case of male-female avatar differences—without using words at all.

Are these choices conscious? They derive from a cultural milieu of fantasy fiction and comic books that dates back to the 1950s. At times it seems that this project wants to overturn a number of social mores, at other times it seems to only perpetuate the common practices of contemporary society. As a Roman Catholic, should I be gratified to see that the concept "religious place" in many of these worlds seems to derive entirely from the great Catholic church-building project of the High Middle Ages? How wonderful it is to enter a building labeled "cathedral" and see massive pillars, lofty arches, and the glorious serene space between them. On the other hand, where is Jesus? Or God, for that matter? The cathedral's message seems to be, "Praise something: Whatever you want, it's up to you." On the other hand, many games have a pantheon of deities representing all kinds of good and evil qualities, and the religious places might be infused with a symbology referencing a specific deity. Still, what is the message behind the fact that a person can worship a God of Evil in a Temple of Evil that looks somewhat like the Cathedral of Rheims?

In my experience, the embedded messages seem to be consistent with the norms of the society that emerges, but it is not clear that the messages actually induce the norms. Rather, since MMORPGs are profit-seeking entities, it seems likely that the embedded messages are designed to make the world comfortable to as many people as possible. This certainly explains the presence of a Temple of Evil. It's not there because the developers are trying to say that Evil is a relative concept and there is no right or wrong. It is there because players want to be in a world where Good and Evil clearly exist and are clearly in opposition. Many players enjoy acting like evil people; it's a nice break from having to be good all the time, and it also seems to speak to some deep-seated awareness of our own tragic imperfections. Moreover, while labeled "Evil," these people usually are civil, even polite. Virtually every "evil" person I have encountered has a story of how they are really very good, but some disaster or spell or betrayal made them go over to the darkness. The MMORPG allows them to go over and revel in the nastiness that is unfortunately part of the human condition, and to do so in a way that actually helps others. A world that includes self-proclaimed and loudly advertised Evil people running about represents a great boon to those who are hungry to fight for the Good. Without Evil people, who could be Good? The implicit message behind the Good and Evil roles in MMORPGs is a rather dramatic rejection of the notion that Good and Evil don't exist. This kind of embedded messaging is yet another source of emotional satisfaction that the world provides.

At the same time, embedded messages do reinforce the norms of the community. Male and female avatars have the same skills but different and, in the case of females, highly erotic bodies; evidently it is expected that men and women should be able to do the same things, but also that they will be having sex with one another from time to time (with a female-as-object dynamic, apparently). Good and Evil are coded into the world, so it is expected that concepts of right and wrong will be applied to actions.

Perhaps the most subtle message in these worlds is that people need one another's company, meaning, it is expected of everyone that they be willing to talk to strangers and possibly become friends.

PERSONALIZED CONTENT AND AI

A final society-building incentive structure worth noting is the ability of the coding authority to provide specific game mechanics that satisfy a player on an individual level. Often this is accomplished through the role-playing mechanics—if I choose to be a warrior, I will be confronted with monsters, mentors, and missions that validate me in that role. Or it might be independent of roles, as in the case of "instancing" content. Instancing occurs when a player triggers the creation of content that is accessible to her and no one else. For example, she may request a mission from an NPC, and the NPC may generate a new dungeon for which only she has the key. At this writing, personalized content is rare relative to communal content, but it is likely to grow in importance as the size and capabilities of world engines grow.

Of course, if the synthetic world was nothing but personalized content, it would be, in effect, our world of social isolation, a lonely single-player game. Because of this, personalizing the content will always be a limited aspect of synthetic world game design. Still, it plays an important role because it allows the world to provide the player with experiences that other players will not have. Even with all of its powerful incentive structures in place and operational, the resulting society may simply fail to provide a particular emotion that the player wants. Not every good feeling derives from society; even the perfectly crafted society will leave us wanting to do some things on our own. To meet that need, most synthetic worlds try to allow some scope for completely individual actions and rewards.

Validating individuals as individuals, in a group context, is a very tricky problem. Take, for example, advancement and status. It feels good to make achievements, accumulate powers, and wave status symbols around. The effect is lessened if everyone else has accumulated the same powers and has been waving the same status symbols around for some time. This isn't just a problem in MMORPGs, it is a core paradox of all human achievement systems: once everyone memorializes himself with a nice headstone, the cemetery becomes a vast field of headstones and no one is memorialized at all. If some status is defined as special, but then given to everyone, no one is actually special. If there are limits on achievement, on the other hand, then some people will be more special than others, creating an emotional burden for those who are left out. As game designer David Rickey reminded us in chapter 2, only 10 percent of the people can be in the top 10 percent along any dimension. How do you make a world in which everyone is in the top 10 percent?

The answer: AI.

With AI, all people in the world are equal, but some people, the player avatars, are more equal than others—specifically, the nonplayer avatars, the AI-driven robots. Players can be allowed to garner all the important achievements, while bots occupy the other 90 percent of the prestige distribution. With enough personalized AI, all of the player avatars can be in the top 10 percent; they all can be made to feel more equal than others. To give a personal example, I will never have as much time for synthetic worlds as, say, a 25-year-old unmarried corporate trainee, because I have other obligations that he does not. Relative to him,

I will never be as rich or powerful in the synthetic world. If he and others like him are my only point of comparison, it will seem that I cannot attain a respectable status in the world; I can't succeed or "win." Still, I can be made to *feel* as though I've won if I do acquire some wealth and power, and if the NPCs then treat me like a rich and powerful person. Thus even if I only attain level 40 in a 65-level game, and even though most other players consider my accomplishment pitiably mediocre, all the NPCs in the world speak of me as a true hero, and man of many accomplishments, a winner. The NPCs form the peer group that puts me on top. True, today, AI delivers these messages in a rather cloying and less than credible way. Nonetheless, this will probably resolve itself into mature respect and admiration as AI advances.[4] Better AI, more than anything else, can help overcome the paradox of a world where everyone wants to be a hero at the same time.

In principle, we can look to AI to contribute any kind of relationship that real people will not. Wouldn't we all like to have a close but subordinate companion, a Robin to our Batman, a page to our Jeanne D'Arc? That's probably why people buy cats. AI pets fill a similar role, except that they can talk and they don't make the mess that cats do. Many people have absent parents. For them, mentoring bots, if designed with suitable sophistication, might fill the gap. That is, they would fill the gap not in the sense that AI will replace fathering, but in the sense that the things a mentor bot says and does will make a father-hungry person feel good. Or this: Wouldn't it be interesting to have a foil, a person who always cooks up new schemes against us, only to be defeated again and again? AI could provide each player with such a personalized enemy. It could provide everyone with a romantic partner, although the long-run consequences are worth thinking about. Personally, I would like to have a home town. AI could do it: Make a place filled with people who are always there, and let me start and end all my adventures there so that I get to know the place well. Let it be my place, so that the people of the village treat me as their favored son. And then let me protect them from dangers and bring them the treasures that heroes bring. Then I would have the feeling that there is one place in the Universe where everyone knows my name and thinks well of me. Like many others, I am a person who might find a relationship with AI quite beneficial.

All of the roles just discussed can be filled by other people in daily life, but it does not always happen in the way desired. Real people won't generally consent to be your assistant superhero forever, but an AI pet will. Real father figures will demand authority, but mentor bots won't. A real human foil can be a serious pain in the neck, but an AI foil can be coded to lay off when he becomes too much of a nuisance. The difficulties of finding good romantic partners need not be expostulated. People in real small towns don't take kindly to itinerant saviors, but well-coded villagers could be more accepting. In this sense, AI can provide some experiences that the social environment on Earth does not.

In sum, the evolution of game development craft has now provided us with a wide variety of tools for building social institutions. These tools have emerged as answers to the knotty problem of creating a place that people like to spend time in. That being the case, it is little wonder that the worlds we build are emotionally enriching, and therefore blend into other parts of our lives.

Blending the Play Space

The designed social institutions of synthetic worlds do indeed have an effect on life outside, if only because it is impossible not to compare their emotional effects to those produced by their equivalents on Earth. The locus of play cannot be contained within the game world itself. Invariably, an entirely separate forum of human interaction grows up around the virtual world, and the struggles and relationships that are generated within the world inevitably bleed over into struggles and relationships outside the world. This general statement is true for literally any domain of human activity that one can name.

Consider, for example, the basic relationships among people. In all synthetic world games, it is common for people inside the game to form into parties of 5–10 people to go do things, like hunt monsters or chat. They trade with one another and give and receive charity. They make long-run friendships. They also tend to play with friends they have met outside the game, as well as siblings, parents, children, and romantic partners. Players organize regular fan meetings to supplement their online friendships with face-to-face contact. Over time, their connections inside the game blend into connections outside of it. The community of users ends up being a community that exists inside and outside the synthetic world at the same time.

There are many other examples of this kind of blending, as the following list, in no particular order, shows.

> **Group formation**. Aside from the hunting or chatting parties, people inside games may form themselves into larger organizations, known as guilds. These are managed by players. Most guilds maintain websites outside the game, where the in-game conversations continue. Guilds also hold Earthbound meetings and attend fan meetings and such.

Conversation. Inside the game, conversation is usually done by chat. The conversations continue outside the game, however, via instant messaging, email, forum posting, blogging, telephone, and most recently voice over Internet.

Events and social happenings. Inside the game, people hold parties, weddings, and dances. People who meet in the game might meet or even get married outside it. Fan gatherings are surrounded with celebratory events. When a player dies in real life, memorials are held in his honor. In the aftermath of the September 11, 2001, attacks on New York City, several synthetic worlds had spontaneous, player-run candlelight vigils.

Politics. Inside the game, guilds find themselves negotiating with other guilds about conflicts of interest. Conflicts between players are sometimes refereed by customer service representatives, put in place by the coding authority for just that purpose. The conflicts that result are often continued on website message boards and in emails among the parties. Mass political statements are made in the game—for example, protest marches to demand a change to some rule. Efforts to change the rules also take the form of petitions and letter-writing campaigns to the coding authority outside the game. The discussion forums at fan sites dedicated to the game are often an incredibly heated arena of intense discussion about the rules of the game. It is forbidden, but not unheard of, for players to protest policies of Earth governments in game chat.

Economics. Inside the game, players work, make or earn things, sell things for cash, and use the cash to buy other things. Outside it, they buy and sell game items on eBay for real money. A dollar exchange rate for most game currencies is established within days of the game's release. I have witnessed auctions for items and services on sale as many as three weeks before a game's release date. Successful auctions can earn thousands of dollars for the seller. eBay's Category 1654, Internet Games, attracts millions of dollars annually in trade for virtual swords, virtual houses, virtual money. And this is only a small fraction of total trade; Asian synthetic worlds are far larger than those in the United States, and I suspect that the amount of external trading they generate is similarly larger. In all, it would not be surprising to me if, by the time this book reaches the press, the global real-money trade in virtual items topped $100 million annually. And proprietary, unpublishable data from inside the worlds indicates that the in-world trade dwarfs the out-of-world trade by a factor of 20. This means that the global sum of trade in virtual items, at markets within and without the worlds themselves, may be as much as $2 billion. If this figure grows, it could begin to have effects at the macroeconomic level in real countries.

Culture. Game worlds are riddled with symbols, ritual, and language. At fan meetings, one sees how symbols have been woven into the lives of the players by being applied to their clothing and equipment. Meanwhile, the rituals of Earth bleed into the game world; the solemnities of September 12, 2001, followed standard Earth forms, even though the environment was decidedly un-Earthlike. Common game usage—"u r teh suxx" means "you stink," roughly—are carried over to email, discussion boards, and general conversation. Indeed, the language of the games is intimately interwoven with the evolution of spoken language across the world. When I receive an email from a student that asks "r u going to lol when i tell my joke?" I know she is asking whether I am going to laugh out loud when she tells her joke, and I only know this because the language conventions of synthetic worlds have entered real-world dictionaries (see http://www.bartleby.com/61/41/L0234150.html).

Violence; conflict; crime. In-game, players hunt monsters and, if the rules allow, they hunt one another. They duel. They meet in arenas to fight for show. They steal too. All of these forms are borrowed from the Earth. On the other hand, some in-game vendettas have turned into out-of-game attacks, even murders. And stealing in-game results in permanent difficulties between players on the outside. Player combat can become a spectator sport as well. Korea has an entire television channel devoted to gaming coverage (Herz 2002). Screenshots and movies are made of in-game action for out-of-game viewing.

Sociology. Norms form in-game and they are expected to be held out-of-game too, on discussion boards, at fan gatherings, and so on. Roles are defined inside and outside the game too.

Solitary activities. Even time spent alone induces blending along the synthetic boundary. Inside the game, one goes exploring, undertakes challenges, inquires and learns about the world. Outside the game, one goes to websites to learn still more, or one buys book-length guides to the games. A not-insignificant amount of time may be devoted to simply planning and coordinating one's time in the game. This can involve planning a large-group activity (hunting a dragon) or simply planning one's own strategy (deciding which skills to enhance first). And I have to admit, when I first began to spend significant amounts of time in synthetic worlds, I often had the eerie feeling in the real world that the people passing by were really nothing more than avatars, just vehicles for the mind of a real person whose true location and condition I could never know.

Sex. You get the idea.

I could continue, but the point is made. Everything that people do in the synthetic world has some effect in the real world as well. The transference is so prominent and frequent that the in-game language has even developed the abbreviation "rl," for "real life." As: "i cant join the castle raid i have a family thing in rl." All users of synthetic spaces face the task of integrating the experiences they have there in their "rl," and as a result the institutions, culture, and patterns of behavior formed inside the world tend to have some kind of influence outside it.

Evolution of the Rules

As one surveys the amount of outside influence synthetic worlds have—significantly changing the real-world institutions that some 10 million people or more are involved in—it becomes evident that this is quite a powerful toolbox. Think of it. Here is a form of practical art, a design skill, that can build places whose effects radiate outward into the daily lives of millions of people. Those who are hungry for connection go there to find groups to join. Those hungry for a sense of mission go there to accomplish things. Those who feel trapped go there to explore. Those who feel dominated by their environment go there to make a difference. A breathtakingly complex system of game mechanics and AI programs provides the user with experiences not available elsewhere. It does this by forming the community of users into a society that does things our Earth society does not. It also provides users with content and AI-based relationships that are hard to find on Earth. In all these ways, synthetic worlds provide users with emotions that can be both good and bad, much like art or any other form of constructed experience. Unlike these other forms, however, synthetic worlds powerfully validate these emotions, by creating them in a community of like-feeling humans.

Given their emotional purchase, it should be no surprise that the social environments within synthetic worlds have begun to meld into the social environment of the Earth. No frontier is truly separate from its homeland; one dramatically affects the other. The rules of the game in synthetic worlds serve only to create a certain kind of society. When that society interacts with the society of Earth, which operates under its own set of rules, the rule sets of both systems begin to change and adapt, as institutional theorists would predict. How the rules evolve will determine what role synthetic worlds will play in the daily lives of people.

It is very hard to predict how MMORPGs and other synthetic worlds may change as they become more popular and more socially salient. Will the core formula of roles, achievement, status, and so on be altered? Or will there always be worlds that offer the basic formula, while other worlds offer something different? It is also entirely fair, indeed incumbent upon us, to ask what kind of worlds there *ought* to be; synthetic worlds are a powerful enough force that they warrant some attention by ethicists and policy experts. Now that this world-making toolbox exists, what should we do with it?

At the moment, however, any questions about the future of synthetic worlds are going to be resolved not by ethical considerations but by profit margins. These places, so far at least, have only been built by private companies, and therefore the synthetic world is going to evolve exclusively according to market forces for the medium term. In order to have a better sense of those forces, the next chapter gives an overview of the supply side of the market for synthetic worlds, the companies and practices that generate the worlds in which these new institutions emerge.

5

THE BUSINESS OF WORLD-MAKING

While the first synthetic worlds were built by individual coders working alone or in pairs, they are now being produced by large teams working within their own sector of the entertainment software industry. In some ways, this parallels the development of the video game industry, where production now most closely resembles that of a major motion picture. As with a film, building a video game requires having a large group of people move several distinct deliverables through a pipeline. Building a synthetic world requires much the same, except that, unlike films or ordinary games, production does not stop when the product is finished. Many industry insiders say that the real work only *begins* when the design is finished, for when the design is done it becomes a world that real people spend time in, and it therefore turns into an ongoing service that needs to be provided on a 24/7 basis. Producing and running a synthetic world is not an easy thing to do; it takes quite a bit of organization, and quite a bit of money as well.

This chapter gives an overview of the supply side of the market for synthetic worlds. It will go over the current state of the market, the major corporate players, and the common production methods and pricing models. Then we will consider market forces that are likely to affect production in the future: boom-and-bust cycles, the likelihood of market concentration, and the possible entrance of noncorporate competitors.

Current Suppliers: Companies and Practices

The current market structure in this industry is the classic combination of a small number of dominant firms facing off against one another, while an army of small, innovative firms push in from the outside. The major players in Asia appear to be the Korean firm NCSoft and Chinese firms Shanda, NetEase, and Webzen

(The9). In the United States and Japan, major players include Sony, which operates its own online gaming division (Sony Online Entertainment, or SOE) and also promotes online gaming through its PlayStation console system. Other US actors include the leader in video game publishing and development, Electronic Arts (EA), and a number of single-world operators, such as Mythic Entertainment, Turbine Entertainment, and Disney. NCSoft now has a US subsidiary. Beyond these firms, there is a large number of potentially powerful new entrants, such as Blizzard Entertainment, and of course Microsoft, which intends to turn its Xbox Live platform into the principal worldwide pipe for all online gaming. Outside the United States and Asia, the synthetic world market is largely one of demand rather than supply; European entertainment firms Ubisoft and Vivendi have made plays in the market, but so far without major success.[1]

Overall, the market has not settled down in terms of its allocations of revenue. Some of the largest firms, especially in Asia, are actually not producers but only operators of games initially produced by smaller firms. In the United States, one model is for developers to make and then run the game, while publishers handle store shelves and billing systems. In other cases, the developer does everything. As a result, the entire revenue stream from the user onward still appears to be in play.

One of the reasons for the ongoing turbulence is that many suppliers initially fail to understand the kind of product they are making. Synthetic worlds are partly a piece of software but mostly an ongoing service (Mulligan and Patrovsky 2003). Computer software companies, however, have a fire-and-forget mentality, and some have had difficulty anticipating the burdens of satisfying thousands and thousands of eager customers, month after month. The politics of running a world—or perhaps the fact that this *is* politics, rather than a simple caveat emptor proposition—seem to baffle more than a few companies that ought to know better. EA's highly anticipated virtual world version of its best-selling game *The Sims* did not do well with players for reasons of poor gameplay, but the company did not help itself by doing things like banning a harmless newspaper that had been set up by University of Michigan linguistics professor Peter Ludlow. The resulting stink ("Virtual Newspaper Faces Censorship, Ban") was interesting enough to outside pundits that Ludlow found himself on national news for a few nights. On the whole, the affair was probably not helpful for EA's bottom line.[2] Aside from these community-relations disasters, we also have the problem that user motivations are not well understood by anyone other than those who have spent a lifetime working with them. It is worth noting that a large number of the stars of the US industry—Mark Jacobs of Mythic, Raph Koster, Gordon Walton, and Rich Vogel of SOE, Richard Garriott of NCSoft—all had a hand in the development and operation of the earliest worlds.[3] New entrants can only raid that expertise or go without it, at least until the industry matures. Until then, synthetic world production will remain an area rife with possibilities for misguided decisions at the senior executive level.

The need for experienced people probably explains the market dominance effects in the industry today. Companies like NCSoft and SOE can rely on their internal expertise, built up from past experience, to avoid making the mistakes that can cause a design to go bad or a service to annoy its users into exile. The other factor that could explain dominance is the cost of developing and running a synthetic world. It is said that one can get a world up and running in the United States for under $5 million, but the guaranteed successes seem to call for much higher initial funding levels, as much as $20 or $30 million. A good chunk of that money might go for a lucrative license, such as Sony's purchase of the rights to implement a virtual *Star Wars* galaxy, an immediate hit. And then there is the cost of the live service, which is quite labor intensive. However, the cost factor is not as imposing as it looks: among the companies that are still on the fringe and trying desperately to get in, one finds some of the biggest companies in the world. Thirty million dollars is not a significant barrier to entry for Microsoft. On the whole, success here still seems to depend mostly on understanding the consumer and having a deft and talented hand at the design controls.

While most executives can probably determine that good design goes a long way in the current market, there are no standard management templates for getting it done. Synthetic worlds, as I said, tend to be designed like video games. In theory, a typical video game production proceeds as follows: An idea is conceived and sketched out in a demo. A team of designers goes off to determine what the player will do, while artists begin to render the environments and characters. Both groups send tasks to the programmers, who are supposed to make it happen. Eventually enough content is built that one declares that an alpha version of the software is available for testing. The alpha tests lead to design changes, which are tested again. The process iterates until management declares a beta version for testing. The beta test continues until management is satisfied with the product, at which point it "goes gold" and is released to the publisher.

With an ordinary video game, these procedures are messy enough. With a synthetic world, they are messier still. For one thing, the ostensible "beta test" in the synthetic world market has evolved into a free-trial phase: once the software reaches beta, companies often open their servers and advertise the game's availability loudly, downloading free software to all who ask. The idea is to get a community of insiders hooked to the game, so that when it goes gold and begins to charge a fee, newcomers will already find an active and vibrant community within the world. It is a very tempting business practice as well; because the game will be an ongoing service, various changes are going to have to be patched in on the go anyway, so why not release it now and fix it through the series of patches we're going to have to make anyway? The risk of doing things this way, of course, is that the nascent community might be exposed to beta software so bad that the game is declared a failure before a single disk is sold. Still, many companies seem to abandon the effort to test the product, preferring instead to release shoddy code that they can patch after the game goes live. In effect, the testing phase of the product seems to go on for months and months after the game is released. For some worlds I've been in, it seems that the testing phase is literally without end: many things are broken and will remain so forever, apparently. All of this merely testifies to the fact that producing an ongoing world experience delivered over the Internet is simply much more complicated than producing a piece of entertainment software for single sale.

If current practices, borrowed from video games, are not exactly the right way to go about managing the synthetic world production processes, it is not clear what would be better. One might look to amusement park and shopping mall production systems, since the services they render are not unlike those of synthetic worlds. Television and radio have a half-century track record of streaming entertainment products into homes. Even the political system is worth exploring for hints; governments, in the end, are the ultimate community-management systems. And so when students interested in a career in this area ask me for advice, I tell them that the standard route is to develop a demo game using their computer skills, but that they might consider instead becoming a moderator for an online bulletin board service, or simply running for office! Best practice in this area is yet to be determined, but when one thinks about the analogous services listed above, a few rules become apparent: don't open the doors until the park is done, works well, and offers everyone a good time; keep new content coming; and don't try to fool all of the people, all of the time.

Pricing Models

While there is a great deal of variety in the structures of firms that are attempting to succeed in this market, there is less variation in production practices, and still less in pricing models. The common model at the moment is a two-part pricing system: users buy the client software and then pay a subscription fee on a monthly basis. Periodically, new content modules ("expansion packs") are released for sale. Over time, revenues tend to fluctuate with user numbers and then spike when new content is released. For worlds that persist for a long time, subscriptions end up being the primary revenue source. Releasing updates is important, however, for marketing reasons; nothing advertises the existence of a world better than its presence on store shelves. The pattern of box sales and subscription fees is nearly universal within the industry.

This homogeneity is probably not necessary; there is actually a very wide variety of business models one could imagine in this space (MacInnes 2002). One possibility is charging fees for in-world goods and services. The users may be informed that running the world requires everyone to bear their fair share of the costs, and therefore certain activities will result in usage charges. Economic theory suggests that content that is being overutilized and congested should be given a price, so as to limit access in a fair way: those who really want the content can pay more for it when it is congested, and that is fair. Perhaps storage space is scarce in this world; then let people face fees when they use a storage facility. Let the fees they now pay in virtual currency, for transportation and so on, be charged directly to the credit card. At this writing, there are at least two worlds with this kind of in-world system of real cash for virtual items (*There* and *Project Entropia*).

Owners could also cast themselves as landholders and earn revenue from renting or selling land to the users. Let the users build everything in the world, but collect usage fees in proportion to the value created on various parcels of land. This is a part of the funding strategy of the innovative world *Second Life*.

Advertising represents another revenue stream (Book 2004), but this one must be handled with great care as it may destroy the reason why people come to the world in the first place. Indeed, all of these approaches to financing can seriously damage the amenity value of a synthetic world if used improperly. Remember, these are fantasy worlds. Too much material from the Earth, or the wrong kind of material, can easily make them very un-fun. So much of the technology and craft of game design is devoted to creating an immersive environment, and it would all be undone the moment the ad for Wal-Mart appears on the castle gates. The same could be said for tax and land-renting schemes: if you can't make it a natural part of the world's lore, you risk degrading the user's immersion level. Handled properly, however, some advertisement could work.[4] There's probably nothing wrong with ads on entry screens; often a great deal of time passes as one waits for various things to load, handshake, and synchronize when entering a world. In principle, those moments might be amenable to product information spots. Or, products can be judiciously placed in worlds, if they fit. No sense having Levi's Jeans in Middle Earth, but they would be a fun enhancement in a Wild West world; why not have Corvettes and Budweiser in World of Elvis?

Revenue enhancement strategies also involve decisions about how much to charge and to whom. If synthetic worlds are like any other group activity, they will be populated by some people who spend a great deal of time in one world and others who switch from world to world fairly frequently. The profit-maximizing strategy in that case is to make sure that the switchers pay less than the stayers; this takes advantage of the lower demand elasticity of those who are not likely to move. Price discrimination may seem distasteful, but it's really nothing more than a policy of offering discounts to people who are more choosy. It's why we have coupons: people who take the time to cut out coupons are obviously sensitive to price, and profit maximization theory suggests that they should be offered lower prices. A simple implementation in synthetic worlds would be to have a sliding scale based on time in the world: everyone gets to pay a lower fee for the first few visits. If they stay, fees move to a so-called "normal" level. The common practice of making the first month free is clearly consistent with this overall pricing strategy.

Finally, one might also attempt to take advantage of market cycles in the same way that hip restaurants do: come up with a great new concept, reap cash while it is still chic, but move on before it becomes tired. For synthetic worlds, oftentimes the first few months are also the most popular, and there may be bandwagon and networking effects as everyone decides that this is the place to be. Over time, these hipness effects dwindle away. Owners could anticipate this dynamic and charge higher prices at first, anticipating price cuts (or simply selling out) when the panache fades. The second owners can earn enough profit to run a respectable business there in perpetuity, but the serious money was all made at the start. On the other hand, the need to encourage networking effects in the first place is what prompts owners to charge low prices at first, and even give the game away for free. Deciding when to raise and lower prices is thus the same kind of dilemma faced by makers of products subject to fashion cycles: charge high to make my product look trendy, or charge low to get the trend going in the first place?

On the whole, there is as much room for innovation in revenue models as there is in management practices. This industry is still maturing.

Slow Growth and the Competitive Cycle

To recall from chapter 2, most analysts predict that sales of video games will rise rapidly for some time, led by the online component of gaming. We're also seeing an increase in the usage of nongame synthetic worlds and avatar-mediated communication systems in general. Analysts argue that the increases can be extrapolated for a number of years; as high-speed Internet and wireless technologies enmesh the globe, the assumed latent demand for these products and technologies will express itself in rising sales. As to whether the untapped demand might be this large, chapter 2 assessed a number of long-run arguments suggesting that fantasy worlds might indeed be desirable for large numbers of people. It seems quite likely that each of the next two or three generations will each be more involved in synthetic worlds than its immediate predecessor.

How will this growth actually manifest itself? First, it is important to emphasize the generational component in the adoption of these technologies. Because synthetic worlds are among the most intensive applications of new media technology, there is a steep learning curve in using them. People seem to have no problem, however, if they have grown up with computers, pagers, cell phones, and video games.[5] Those of a certain age, on the other hand, find the whole thing baffling. As time passes, a larger fraction of the population will fall into the former category and the demand for synthetic world access will gradually grow.

The significant word in that prediction is *gradual*: unless something dramatic changes in the user interfaces of these worlds, their growth will not be like the twentieth century's rapid adoption of revolutionary media such as television. The penetration rates will differ because of the difference in learning curves. You operate a television by turning two knobs. One knob gets a moving picture going. The other changes what picture you get to see. If you're hard of hearing, there's a third knob that makes it louder. Gomer Pyle could operate a TV.[6] And that meant that TV was able to expand throughout the world's population as fast as RCA and Zenith could make CRTs. Not so with synthetic worlds. Driving an avatar in hostile conditions is a skill that takes time to learn.[7] While there is some chance that the spread of gaming console systems with online functionality—which make an effort to reduce the plethora of buttons and levers one must master to get by in these places—will speed up the growth rate, it will probably not have a significant effect. Much of what is new in a synthetic world does not involve the interface. Negotiating the embedded social system takes time; this is a party in a play, not a moving picture. As a result, one should not expect explosive growth in this sector.

Moreover, on the supply side, the growth will almost certainly not be steady. Rather, it will follow the boom-bust-boom pattern of many new technologies. As I write this, there are one or two dozen obviously successful synthetic worlds in operation, but perhaps over 100 in development. The year 2003 saw a number of highly touted new worlds fall flat; if this is a growth sector, one might ask, why are so many of the latest additions doing poorly?

On the one hand, this is perhaps a moment to remember Carl Jung's dictum: "One of the most difficult tasks men can perform, however much others may despise it, is the invention of good games." Making a game that is this big, this complex, and also fun, for thousands and thousands of people playing with *each other*, is surely a great creative and intellectual challenge. A more specific explanation, however, has to do with the nature of synthetic world development and its cost and revenue structure. Note, for example, that we have only seen a very few of these places close their virtual doors. That is an extraordinary fact in an industry where 95 percent of the titles are expected to fail and disappear within weeks. The trend in MMORPGs is completely different: the world is developed for three to five years, released, and then maintained seemingly forever. A flop in this market is not a world that closes down—with rare exceptions, none of them do that—it is a world that lives on but does not have many subscribers.[8]

This pattern can be traced to the unique nature of costs and revenues from world-building: Worlds cost a great deal to make but not as much to run.[9] Meanwhile, most revenue comes from subscription fees after the world is built. As a result, it does not take much in the way of subscription revenue to overcome ongoing operation cost. Once a world is open, then, you might as well keep it open, because ongoing operations bring net revenue to the company. For a world to be *profitable*, however, that stream of net operating revenue has to eventually overcome the large capital cost of building the world in the first place. When a world falls flat on arrival, the net revenue from subscriptions is a trickle, not a stream, and the whole project, while still alive, has turned out to have been a losing proposition. This has been the fate of several new worlds as of this writing, and will undoubtedly be the fate of many more. Indeed, by the time this book is published, it would not surprise me to find that the market for synthetic worlds is being described as a complete bust, yet another new-media hoax, hokum, and hype.

I would argue against that view; rather, these developments are a natural pattern for any good with this combination of cost, revenue, and demand. Demand grows slowly in this space, probably more slowly than technological innovation on the supply side. When these worlds first appeared, the first few were obviously very profitable. When *Ultima Online* and *EverQuest* had their success in the late 1990s, everyone and his avatar decided to make a world. Building a world takes several years, and when all the post-*UO* worlds spilled onto the market four years later, there was a glut: the demand for worlds had risen by perhaps 50 percent while the number of worlds went up 500 percent. But because you don't need many subscribers to keep a world going, none of the weaker worlds have closed their doors. Thus the market recently has seen dozens of cancellations and poorly received new releases, punctuated every six months by a genuine success. Meanwhile, the global numbers continue to increase, quarter by quarter. Each new success seems to add its population to the industry without detracting significantly from the population of current entrants; otherwise, older worlds like *UO* would have folded long ago. This indicates that the demand must be increasing, but growing less rapidly than supply.

Even in a down market, on the other hand, there is room for success. Blizzard's *World of Warcraft* broke single-day PC game sales records at its release on November 23, 2004. As this book goes to press, it is on target to reach several hundred thousand subscribers.

Whatever trauma this boom-to-bust-to-boom cycle may induce in the development community and the popular press, in fact, all is well from the consumer's standpoint. The economist and sage Joseph Schumpeter (1945/1984) long ago alerted us to the fact that the best thing about an evolving economic system is that it destroys mediocre things. Therefore, let there be a glut of worlds, and may the best worlds win. The quality and quantity of available fantasy worlds are both clearly rising. The fact that the market falls into a boom-and-bust cycle, especially at the start, should not blind anyone to the long-run forces behind this technology.

Focusing on the long run, then, where do synthetic worlds fit into the economy? Here are some competitors that may be in trouble:

Passive media entertainment. Many gamers say that playing games only required cutting one thing out of their lives: TV. Data from Nielsen Media Research indicate that TV viewing among 18–34-year-old males has fallen by more than 10 percent in the viewing seasons 2002–2003 and 2003–2004 (Rose 2004); Burbank wonders where they have gone, but Austin (the center of the multiplayer gaming industry) knows. And if we were to return to the 1970s and tell contemporary pundits that the new century would see many people abandoning their TV sets in favor of an interactive and social form of entertainment, I'm sure they would have jumped for joy. The glory days of that horrid car-selling box in your living room are perhaps over. Indeed, DVR recording technology is turning it into an interactive medium itself. Other forms of passive media—films, books, spectator sports—might be affected too. The open question here is whether the average person would really rather be doing something than watching it.

Travel and tourism. When Tahiti is only a few clicks away, why take a flight there? When I already own a ship that can fly me to Alpha Centauri, why support a space program that's just getting to Mars? This is not to say that NASA's work is unimportant work; I'm only pointing out that its support in the populace may weaken as fantasy space travel starts to feel more and more like the real thing, without the costs and complications.

Communications. Avatar-to-avatar communication can offer everything that voice communication can, and it also offers facial expression and body language. It requires less bandwidth to communicate gestures than video does. Moreover, people may prefer to have a simulated self do the talking rather than the real thing. And avatars are a very intuitive way to implement social software: with an avatar interface, not only can we both write on the white board that appears on your computer and mine, we can also gesture to it. And with an avatar, you can mingle in a space. No other technology offers the same superior combination: all of the good things about face-to-face communication, with none of the bad.

User interfaces. Running a computer is still rather difficult today. The wizard who answers to your click on "set up new network connections" is a wizard in name only. Why not make him a real wizard, with a gray beard and a pointy starred hat, who sets up connections for you when you ask him to? That would certainly be more intuitive than clicking and typing and clicking and typing. As for daily work tasks, a person connected to an avatar can have the avatar summon a virtual typewriter and open a virtual mailbox. If there's a problem, the user can get some help by talking to an AI in avatar form. There are already synthetic worlds with embedded email, instant messaging, and web access. There seems to be little that we do with our computers that we could not do in avatar form. And we may prefer the avatar form for numerous reasons; perhaps it is the most intuitive way to translate body gestures into commands.

In sum, depending on the preferences of average people, synthetic worlds may make an impact in several important areas of the economy.

Market Structure

If synthetic worlds do have an important economic impact, it is of interest to consider who will own them or, more precisely, how many people will have their hands in the profit stream. The question is interesting because synthetic worlds have features that make them subject to both monopolistic and competitive market pressures. Their ability to host large social groups give them the same kind of network externalities that, in other contexts, typically lead to domination by a single provider. On the other hand, the consumer would probably prefer to have a choice of worlds and dabble in one or another as her tastes dictate. It's Metcalfe's Law versus variety as the spice of life.

Examined in the abstract, synthetic worlds fit best in the subfields of economics concerned with *public goods*, markets for things that are consumed by more
than one person at a time.[10] Two subfields of particular relevance are the theory
of local public goods and the theory of club goods. A *local public good* is a good
provided in one jurisdiction and enjoyed by everyone who lives in that jurisdiction; an example is elementary school education. Theories in this area address
how people sort themselves by jurisdiction: those who desire good schools rather
than disposable income will go to a high-tax district; those who prefer to have
income rather than schooling will go to a low-tax district. Like local public goods,
club goods are amenities that can be shared by many people and require choices
about what club (i.e., jurisdiction) to join. With club goods, however, the analysis recognizes that there may be some congestion in the enjoyment of the good.
As a result, the theory talks about not only who will join what club (which is the
same question as who will live in what jurisdiction), but also about what fees to
charge and what entry limits to impose, to handle the congestion problems. Club
goods are probably the closest analog to synthetic worlds in economic theory.
With synthetic worlds as with the clubs of this theory, people have a number of
options in terms of where to be, and they know that when they go to the place of
their choice, they will be sharing the benefits with others. Like clubs, synthetic
worlds have a public good aspect—the shared fantasy space—as well as the potential for congestion costs in the form of lag, wait times, griefing, and other
nuisances that arise when a world is overcrowded. Moreover, like clubs, synthetic
worlds have solid doors; it's possible to prevent people from gaining access unless
they pay a fee or meet some requirement.

With the same abstract structure as synthetic worlds, then, club goods also
exhibit both networking effects and congestion effects. In club good theory, the
networking aspect comes from the fact that the good gets better when there are
more people using it: no club is fun if you are the only member. The congestion
effect recognizes that there can be too much of a good thing: no club is fun if
there are so many people that you can't do anything there. The rules of access that
we can derive involve opening the door to some people but not everybody; there
is an ideal size. Our policies should try to keep the club population at that size.
This means that completely open access is a no-no: suppose there is an open-
access club in which the ideal number of people is 100. Having 99 people is a little too small a party to be ideal, but having 101 imposes a little more congestion
than is ideal. Let's say I am person number 101. If I join the club, I make it a club
of 101 people, which makes it a worse club for everyone. However, the reduction
in value is not that great, to me personally, so the club is still something I would
want to join, given that access is free. In effect, I ignore the fact that my entry

imposes a cost on every other member. As a result, I do join the club, and so does person 102, and also person 103, and so on, all of them ignoring the costs they impose on everyone else. As a result, the club ends up having significantly less value for all its members; open access results in too much congestion.[11] To avoid this problem it is necessary to restrict access, by imposing a membership fee of some kind. The right fee keeps the population at the right size, considering not only the demand for the services of the club but also the cost of their provision, including congestion costs.

Thus the theory predicts what size a club should be, based on the amenity it provides as well as the way population sizes turn into congestion costs. And if we also know the total demand for this kind of good at the optimal fee levels, we can predict the number of clubs.

For example, consider an athletic club with a swimming pool. If the club has one member, the club's services are not a very good deal on the whole. First, the one member has to pay the entire cost of running the club. Second, there is nobody else sitting around the pool to talk to. Now if the club attracts more people, the cost per person falls and the value of club membership rises: each member still has access to the pool, and it is more fun because there are other people there. If the club attracts too many people, however, say, hundreds of thousands, then the club is once again not a good deal. The cost per member is very small, but one cannot actually get into the pool because it is filled up with humans, stacked in like sardines. The economic theory of club goods will allow us to find the right mix of access rules and fees that keeps the population of the athletic club at just the right level, all the time. Once we discover those rules, we will know how many athletic clubs the market can support. For example, suppose that we have a city of 4,000 fitness enthusiasts and it turns out that the optimal size of a club is 5,000 people. Then we know that this city will have only one club: the bigger the club, the closer it is to the optimal club size, and therefore the better is its product; it will beat out any competitor. Conversely, suppose the optimal club size is 500 people. Then there is room for eight clubs in this city. Moreover, if there is some diversity in fitness styles—free weights, tae-bo, swimming, tennis, yoga, sipping beers by the pool—we can expect that the eight clubs will be different, each one serving a niche of the population with a product that best suits its desires.

To give an example with numbers, suppose we are talking about nightclubs, and suppose the ideal crowd in a club is 200 people in a space of 5,000 square feet. We work out the details and find that you can get 200 people into a club of that size by charging an admission fee of $12. We also determine that the net revenues of 12 × 200 = $2,400 nightly, plus the bar tab, are sufficient to earn profits from a nightclub with this size. We can then analyze the market demand to determine that a total of 10,000 people will go out clubbing when the price is $12. Therefore, the market can support 50 clubs, and diversity of style will determine what kind of music each will play.

Synthetic worlds are like these examples in that they provide an amenity whose value first rises with the number of users and then falls as the worlds become congested. These congestion effects, by the way, are not necessarily technological in origin. True, bandwidth problems do arise when 10,000 characters are trying to run through the same space. But congestion is also an emergent property of space on Earth, where these bandwidth issues do not arise. Congestion is really an economic phenomenon that happens when there is a good that many people can access but where each person's access degrades the quality of goods for others. When congestion occurs, improving technology really will not help; building more lanes on the freeway does not magically undo the fact that freeways are open-access systems in which one person's use slows down everyone else. There will be congestion effects in synthetic worlds as long as Zeroax the Mighty and Wealthy Dragon can be killed by anyone at any time. The world will always be more fun if there are some people in it, but if there are so many that Zeroax gets killed all the time, I will never get my chance, and the world is therefore a congested place.

Synthetic worlds are also like club goods in the sense that not everyone likes the same club. Different clubs offer different amenities and will have different clienteles. This is also efficient; ideally, there should be enough clubs that everyone finds that their desired amenities are provided by some club at a price they can afford. Clubs allow people to share goods that are better when shared, without imposing the same good on everyone. The critical mechanism here is sorting. If you set up a wide variety of clubs, people will sort themselves into the clubs that are right for them. The finely manicured golf course will be provided by the expensive golf club, and those who want the more costly course will have to pay a higher fee to get it. The course with turf like asphalt will be provided by a less ambitious and less expensive establishment, and those who don't mind a low-quality round of golf will pay a low fee. This is Tiebout's insight (1956): The population sorts itself into those who are more and less willing to pay a great deal for a shared amenity, and each group gets what it wants. The application to synthetic worlds is this: synthetic worlds provide a wide variety of things to do, from shooting games to simple conversation to complex, AI-enhanced amusement spaces. Some of these things are cheap to provide, some are expensive. Who knows what kind of activities they will offer in the future. As the number of worlds grows, the population will be able to sort itself into desired worlds with finer and finer detail.

This assumes, of course, that there will be increasingly many worlds to choose from. The economic theory of clubs does point out, however, that it is possible for one club to gobble up the whole market. This can happen if the right club size (considering both user interest and costs of operation) is very large, and if all the people share roughly similar tastes for the amenities that the clubs can potentially provide. In other words, if the optimal size of a synthetic world is 10 billion people, and everyone on the Earth wants to be a wizard or a warrior, then a huge synthetic world based in Tolkien lore could take over this entire market.

However, the conditions that lead to monopolization don't hold for most clubs, and they don't hold for synthetic worlds either. First, it is clear that synthetic worlds offer widely different benefits to different people; there is no homogeneity of tastes here at all. Not only are people different in terms of basic motivation (explore, socialize, kill, etc.), they also differ in terms of the fantasy atmosphere they desire (medieval, suburban, outer space, wild west, Vegas, etc.). Second, there are no returns to scale in world-building. The biggest world is not ever going to be both cheapest to make and also most fun to use. Constructing the right atmosphere in a synthetic world involves paying attention to content and AI, both of which are labor-intensive processes, and labor is *the* expensive factor. True, you may be able to design a program to produce endless content and AI, but it will only produce endlessly repetitive and thus endlessly uninteresting content and AI. Thus, while MS-DOS was able to become the dominant OS software, it is unlikely that MS-DOS-WORLD would become the dominant synthetic world. There are natural limits on the size of any one world, limits that do not exist for things like basic operating system software.

Indeed, one can already see significant partitioning in the market. New worlds tend to target different segments and, as mentioned, they tend to add their populations to the market rather than take users away from extant worlds. The portfolio of available worlds has risen dramatically in just a few years and seems likely to do so for some time. There is no evidence at the moment that only one or two worlds will survive.

At the same time, there is strong evidence that worlds are local monopolies in the same way that a club can be. Once you have paid your membership fee, you are, in a sense, trapped in your current club, because going to a different club would involve high switching costs. With synthetic worlds, switching costs take three forms. First, if you are going to another world, you have to pay a new set of fees. Second, synthetic worlds unquestionably exhibit network effects, first because they are social—if your friends are in world X, you want to be there too—and second because they are a proprietary communications channel. That means that if you switch worlds, you lose the value of the network you've been in.

Third, the advancement and reputational systems result in the accumulation of assets that cannot be transported out of the world, making it expensive to leave.[12] With high switching costs, synthetic worlds can lock in their user bases to some extent, which means that they enjoy some monopoly power over them (Shapiro and Varian 1998). It is similar to the monopoly of the snack food stand at the movies: once you've entered the theater, they are the only food providers, and they charge accordingly: $5.00 for 50 cents' worth of popcorn. Still, as with theaters, the pricing power of synthetic worlds is strictly local, and each world remains locked in competition for your time with other synthetic worlds. Club theory shows a market of competitive of local monopolies like this will provide the goods and services that customers desire at a price that is very close to the long-run marginal cost. In other words, the market may have numerous local monopolies, but it is not broken in the sense that economic theory uses; there are no grounds here for government intervention or oversight.

Thus, these theories argue that the production of synthetic worlds is likely to remain competitive despite the network effects that arise from their social and communication aspects. This does not mean that the *operation* of these worlds will remain competitive; it is possible that all of the pipelines between the developers and the customers might be dominated by one firm. But this involves the much larger question of service provision over the Internet; will it be the case that, say, the Xbox Live platform becomes the main conduit by which all synthetic worlds stream into the home? For that to happen, it seems to me, it would be necessary for Xbox Live to be the main conduit by which *all* digital content streams into the home. And it is not clear to me that the provision of digital information products is subject to increasing returns to scale on either the demand side or the supply side. One does not hear many analysts predicting that the cable, telephone, wireless, and satellite ports into our living rooms are all going to be dominated by a single firm someday. Unless that happens, there will always be open channels by which new synthetic worlds will be able to deliver their content.

In general, then, while the market for production and distribution of synthetic worlds floats somewhere between monopoly and perfect competition, it is close enough to the model of competitive clubs for us to draw some conclusions. First, there will always be competition between worlds, and no profit margin will ever be entirely secure in the long run. Second, the market will provide as wide a variety of worlds as people are willing to pay for. Third, populations will clump up in the way they do for clubs and cities: a few places will be quite popular, others will be less populated but still viable, still others will scrape for membership. Fourth, there will at times be lucrative temporary monopolies. The first company to discover a latent desire for some kind of experience will be able to lock in a large number of users. It will take competitors several years to develop similar worlds of their own. In the meantime, that first company will have significant pricing power and a comparatively rich revenue stream. It will not go on forever, however. The near-term future of this market thus seems to be one in which a slowly growing pie is shared by a slowly growing number of major players.

Providers

There is one wrinkle that might affect the gradual evolution and expansion of the synthetic world market, and that is the possible entry of other, nonmarket providers.

One possible entrant is the state. Synthetic worlds are a powerful technology, one that completely embeds the user in a world of the designer's choice. It is conceivable that some governments might find this dangerous and seek to regulate the sector. Alternatively, they may provide their own synthetic worlds and ban access to all others, effectively monopolizing the market. Doing this would require deep controls on all streaming media channels, something that would be hard to do in most countries but not all. China comes to mind as a looming battleground; Korean firms hoping to release synthetic worlds in China already must gain approval by state ministries. One wonders how much fantasy an autocratic government can tolerate. One wonders also whether autocrats can resist the temptation to makes fantasies of their own and steep their unwitting populations in them.

Taking a more optimistic view of the state's objectives, we should also say that synthetic worlds represent a technology that can be useful in the provision of important public services. Schools can use this technology in the classroom to teach via immersion, at a comparatively low cost. An early effort in this direction is *Quest Atlantis*, in the School of Education at Indiana University. Kids from around the world are able to meet up in this space and go on quests that involve environmental health issues. A second effort underway is *Revolution*, which is being produced by the Comparative Media Studies lab at MIT. This world will present a detailed replica of Williamsburg, Virginia, in the American Colonial era. *Second Life* plays host to architecture classes. The educational power of this technology is hard to miss.

Beyond the education context, agencies may build worlds to support basic research into phenomena that are hard to study in real societies. If you are wondering what a change in a certain virus might do, the place to study that is not with real people! But that kind of research could easily be done in a virtual society with no harm. Imagine how much better the last 300 years would have been if political theorists had had synthetic societies in which to test their ideas of state before unleashing them on an innocent polity. The opportunities for research in all the social and health sciences are, again, hard not to see.

Synthetic worlds might also play a role in basic governmental functions. Security agencies may build synthetic worlds as cost-effective training grounds. International agencies may find that the best way to hold large meetings is not to gather in one spot but to build synthetic meeting places. Would air traffic control be easier if the controller stood as a giant avatar in a virtual world while little plane-avatars flew around her? Would driving be safer and more civil if other cars were rendered as avatars to one another, with open communication channels among them?

Nongovernmental organizations and nonprofits may also become providers of synthetic spaces. While, as with government, the technology may be attractive as a way to execute the organization's duties, I suspect that nonprofits would find the messaging power of synthetic worlds to be their most attractive feature. If you want to make a statement, especially to the young, you could embed it in a fun virtual world and let their minds soak it up. For example, to date, synthetic worlds have sent mixed messages about gender discrimination by giving male and female avatars the same skills while still highlighting the erotic features of female avatars more than male ones. The message can be unmixed; just create a world in which both genders are equally skilled and equally objectified. Want a world that surrounds visitors in your religious views? You can build it. Concerned that a disadvantaged group does not have access to a Very Good Thing? Make a world where everyone can get that thing for free. Have a hope for a different future if some policy were to change? Build that future. If you can craft a social world that people like, you have just made a powerful argument for the policy decisions and cultural attitudes implicit in the world's design.

A final provider worth noting is the Provider of the Whole. It is possible that world-building tools may become ubiquitous and easy to use, not unlike file-sharing software. Perhaps everyone will be able to build a small corner of a synthetic world and host it on their own machines. Or perhaps some rogue copy of an existing world will be liberated and made available for free on an ad hoc peer-to-peer network. Something like this has already happened; savvy hackers have used the client software of virtual worlds to reverse-engineer the server-side software, afterward setting up rogue servers that one can access for free. While these rogue worlds have not seemed to function very well—they apparently are unable to replicate the database functions and customer service side of the business very well— their existence makes the point: it is possible that through the combination of open-source software and decentralized networking, worlds may simply begin to emerge on their own, with no owners or controlling authority. This kind of provider, or un-provider, presents serious security issues. If things happening inside synthetic worlds have negative consequences for people outside of them—as has already happened—how would the rogues inside a rogue world be brought to justice? This issue is considered again in chapter 11.

If we now look to a future in which we have, on the one hand, a competitive market with a sizeable number of virtual worlds and, on the other, a substantial palette of worlds being operated by governments, organizations, and their own users, it might make sense to develop protocols for handling relationships among the worlds. Several worlds might find it advisable, for example, to allow users to transfer assets among worlds in their consortium, including avatar capital. Ideas like this have already been proposed by some start-ups, such as PlayVault and the Gaming Open Market. The idea would be that once a user has advanced greatly in World of Hedgehogs, she will face large switching costs if she wants to try out World of Wombats; if the two worlds agree to allow users to switch costlessly between their worlds, however, they make their consortium a more attractive option relative to their competitor, the always-popular World of Higher Mollusks. Higher Mollusks may then join the consortium to protect itself from its archenemy, World of Certain Subspecies of the Yeast Family. In this way, groups of cooperative worlds may form, with, indeed, the possibility that one consortium may become dominant. There are some mechanisms that probably should be industry-wide; for example, all synthetic worlds certainly would benefit from the existence of reputation systems that were portable across all of them. The fact that a user has been permanently banned from one or two worlds is a fact of interest to all worlds. So are facts involving the in-world accomplishments of very active users. All providers in the market have an incentive to develop protocols involving these kinds of shared interests.

To sum up the current state of this market, I will have to confess that as a consumer of synthetic worlds I view the situation today with a great deal of satisfaction. There are already more worlds, with more variety, than I could possibly ask for. And as long as there is money to be made building synthetic worlds, more worlds will be built. If other organizations get involved, my palette of choices will only expand. If ad hoc peer-to-peer worlds appear, I may be able to visit virtual spaces that evolve according to their own internal dynamic. In other words, I see a future of increasing choices, increasing quality, and an increasingly broad range of possible services being provided, from entertainment to communication to education and research. From the standpoint of the individual user, the future is bright.

Thus, a certain excitement about possible applications is the proper tone as we come to the close of part 1. My objective in the book is to persuade a serious thinker to consider the implications of this technology; a basic tour of the space, which has been the task of part 1, outlines a vibrant technology that seems to have more potential than has been realized as yet. The behavior this technology induces is quite bizarre in some ways, as indicated by chapter 1's summary of daily life inside a synthetic world. Yet in chapter 2 we saw just how many people already find this way of life attractive enough to pay for it, the minimum figure being at least 10 million. We saw some reasons why that number seems destined to grow, at least in the near term. In chapter 3 we saw that technology does not seem to present any long-run barrier to that growth, and in chapter 4 we saw how the technology has begun to spawn unusual institutions and patterns of behavior that already spill out into the real world, spillages whose meaning will increase as the underlying technology spreads. And finally in this chapter we have assessed conditions on the supply side, coming to the conclusion that there are many more opportunities for this technology than have yet been realized or even conceived. These new opportunities are credible; the technology is established and stable, and millions of people are already taking advantage of past opportunities that have been seized. The emergence of still greater opportunities, in my opinion, is sufficient by itself to warrant attention from serious thinkers at the top of all kinds of organizations: companies, media groups, agencies, universities, founda- tions, families. I doubt that those on the top have time to read books like this, but perhaps those in the middle, those with a vision, might be able to use this book and especially its first part to make their case to the upper echelons. Yes: there is something worth looking at in this sector of human affairs. Something serious is happening within games.

If synthetic worlds do grow, they will have an impact on everyone and every- thing, just like the auto and the TV. The task of part 2 is to consider some of these macro-level implications.

PART II

WHEN BOUNDARIES FADE

IN THE FIRST PART OF THIS BOOK, I ATTEMPTED TO INTRODUCE a hardheaded reader to the phenomenon of synthetic worlds. I tried to treat these places with more gravity than they usually receive. Even if you've heard of this kind of activity, and I am not assuming you have, you're more likely to have connected to it through mainstream media reports than first- or second-hand knowledge. The typical media report about massively multiplayer role-playing games (MMORPGs) and the like has very much a gee-whiz feel to it. The man-bites-dog part of the story is usually something along the lines of, "Would you believe, people actually treat these gold pieces like real money!" The implied subtext is that only an idiot or a lunatic would do that. And then four pages later, the same newspaper reports in complete sincerity that a celebrity homemaker has been convicted of insider trading, a development said to have *grave* implications for her media empire. You would walk away from the paper thinking that the demise of Martha Stewart Living Omnimedia Inc. is more important than the emergence of this MMORPG thing, whatever it is. My task so far has been to show you what the MMORPG thing is, on the inside, so you can make a reasonable judgment about it without having to spend hundreds of hours online. In my view, synthetic worlds are an emerging technology with considerably more importance than a cooking show.

In the first part of the book, two key conclusions emerged that should be kept in mind going forward. First, it is true: gold pieces are indeed treated like real money, by real people who are neither slow-witted nor insane. There are lots of people doing this, in fact. At least 10 million people pay for access to synthetic worlds as I write this, and there will be more by the time you read it. The values generated within these societies, as I argued in chapter 2, have no less and no more authenticity than the values you and I hold in the allegedly "real" world. Value is a social construct. It will be what it will be. We cannot control it or wish it away. And therefore if large numbers of people begin to feel as committed emotionally to their virtual existence as they do to their Earth existence, the values emergent in cyberspace will begin to matter to us all.

The second thing to remember is that some kind of shift in social salience, by which the synthetic world comes to bear as much weight as the real world, is likely to happen within the next few generations. I tried to get at this from as many directions as I could: stock market analysis, business model assessments, cultural criticism, postmodern social theory, technological evolution, institution theory, club theory, the possibility of state intervention, a theory of efficient communications. From each separate angle, it appeared that some degree of growth in this phenomenon was probable. The demand will be there, the supply will be there, and the technology is there already, meaning that both commercial and noncommercial actors will find themselves building worlds upon worlds according to their separate objectives.

Part 2 of the book takes these two conclusions and asks about their implications for many of the things we now deem important in the real world. The topics to be covered are generally in the area of political economy, broadly understood: governance, law, business, the economy, terrorism, national security. It begins with a chapter that briefly describes the channels by which events in the synthetic world and the real world affect one another; the metaphor of a "porous membrane" is invoked, a boundary that defines and separates two organs but does not completely inhibit passage between them. Chapters 7 and 8 describe the emergence inside synthetic worlds of new business patterns and new markets, respectively, with an eye to their external consequences. Chapter 9 considers the nascent politics of synthetic world communities and the ongoing governance troubles these communities have. Chapters 10 and 11 consider the darker side of this technology, the potential for criminal and terroristic use (10) and the difficulty of effective responses (11). Throughout these chapters the focus will be on the possibility that an emergent synthetic frontier may, in effect, march toward nationhood and sovereignty with the same unsettling effects on the "Old World" as the emergence of frontier nations has produced in the past.

6

THE ALMOST-MAGIC CIRCLE

Following on the overview of synthetic worlds in part 1, the first task in part 2 is to explicitly discuss the relationship between synthetic worlds and our world. I suppose the easiest distinction to make would be that the synthetic world is not real, but our world is real, and there is no relationship between the two. If I felt that were the case, I could stop this chapter right here. Indeed, I could give up the whole manuscript and go do something more entertaining. Unfortunately, the reasoning laid out in the first part of the book has convinced me that the distinction is not as clear as all that. There is certainly a relationship between the synthetic world and the real one, and it is quite real on both sides.

In this chapter I use a metaphor that I've found quite helpful in thinking about synthetic worlds: the membrane.[1] The synthetic world is an organism surrounded by a barrier. Within the barrier, life proceeds according to all kinds of fantasy rules involving space flight, fireballs, invisibility, and so on. Outside the barrier, life proceeds according to the ordinary rules. The membrane is the "magic circle" within which the rules are different (Huizinga 1938/1950). The membrane can be considered a shield of sorts, protecting the fantasy world from the outside world. The inner world needs defining and protecting because it is necessary that everyone who goes there adhere to the different set of rules. In the case of synthetic worlds, however, this membrane is actually quite porous. Indeed it cannot be sealed completely; people are crossing it all the time in both directions, carrying their behavioral assumptions and attitudes with them. As a result, the valuation of things in cyberspace becomes enmeshed in the valuation of things outside cyberspace.

In other words, we find human society on either side of the membrane, and since society is the ultimate locus of validation for all of our important shared notions—value, fact, emotion, meaning—we will find shared notions on either side as well. When a society in cyberspace holds that a certain glowing sword is really and truly magical, in the sense of having great and extraordinary powers, that judgment is not only impossible to deny within the membrane, but it starts to affect judgments outside the membrane too. By this process, virtual things become real things; when most people agree that the thing has a real value to somebody, it genuinely does have that value. It is not virtual at all any more, but real and genuine. That is how diamonds come to be really and truly valuable, not just virtually so: when many people trade hours of their own work in order to determine what fingers diamonds will adorn, their value becomes undeniably real. And this process of social validation, through mechanisms like time inputs and the like, necessarily creates value that is relevant on both sides of the boundary between the worlds.

I would argue that these processes of value creation have advanced so far, even at this early date, that almost everything known as a "virtual" commodity—the gold piece, the magic helmets, the deadly spaceship, and so on—is now certifiably real. Indeed, as I argued in the introduction, the term *virtual* is losing its meaning. Perhaps it never had meaning. The things happening online have always been literal human things; there was never anything metaphorical, as-if, or subjunctive about them. At first it may have been convenient in many ways to think of networked human interaction as only a model of the real thing. Now, however, and specifically in the arena of synthetic worlds, the allegedly "virtual" is blending so smoothly into the allegedly "real" as to make the distinction increasingly difficult to see.[2] There's nothing revolutionary in this, though. It is merely a recognition that these things were always as real as anything else in the human culturesphere.

In this chapter I will discuss three areas where this blending across the membrane breaks down the easy distinction between real and virtual. The three areas are markets, politics (specifically the politics of fairness), and law. In each area, one can see that institutions outside the membrane have begun to formally validate institutions inside the membrane. In each case, it will be seen that the process by which this validation is occurring is driven by an interesting new behavior pattern on the part of synthetic world users: they have begun to see no line whatsoever between their online activities and their offline activities. This is not necessarily because they are immersed completely in the synthetic space, although this may often be true. Rather, it is because the distinction between the putatively virtual and the putatively real is a nuisance to them. Tellingly, they and their colleagues try to live without it, and this more than anything is what makes the membrane porous.

eBay

The blurring of real and virtual is perhaps nowhere more obvious than in the pricing of goods and services that exist only in synthetic worlds. World-builders always intended for goods and services to have prices and markets inside the world, in terms of gold pieces and credits and so on, but they seem not to have anticipated that these things would acquire robust markets in dollars outside the world. At this writing, the online auction site eBay hosts about $30 million annually in trade for goods that only exist in synthetic worlds.[3] Much of this trade involves currencies, which means that eBay is effectively hosting a foreign exchange market for synthetic world money. The dollar exchange rates are robust and not uncommonly higher than those of Earth currencies. For a good part of 2001, the "Platinum Piece" of *EverQuest* was trading at 100 to the dollar when the yen was trading at 120 to the dollar. Another significant chunk of the eBay market involves the trading of user accounts, effectively a market for services. While most world owners oppose this trade verbally, they seem to believe that not much can be done about it. Wars on trade are difficult to win.[4]

By now, no one in a synthetic world bats an eye over the idea that it might cost about 100 of *EverQuest*'s platinum pieces to get one US dollar. As mentioned in chapter 4, online auctions of game items begin to appear weeks in advance of the game's release. Every major virtual world of which I am aware has an active eBay market. Typically prices are $50 to $100 for gold pieces in lots of thousands, and $200 to $500 for user accounts with well-established characters. With currency trades, you send the seller the dollar payment and arrange to meet in the game. Once payment is sent, you go into the game world and meet with the avatar of the seller, who hands over the gold pieces. Buying accounts is somewhat different; after winning the auction and sending payment, you receive an account name and a password from the seller. These keywords allow you to log into the world as that seller, which means you have access to all the characters and equipment he has developed. Once you are in, you change the password on the account, and it is yours forever. Engaging in this trade has been normal and commonplace throughout the synthetic world.[5]

Is this market legitimate in the same way that outside markets are? You might wonder why you trust the sellers to deliver the goods and passwords as they promise. But that's not a question for synthetic worlds, that's a question for eBay. Why does anyone send the Hummel figurine after you send them payment? eBay and other sites have methods for raising trust online, and they work (Kollock 1999b). eBay, at this writing, does over $14 billion in sales annually. It's the most successful market in the history of humankind. There are no grounds for doubting that the online markets for virtual items and services are legitimate markets.[6]

The existence of these markets, however, has interesting effects on synthetic worlds. For one thing, the economy becomes difficult to control. Suppose a world that is no more or less fun than other worlds suddenly offered easy gold pieces for all players. In El Dorado, it is proclaimed, gold now grows on trees and can be plucked by anyone. El Dorado gets many new players, of course, and existing players get many more gold pieces. Meanwhile, the value of the El Dorado gold piece on eBay would fall as that market gets flooded with them. While people in El Dorado now have more gold and hence better equipment, the dollar value of that gold and equipment would have fallen. Of course, people will continue to leave other worlds (World of Poverty, World of Want, Earth, and so on), as long as El Dorado offers the better deal. Each move further drives down the dollar value of El Dorado's items and gold on eBay. The process continues until, once again, the dollar value of earnings in El Dorado is no higher than in any other. It's just an example of the economic *Law of One Price* applied to the low-skill labor market represented by synthetic world economies. Dollar-valued earnings in all worlds must be equal; population flows and exchange rates for currency will equilibrate them. El Dorado's search for popularity through easy gold is quickly frustrated by a reduction in the dollar value of the gold.[7]

The possibility that unskilled labor markets may affect the value of playing in a synthetic world may seem strange, but the idea has been corroborated by recent events. We know now that, in several synthetic worlds, unskilled labor has been hired to do nothing but mindlessly farm the world for gold pieces, say, by killing monsters and looting their treasures of coins over and over and over. The gold is then sold on eBay. In worlds where this practice has developed, the value of gold pieces against the dollar rapidly drops and, therefore, the value of assets obtained by everyone in the game drops as well. This is exactly what the market logic predicts: when new unskilled laborers from the third world begin farming loot and selling it, they drive down the wages of those who had been in the world before. In a way, we have only learned that the synthetic world is something of an instantly globalized labor market.[8]

Indeed, the presence of outside markets presents a serious problem for world design on a more general level. A synthetic economy is more fun if it rewards hard work with a rags-to-riches story line. It's also more fun if it undoes the injustices of birth on Earth: everyone starts with the same rags. Both features are damaged when wealthy heiresses can buy mountains of gold pieces and advanced accounts online. eBaying, as the term goes, seriously damages the fun factor of the world. Since the world-builders are trying to sell that atmosphere as part of their product, they would be justified in defending their world from anything that damages it.

eBaying could be reduced, and perhaps eliminated, with a combination of policies. First, note that every eBay transaction involving goods and currency requires that two avatars meet in the world, with one giving the other valuable items in return for nothing. Accounts that repeatedly engage in this kind of charity ought to become suspect. The trade also implies that someone (the recipient) is suddenly getting much richer, seemingly out of thin air. A policy of high progressive taxation can automatically and fairly reduce the value of these kinds of transactions to the recipient, making eBay a less valuable tool for advancement. Third, world-builders could deploy tactical media strategies, such as fraudulent auctions that lessen the reputation of sellers in the eBay market. Lastly, they could deploy investigators and have a formal trial process. In all of this, the cooperation of eBay or any other market-maker cannot be assumed. If eBay were to cooperate in a way that was critical to the operation, users would move the market elsewhere. eBay tried to help *EverQuest* control sales of its goods, and the market simply moved to a different site, PlayerAuctions.com. It would be costly to take steps against the external market, but it might be necessary if the damage to the game's basic lore becomes too severe.

How eagerly the coding authority should go after the online auction market is a question I will leave to other writings, but there can be no question that the existence of these external markets makes every good inside the membrane just as real as the goods outside of it.[9] It is frankly impossible to deny that the gold pieces of fantasy worlds are money, just like the money in your pocket. They are sustained by exactly the same social mechanisms and perform exactly the same functions. But if these points are not persuasive, surely the fact that gold pieces can be used to buy dollars reveals something of significance. We may still debate whether many of the features of synthetic worlds are real, but there can be no debate about money and the prices of things there: they are as real as real gets.

Politics and Fairness, Inside and Outside

After money, another avenue of shifting reality in synthetic worlds involves the politics of fairness. In synthetic worlds, politics is inevitable. Users are a community of interests who are affected by the decisions of a coding authority, usually the game developers. Here I will focus on decisions regarding the roles users occupy. Chapter 4 described the fact that players are often specialized into different economic and social roles, and it turns out that these roles generate political tensions. Often it takes quite a bit of time to fully inhabit a role, which tends to lock a user into the role once it has been attained. It takes so long to build an avatar into a powerful wizard that, once the pinnacles of wizardry have been attained, it is very costly to switch to being a warrior. Should something happen to the conditions of being a wizard—say, a formerly powerful spell gets weakened—all those who are settled into wizarding as an occupation experience a genuine loss of well-being. Similarly, if you are a level 65 wizard and the coding authority decides to make the level 65 fireball spell into a veritable cloud of utter annihilation, you experience a genuine increase in well-being: all wizards are more powerful and they will reap the status rewards that result. As a result, it is very common for players to complain and plead for improvements in their class or race or occupation.

What is interesting is that while there are many sanctioned avenues by which one can communicate with the coding authority, the far more common practice is to use public forums to make critiques and suggestions about how the world should be changed. These suggestions, often appeals, are aimed directly at the coding authority, in recognition of the authority's dictatorial powers. While many of the petitions are of a customer service flavor—"the game client crashed and I lost my loot, please fix it"—others are exercises in the finest tradition of political philosophy. The arguments are almost always couched in terms of fairness. The game world should be "balanced," it is said, so that all users face the same level of challenge in meeting their goals. Particularly powerful and easy avatar types should be *nerfed* (reduced in power). Those that are weak should be enhanced. The debates rage endlessly in online discussion forums, whether they be ones established by the coding authority for just this purpose, or independent sites established by fans. The point is that these debates, which really do involve legitimate political interests, almost always occur outside the membrane rather than inside it.

The presence of political clamor outside rather than inside is interesting because, in my experience, it often works. In many cases, the coding authority acts like a chastened dictator and bows to the expressed wishes of the people. Rules do get changed. The reason is not hard to see, and explains why the campaigning occurs "in public" as it were: these are profit-oriented companies. If something is very unfair, developers have every incentive to change it so as not to lose subscription dollars. And by making their criticisms known through outside channels, where potential game-buyers might see them, the agitators tap into the most effective pressure available. This is not to say that there is no political activity inside the membrane; synthetic worlds have been hosts to protest marches, sit-ins, mail campaigns, petitions, and even violent revolt. In the early days of *Ultima Online*, disgruntled players marched to the King's throne, stripped off their avatar clothes, and proceeded to vomit on everything. In the face of such earnest, if repulsive, expressions of distress, many a ruler would consider granting their requests. When descriptions of the event make their way onto the Internet, however, and thence to the pages of the *New Yorker* (Kolbert 2001), even the worst tyrant, if he is profit-seeking, must yield.

When users take their in-world political concerns to out-of-world forums, they break down the distinction between virtual and real in a very radical way. In this case, it is the ordinary pressures of commerce outside the membrane that give voice to political pressures generated by situations entirely within it. To maintain some kind of distinction between the virtual and the real here, it would be necessary for each petition to carry a disclaimer: "Recognizing that the issues I am about to discuss are only hypothetically important, on the as-if assumption that the affairs of a society in a synthetic world really matter, I hereby suggest the following . . ." No one bothers. The entire discussion proceeds on the assumption that the coding authority's interest in pleasing those who pay for the world with US dollars is sufficient to turn the virtual concerns into real ones.

The response of most coding authorities to these requests is interesting in that it usually refuses to recognize the role of outside pressure. Typically, if a change is made, it is never attributed to the vocal protests of users. Rather, a broader appeal to fairness or balance is made—"We felt that Wizards were becoming too over-powered with their use of the Staff of Stupidity, so we reduced its damage." One suspects that the coding authority hesitates to admit that the external protests are effective, lest they face even more of them.

Yet this choice is not without its costs. The external forums are really the only place where the coding authority can be frank with the users; inside the membrane, it would be a violation of the fantasy to explain why the rules behind the fantasy are set as they are. And what if some of the things that users complain about are caused by forces that are not actually under the coding authority's control? By failing to become a political actor on the outside, the coding authority cannot deflect blame that it does not deserve.

Fairness issues, especially, are an area in which most coding authorities are criticized unjustly. Many of the seemingly unfair things that people complain about in a synthetic world are actually the result of the ebb and flow of labor markets inside and outside the membrane, over which the coding authority has no control, of course. The Earth labor market effects appear because, as noted, users can choose what roles to inhabit, and the returns available to a particular role will depend on how many people are playing that role in the synthetic world at a given time. But this headcount itself is affected by the returns; if they are high, many people will begin to enter that role. And inevitably, this entry will drive down the returns available in that role. The critical thing here is that the entry effect will depend on conditions both inside and outside the synthetic membrane. And thus, when the social esteem of some role plummets because lots of new players are choosing to enter the role, competing away the profit margins it affords, none of that is the fault of the coding authority; it will be blamed, of course, but not with any justice.

Let me spell out this argument in a bit more detail. The first choices people usually make when entering a synthetic world involve the kinds of skills and powers they will have. The coding authority allows some diversity in these skills and powers, because this diversity is integral to providing a rich, complex, and fun social environment. The coding authority also, properly, allows all users to choose whatever roles they please, because this is only fair. Users can therefore sort themselves into the roles that they prefer, which is a good thing.

Now consider the fact that any user's enjoyment of a synthetic world depends on two things: the fun they get out of it, and the earnings they get out of it. Earnings (or wages—I'll use the terms interchangeably) are the result of labor hours devoted to gathering resources from the synthetic world; it is expressed in dollars and can be thought of as the dollar price of the resources, as if that loot were to be sold on eBay. Fun is, well, just fun; some modes of gathering are entertaining and fulfilling, others are boring. With this in mind, total compensation of a synthetic world can be expressed as follows:

$$\text{Total Compensation} = \text{Wage} + \text{Fun}.$$

Labor economics tells us that jobs that are more fun should have lower wages. The theory of *compensating wage differentials* says that those doing unpleasant jobs must be paid a higher wage than is otherwise available for someone of that level of skill; the workers must be compensated for enduring the unpleasant work conditions. Similarly, a nice job often pays poorly. Just look at professors. They spend most of their time just thinking and chatting with respectful young people, a kind of job that lots of people probably enjoy doing. There's a great deal of supply available to fill these positions, and not so much demand for people to be doing them, hence the wage tends to be lower than it would be if the work conditions were not so pleasurable. In general, when the Fun component of compensation rises, the Wage component goes down to compensate, and vice versa.

This is where the problems emerge for synthetic world-builders seeking to balance the fairness of different roles. If they make a role more fun, more players will enter it. If more players enter it, the earnings available in that role have to go down because of the new competition. Theory predicts that the total compensation of Wage + Fun will remain unchanged. If the coding authority does something to make a class less powerful, people will leave it, driving up that class's earnings and, again, leaving total compensation unchanged. If you are wondering where all these extra players are coming from, that is, the ones who make these wage adjustments happen by entering or leaving the synthetic labor market, the answer is that they come from the labor markets of Earth. On Earth too, total compensation is given by Wage + Fun. True, the Wage part is bigger and the Fun part is smaller, but the formula is the same. And if someone makes a synthetic world activity more fun in some way, that activity becomes marginally more attractive than time spent in Earth activities. So people switch their time accordingly, leading to the wage changes inside the membrane. The net result of this process is that the coding authority may get blamed for making things unfair, when in fact the forces in play are far beyond their control.

Now, these are long-run effects, it should be remembered. It takes time for a social system based on these roles to adjust. It can be months before a wave of newly minted wizards ascends to the level of power necessary to compete with the old wizards for work and resources. Still, these are clearly the forces at work and, even if they act only in the long run, they demonstrate that fairness and balance are affected as much by decisions in markets outside the membrane as by the policy decisions of the coding authority.

The somewhat good news, however, is that the sorting processes just described could, given time, also automatically defuse many of the political tensions regarding unfairness. If druids are fun and powerful, there will be many druids and nothing will be special about being one; the goods and services that a druid supplies will be in abundant supply. Fun will be high, but compensation low. If clerics are weak and not very fun, they will be hard to find and handsomely compensated for the services they do provide.[10] Fun is low, but compensation is high. Suppose that initially clerics and druids enjoy an equal total compensation level. If something happens to make clerics more powerful and druids weaker, the population will shift away from druids and toward clerics, thus lowering the fun factor and earnings of clerics while raising those of druids. If on the other hand druids become more powerful, the population shifts in the other direction, away from clerics and toward druids, lowering compensation to druids and raising it for clerics. Regardless of what happened initially, the population shift must continue until the total compensation of druids and clerics is equal again.[11] This player-sorting mechanism will always move the system toward balance automatically, so long as every role has something to provide and there are no barriers to roles based on player skill or certifications.

And yet despite the possibility that systems will adjust and create balance on their own, we see coding authorities constantly embroiled in battles about these issues. The reason is, again, political. No one wants to wait for a system to move toward social justice on its own. Very few people are satisfied with ideas like sorting and healthy competition as an explanation for the decrease in well-being they are suffering. As with all political debates, no one wants to wait for "eventually" to come around. And therefore political pressure builds outside the membrane, and coding authorities pay attention to it (although often without admitting to that).

Whether they admit it or not, coding authorities do face the reality that the political tempests in the teapots they've made are, in fact, very real political movements that can exert very real political pressure. And in so doing, these movements reveal one route by which the affairs of synthetic worlds become validated by the outer world. The political mechanism works because users are choosing how to spend their time, and this includes their time in roles on Earth. Saturday's Wizard is an Accountant on Friday and a Lector on Sunday. Switching from Accountant to Lector has never raised any eyebrows, and increasingly, doing a stint as Wizard in between is no longer surprising either.

Law

In the history of virtual worlds, you have to go back to the days of text-based MUDs to find the very first examples of scholars realizing that the events inside the membrane were not at all fictional. As it happened, the first events that seemed real involved the law. Julian Dibbell, having spent some time in an early MUD called LambdaMOO, was the first writer to report that something as serious as real crime, in fact a cyber-rape, could happen in an online space (1999). Later, legal scholar Jennifer Mnookin explicitly tracked the emergence of law-like forms and practices in the same MUD (Mnookin 2001). These days, thanks to the arguments of Larry Lessig and others, the notion of cyberspace as a unique legal jurisdiction is no longer novel (Ludlow 2001). And now synthetic worlds have themselves become the subjects of an explicit legal analysis. Lastowka and Hunter (2004) trace the growth of these worlds as legal forms and consider their legal status in broad terms. Balkin (2004) warns that commodification of these spaces will effectively erode any special legal protections they may enjoy. Kerr (2003) makes explicit the distinction between the outside perspective of virtual worlds (wires, computers, graphics cards) and the inside perspective (the experience of a user when in the world); increasingly, law and policy are coming to recognize the value of the intangibles that exist only in cyberspace (Mueller 2002). As we will see in chapter 9, Raph Koster's Declaration of the Rights of Avatars is a formal statement that the events of these worlds are, in effect, well worthy of legal attention.[12] A moot court that involved exactly this kind of question, held in Las Vegas on July 30, 2003, before US Circuit Court judge Philip M. Pro, concluded that the objects in play in synthetic worlds were valuable under the law.[13] Chinese courts have come to the same conclusion—not moots, but actual courts.[14] And so legal opinions have evolved from recognizing the potential reality of a rape in cyberspace to the potential reality of a theft there. When legal scholars assert that the destruction of $1 million of magic swords is real damage, real loss, responses by real courts become possible.

One of the critical issues here is the nature of property. If I spend thousands of hours developing assets of various forms (equipment, real estate, and avatar capital), is it not mine? Rules against eBaying currency and character accounts seem to go against the general notion that we are free to dispose of the things we make. The synthetic world is just a piece of software that allowed me to make Sabert, the Wizard, just as Microsoft Word is allowing me to make this book. Microsoft does not own my book; why does El Dorado own Sabert?

The coding authority would claim that this is all regulated in the End User Licensing Agreement (EULA) and the Terms of Service (ToS), to which I must agree every time I use the world. My every click is labeled in those documents as "uploaded content," and by clicking "Yes" I expressly disclaim any right to it. Of course, I also agree to things like abridgments of speech and being required to follow any and all instructions of any representative of the coding authority, emergency or no. These kinds of requirements have not yet been subjected to serious court challenge, but that day is surely not far off. Rather than relying on these documents, a more solid justification for limiting the right of free disposal of digital goods would rest on the user community's interests in preserving the world's atmosphere, mentioned in the discussion of market controls above. The argument would be even more persuasive if the community's interests had been validated and expressed through some unbiased consensus-building process. If a parliament of users passes restrictions on the sale of currency and goods and accounts for Earth currency, it seems to me, the coding authority would be quite justified in restricting that activity.

The fact that this discussion takes place at all presumes, of course, that the El Dorado gold piece is a valued thing under the law. An interest is an interest is an interest, wherever it occurs. Here, we see that the obvious economic value of the interests present in synthetic worlds has led to some notion of value under the laws of Earth; law is another site where virtual and real are blending together.

The Self-Affirming Culture of Gaming

In these three examples, we have seen that economic, political, and legal activity that crosses the membrane between synthetic worlds and the Earth serves mostly to blur any distinction between what is synthetic and what is Earthly. This argument may be applied more generally to the world of gaming as a whole. As the industry has evolved from board games to the creation of entire new worlds, the cultural milieu in which its products are experienced has expanded well beyond the card table on a Saturday night. Games are becoming such an integral part of daily life that the distinction between game and life may be fading as well.

Consider the prospects for ubiquitous computing mentioned in chapter 3. One of the early applications of ubiquitous computing will doubtless be ubiquitous gaming. If gaming is truly ubiquitous, what distinguishes it from daily life?

One sees gradual growth in the culture of gaming in many different practices and behaviors. At this particular moment, I am flying in a plane whose pilot is receiving flight path instructions from an air traffic controller—a good one, I hope—somewhere down there. At the same time, I know there is someone flying a simulation of this plane or one like it, on a similar flight path, and that person is also receiving path instructions from a controller; all of this is happening through VATSIM.net, the virtual air traffic simulation system. Through VATSIM, ordinary people have come together as a network of pilots interacting with air traffic controllers to produce a vast, organic simulation of actual air traffic. Flight simulation, in other words, has taken on a massively multiplayer format, and hundreds of ordinary people fly long, ordinary flights under the watchful eye of other ordinary people. All for fun.

If we move to the world of combat flight simulators, we find tens of thousands of people forming into squadrons to fly small-group missions against AI or human opponents. In the world of multiplayer first-person shooters, thousands come together in small teams to relive the horrors of the wars of our past or wars we have only yet imagined. All of this activity is coordinated by active communities based on websites, email, instant messaging, and voice over Internet. It is occasionally charged by face-to-face meetings as well, at fan gatherings, or in the form of romantic trysts. Meanwhile, social gaming grows gradually. Certain venues, such as PC Cafes, host walk-in players interested in gaming with one another;

at this writing, Korea boasts some 25,000 PC Baangs (Herz 2002). Not all of this meeting up is about physical togetherness, mind you; for some gamers, the Internet is just too slow. If everyone can bring their high-powered machine to one location where they can link to a local high-speed network, the gaming is better for everybody.

The broader implications of emergent playlife communities could be significant. The political movements that happen inside and outside games are, at the moment, mostly about games. But there is no reason to expect that these communities will always limit their political activity to game-related issues. If there is a "cyberdemocracy" movement, or any online political movement at all, perhaps it will have to make use of synthetic world technology to get its message to the masses.

Increasingly, the gamer's daily life involves shifting frequently back and forth between different activities, some of which can currently be identified as the "game," whereas others are called "life." But when I am sitting at my computer at home, chatting to my friend Ethelbert, who happens to appear on my screen as an Elven Mage, we are just as likely to be talking about the weather as we are about Magecraft. Perhaps we are also talking to our mutual friend Shotgun Edna by voice over Internet, and she is inviting us into a game of first-person World War II shooter action. Meanwhile, I am in an instant-messaging conversation with my friend Rowena, who wants to get together for a card game Saturday night. Ethelbert is reading an email from the administrator of another synthetic world, informing him that he has won an in-world auction for 600 slats of wood for 50 gold pieces. A similar email from eBay informs him that he has won an auction for a nice Magritte print for $50. With all of this going on, where exactly is the line between game and life? Perhaps someone might be able to make distinctions, but Ethelbert and Edna and Rowena and I, who share a common set of assumptions about the rituals and symbols of our game-infused environments, would probably find them too nit-picky to implement. Imagine if someone were to insist on the following rule: if a rabbit attacks Ethelbert and I help him by casting a spell, we are "in the game," but if we are not actually interacting with the synthetic world, but rather only with each other, then we are "in life." One could always divide things up that way, but for the purposes of living with both the Earth's weather and the fearsome Wererabbits of El Dorado, it's not worth it. Our culture has moved beyond the point where such distinctions are helpful.

Thus this chapter ends with the point that the membrane between synthetic worlds and daily life is definitely there but also definitely porous, and this is by choice of the users. What we have is an almost-magic circle, which seems to have the objective of retaining all that is good about the fantasy atmosphere of the synthetic world, while giving users the maximum amount of freedom to manipulate their involvement with them. Because of these properties, it seems more than likely that synthetic worlds will never be completely marginalized; the routes between them and daily life are too well-traveled. Now that this point has been made, it will perhaps make more sense that we will be spending a few chapters talking about the impact of this technology on issues of daily life. Because the two worlds are destined to interact, some attention should be paid to the broader economic, political, and security issues that will certainly arise.

7

FREE COMMERCE

Throughout part 2 we are pointing our attention to the effects of the synthetic world on our world, which occurs mostly through the blurring of lines between the two. In the last chapter we had a quick look at three avenues by which this blurring occurs: markets, political pressures, and legal opinion. These avenues and others are responsible for putting the synthetic world inside an almost-magic circle rather than a truly magic one, and the consequence seems to be that those who travel back and forth seem to gradually stop reminding themselves that the events in the synthetic world are supposed to be some kind of fantasy. In chapter 2 I argued that, at some deep level, those events are no more fantasy than the fantasy of daily life, but the point I am driving at here is that the fantasy in the synthetic world is supposed to be a *different* fantasy, one that proceeds according to different rules than the rules we have here on the outside. The porosity of the membrane, however, means that the rules of play inside and outside influence one another, with unpredictable results for both.

The remaining chapters of part 2 are going to focus on specific phenomena, a topic-by-topic review of some of the more noteworthy consequences of having a porous membrane in place rather than a solid one. There are many more consequences than can be addressed here, but I hope to discuss effects that are of more than passing significance. In this chapter we begin with a discussion of business—specifically, the fact that people have already begun to set up businesses inside synthetic worlds, businesses that capitalize on an intimate knowledge of daily life there in order to earn sizeable real-world incomes.

Some Corporate PR

Taggart Transdimensional seeks to better serve the universe via complete
vertical integration. The main business lines of the company are split between the basic disciplines—Mining, Industrial, Trading, Defense, and Financial . . .

Unique Financial Department. The corporation has a broad array of financial
services available. More information can be found in our Financial section, but
a short discussion of the venture capital arm is described below.

Our financial department will enable intra-company venture capital investments. This practice, a fundamental tenet that we feel makes this corporation
unique, allows many benefits:

- Any group of employees in the company can approach one of our fund managers and request money for a venture. This money will be repaid pursuant
  to the terms of the deal.
- Divisions that want a particular mineral mined, component built, etc., can
  attract groups of employees to do so by investing money in this effort. This,
  in a sense, is an intra-company mission generator.
- Individual employees can invest in as many of these funds as they wish to
  supplement their income.
- Other corporations can invest in these funds to diversify their holdings.

(From the corporate information page of TaggartTransdimensional.com.)

This brief excerpt from the website of Taggart Transdimensional Incorporated
(TTI) certainly makes it seem like an innovative corporation. Instead of top-
heavy central control, the managers would like to see the corporation expand
through the entrepreneurial activities of its employees/members. You might think
that this kind of company would make a good investment, but before you call
your broker, you should be aware of TTI's base of operations. The company does
most of its work in outer space, you see. Not Earth's orbit, actually, nor even our
solar system. TTI operates *out there*. Way out there in fact, on the other side of the
galaxy. With current technologies, we couldn't fly to TTI's corporate HQ within
the lifetimes of 100 biblical patriarchs.

Of course, we don't have to fly there ourselves, we can ship an avatar to the place
in a matter of seconds. TTI operates in the corner of the galaxy being built and maintained by *EVE Online*, a space-themed MMORPG. It is unique in its encouragement

of corporate forms of governance. The thought experiment is this: Suppose a corner of the galaxy opened up in which there were no countries, no kings or parliaments or despots, but only corporations. The corporations would—finally!—be free of the oppressive interferences of humanity's lesser beings, and their members could advance the species in a glorious whirlwind of unregulated entrepreneurial capitalism. EVE has been designed self-consciously as a paradise for followers of Ayn Rand.[1] Not surprising that corporations such as TTI have emerged.

What then do we make of the fact that one can speculate for the ores of EVE's galaxy on a completely different market: eBay? As I write this, I have a browser window open to eBay Category 1654, Internet Games, the category where most sales of virtual items happen. There are a large number of *EVE Online* auctions. Here's one for Megacyte. We see there are 8,000 units for sale; the opening bid was $19.95; 13 bids later the price has risen to $152.50 and we have three hours to go. If we didn't want to buy our Megacyte at eBay, we could instead buy EVE currency here—20 million "ISK" for only $35—and use it to buy our Megacyte in the game.

One wonders whether TTI has a hand in this market as well. It seems to be a profit-oriented company that is willing to fund the investments of its members, wherever they might be. Some might be on faraway Earth. No matter; capitalism loves to explore.

The Entrepreneurial Landscape

If it did mix in-game commerce with out-of-game commerce, TTI would not be special in any way; indeed, there are now several companies taking advantage of the mix between in-world and out-of-world markets. Perhaps the first was a company called Blacksnow Interactive Inc., which made its business from buying and selling items from *Dark Age of Camelot*. When threatened with expulsion from the world in 2002—Mythic, the world's owners, are especially vigorous in defending their world's atmosphere from the effects of out-of-game commerce—Blacksnow sued. The suit was later tossed out of court, apparently because the company failed to make its court dates, but the prospect of commercial and legal conflict between owners and entrepreneurs was clearly demonstrated.

During this same time period a company called Yantis Enterprises Inc. built a thriving business buying and selling items from *EverQuest*; its site, MySuperSales.com, would display thousands of items and currencies for sale. Yantis was better than eBay; on eBay you'd have to deal directly with some other player, but through Yantis you could take advantage of a professionally trained staff that would handle financial issues, customer service, and so on; when you bought through Yantis, your goods would be delivered on the spot.

Soon a new entrant in game item trading emerged, Internet Gaming Entertainment Ltd. (IGE). Like Yantis, IGE raised the bar in terms of business professionalism. IGE obtained positive ratings from VeriSign, BizRate, and SquareTrade. It expanded its coverage to all of the major North American synthetic worlds. It took advantage of the global reach of synthetic worlds by setting up shop in Hong Kong. There, a small army of technically savvy but low-wage workers could field orders, load up avatars, retrieve stored goods, and deliver them wherever necessary. As I write this, IGE uses eBay as advertising, posting sales auctions for all shards of almost all synthetic worlds, each auction pointing clearly to the company's website. Once a buyer gets to the website, purchasing virtual items and currency is just as quick and easy as buying a book at Amazon.com. Select the items you want, put them in your shopping cart, and head for the checkout. After your payment is confirmed, load your avatar in the game and wait for a message from your friendly in-world IGE rep, who will quickly bring your goods to you. This business model simply takes everything we know about customer satisfaction and applies it to virtual-item sales, or RMT — real money trade.

By all accounts, this strategy has been enormously successful. IGE now maintains its world headquarters in midtown Manhattan and throws lavish dinners for MMORPG cognoscenti at game conventions. They bought out Yantis for $10 million. The idea that someone can actually make decent money trading items was directly tested by writer Julian Dibbell, who spent the year 2003 attempting to earn as much from virtual item sales as he does as a journalist. According to his blog "Play Money," Dibbell was able to accumulate monthly earnings of more than $2,000 for an entire year. And the market that enables earnings at this level, according to most estimates, is growing exponentially.

In the wake of IGE, several interesting start-ups have been founded. PlayVault offers to all synthetic worlds who join their consortium a matching service, so that users who want to move from one world to another can in effect transfer their wealth with the sanction of the world's owners. The Gaming Open Market allows anyone to post buy and sell and trade orders for all synthetic world currencies, again allowing users to more easily transfer wealth among worlds. Virdaq specializes in price reporting: folks who broker items and currency through their site have access to sophisticated price dynamics statistics, so as to avoid being duped. Other companies specialize in reporting prices from within game worlds; they code bots who automatically access internal market data and post the findings to spreadsheets. It seems that a mob of entrepreneurs is hovering around all this market activity, trying to think of ways to capitalize on it.

Yet for all its success, IGE and its competitors are not fully accepted within the gaming industry. Game developers in general seem to wish that IGE and the market that feeds it would go away. For the fact is, the developers are trying to build a fantasy existence, and the idea that not only is this alleged fantasy irreparably intermixed with reality, but that some outsider can make millions off of that fact, is troubling.

From a neutral standpoint, one can see merit on both sides. IGE merely capitalizes on natural market incentives. On the other hand, the fantasy atmosphere of synthetic worlds is their most precious object, and the crass marketing of goods and currency endangers it quite terribly. A debate has emerged among legal scholars about the legal standing of these trades. On the one hand, the End User Licensing Agreement (EULA) that all players digitally sign off on when using the world often dictates that selling game objects for real money is against the rules. On the other, most traditional notions of property hold that objects that I create belong to me. Another issue is the fact that the EULA seems never to be enforced; this trading goes on night and day, yet (with significant exceptions, including companies like Mythic Entertainment and Blizzard Entertainment) developers don't make much of an effort to stop it. Thus on the one hand, the trade is against the rules, but on the other, it doesn't seem to encounter strong opposition.

If the EULA is ignored, however, and virtual-item trading becomes accepted, some very interesting consequences come up. For what, then, distinguishes my sale of a magic wand for $10 from my sale of a T-shirt for $10? And yet I have to pay a tax on the latter transaction; why not the former? Moreover, in order to be licensed to sell a T-shirt, I have to meet all kinds of regulations and laws. Why do these regulations and laws not apply in cyberspace, if the commercial activity is basically the same? A synthetic world that admits an equivalence between its internal commerce and the daily commerce of the external world will have to be asked to submit to the same rules of the game that external firms do (Balkin 2004). Developers could be held liable for server crashes that destroyed database items which, if they are held to be just as valuable as their free-market price indicates, could amount to hundreds of millions of dollars in damages. Setting liability aside, the commercialization of what was supposed to be a fantasy would destroy the differentness of the synthetic world quite completely, a disaster in my opinion.

Developers rely on the EULA to defend the membrane; since everyone who enters the world has digitally agreed not to engage in external commerce, they say, the values that appear only through the external commerce can be ignored. Gold pieces, they will say, are game pieces only and have no real-world value, because the EULA forces everyone to agree to that understanding in advance. Unfortunately, the EULA may not be as strong a tool as they hope. The recent Chinese court case mentioned in the last chapter illustrates why.[2] A hacker broke into the database of a popular synthetic world and transferred several choice items from the account of another player to his own. The player asked that his items be returned; when the company refused, citing rules of the game that prevent the owners from arbitrarily transferring items, the player sued. Using prices in external markets, the court was able to establish that the virtual items were worth $1,200 and ordered the company to return the items. The point is that the case did not seem to involve any arguments about a prior contract by which all parties agreed that virtual items have no external value. The value was tangible on external markets, and the judgment for compensation followed. In a somewhat different case in the United States, the "It is only a game" argument has been raised but then rejected on appeal.[3] I am not a legal expert, but it seems to me that courts may pay more attention to actual harms than to the EULA, unless a firm precedent or law supporting EULAs can be established (Castronova 2005).

Taking a view from 60,000 feet, it seems clear that a new form of business enterprise is emerging. The interests of companies and customers now straddle this strange semiporous boundary, and it is not easy to decide how conflicts of interest should be resolved. It is never a good idea to arbitrarily dampen the force of legitimate and honorable profit-seeking. On the other hand, if we determine that all synthetic worlds are really nothing more than shopping malls, something very important will have been lost. Developers have every right, in my view, to try to keep the fantasy aspects of their worlds pure.[4] What is needed now is a new set of regulatory and legal understandings, ones that take advantage of these new forms of business without damaging the synthetic worlds from which they derive value.

Future Competition

As these developments move forward, it seems that most traditional businesses remain somewhat flat-footed. That's understandable. A book on ecommerce strategy published in 2001 explained to executives that, on the web, you can use a mouse to point at a picture, and when you click it, you get a new page of info related to the picture you clicked on.[5] Oi! The executives who were the target of that book really need to get up to speed. But rather than criticize senior executives, perhaps we need to be aware that things are moving too rapidly for people at the top of any organization to keep up. Their job is not to go out and find minute seismic shifts, their job is to plan for the consequences of shifts that their employees are reporting. Here in the post-bust phase of the Internet boom, we re-awaken to the reality that the Internet kept going while we gave it up for dead. Just when the top echelons begin to grasp the significance of Google and the MP3 revolution, along comes this guy—me—who says that *Dungeons and Dragons* has become a real place and some little company is making millions off of it already. That kind of idea, I admit, is going to be a little tough to swallow for quite a few years. I do not think that many traditional firms will be moving into this space right away.

This of course opens opportunities for start-ups to become the established leaders. Certainly the independent developer companies, such as NCSoft, Blizzard Entertainment, Mythic Entertainment, and Turbine Entertainment, have a chance to become major entities. Interestingly, some large firms that want to be involved here, such as Microsoft, are having trouble finding a toehold. But beyond the development role, there are other opportunities opening in this space. In middleware development, for example, there are only a few start-ups, such as BigWorld and Butterfly.net. The synthetic world *Second Life* might count as a middleware start-up, since their business plan allows anyone on the outside to buy some of their virtual land and use their scripting language to build things on it. *Second Life* also allows users to retain property rights and, as an effect, profits on the things they create. I think there are opportunities for customer service companies to take over the user management side of ongoing synthetic world operations, since this is a tough job that most developers and owners take a long time to learn how to do well. There's one bona fide consulting firm at the moment, the Themis Group. All in all, this market remains open for innovation and the niches are being occupied by comparatively small enterprises.

That is the situation in the near term; if we think longer term, the emergence of corporate commercial activity in this space begins to raise daunting possibilities. Suppose the level of financial transactions in synthetic worlds reached the point that a major investment bank comes to believe that a serious profit opportunity is present. It considers opening a bank somewhere in a synthetic world; people could come by with their avatars and exchange their game credits for dollars, yen, or gold pieces as the case may be. Having obtained the agreement of the developers of some world, the bank sets up operations and then goes to file its papers—where? What jurisdiction covers the bank's operations? Perhaps none; and if so, a tax- and regulation-free mode of operation becomes possible. Operating only in the synthetic world, this bank could become a cyberspace version of the Cayman Islands. With sufficient cash volume, potentially produced by millions of ordinary players as they deposit their gold pieces and dollars in the bank's vaults, it could become an important source of external, no-questions-asked funding for all kinds of enterprises. The same is true of all commercial entities, not just banks. If synthetic worlds become a place that just about everyone visits, the flow of trade that passes through cyberspace will be quite substantial, and those companies that go "out there" and take advantage of it may find themselves operating in a libertarian's dreamland. In other words, the longer-run vision of *EVE Online* and TTI Inc. is not just a pipe dream: we cannot predict how the emergence of fantasy worlds with real economies will shake up the relationship between business and government.

A Corporate Petri Dish

In facing this future, we can expect business know-how to emerge and take advantage of opportunities as they appear. But we have to recognize that it may not be Earth firms who do the innovating. Rather, it may be the case that the unregulated frontier encourages such a wave of innovation and reorganization that new practices are more likely to be discovered out there than in the ordinary world. Beck and Wade (2004) argue that the common practices of the gamer generation will change business forever, and synthetic worlds are one conduit of that change. What if the leaders of TTI have come upon a truly path-breaking form of corporate organization? They will certainly make good money within *EVE Online*, but the more significant possibility is that they may port their system into the markets of Earth and make money here too. Indeed, we can and should view synthetic worlds as essentially unregulated playgrounds for economic organization, and therefore it is more than likely that if there are ways of running things that humans have not yet discovered, they will first be discovered in cyberspace. Synthetic worlds are a lab for corporate practice; we may learn as much about business in the information age from them as from any other source. The sheer volume of trade today is not large, of course, but this technology may eventually enable a great deal more commerce than it does today. One can imagine lattices of synthetic worlds in which avatar-mediated interaction drives the purchase and sale of a large portion of the goods we consume, digital and otherwise. Perhaps the future Wal-Mart Online has aisles and items, just like the neighborhood store, and you use your avatar to go shopping and examine items. It also has a teller machine and even an insurance office. It's funny that the teller machine says "Bank of America" but the insurance office says "Sabert's CyberSurance." But that's because Sabert figured out how to do insurance in this space before AllState did. The still-unregulated commerce within synthetic worlds may be the test bed on which many new practices are discovered.

In sum, we see that the interactions through the membrane around synthetic worlds lead to an unusual combination of commercial opportunity and innovation. These interactions also pose dangers for the very worlds on which these opportunities depend. If synthetic worlds become commercialized completely, the golden goose will be dead. For as entertaining as Wal-Mart Online may become, it will never have the drawing power of the world of my dreams. And if you exploit my dream and make it into a Wal-Mart, I will be very, very unlikely to go there any more. The way ahead is to preserve the dream worlds by whatever means necessary, leaving the world of for-profit actors to take care of itself—something it does very well.

Having now considered the evolution of external markets to some degree, the next chapter turns our attention to the evolution of internal markets, the economies within the dream world.

8

THE ECONOMICS OF FUN:
BEHAVIOR AND DESIGN

Interlude: What's Happened to Reality?

The commercial, political, and legal considerations of the last two chapters showed how ordinary notions of reality get warped once the synthetic world appears. At first, you might have said that the things on the Earth are real and the things in a synthetic world are not. Then you notice that money in synthetic worlds has all of the features of money outside synthetic worlds, and this fact (plus the political and legal validations that synthetic worlds receive) makes you conclude that everything is real, both inside and outside the membrane. And this is well in accord with the views presented in chapter 2, where play theorists were said to view daily life as having elements of play, and where media psychologists were said to have shown that treating events in the synthetic world as real is all but involuntary. But then in the last chapter, when considering the effects of commercialization on synthetic worlds, I gave arguments for keeping the membrane as solid as possible, lest crass market forces erode the precious fantasy atmosphere. But if everything inside and outside is equally real, how can there be any fantasy atmosphere to protect? Isn't it inconsistent to claim that events inside a synthetic world are real, but that they are also unreal?

Well, no. It's just that the word "real," handy as it is in some contexts, is not very helpful here; the meaning of this word truly does have to be warped to capture the complexity that synthetic worlds present. Synthetic worlds are both real and unreal. They are real in the sense that they matter to people. They are also real in the sense that the institutions we find within them can be traced back to very ordinary human impulses. But they are unreal in the sense that the resulting patterns of behavior there are potentially different from those on Earth. Consider sex, for example. Sex in synthetic worlds is real; the courtship is real, the passion is real, the orgasms are real (Dibbell 1999; Taylor 2002). Institutions like dating, gift-giving, and marriage are also real. What is not real, in the sense of being not like things in daily life, is the fact that by switching avatars, you can have sex in all four quadrants of the human pairing possibilities graph (M/F, F/M, M/M, and F/F) *with the same partner.* This variability in avatar-mediated pairings may be a good thing or a bad thing, but it certainly is a new thing, and we have no idea what its long-run consequences may be for human social relations.[1] There is no question that it forces us to enter into a whole sequence of very complex rethinkings, which can be very disorienting.[2] But while this rethinking is going on, it would be a shame if something were to happen at this early stage—say, a regulation that no one can use an avatar with a gender different from that of their Earth body—that makes this new form of behavior disappear. Therefore we should be careful that our awareness of the realness of things inside synthetic worlds does not cause us to treat them so much like daily life on Earth as to destroy the unrealness they also exhibit. The membrane is porous, but that does not mean we should puncture it willfully or remove it completely.

In chapter 2 I warned that synthetic worlds were, in a sense, play spaces and nonplay spaces at the same time, and that this level of complexity would be necessary to hold on to throughout the book. Here in part 2 we begin to see the practical consequences of failing to hold on to that complexity. If we think too simply, we perhaps think of synthetic worlds as a meaningless fantasy land and assume that no one in their right minds would care what is happening there; and then a small, energetic company like IGE comes along and grabs the first niche in what might become a massive and lucrative market. Or, being too simplistic in the other direction, we think of synthetic worlds as just an extension of daily life and assume that no one in their right minds would fail to see that everything is real there; and then judges start handing down opinions by which a game company is held liable because Ozgord the Ogre stole $200 worth of virtual gold pieces from Migdan the Midget. Either/Or thinking does not work here. The phenomenon requires some subtlety in treatment. We need to be able to make astute moves like IGE's without bringing contemporary tort law into Middle Earth, where it most certainly does not belong.

The subtleties required will eventually be incumbent on professionals in many disciplines, but given that my highest degree is in economics, it is there that I would like, at first, to consider what those subtleties might entail. In fact I think the economic activity inside synthetic worlds is an especially revealing case of the warping of the word "real." I am certain that one could write similar cases for other disciplines and phenomena (and I imagine those cases will be forthcoming eventually), but in this chapter I would like to focus on the very ordinary, and yet the very extraordinary, economic forces that synthetic worlds produce.

There is one other reason to focus on synthetic economies at an early point: the economy is in fact an integral part of the fantasy. Nothing makes a world feel more alive than an active market system. Developers seem to recognize this. With very few exceptions, every synthetic world has a set of user institutions, game mechanics, and AI systems that collectively constitute an economy. Most worlds tout the existence of an economy as an important selling point: "This amazing new world has an entirely player-driven economy, where items you find or make can be bought or sold to other players! You can be a merchant if you want; buy low and sell high, and you can make yourself rich!" Once the world is launched, discussions of the economic system often occupy center stage in the game and on discussion boards. Indeed, because of the critical role that prices and wages play in the fantasy, there seem to be as many self-proclaimed experts on the economy as there are players.

Among these interested users, it's quite common to read that a world's economy is "broken," although that judgment is usually based on a misconception of what an economy is. Economists would prefer the following language: "The economic conditions of this world are not what I want them to be." And certainly, comparatively few of the economies in the current group of MMORPGs seem to operate in the best way. There seems to be a knowledge gap; it seems to me that adhering to a few simple doctrines would make the economies function much better. It's arrogant to say that, of course, since I've never developed a virtual economy myself. I recognize that I am explaining to the islanders how to cast their nets. Consider the arguments I present as food for thought, then: the honest opinion of an outsider who has thought a great deal about economics while spending a great deal of time online. It's not that I sought out synthetic economies to study; synthetic economies just exist, everywhere, in the games I play. Indeed, despite the pride with which marketing departments proclaim the existence of a real economy in the worlds they are promoting, it is very hard for me to conceive of any persistent community of people that would *not* have an economy. I don't think it's possible, as a review of some basic economic principles should help make clear.

What Is Economics?

Synthetic worlds are so complex that it's necessary to start at the beginning, with basic definitions. Economics is usually defined as the study of choice under scarcity. The idea is that any human being has desires, and that these desires can never be fully satisfied with current resources. Resources are scarce, and that forces us to choose where to allocate our resources so as to obtain the best mix of desires that we can. The problem of choice under scarcity is not some rare condition, it is in fact inherent in our physical natures. If the amount of food in the world tripled or quadrupled or grew by 100,000 times, food would still be scarce because it would still have a positive price. That price might be low—one millionth of a penny—but it would still be positive. And that means that every cheeseburger I eat is going to reduce the resources I have for other things. I will still have to decide how much to spend on food, which means, collectively, all humans will have to decide how much of our resources to expend creating food to eat. Scarcity emerges from the fact that the Earth only has so much stuff on it, and this stuff can only be made into a certain portfolio of things to eat, drink, wear, and play, while my desire to eat and drink and wear and play is virtually limitless. Indeed, time is perhaps the ultimate scarce resource. We only live so long. If we had one million Earths, we still would not be able to do and have absolutely everything we can imagine. No, we would have to choose how our time is allocated. That's what economics involves—not money or markets per se, but constrained choosing.

Like the rest of us, users of synthetic worlds have to choose how to allocate their time. They have to decide what worlds to visit, and, once in the world, they have to decide how much time to spend doing different things. It's part of the deal we all got when we became human beings. Thus, choice under scarcity happens whenever a human decides what to do. The economy "happens" in that moment. In other words, *every synthetic world has always had an economy*, without exception.

In fact it would be impossible to design a synthetic world without an economy. If you create a 3D space with things to do and then admit people into it, economic decisions will be made. The mere fact that the developers have put gold pieces and markets into the world does not mean that they have created an economy; it was already there. And the mere fact that gold pieces aren't worth what they used to be, or that the price of something has gone up or down, never means that the economy is "broken." The evolving lattice of individual choices is just having an effect on things; the numbers by which we observe the economy are changing, but the economy is always existing and functioning like a genuine economy. The economies of these worlds, as a matter of fact, are not just "functioning like a genuine economy": they *are* a genuine economy.

Much of the confusion in discussions about economic topics stems from common misunderstandings about what an economy is and what it is not. Among users and developers, a great deal of energy is expended discussing things that are only the outward manifestations of underlying economic processes. Consider money. Many people treat money as *the* economy. Synthetic world user hand-books, under "Guide to the Economy," often write something like "In Castrovia, 1 gold piece equals 10 silver pieces, which equals 100 copper pieces." This is a largely irrelevant fact, at least as regards the economy. Money is just a convenience for recording choices and their effects. The economy is the choices, not the money by which I register the choices. If at some point the price of some object changes from 1 gold piece to 1 million gold pieces, that fact, in itself, is of no consequence. The price simply states a rate of transaction that by itself has no implication for anyone's well-being. If houses cost \$100,000 and I am being paid \$60,000 per year, I am in the same situation as I would be if houses cost \$1,000,000 and I were being paid \$600,000 per year. True, an understanding of the economy involves understanding monetary issues. But the things we care about involve not money per se, but the underlying conditions of choice under scarcity that monetary accounting allows us to measure.

Thus right from the start, this view that economies of synthetic worlds are somehow capable of existing, or not existing, or of being broken, or not broken, stems from a fundamental misunderstanding of what economics is. Similarly, only those who have never grasped the fundamentals of the discipline can hold the view that the economy of these places is not a "real" economy. So, let's dispense with these ideas immediately. Synthetic worlds do have economies; they are as authentic as the Earth's economy; and they have this authenticity simply because time is scarce, a feature that no design document can alter.

That having been said, it is fair to ask what kinds of phenomena are usefully subsumed under economics. Following the choice-under-scarcity paradigm, we would want to include all decisions in which users allocate their resources to different ends. This includes such things as labor supply (work), consumption (buying things), and investment (accumulating physical or avatar capital). It absolutely includes exchange between users. At the macro level, economic issues include the structure of institutions that support the economy: market-making, monetary policy, transportation, and banking. These issues are at the core of an economic study of synthetic worlds.

What's the Objective of Economic Design?

On Earth, we guide economic policy choices by reference to theories of ethics. At the risk of grotesquely oversimplifying, we could note that one of the most popular is utilitarianism, which holds that the object of policy is to maximize the collective well-being of the populace, where well-being is in the eye of the be-holder. Another is Kantianism, which holds that there are absolute goods and bads, with the worst thing you could do being to treat another human being like a thing rather than a person. My own leaning is toward a concern for the dignity of the human person, a post-Holocaust concept with roots in both Kantian thought and the medieval religious conception of the common good. I am no ethicist and the specific schools are not important; rather, the idea is that, in the real world, you are supposed to take a school and do economic policy with an eye to the objectives it dictates.

The game development industry takes all of this and throws it out the window. It's probably a good thing. When you are designing a game, the objective is FUN! People should be happier after playing a game than they were before. The fun objective could in principle be traced to a utilitarian concept (maximize the to-tal fun of the people), and a reasonable argument for doing that would be that almost all worlds today are run by profit-seeking enterprises. Maximizing profit could be taken to be equivalent to maximizing fun for lots of people. While this looks like a utilitarian approach to game design, it would be a mistake to assume that game designs emerge from a desire to maximize happiness. Profit motives in themselves do not, in fact, imply that the items produced will maximize happi-ness for the greatest number of people.[3] Moreover, game designers themselves are driven by more than profit. Fun is a legitimate objective all by itself. One gets the feeling, when playing many games, that the thing exists only because the people who made it thought it was a blast to play. Indeed, those are often the best games. But then, not everyone has the developers' tastes. In designing for fun, developers may or may not meet some overarching policy objective. Or perhaps we need to admit Fun as a legitimate guide for policy.

Rather than try to impose an ethics on the industry, let's take the fun objective as given and work within it. If the objective of game economic design is to pro-vide a system that, rather than meet some condition of philosophical ethics, sim-ply enhances the user's fun level, that puts us at an odd moment in this story. I, Castronova, PhD Economist, with over a decade of experience writing, teach-ing, and speaking about questions of Economics and Public Policy, must now answer the following question:

What Makes an Economy Fun?

Never has an alleged expert been less prepared to answer a legitimate and impor-tant question in his area of expertise. I can honestly say that this is the hardest economic policy question I have ever encountered. What makes an economy fun?

If I have little of substance to say about that, I can always blame my colleagues: There is no research on this question in my discipline. We have endless research about whether an economy is efficient, whether it is just, whether it is productive, wealthy, growing, balanced, or constrained, but we have no research on whether it is fun. You see, the dismal science has not considered the possibility that the economy might usefully be considered as an entertainment product, even though on reflection that might be its core purpose. But economics has no concept for *fun*. The closest thing it has is *utility*, which is a numerical index showing the distance between our current state and our ideal state. I suppose if you do something fun, your utility index will rise—you got closer to your ideal state. But an increase in utility does not measure the change in happiness, the joy, the sense of emotional satisfaction, that comes with *fun*. As mentioned in chapter 2, the relationship between economic events (changes in income) and happiness is fairly complex (Easterlin 2001; Castronova 2004). For example, Frey and Stutzer (2001) report that changes in income have less effect on our happiness than changes in our ability to engage in politics. Is there a connection here to *fun*, to the play impulse of Piaget and Huizinga? Perhaps. But economics, at the moment, is not in a position to comment. With happiness being such a problem for us dismalists, how does the economic policy specialist handle *fun*?

Since there are no precedents (of which I am aware) in academic literature, the only approach to this question seems to be a combination of the developed wisdom of the game design community with some personal intuition about what makes game activities enjoyable. Game designers spend almost all of their time thinking about creating fun, and we can see in their successful products actual examples of fun at work. Some sensitivity to economic and political history is also useful here. Humanity becomes obsessed with certain things for certain reasons, and perhaps one of them is because engaging with those things is usually fun. What is it about the stock market and recall elections that attracts so much attention? Perhaps playing stocks and screaming for someone's head are fun games above all else.

What follows is a tentative list of features that can make an economy fun, based on my experience and understanding of both economics and games; there is also some support for them from the field of hedonic psychology—for example, the idea that work can be enjoyable (Kahneman, Diener, and Schwarz 1998). This material also draws on the vast grey literature of game designer interviews and columns on the Internet, much of which is summarized in the relevant chapters of such design guides as Bartle (2003) and Mulligan and Patrovsky (2003), and at Raph Koster's website.[4] The list of fun features here overlaps to a considerable extent with those of the design community, but I've tried to put them in order from most to least important from my own point of view as an economist and a player.

1. CONSUMPTION AND ACQUISITION

The most fun thing about the economy is getting something you've come to desire. When you buy something, the fun comes from several sources. Certainly, you enjoy the uses of the new object; it does things for you that you could not do before. But it is also fun simply to go around and collect information about qualities and prices, and then make a choice about which thing to buy. That is, the very process of making a choice under scarcity is enjoyable. It is a puzzle whose solution is often satisfying in and of itself. A third source of fun is the wearing and using of the item, which can earn all kinds of social notice and respect.

Beyond shopping is the joy of acquisition, the accumulation of an empire of objects. That acquisition is an important source of fun per se is amply demonstrated by a story from the early days of *Ultima Online*, when the world allowed unlimited storage of items for free. Someone decided it would be fun to have shirts, indeed a great many shirts. He somehow acquired and stored over 10,000 of them, for reasons unknown.[5] Just having things is enjoyable.

2. FAIR RETURNS TO WORK AND SKILL

A second fun thing to do in an economy is to go about activities that may or may not be fun in and of themselves, but then get a great reward for them. People seem to enjoy expending their time and effort, even in quite boring tasks, and getting something nice as a result. They also like being rewarded for being good at something. If a job is handed out by some mentor-figure NPC, doing it can make you feel like an important person. If the mentor manages to sweep you up in the emotional content of the quest, doing the work can make you feel like a real hero. Wouldn't we all like to have a boss who convincingly explains that our work is of dire importance? As for work itself, there seems to be much fun in doing things that are in themselves unpleasant and difficult, if the successful completion of those things can be worn as a badge of honor. The reward, in other words, doesn't have to be a useful or fun thing in itself, it need only be an obvious outward sign that the wearer of it has done some difficult work to get it.

In contemporary synthetic worlds, it is not uncommon to find large numbers of people who do a mundane, unchallenging task over and over, for literally hundreds if not thousands of hours, just in order to gain some kind of advancement or reward. In my early days in *EverQuest*, I spent a great deal of time near a ruin that also happened to be the place where a certain NPC would appear extremely rarely and unpredictably. The NPC carried an item, the Glowing Black Stone, that was of some value to wizards. I began to notice that every day, as I was going about my business, I would see one person sitting near the ruin, for hours and hours, doing absolutely nothing. After conversing with the person, I learned that he was a very powerful character who decided he wanted the Glowing Black Stone and had come to wait for it. In game parlance, he was "camping" the item. So he sat there, doing nothing at all, for hours every day. It went on for weeks. Finally the NPC appeared and the player got his Stone and went away. Word apparently went out that the Stone camp was now open, because the very next day, someone else appeared to wait for the next one. Having a Glowing Black Stone was apparently quite a badge of honor—if you had one, it showed that you had survived a horrifically boring experience. People seem to find even the most onerous tasks enjoyable, if they provide some kind of suitable reward. The mere fact that the reward is rare and visible may be enough.

As for returns to skill, people unquestionably enjoy working to develop their own abilities and then have those abilities observably compensated. We can distinguish between the skills of the person and the skills of the avatar. For the person, rewardable skills could include puzzle-solving, figuring out riddles, developing eye-hand coordination, and learning combat tactics. For avatars, the skills could really be anything: Swimming, Carpentry, Animal-Taming, Baking, Axes, Siege Equipment, Hairdressing, Lasers, Jumping, Healing, Sneaking. All of these and many hundreds more exist in synthetic worlds right now. Interestingly, the fun effect of rewards to skill does not seem to depend on where the skill resides. Users seem to enjoy having their avatar's rated skill at Archery go up as much as they enjoy feeling their own prowess at finding, targeting, and engaging prey going up. Indeed, the fact that the Archery skill is an observable rating makes it a more fun skill to raise—how do I know that I personally am a better archer, after all? But if my avatar's Archery skill goes up, the computer will send me an explicit message to that effect: "Your skill in Archery is now 87!"

3. CREATION, OF THINGS AND OF THE SELF

A third aspect of fun in an economy is the joy of creation. Whether the result be a commercial empire or a simple tunic, it is enjoyable to make things. An economy is fun if it allows people to combine basic items into more complex items. If those items can exhibit the worker's craft, so much the better. Personalized, artistic items are the most fun of all. The rags-to-riches phenomenon seems to enchant many people; it is apparently very enjoyable to start with nothing and then make yourself into a powerful, wealthy person. And it is fun to do this according to your whims, to be your own boss.

4. MISSION AND PURPOSE

A fun economy gives people a meaningful role to play. The role should be individualized, because no one likes being a cog in the machine. At the same time, the role should be a critical part of the entire system, so that the worker feels needed and important. Moreover, economies generate even more fun if they are seen in competition with another economy at a macro level; each worker in Castrovia can see his work as a contribution to the greater goal of making Castrovia the wealthiest nation in the world.

5. ROBUST COMPETITION UNDER EQUAL OPPORTUNITY

Fifth, many people find competing with other people to be fun in and of itself, even if the object of the game is arbitrary. At the same time, the competition should be fair. If the game is about accumulating power in a synthetic world, then everyone should start with a similar set of resources. After the start of the game, the rules should not change arbitrarily to favor one person over another. At the same time, a competition is no fun if the opponents are not at least roughly comparable in power.

6. RISKS AND BARGAINS

Everyone loves a little gamble now and then. The economy should have some uncertainty in it, and luck should play a role. That is, independent of skills or choices, a user should have some actions rewarded and others punished just because of the roll of the die. Ideally, the risk system should reward rational odds-making and betting; it should be the case that a smart player will gradually learn when to take chances and when to walk away. Risk, especially downside risk, also raises the level of emotional investment people seem to have. A world without risk is not just boring, it is empty of things to cherish.

7. PROPERTY AND CRIME

Owning things feels good. A fun economy allows you to feel that you own a little piece of the world, that you have some special item or land that is all yours. On the other hand, having things stolen feels bad, while seeing criminals brought to justice feels good again. Committing crime is a fun activity for some people. Evidently, crime is a cat-and-mouse game that clearly fascinates people, judging from passive media genres. A fun economy should have property, theft, and jail too.

8. CHAOS AND HISTORY

Finally, a fun economy should have major events and epochs at the macro level. Pure stability is boring. As evidence, we can point to the fact that the recessions in my memory (1973–1974, 1980–1982, and 1991–1992) were each milder than the last and yet were treated as increasingly more disastrous. It's as if we *want* to feel like something terrible is happening in the economy. It gives us all a sense of history, that the world is changing and we are witnesses to momentous events. While no one would wish a Great Depression on the world again, it did occupy everyone's attention for quite some time. A synthetic economy that went through the usual business cycles but occasionally flared up in a serious way, toppling empires and tossing people around in the income distribution, would certainly keep everyone energized. It would also generate significant social mobility, an integral part of ensuring equality of opportunity, robust competition, and rags-to-riches experiences. I suspect that many experienced developers would cry out that players *hate* having their prized accomplishments dashed because of what seem to be arbitrary cycles in society. Yes, that's what they say, but are we sure that they would prefer a stable world to an unstable one? Perhaps it is more enjoyable to put things together in an environment where one's future is not assured. Yes, if everything collapses, the users will be angry, but will they abandon that world for a place where nothing at all ever happens? The very act of yelling at God may be fun in itself—so long as you're yelling about fantasy disasters rather than Earthly ones.

Considering all these criteria, it is evident that Earth economies have done fairly well along a number of dimensions. Can synthetic economies do better? They have a number of advantages over the Earth economy. In synthetic economies, physical resources can be provided in any quantities at any desired cost, meaning that the price of any good can be set at almost any level. Rudimentary services can also be provided in any amount, at any cost, so long as AI is complex enough to master the duties required. The technology of production can be structured in any way desirable; we are not limited by the fact that a certain quantity of water heated to a certain temperature can only produce so many pounds of steam pressure. In synthetic economies, the only limits on the things, people, and protocols of economic life are provided by the time and skill constraints of the users.

Not everything is easier with synthetic economies, however. If the world's security breaks down, it is possible that users may use hacks and cheats to create goods to which they have no right; this practice is known as "duping." An early example of this happened in the first graphical synthetic world, *Habitat* (LucasArts; see Morningstar and Farmer 1990). The designers had set up bots to buy and sell unlimited numbers of items at fixed prices. One day they unthinkingly set the buy/sell price of an item to be X tokens at one bot but $X + \varepsilon$ tokens at another bot a few minutes away. Several users spent the night shuttling back and forth between the bots, earning ε per item per trip. They generated thousands of tokens of money in the process. In contemporary synthetic worlds, any such price discrepancy could be exploited by hundreds of thousands of people.

A second problem arises because the interface is implemented by a programmable technology; therefore any acts that can be automated in principle are easy to automate in fact. Make one mistake in your economic design, and users will "macro" it: write programs and set up server farms to mine it on a 24/7/365 basis. Moreover, if the actions required to exploit a situation can be automated, programs can be written on the client side to repeat these actions endlessly. Macroing is a serious issue because it allows a user to have an avatar work away endlessly at some menial task while the user goes out for a cheeseburger. In effect, it allows the user to act as though he is able to spend 24 hours a day in the world; if the economy is not designed to deal with that kind of labor supply, it might cause undesirable effects. A related problem involves the use of bot avatars. It is not uncommon for a user to own two or more accounts in a world, one that is his main avatar and the others to do noting but menial, macro-able tasks to support the main avatar's activities.

A third category of problems are bug exploits. Suppose a certain scary monster carries an item that is supposed to be very rare. The monster himself is not rare, he is just very hard to kill. As is common with many monsters in these worlds, if he is killed, he re-spawns at a certain location 30 seconds later. One day, players discover that a bug in the monster's AI causes it to die whenever a nearby warrior character in a purple hat looks at the moon and says "bodacious!" three times. When word of the bug spreads, warrior characters stop whatever else they are doing, put on purple hats, run to the spawn point of the monster, and start chanting "bodacious!" while turned to the moon. Every 30 seconds the monster appears and dies, coughing up the supposedly rare item every time. The first warriors to get the item get rich by selling it; in time, however, the item becomes as common as junk.

The basic point is that one should expect users to manipulate all technology at their disposal to achieve the ends they desire, many of which will have an effect on the economy that is not desired by the designers. Since the designers are trying to provide a community of people with an amenity that the community wants, it is important for the designers to have control over the quality of that amenity. Design of the economy plays a role in that.

In an ideal synthetic economy, for example, every choice would have to be a choice that a human being makes while sitting at the computer. That rules out play systems that involve rote steps, which are fairly common at the moment:

> Click on one unit of Hide. Drag the unit of Hide onto the crafting tool. Click on one unit of Thread. Drag the unit of Thread onto the crafting tool. Click on Tunic Pattern. Drag Tunic Pattern onto the crafting tool. Click "Sew." Retrieve Tunic and Tunic Pattern. Your Sewing skill is now (2)! Click on one unit of Hide. Drag the unit of Hide onto the crafting tool. Click on one unit of Thread. Drag the unit of Thread onto the crafting tool. Click on Tunic Pattern. Drag Tunic Pattern onto the crafting tool. Click "Sew." Retrieve Tunic and Tunic Pattern. Your Sewing skill is now (3)! . . . Click on one unit of Hide. Drag the unit of Hide onto the crafting tool . . . Your Sewing skill is now (382)!

And you're thinking about blowing your brains out. No wonder people write macroing programs! These systems not only are easy to macro, they should be ruled out anyway for gameplay reasons.

In other words, designers already have incentives and strategies for handling bugs and dupes and exploits of various kinds that affect the economy. In what follows, I will set these issues aside and focus instead on some broader principles.

Principles of Synthetic Economy Design

Indeed, despite the fact that things that can go wrong in a very dramatically digital way, the controls that designers have over virtual economies do allow them to build a fun economy, and many of the economies I've experienced, despite being declared "broken" by many fans, have actually been quite fun. And it is too easy to say, "All you have to do to make things better is apply the basics of a college-level economics course." I've taught that course dozens of times, and I can assure you that the material delivered there is already pretty disconnected from the economies of Earth, let alone cyberspace. Many people believe (me included) that economics is fundamentally out of touch with the mindspace of real people. So if you are thinking of starting your own world, don't grab an Econ 101 text, whatever you do. Applying material that is already too abstract for Earth to the specific example of a synthetic economy is a stretch that is not easy to make. Rather, turn to world-building veterans, such as Richard Bartle (2003, pp. 297–316) and Raph Koster, who have graciously written down their own set of practical principles for economic design.

What follows here is often consistent with this accumulated wisdom, but it is not completely consistent. The accumulated design wisdom often has the feel of being a work-around or patchwork solution; my hope in this section is to give broader principles of design that will make patchwork unnecessary.[6] This is done by listing a series of fun-oriented design objectives, derived from the activities outlined above, and then discussing how those objectives might be achieved.

1. Objective: Make sure there is economic activity.
Tools: Specialization and gains from trade; no lucrative self-reliance strategies; consumable goods.

To get any fun to happen at all, you need to have an active economy to begin with. The key to generating economic activity is trade. Trade constitutes a large part of social activity on Earth and should do so in a synthetic world. Trade allows people to have fun buying things. It brings strangers together, to do something other than fight. Its broader effect is to make your world feel alive. Make sure trade involves conversation, chatting, shouting, verbalizations that can be overheard. It's the buzz of the city—more than that, it's why cities have buzz; it's why there are cities.

Creating economic activity is easy: specialize economic roles, and trade will follow. Specializing roles lets people feel unique and needed, which is fun, but it also makes trading worthwhile. The economic theory here is that *specialization and gains from trade* are what make economic activity grow; we owe the idea to Adam Smith, the founder of the discipline. The idea is that trade happens because both parties gain from the trade. Each person has something the other wants, and more trade happens if each person can satisfy her own wants to a very limited degree but can satisfy specific wants of other parties to an extreme degree. If I have 10,000 shirts and nothing else, and if I have a need for a broad variety of things besides shirts, I have to do a lot of trading—I have way more shirts than I need and not enough of lots of other things.

How do you make it so that each avatar has lots of one thing and almost nothing of everything else? You make sure they have lots of needs, first of all, and lots of different kinds of needs. Anyone who gets 10,000 shirts and doesn't trade them needs to start feeling hungry. An avatar needs clothes, food, equipment, housing, transportation, entertainment, and anything else you can come up with. Then design production so that any one avatar can only create a small fraction of this portfolio of needs. An avatar can make thread but not cloth, steel but not armor, pies but not berries.

You cannot allow anyone to be self-reliant without trading. People *can* be self-reliant in the sense that they can, as a single individual, generate enough income for themselves to buy all that they need—that is, without having to cooperate with others (in teams or groups or whatever) to get ahead. But for economic activity, you need to make sure that this self-reliance happens in a certain way—namely, the individual in question must specialize in one activity (beet farmer, rabbit hunter, dressmaker) and then earn enough income from that activity to buy everything else she needs. In other words, economy activity does not require that people form into collectives or teams or firms, although one could structure things that way if one wanted to have people building things together. Rather, economic activity requires that no one person finds it sensible to make everything she needs for herself, without trading with others.

It's also fairly important to ensure that the needs have to be met by consumables rather than durables. *Consumables* disappear when used the first time, *durables* don't. An economy based entirely on durable goods does not need as much production or trade as one based on consumables. Once you buy something, you don't have to buy it again. An economy based on consumable goods, conversely, generates a constant flow of needs that are met by a constant flow of production. A durable good may depreciate, of course, and as it does so more rapidly, it becomes more like a consumable. By all means, there should be no goods that never depreciate; these items would not be durables, they would be "permables," quite rare on Earth but unfortunately ubiquitous in synthetic worlds, whose production destroys all future demand for itself.[7] You don't want to do anything to choke off the demand for goods; make sure everything disappears eventually.

A third aspect to mention is that the structuring of production roles is critical in making players feel needed and having a sense of mission. By giving each player a large palette of needs, but the ability to only supply one of them, you guarantee that each player will be providing a unique and valued service to others. True, some economic roles will be more fun than others; as explained in chapter 6, when that is the case, more players will try to occupy them, driving the net return of that activity (money plus fun) down to the level that other activities receive. Players will have a choice: do a fun economic task (explorer, dancer) in heavy competition and not get paid much for it, or do a fairly unfun economic task (beet farmer; economist) under little competition and get paid much for it. Allowing players to choose specialized economic roles in this way adds to both the diversity of experience and its sense of legitimacy.

2. Objective: Consciously locate and publicize economic activity.
Tools: Strategically placed transportation hubs; resources distributed geographically; open communication for trades.

Nothing is more eerie than a large, unpopulated city. It happens often in the cities constructed in virtual worlds, because the cities have no economic rationale and hence no economic activity. They are large, beautiful, empty spaces.

Meanwhile, somewhere out in the countryside, all the players have accumulated somewhere to conduct their marketing activity. In the first few years of *EverQuest*, the main market was located in a tunnel in the wilderness because that happened to be the main route by which people traveled; a nearby city was evidently built to feel like a capital but was usually empty simply because the tunnel was the most direct route through that area. Getting people to congregate for market purposes requires that transportation practices be respected. The most likely spot for a market is a place where popular routes intersect. It might be wise to code the world so that markets can be built by the players; that way, real market-like places can emerge anywhere that the player community wishes. Ideally, players should always be able to access the market, anywhere and at any time, to observe prices and to place buy and sell orders. Travel and shipping of goods, and service performance, are what would then make a market exist in one or two geographical locations.

The path of transportation routes will depend on the location of resources. If you want large and active markets to happen, you should put geographic distance between the resources needed to make things. Let the berries be numerous in one region and the wheat be abundant in some other. Then anyone wanting to make fruit pies will have to travel, carrying berries to get wheat or wheat to get berries. The most likely outcome is for some central spot to emerge as the efficient point of exchange. If you decide instead that, for convenience, all the things a person needs to make pies should be located close to one another, don't expect many bakers to be involved in the economy; people will gather berries and wheat and make pies themselves. Similarly, if you allow easy transportation to any spot in the world, what is to stop someone from making a short trip to every region that holds the goods she needs? Again, don't expect her to contribute much to your economy; she is doing fine all by herself. Convenience for the individual player hurts trade activity.

To generate buzz and a sense of life, economic activity should be noticeable by third parties. An economy based entirely on private messages is a quiet economy and it makes for a dead world. There should be places in the world where trades can be seen and heard. Or, there should be ongoing worldwide reportage about trades as they happen. The most exciting urban spaces on Earth have grown up around active, open markets. Trading of all kinds of goods is openly reported on an ongoing basis. Trade should be public in synthetic worlds as well.

3. Objective: Generate earnings and investment.
Tools: Resource endowments; production function.
To participate in all this trading activity, the player has to be able to buy things, using money earned from selling something—ideally, one specialized thing. How are those earnings obtained? I'll work with symbols for a moment, then provide

an English translation. For beginners, one thinks of earnings as a linear function of hours of work: $Y = w \times L$, where Y is income, w is the wage, and L is hours of work. But this system of wage payments is only the result of a labor market that manages an underlying production process. Here's how it goes. A production process generates q units of some good according to the function $q = f(K, L)$, where f is the production function, K is the amount of physical capital, and L is the amount of labor input. Let's assume for now that the amount of capital, K, is fixed; we will get to that in a moment. Now, the output q is sold on markets for the price p. Therefore, the revenue produced by this process is $p \times f(K, L)$. The money to be made from adding another worker to the process, known as the *value of the marginal product of labor*, is $p \times \partial f(K, L) / \partial L$, where $\partial f(K, L) / \partial L$ is called the *marginal product of labor*, the additional output that one more unit of labor can produce. The value of the marginal product of labor is, in effect, the demand curve for an hour of your time. A person who knows this production process and owns the capital to run it can hire you as part of L, insert you into the process, and let you produce the additional product that you will produce (the marginal product). He then sells that additional production for p, meaning the formula $p \times \partial f(K, L) / \partial L$ shows how much money the owner can make from having you around. It's therefore his maximum willingness to pay for your services, which means it is his demand curve for your labor. Following the *Law of Demand*, the employer's willingness to hire labor is inversely related to the wage that is demanded: when wages rise, employers hire fewer workers.

Now, you and your fellow laborers have a supply curve too, and where your collective supply curve meets the collective demand curve of all the people managing the process $f(K, L)$, a market equilibrium occurs that sets the value of the wage (w) as well as the total amount of employment. Let's indicate the specific amount of equilibrium employment by L^*. Then we have the wage being determined by the formula

$$\text{The Wage: } w = p \times \partial f(K, L^*) / \partial L.$$

English translation: the wage equals the amount of product that one hour of work can produce, multiplied by the selling price of the product under current market conditions.

In synthetic worlds, the production process is an inherent feature of the world, available to all, and the requisite capital is in the hands of the individual avatars. The economy consists of thousands of one-person firms, each with its own stock of capital and one laborer. It doesn't have to be this way—one could very easily have explicit firms where one person or a group of shareholders hires groups of avatars to do work for them. But it seems that one of the attractions of the synthetic economy is that it can be designed so that everyone can be independent, can be their own boss. There is most likely a strong latent desire to do this. Certainly, Earth's economy is not very strong on that point; there are too many risks to being an entrepreneur, and so most people work for others. Synthetic economies don't need to operate that way and, in practice, such an arrangement has not been a popular design choice. Therefore, let's assume that avatars will remain independent owner-operators of their own little firms.

Let's work with the production function a bit to make it more relevant to this special case. In synthetic worlds, output (q) is going to be some object—pieces of loot from a hunted monster, items that have been crafted, rewards from quests. This good is produced by the player, who expends her own time (L) to get it. Her ability to get the good depends on four other factors: her skills as a player, or *human capital*, H; her avatar's skill levels or experience levels, or *avatar capital*, A; her avatar's gear, or *physical capital*, K; and the number of monsters, crafting inputs, or quests provided by the world, or *resources*, R. So we have

Production: $q = f(L, H, A, K, R)$.

Assuming there is lots of trade activity going on, the objects can be sold at a price p, so that the avatar's earnings are

Earnings: $p \times f(L, H, A, K, R)$.

English: The player has complete control over her own labor input (L), and her own skill level (H) is a combination of her innate abilities plus the amount of time she is willing to spend to learn the game. The developers control how easy it is to increase avatar skill levels (A) and the amount of in-world gear (K), and they set the amount of in-world monsters and quests (R). World-builders have to manipulate A, K, and R to make earnings higher or lower, as desired. Note that if the price of the good being earned (p) can be controlled and stabilized, then an increase in the ease of obtaining some good (i.e., an increase in the rate at which loot drops from monsters) means a real increase in the income of the player. Indeed, a valuable good, with a high price, can also be a common good, owned by everybody; it's just a way for the designer to give all the players higher incomes. If the price cannot be controlled, however, increasing the drop rate or availability of the good will drive down its price. If it is not rare, any supposedly valuable item will, in fact, be cheap.

If we assume that R is fixed, economics tells us that the added earnings one can make by adding a unit of any of the other inputs will decline as the level of that other input rises. This is known as the *Law of Diminishing Marginal Productivity*. It means that if the player works long hours at the game, each additional hour should contribute less and less to earnings; the player gets tired and bored and runs out of quests to do and monsters to kill. Similarly, adding better and better armor to an avatar that works only so many hours, and has only so much skill, may always raise earnings but it will have a smaller and smaller impact as the armor gets better. If I have a level 1 character, he can be made more powerful if given level 2 armor, and he can be made even more powerful if given level 3 armor, but the impact of going from level 2 armor to level 3 armor is not as big as the impact of going from level 1 armor to level 2 armor.

While it might seem possible to code the world so that diminishing returns do not occur, the fact that the world has a limited size will eventually impose some kind of diminishing returns; there are only so many resources (R), and eventually the player's earnings will not rise much when one single input is increased. If the level 1 avatar above goes from level 299 armor to level 300 armor, the impact on her earnings will be minimal. In textbooks, the *eventual* aspect of diminishing marginal productivity is often stressed: at times, adding extra units of input can increase marginal productivity, but *eventually* . . . This feature, while it seems frustrating on the Earth, actually contributes to a fun game. Diminishing marginal productivity can fight against player tendencies to maximize one aspect of their avatar at the expense of all others; with each aspect having diminishing usefulness, no one characteristic makes the avatar "uber," as the saying goes. Rather, the player is forced to find a balance of all aspects to generate the most earnings.

In final translation, then, this production function approach reveals that we allow players to gather earnings as the result of two kinds of activity: the direct application of time to productive activity (L), on the one hand, and the indirect application of time to investment in building her own skills as a player (H), the experience or skill level of the avatar (A), and the quality of the avatar's equipment (K), on the other. Making these activities fun requires that the earnings appear fair, meaning that there should be enough resources available to farm and also a market for the goods that are produced (Objective 2, above). There should also be a reasonable return to investment: raising the capital components H, A, and K should all increase earnings power. At the same time, the rewards should not be too high, otherwise the game world is not very challenging. The exact form of the production function should be a fairly complex and therefore fun puzzle; players should be rewarded for spending time thinking about how to allocate their time and earnings to maximize their earning power. It is not so much fun if the answer is "maximize your Strength attribute and ignore everything else." Recording the inputs as numerical quantities and making them visible to the player, as is commonly done, is a major advantage of synthetic economies over Earth's economy, where you can have a hard time knowing how good you are. In a good economic design, one can have fun taking what one knows about skills and markets and trying to determine the best earnings-yielding build for your character.

4. Objective: Generate the value of things, as well as history and chaos.
Tools: Merchant AI.

What should prices be? Presumably this is a design issue of great importance. It is absolutely critical to the atmosphere of most games that certain objects be very valuable and others less so. When an allegedly important item (Julian's Amazing Wand of Wizardry) is as cheap as trash because the price system has failed to validate it, the immersive lore and atmosphere of the world is degraded. Since valuation and merchant AI is a fairly critical topic, and also one that sits uniquely at the intersection of economics and synthetic world design, we should consider it in some depth.

Merchant AI is frequently used in synthetic worlds. Often its purpose is to create the feeling of economic activity, but the effect is deceptive. Merchant bots cannot generate economic activity, because economic activity is about trade, and trade only exists between human beings, i.e., players. When Sabert digs up a few gems and sells them for gold to an NPC merchant, he has actually contributed nothing to the world's economy. Sabert simply exchanged his gems for gold; it's as if he dug up gold instead of gems. Economic activity only happens when Sabert trades his gems (or gold or whatever) to another player for something else.

What do AI merchants do, then? Typically, they are coded to offer unlimited amounts of some good for sale at a set price P_S, and to buy unlimited amounts of the good at a set price P_B. The prices are expressed in the world's currency (gold pieces, credits, or what have you). The price difference $P_S - P_B$ has to be positive; if merchants paid more for items than their own sales price, a player could make gold with every transaction. Write a macro and you can endlessly pump new money into your account. Let's assume the designers have prevented all such opportunities for macroing. Therefore, with $P_S > P_B$, we have the following:

- P_S is the upper limit on the price of the item in player-to-player markets. No player will buy the good from another player at a price above P_S because he can go to a merchant and buy it there for only P_S.
- P_B is the lower limit on the price of the item in player-to-player markets. No player will sell the good to another player for less than P_B because she can go to a merchant and get at least P_B for it.

This code creates a number of problems, but the principal problem is that it assumes there can be an infinite supply of something and an infinite demand for it, and at different prices no less. This kind of infinite-good assumption only appears in economics when the market in consideration is very small relative to global markets. In such *small, open-economy* theories, one assumes that the local economy is so small that no amount of exporting or importing will have any impact on the global price of a good. Thus, from the standpoint of domestic producers and consumers, it is as if the good can be bought or sold in infinite quantities at the global price. If the local or domestic economy's price would normally be below the global price, the local country exports goods to the global economy. If the local price would normally be above the global price, the local country imports goods from the global economy. As imports or exports compete with domestic supply or demand, respectively, the competition drives the local price either up or down until it is equal to the global price.

The critical point here, however, is that there is one global price in the open-economy theory, not two. In contrast, the typical merchant AI seems to assume that merchants have access to two global markets, one where the price is high and the other where it is low, and the twain never meet to arbitrage away that price difference. Not only is this completely unrealistic, it also reduces the fun that can be had by players, who but for the dominance of merchant NPCs could conceivably play a role as an importer or an exporter. Instead, most "economic" activity in worlds with this kind of merchant AI is not really economic activity. Instead, the players use merchants to turn their item loot into gold pieces at price P_B, and when they get enough gold, they buy what they need at price P_S. Of course, if the two prices are very far apart (as they are in games like *EverQuest*), then there are incentives for players to trade items to one another. If the prices really are that far apart, then it is as if merchants are very stupid; fittingly, they also play no role in shaping the economy. Overall, then, the nearly ubiquitous two-price open-economy system is fraught with problems.

There are three ways of handling it. (1) Get rid of merchant AI. (2) Explicitly model this global market, its prices, and the access of merchant bots (and players) to it. (3) Get rid of the global market assumption and hence limit the willingness of merchant bots to buy and sell goods.

The first method, while it directly eliminates the problem of trying to make economically sensible game AI systems, throws an important baby out with the bathwater. Having a purely player-driven economy is not necessarily the best economy that there is; meeting the objectives of fun requires having an economy with social mobility, chaos, and bargains, but not too many of those nor too few. It has to be the right amount, and that requires management. Management requires tools, and merchant AI is an important tool. Note that there are two ways of removing merchant AI from the economy: you can just not have any buy/sell bots in the world, or you can code them to be incredibly stupid (as mentioned above), willing to pay only 1 gold piece for an item that they then try to sell for 1,000 gold pieces. Such merchants get no business of course; they are effectively out of the economy. Either method does force the economy into the hands of the players, but leaves designers with much less control.

The second method would require that merchant bot sell and buy prices be the same, or at least close to one another. The price difference $P_S - P_B$ is the merchant's profit margin, and in a competitive economy, it should be fairly small. It represents the costs the merchant faces to run the business, including the cost of his own time, his wage. While these should not be zero, they should not be all that big either, certainly not so big as dissuade the players from using the merchants for their buying and selling needs. Ideally the merchant's hourly wage should be similar to the players' wages, derived from their production function.[8]

If merchants make decent wages and offer sensible, competitive prices, under method 2, where then would be the scope for player participation in the economy? Why won't every player use bots to do all of their selling? The answer is that they will, of course, if there are merchants on every street corner who stand willing and able to buy every single thing in the economy. This is also a common practice in existing worlds: place merchants everywhere. It is a matter of player convenience; players want to be able to turn their loot into gold at once, and the player-driven economy is apparently not trusted to perform this function. If merchants are everywhere, and if they offer sensible prices for all goods, then there will be no player economy. Something has to go, and the usual design choice is to eliminate sensible prices rather than limit the availability of merchants.

This is a mistake, because prices are extremely important and should be at the core of the economic design. They are the sole source of information about value in the economy and they ultimately determine a large fraction of the decisions people make. Therefore, if it so happens that bots are too attractive as merchants and are preventing player-to-player trade, then they should be made less attractive through means other than prices; they should not be made stupid, they should be made rare. Merchants can be placed at the corners of the world (which would make sense if we are thinking of them as export/import agents); they can be made curmudgeonly. At the same time, player markets can be made more attractive through means other than the price as well. They can be located and publicized well (Objective 2, again), and storage and buy/sell ordering technologies can be used to overcome the problem that players are not always in the world at the same time. It is important not to use price controls to push trade away from merchants, because this distorts prices and also sacrifices some of the control that merchants might have over them. Rather than ruin merchants to push trade away from them, systems of trade among players should be made so fluid and convenient that trading with other players is much easier than trading with merchants. Allow players to check prices and place buy and sell orders from anywhere.

Implement an explicit shipping system so that goods and orders and gold can easily get to market and back. Then merchant prices can be kept sensible, as a kind of backstop or final arbiter of value at the edges of the known world. If prices in player markets get out of control, some players will surely take caravans to the faraway merchants and thereby arbitrage the price problems away.[9] Indeed, in the economy of worlds like *Final Fantasy XI* and *EVE Online*, there are distinct markets in distinct regions, and players are known to arbitrage price differences among them as a conscious part of their gameplay.

If we assume, then, that merchants are not everywhere but are hidden away at corners of the world, and that rather it is player markets that are ubiquitous, we can proceed on the assumption that the merchant buy and sell prices are roughly equal. These prices then become roughly equivalent to a global price in the small open-economy foreign trade theory mentioned above. It is a useful approach because it now allows the designer to manipulate the economy by changing global prices. They can guarantee that a good is rare in the synthetic world by setting its global price to be high. Perhaps the merchant who makes that price effective is difficult to reach, only appears at certain times, or only deals with players who achieved mastery in some kind of merchant skill class, but his existence still makes the price effective. The players who are in the lucky position of being able to deal with that merchant can sell the goods to him in infinite quantities at high prices. They will therefore be willing to buy the good from other players in large quantities for prices nearly as high; the difference compensates them for the trouble of dealing with the merchant (who is far away, frequently absent, or simply curmudgeonly). The in-world price of the good stays high, as desired, and players fill most of the links in the chain of trade, as desired. The open-economy strategy can be used effectively to make merchant AI into an economy-management tool.

The third strategy above abandons the open-economy approach and replaces it with the notion that merchants cannot buy or sell goods in unlimited quantities. The merchants simply buy and sell goods at some fixed price, up to a limit imposed by how much money and how many items they begin with. This strategy effectively turns merchants into a source of liquidity only, in the sense that the only real thing they contribute to the economy is the service of turning items into gold pieces and vice versa. Unless there are hordes of merchants, their limitations in terms of stocks of goods and money will prevent them from having an effect on overall market prices, whatever prices they are coded to offer. If, for example, a merchant is told to pay a great deal for a certain magic helmet if one is ever offered, but only if his current cash allows it, he will not purchase many of those helmets. Their transactions, even at those high prices, will represent a bargain for the seller, but it will be a one-shot effect, not a general increase in the price of those helmets throughout the synthetic world. Of course, the designers could periodically restock the merchants with items or gold, but this would be the same as the import/export model: new cash and items appear from nowhere, which means, "from abroad." If one truly cuts off the economic system from outside, and thereby imposes realistic limits on the amounts that merchants can buy and sell, then merchant AI will not play much of a role in the shape of the economy. And while this is not necessarily bad—it does guarantee that the economy is entirely in the hands of the players—it does mean that the designers have surrendered much of their control over the value of things.

To compare the three strategies, let's recall that the ideal situation would be for the designers to have some control over prices, through the operation of merchant AI, but not in a way that stifles player economic activity. The second strategy, which treats the merchants as marginal but influential export/import agents, seems most likely of the three to achieve these goals. It allows merchants to have an effect on prices without eliminating the need for player-to-player transactions; the merchants offer sensible prices and the players must take the goods, through a series of trades and transports, from the harvesting areas to the docks. By raising and lowering the global prices at which merchants import or export, goods in the world can therefore be made more or less valuable.

Indeed, the designers can introduce a measured amount of chaos by gradually changing prices up and down over time. This kind of chaos is an important contributor of fun, and can be used to move players from one activity to another as the relative payoff of the activities changes. Global prices can also be used to keep things stable, too; if player activity threatens to makes a good too rare or too abundant, the fixed global price ensures that the rare goods end up being imported and the abundant goods get exported. Moreover, by manipulating merchant geographic placements and attitudes, the designers can change trade routes and the income distribution; some who had a lucrative monopoly on a certain trade may one day find it is not worth so much. These parameters can even be set into some kind of historical cycle, so that macro-scale events can be designed ("the winter of 2377, when food was so hard to find").

The essence of the second strategy is to allow merchants to buy and sell unlimited quantities at one fixed price, but to do so in a way that still allows for a player-to-player market. Perhaps the easiest way to do this would be to explicitly model the export/import process. Ships periodically come in to some port. When a new ship arrives, it is laden with cash and items. Players who are on hand can deal with the ship's merchant and buy and sell items, as well as place buy and sell orders for future shipments. The ship sails away again, laden with new cash and new items. The designers, meanwhile, keep an eye on the outstanding orders and send more or fewer ships as needed.[10] By playing around with the timing of ships, the designers can introduce business-cycle effects; maybe spices become rare for a while because storms off the coast of Zanzibar have delayed ships from that region. Perhaps players well-skilled in Meteorology might have predicted the storms, stocked up on spices, and are now in a position to make a killing. That would be fun.

At the same time, players who do not want to wait around for ships at the far edges of the world can buy and sell their goods at the centrally located, well-publicized and convenient player markets; there, broker players will buy and sell goods and then make trips back and forth to port to await the ships. The system would set the prices of different goods at the levels the developers wish, while maintaining a vibrant economy among the players. It works simply because this codes merchant AI more precisely into the export/import role it must play, and as a result, the synthetic economy assumes the nature of the small open economies we have on Earth: the Earth sets the price, and the small open economy reacts to it.

While strategy 2 (import/export merchants) has distinct advantages, it should be noted that exactly the same kind of global price-controlling effect could be done, and in fact has been done frequently, with strategy 1 (no merchant AI at all) or strategy 3 (limited merchant AI). The trick here has been to control the rate at which goods enter the world. If a certain type of grain is only obtained when a certain scarecrow is defeated as part of a certain quest, one can make that type of grain more or less abundant by changing how much of it appears when the quest is completed. The *drop rate* of the item will inevitably affect the item's price, but only indirectly. Now, it is possible to manage prices by changing how frequently things appear, but it is a very cumbersome affair; to keep prices at the right levels, one would have to pay close attention to what all the players are doing and adjust drop rates downward when players overfarm something and upward when they underfarm it. As an economist, I am reminded here of the debates regarding rules versus discretion in macroeconomic policy. Advocates of rules say that policy should be directed toward establishing a more or less fixed rate of growth in the money supply, corresponding to the long-run rate of economic growth, and letting the economy self-adjust to it. Advocates of discretion say that policy should pay close attention to current affairs and increase the money supply when the economy is slow and decrease it when the economy is fast. I can't do justice to those debates here, but the point is that fixing a global price system in a synthetic world and sticking to it—while expecting the economy to make adjustments on its own—is in the flavor of a rules-based policy. Micromanaging drop rates to try to get prices where we want them to be is more of a discretionary policy. Personally, I favor the rules-based approach; an economy is hard to micromanage well.

*5. Objective: Control the per capita capital stock (especially among weaker
players) and, as a corollary, the value of the currency.*
Tools: Loot code; merchant AI.

One possible objection to the fixed-price scheme just presented is that it would
swiftly be overtaken by inflation, which has been endemic in every synthetic
world ever built. True, the merchant import/export idea might guarantee that the
price of a Steel Rapier was always 5 gold pieces and the price of a Helm of Power
was always 500 gold pieces. But will the amounts "5" and "500" always mean
"moderately expensive" and "very expensive"? As money floods the world, won't
both of these items become incredibly cheap?

The answer is, "Not if the value of money is handled well." To understand why,
consider the fact that in most worlds, goods and money come into the world
through player actions. For example, in many worlds, hunting mobs (mobile
objects, basically, monsters) is one of the main activities. When a mob is killed, it
drops some kind of loot and the players pick it up. It's often a few pieces of currency plus some kind of useless item—rat whiskers, griffon claw, a rusty spear
that no one would use. The useless items, in most worlds, are good for one thing
only: you can take them to merchants, who will pay money for them. Thus,
because of the standard merchant AI, most loot really just reduces to an amount
of cash. The entire system of play involves players going into the world and, in
effect, minting coin for themselves.[11]

At the same time, this hunting activity (and other player activities) also produces valuable items, such as coveted magic spears and glowing helmets and laser
guns. As time goes by, these coveted items begin to accumulate in player invento-
ries. Indeed, in most worlds these items tend to be the "permables" mentioned
above, goods that (unrealistically) never depreciate in value. As the world fills
up with these goods, and with cash, a phenomenon commonly known as
MUDflation occurs: the prices of some goods plummet while the prices of others
skyrockets.

While it must be said that the term MUDflation (which dates from the original text-based multiuser domains) reflects a fairly significant misunderstanding
about what inflation actually is, it does have something to do with it. The phenomenon in question actually is the result of two things: a gradual increase in the
price level, which *is* inflation, and a gradual increase in the amount of physical
capital per player (K in the production function outlined above), especially
among relatively weak players, which is not inflation but a real increase in earning power. Both are interesting problems.

First, the inflation part. As players mint more and more money into the world,
it has a fairly predictable effect of raising the overall price level in the player-

to-player market. With more money chasing the goods that players have to sell, the price level must rise. To see this, let Q be the quantity of goods that players sell to other players, let M be the total amount of money in the economy, let P be the price of the goods, and let V be the *velocity* of money. Velocity is a constant that measures the number of transactions a given piece of money is used for in a fixed period of time; its level is set by the locations of markets, how the banking system works, and so on.

Economists have developed a *quantity theory of money* to explain how the price level is determined in a simple economy like this one. The quantity theory says, basically, that the quantity of money available determines how high prices must be. The conclusion is based on an *equation of exchange* that must hold in any economy:

Equation of Exchange: $MV = PQ$.

That is, the amount of money (M) times its velocity (V) is the total amount of cash that is used to buy things, and this of course has to be equal to the total amount of cash that is received from selling things, which is PQ. With velocity being constant, we can rewrite the equation as

$$P = MV / Q,$$

which means that, for any fixed level of goods to be traded (Q), the price level will be higher as the amount of money available for trading is higher. For example, let's say the velocity in Gondor is 1, so that each gold piece gets used in about one transaction per day. Let's say that in any given day, players in Gondor kill five dragons, and each dragon has one DragonScale Breastplate. Let's further assume that of the five breastplates, three are immediately used by players—they are fine armor—while the remaining two are sold on markets to other players. With only two being sold, we have $Q = 2$. The equation of exchange says that if there are currently 500 gold pieces (gp) in this economy, the price of the breastplates will be 250 gp. If something happens to raise the number of gold pieces to 12,000, the price will be 6,000 gp.

The prices of objects must rise as the amount of money available to pay for them rises. Therefore, any process that raises the amount of money in the system without raising the number of traded goods (Q) will inevitably raise the price level. Specifically, the act of killing monsters and looting cash from them is always an inflationary act; it brings money into the world without increasing the number of goods that players will trade with other players. Similarly, selling a good to a merchant for money is also always an inflationary act: it pulls gold into the economy while pushing an item out of it. If the item was junk anyway, Q is unchanged; if the item was tradable to others players, it's even worse, because Q goes down. If inflationary acts are not balanced by deflationary ones, then the amount of money in the system rises and, with it, the price level. This is one half of the MUDflation phenomenon.

The other half is a per capita increase in K, the physical capital of the avatar. Players who spend time in a synthetic world gradually get better and better gear as they play, and they regularly replace their old gear with new gear. The old gear gets sold to merchants—thus increasing inflation—or it gets sold to players. Indeed, gear sold to players tends to follow a specific flow: as players become more advanced, they acquire better equipment and sell their old equipment to less advanced players, who in turn sell theirs to still less advanced players, and so on. The gear flows down the power stream, while cash flows up it.

Now, in worlds where gear never decays or does so very slowly, the stock of physical capital in the world generally rises as time goes by.[12] As it does so, the real price of gear generally falls: players keep killing monsters and looting new gear, continually increasing supply. As the real price of new loot falls, players with lower and lower earnings are able to buy them. Eventually, weaker players can begin to afford very advanced items. As the cash flows upward and the equipment flows downward, the net result is that the most advanced players are often sitting on very large amounts of cash, while the least advanced players often have very good equipment. And since avatars with wonderful equipment find it easier to obtain loot than those with rudimentary gear, the task of killing and looting monsters (or completing game objectives more generally) is getting easier and easier, especially among the newer players.

The increase in equipment stocks represents a real increase the return to an hour of work in the world; K is going up. The players are becoming more and more wealthy in real terms, but the inflation effects often mask this or distort it. This is because both the amount of money and the amount of equipment capital is rising at the same time. Thus, the overall price level is rising, but in a strange manner: the price of high-end goods is going up rapidly because of all the cash accumulating among powerful players, while the price of low-end goods is actually falling because of the equipment supply that is accumulating among the weak players. For example, a simple sword may see its price fall from 10 gp to 8 gp, but meanwhile, the Vorpal Sword of Uberness has its price rising from 1000 gp to 5000 gp. This combination of inflation masking a real increase in the capital available to the average player is the core characteristic of MUDflation.

Both parts of the phenomenon are a problem. Inflation is perhaps less of an issue, because the things that determine happiness are not prices but real goods. If inflation affects the production or distribution of real goods, however, it does become a problem, and it may do so in this case. If a player has been planning for months to obtain some item and sell it for a certain amount, she will be distressed if inflation has eaten away that value.

A gradual rise in physical capital at the low end, however, is always a serious issue. It means that a new player on the day a world is launched faces a very much more difficult uphill struggle than a new player who comes on board later. The later player can buy lots of nice equipment to start out with that the early player could not get. This violates one of the core fun requirements, which is that there should be equality of opportunity in the world and a rags-to-riches story line in the economy. Certainly, no developer would want to consciously build a game in which the challenge level was out of control and gradually declined over time; if anything, one would think that designers would like to gradually increase the challenge level as the player population becomes more familiar with the game's various secrets. Nor do we want the economy to provide people with nothing but a riches-to-riches narrative; that's basically what most middle-class people have on Earth. A final problem is that this phenomenon eventually encourages players to do nothing but gather loot, by whatever route is easiest. There is no point to hunting down the dragon that carries the Vorpal Sword of Uberness, because there are already so many copies of it floating around that it's much easier to just get money and buy one.

There are a few rules that can reduce MUDflation for developers who wish to do so. First, you could control the money supply, and a critical element of that is that players should not, in general, be able to mint money as they please. The practice of rewarding players with gold for their accomplishments is an ancient one in the gaming world, but it makes it quite difficult to manage the monetary system. Psychologically, yes, players do need to get some reward for doing things, and a gold piece or two might seem the easiest way to do it. The problem is that gold pieces are not just shiny things, they are the unit of currency. Coding the world so that monsters produce gold when killed is a recipe for inflation. Money should only come into the world at specific times and in specific amounts that the developers desire. Indeed, the amount of money needed depends only on how many transactions are going on. Developers should design and track specific inflation indices and take money out of the world when the price level rises. It will surely rise in a world where gold is a common reward and there are not many transactions between players. Indeed, in many worlds players are very self-sufficient; they generally use equipment that they obtained directly, by crafting it or taking items from beings they have hunted. None of the goods are traded to other players. In such a world, there should be no money at all. Only so much money should be in the world as is required to support the current level of trade. And loot should consist only of items players will either use themselves or trade. No junk. Certainly, merchants should not be willing to pay positive sums for items that players do not want. Remember the *I* in merchant AI: Only stupid merchants would buy junk.

Second, every inflationary transaction has to be countered by a deflationary transaction. If merchants frequently buy things from players, they must also frequently sell things to players. Designing a world in which the main role of merchants is just to buy junk from players, and not sell them much of anything at all, is to make the merchant system a money pump. Only by selling things to players can merchants lure money back out of an economy. If merchants are coded to be a generator of cash in a world, they have to be given ways to suck it back out again. And if some cash is to be given to new players, it should be only so much as is needed to restore the cash lost when old players close their accounts.

Third, to prevent the accumulation of equipment at the low end, the prices of low-end gear must be stabilized. One way would be to have items decay fairly rapidly; in a world where everything is a consumption good rather than a durable good, there are no stocks to accumulate. Another way would be to have an active export market that always keeps the price of rare items elevated. That way, when Sabert replaces his Vambraces of Toughness with the still-better Vambraces of Invincibility, he can sell the Toughness ones to foreigners, effectively shipping them out of the economy. Otherwise he may just give or sell them to a low-level friend.

In general, the goals of stabilizing prices as a whole, as well as the challenge level of the game, can be achieved with the same import/export AI strategy deployed above to set the value of specific things. One could keep the price system fixed at the global level, so that the simple sword will always cost about 5 gp on the street and the Helm of Power will cost about 500 gp. The point here is that fixing prices globally also prevents inflation. If for some reason excess money gets pumped into the economy, it will raise the local price level; the prices of all local goods will rise. However, players will start to buy less often on the local market, preferring the global market instead, while the same reasoning will cause them to sell more often locally. Both forces drive the local prices down to the global levels. When players buy more things on the global market, and sell fewer things, they effectively ship money out of the local economy, thus restoring the money supply. Basically, in the equation of exchange, we fix P by using the global markets. With P (and V) fixed, $MV = PQ$ means that any rise or fall in M will be self-corrected through flows from the global markets, Q. It also means that if Q changes, M will change automatically to restore the balance. If there is an excess amount of traded goods, some will be sold abroad, thus raising M; if there are fewer traded goods, some will be purchased from abroad, lowering M. These flows ensure that the price of goods between players will always be near the global price. And that, in turn, ensures that the real value of goods and their relative accessibility to players will not change over time except by design.

6. Objective: Introduce social mobility.
Tools: Earnings; merchant AI; risk; progressive taxation.

Of course, the preceding does not do anything about the fact that a player who spends a great deal of time in the world will gradually gain more and more equipment, money, and power. That's a good thing, too. One of the fun things about an economy is that it rewards work, and lets a person feel pride in his accomplishments. The danger in a synthetic economy is that, unlike the Earth economy, there may not be enough room at the top. On Earth, there are so many people, so many places, and so many things, that no one ever seems to feel that they have gotten rich enough. In synthetic economies, by contrast, the entire population can come to feel that it has bought every item and visited every place in the world. Once the rags-to-riches narrative has reached its happy end in riches, what else is there to do?

It is not clear that this is a problem. Well, from the standpoint of profits it is a problem, because one never wants players to feel they have done everything they can do, and leave. But from the standpoint of individual well-being, perhaps that is exactly what should happen. It is probably not a good thing for a person to spend an entire lifetime in one synthetic world, nor is it good to keep people on endless treadmills, where they never hear the words "Thank you! You are finished. Good job. Go home."[13] All good things must come to an end. But if we conclude that we want players not to get bored at certain points, then it could be a problem if the economy has some kind of cap on it. The problem occurs, however, only because in most synthetic economies at this writing, achievements are forever secure once made. Once the rich become rich, they remain *the rich*, forever. On Earth, there is much more income mobility than that, and so perhaps some mobility should be implemented in synthetic economies as well.

Introducing mobility is complicated by the practice, mentioned several times already, that synthetic economies tend to be based on durable stocks of goods rather than ongoing flows of consumption. If the entire economy is all about the production and acquisition of items that never decay, once I have many items, I am rich forever. Making me un-rich, putting my wealth at some risk, has to involve some kind of theft or loss mechanism; someone or something has to destroy the goods I own. And that is not very fun. However, in an economy based on continual flows of new goods that disappear when consumed, a person can be rich only so long as she maintains a constant flow of income to support the flow of consumption. That person's riches can be put at risk by anonymous economic forces that reduce the flow of income to a trickle, and this seems to be fairly fun for a number of people. Many are the watchers who keep an eye on changes in the economy to make sure that they are invested in the right income flows; it is a hobby that seems to obsess large numbers of people. It's much more fun than watching for thieves and tornadoes; it involves strategic thinking and a subtle understanding of the way markets work. If you are good or lucky at it, you may go from being a moderately rich person to being a most rich person for a time. If you have a streak of bad luck, down you go. Economic achievement, even at the top end, would be about actively maintaining a portfolio under chaotic conditions; the game is not over when you have furnished your avatar with every top item there is, you must continue to pay attention. This idea could actually be filed under a simple heading: increase the importance of income at the expense of wealth. This will generally make the economy more mobile, and more fun.

Merchant AI and the price system are the critical tools for achieving some of the required chaos in income streams. Each player should be able to receive income from different sources, and fluctuations in prices should affect those sources. The economy of *Star Wars Galaxies* already achieves this kind of variability; resources are spread out on a map and they can run dry. In addition to letting resources run out, why not add weather effects? Those who have worked hard to build up their contacts in the spice trade are hurt when storms strike Zanzibar; when the storms subside and the spices flow in again, they reap excess returns. Why not have merchant players undertake long and difficult caravan or sea journeys to strange foreign lands? If they can get back safely, they make a great deal of money; if they don't, they can lose their entire empire. That kind of risk-taking is definitely fun.

Even with considerable economic fluctuation, there is still the possibility that some players will become so rich they do not know what to do with themselves or their money. Sitting on stocks of millions of gold pieces, with nothing to spend them on, the player may be tempted to liquidate their entire wealth by selling it all at online auction sites (see chapter 6). There are different ways of answering this problem. First, even the most powerful player needs to have a use for his money. Proper management of the money supply should prevent a gradual accumulation of cash in the world. By properly specializing economic roles, and by ensuring that most goods are nondurable, even the most powerful player will have to buy and sell things on a continuing basis to maintain his position. Adding risks of economic downturn to the world also gives every player an incentive to hang on to some reserves of cash and equipment.

Still, if all else fails and players begin to acquire more power over the world than the designers intend, there is a simple solution: progressive taxation, taxes

that land more heavily on the rich than the poor. Many games have AI government systems, with factional politics and cities and so on. In principle, all of these
entities provide services to the players. They make safe zones, staffed with powerful guards, so that players in trouble can find sanctuary. They provide banking,
storage, and transportation systems as well. A general rule in economics is that
nothing is really free. A corollary states that the person who enjoys the use of a
good or service should also be the person who pays the full cost of its provision.
When goods are provided for free, the economy suffers; the good is too-heavily
demanded, in the sense that our individual decisions don't take into account the
fact that the good is costly to produce. Yet in most synthetic worlds, these banking, storage, and transportation services are provided for free, or for only a nominal fee. There are predictably strange results, as in the case of the man who
hoarded 10,000 shirts in *Ultima Online*. Or, people teleport themselves willy-nilly
across hundreds of miles. Why not charge for these things? And, why not charge
more to people who have more? The job of protecting a precious gem is surely
more costly than the job of protecting an old axe; a player who places a gem in a
storage space should pay correspondingly more. No service provided by AI to the
players should go uncompensated; it's *AI* after all.

7. Objective: Recover from breakdowns.
Tools: Merchant export/import AI; progressive taxation.

What if something goes wrong? What if players discover a way to mint a million gold pieces a day and do so for weeks before being found out? Well, first of
all, it would make those people rich. They would go spending their riches in
player markets and in AI-based import markets (if they exist). It's all right; people get rich unfairly on Earth and it seems to contribute to the fun, especially if
there's income mobility. One day they will lose it all again. And none of this needs
to affect the price system or the price level, because those could be fixed and
maintained globally. If, however, the price system is not being maintained in this
way, the breakdown would not only make someone rich, it would certainly flood
the economy with gold and new equipment. In that case, it would represent a real
increase in the average wealth of players. In effect, it would be like Spain discovering the Americas: overnight, a new source of wealth. Sure, there was inflation
and less incentive to develop the kind of society that could exploit the industrial
revolution when it came around. But for a few hundred years, it was a fun party
for the Spanish upper class. What's not to love?

The problem, of course, is that this is an unfun outcome for everyone else. If
the price system is not being maintained, the result is a permanent increase
in MUDflation with these particular players becoming relatively much more

wealthy. If, conversely, the price system *is* being maintained, these players still become more wealthy, even if there are no MUDflation effects.

What is the answer to a rapid increase in wealth that is generally considered to be unfair by almost everyone? Well, perhaps it would be wise, as a general rule, to put very high tax rates on acquisitions of wealth and income that far exceed the norm in the world. If this kind of a tax is in place, it would prevent anyone from rapidly increasing their wealth or income, by any means or process. It would not matter if it is a bug in the code, or some ingenious strategy that the coders did not realize might be possible. It would not matter if the new wealth came from some outside source (eBay). The point is, it would be an accumulation of wealth that is happening more rapidly than the designers (keeping in mind the entire player community) want wealth to be accumulated. The designers are trying to provide players with a world whose challenges are to be overcome at a certain rate. If anyone discovers a way to overcome the world at a ridiculously rapid rate, whether through exploits, or bugs, or dupes, or macros, or buying things with US dollars, that practice becomes a serious problem for the world's design. No puzzle is fun without a challenge. The exploiting practice has to be corrected. Designers can therefore justify the progressive tax as their stop-gap mechanism, with the justification that you'll get the 98 percent tax rate if and only if you make over 500 gajillion gold pieces in an hour; "Think of it as our way of saying, 'However you did it, and we don't really care, we define it as not being fair play.'"

A heavy progressive tax makes sure than anyone who finds the easy answer to the puzzle has no reason to implement it. You can always do a crossword puzzle quickly if you wait a day and look at the answers first. A heavily progressive tax takes away anything you might earn from doing that. And in that case, why not just work the puzzle the way its designer intended? This kind of tax not only removes the consequences of an exploit, it also removes the incentive to find exploits in the first place.

From Economics to Politics

Many of the ideas just reviewed would be very controversial if implemented within an existing synthetic world. Not many of them have even been tested, and the person proposing them has never designed or handled an actual synthetic economy. Whether or not a user base would accept them and find the results fun is partly a political question, in the end. Consider it: the whole idea of a progressive tax is a political one, bound to be popular with some players and very unpopular with others, since it implicitly invokes a judgment about fairness. Yet this is just another element of the warping of reality that synthetic worlds cause: they place designers in the unenviable position of being God (in charge of Nature), and State (in charge of Justice), and Jester (in charge of Fun), all at once. Each of those hats is tough to wear; wearing all three well is quite a hat trick. Implementing an economy well requires juggling objectives in all three areas, and in the end, designers must make controversial decisions. They will therefore often find themselves attempting to justify their actions according to all three roles. To justify actions, however, the powers that be really should focus on producing legitimacy. Legitimacy comes from decision-making systems that those affected are willing to accept. It is a matter not of fun per se, but of politics, and as the next chapter will show, systems of legitimate decision-making also have been affected by the warping of reality around the synthetic membrane.

9

GOVERNANCE

After business and economics, another realm in which outlines are blurred in noticeable ways by synthetic worlds is politics. Chapter 6 gave an initial example of strange politics at work, in its discussion of fairness issues and how they drive powerful if informal political movements outside the synthetic world. There, the point was to illustrate how the movement of interests back and forth across the membrane tended to validate community interests involving virtual occupations. In this chapter I consider a different dimension of politics, the issue of governance.

As with economic activity, the existence of political activity in and around synthetic worlds is not something we should be surprised about. Where there are people, there is an economy and also a polity. However, while to my knowledge no one has written about economic issues as they appear in cyberspace, many have written about political issues. There is already a growing literature on the problems of maintaining social order in cyberspace (Rheingold 1994; Smith and Kollock 1999; Mueller 2002; see especially Reid 1999 and Smith 1999), as well as increasingly sophisticated thinking about the nature of sovereignty and law in cyberspace (Lessig 1999; Ludlow 2001). Even though the issues of community management are well-known, world-builders (actually, their marketing departments) sometimes proclaim that their world is unique in that it allows "player politics." In truth, of course all worlds allow player politics whether in the synthetic world or somewhere else. Any collection of people will have conflicting common and individual interests, and some politics or other will have to be generated so as to regulate those conflicts. One could argue that the code of a synthetic world is effectively its law, but we will see that there is more to the state than just code in these places.[1] However, the unusual forum in which politics occurs here seems to have a dramatic effect on how things work. In particular, there are issues of ownership and governance that wrinkle the affairs of state significantly. This chapter will describe some of those wrinkles.

Good Governance

Synthetic worlds are a fascinating phenomenon from the standpoint of political theory. Here you have collections of ordinary people thrown into a fantasy environment with varying degrees of communal institutional depth (i.e., group structures, clan structures, voting systems, etc.) including, in some worlds, no depth at all. What kinds of governance do these people generate?[2]

This question is of relevance to issues that are as old as political theory itself. In the modern era, most political theory would predict that if you were to set loose a crowd of people into an untamed synthetic wilderness, some sort of limited government would arise. Going back to Hobbes's *Leviathan* (1651), most conceptions of proper governance have held that we have governments because we want them. If we had none, we would not like the way life would be: nasty, brutish, and short. We therefore have a collective interest in supporting a sovereign, who has the power to coerce individuals to promote the common good. The legitimacy of the sovereign derives from the services it provides to the community. Of course, the mere fact that the government *may* be legitimate, because it is necessary to manage common interests, does not mean that all governments with power in fact are legitimate. There is really no guarantee that a given government will necessarily serve the common good at all. For that, the government must be structured in a certain way; its powers must be restricted and, to the extent possible, harnessed to the interests of the population. Restricting powers, of course, makes a government less able to serve any end at all, including the end of promoting the common good. Therefore a balance must be struck between the ability of the government to act and the requirement that those actions be seen as legitimate services in the eyes of all citizens. The US Constitution reflects intense debates at the time of its founding about the nature of power restrictions and the will of the people. Contemporary democratic thinkers recognize that systems of checks and balances and popular elections can be singularly inefficient, but almost everyone agrees that these kinds of systems offer the best possible sovereigns (Dahl 1991). Many other schemes have been tried, with unquestionably disastrous results.

Taking as given the discovery that good government is government of significant but limited power, political scientists now devote much attention to systems of incentives for gaining and holding power. As mentioned in chapter 4, they have developed the concept of *institution* as the "rules of the game" governing all collective human action. The premise here tends to be that any individual will exploit any power to her own ends, to the maximum feasible extent, unless constrained in some way by a countervailing incentive. For example, all elected politicians will seek re-election; to do so, they must make themselves popular to the voters; to do that, they must provide services to them. Thus each voter's voice in Leviathan's ear should, as a general rule and over the long haul, be at least mildly related to that voter's interests. And that seems to be the best we can do. At the very least, systems of democratic governance are peaceable and largely unintrusive. Perhaps because of these features alone, the democratic method has now become the dominant mode of authority on Earth.

Thus, on the whole, the lessons of political theory and practice on Earth would suggest that the people of cyberspace, like people everywhere, would desire some kind of limited, effective, democratic governance for the proto-states they are building. Synthetic worlds are indeed a fascinating test bed for ideas about how to govern, just as they are for ideas about business management. Hobbes posited a "state of nature," a world with no government, as the initial condition from which the game of government supposedly arose. Synthetic worlds don't really seem to have any explicit government, so we might think of them as a state of nature. Leviathan should have appeared by now, but perhaps he has been replaced already by a system of democratic constraint, as the theory predicts.

Strange Governance

How strange, then, that one does not find much democracy at all in synthetic worlds. Not a trace, in fact. Not a hint of a shadow of a trace. It's not there. The typical governance model in synthetic worlds consists of isolated moments of oppressive tyranny embedded in widespread anarchy. Basically, the state of nature is never allowed to occur. There is a tyrant in place from the beginning, but an extraordinarily inactive one.

Swarthmore historian Timothy Burke, an expert on political economy issues in contemporary MMORPGs, explains why (Burke 2004). Burke considers the idea of sovereignty in these places and imagines it might be located in any one of three places: in the developers, in user organizations, or in an artifact of gameplay— that is, a player-parliament. Burke concludes that sovereignty is presently not found in any of these places in the vast majority of current worlds. The closest candidate would be the developers, but the relationship between this ostensible sovereign and the state it supposedly rules is, as he writes, "where the virtual state in MMOG gameworlds gets both seriously interesting and seriously weird." For reasons involving business competition and the like, the developer-state does not make any effort to legitimize its rule through, say, effective lines of communication or transparent decision-making processes. The net result is a rather mysterious kind of authority, a God whose interest in the people is hard to understand.

In other words, the tyrant here is the coding authority, which reserves for itself dictatorial power over everything in the world. Its basis for government comes from the End User Licensing Agreement (EULA) and Code (or Rules) of Conduct (CoC) documents to which every user agrees when entering the world. To let the reader have a flavor of the content of these agreements, exhibits 1 and 2 at the end of this chapter reproduce a typical set of terms, these having been taken from the popular game *Star Wars Galaxies*. The terms reproduced were those in force on July 4, 2003. They are the law of the synthetic world. Indeed, their tone broadcasts "LAW" and their length testifies to the complexity of managing the common interests of hundreds of thousands of players. I also include the documents in their entirety to emphasize the fact that no user enters the world fully cognizant of what the EULA and CoC require. No one reads them. They click "yes" and go on their way.

What is interesting about these documents is that while they do solicit the consent of governed—you don't have to agree, after all—they offer no due process of enforcement or amendment. This is *Diktat*: Take it or leave it. Of course, once a user has spent thousands of hours in a world building up valuable assets and friendships, the "leave it" option becomes quite unattractive. Persons in that position, at that point, are being governed by a de facto dictatorship. Even freedom of speech is in doubt—note the clause against "sending excessive unsolicited tells [messages] to a CS Representative." Send too many letters to your representative in government, and you may wind up being deported.

On the other hand, this is an odd despotism, and one that might be quite benevolent. After all, this despot is in intense competition with other despots for your entertainment dollar. Being a nasty despot rather than a benevolent one will cause the citizens to move away eventually. Thus, because they pay a subscription fee voluntarily, the people do have some power, perhaps more power than an individual vote gives them. For the tyrant, losing citizens means losing revenue. Perhaps, then, this is the best possible form of government: a highly efficient despotic regime that, thanks to competition with other despotic regimes, does its best to provide legitimate services for the people.

On still another hand, one looks long and hard to see any governance in synthetic worlds at all. In my experience, and I believe this to be a general truth, actual governing moments happen rarely. I have never even seen one; I've never seen a customer service representative actually do anything. I've had perhaps two conversations with a customer service representative, and both ended with, "I'm sorry, there's nothing that can be done about that." I have heard tales of customer service representatives doing things, but not in my own personal experience. Thus, from my perspective as a long-time player, not despotism but anarchy seems to be the de facto form of government in synthetic worlds. No one is in charge. If there is order, it is spontaneously generated by the player community. If the community of players does not spontaneously generate and enforce a norm for or against some behavior, it goes unregulated. And in my experience, quite a lot of bad behavior is unregulated, far more than on Earth. Indeed, it often seems that anything that people can get away with, they do.

Two classic examples of political breakdown are the cases of player versus player combat, and of role-playing shards. Player vs. player combat, known as PvP, is something of a holy grail to world designers: they would like to have it happen, but they haven't been able to implement rules that allow it to happen in the way they desire. The concept of PvP is pretty natural. The players have weapons and damage-dealing spells designed to help them kill monsters, but there is no logical reason why these things could not be turned against fellow players. It would seem that allowing violence among the players would produce fun gameplay and also add to the social cohesion of the world. If someone swears and you don't like it, you can just kill them.[3] *Ultima Online* allowed PvP early on, but the effect was not less swearing, it was more death. Lots more. Onlookers, including some of the developers, were shocked to discover that there are people who think it is fun to do nothing but kill other players over and over and over. Rather than just play the game and use PvP option sparingly, players and entire guilds devoted themselves to the study of how to track down and kill innocents, just for kicks. World populations plummeted. *UO* experimented with reputation point systems (to define outlaws) and the like, but in the end, the designers felt forced to implement controls on the PvP system.[4] Controlled PvP has now become the norm in the industry. Controls include designating certain shards as completely non-PvP, and also designating certain areas within the world as PvP-disabled. The lesson here is that players, given the opportunity to use weapons and spells against one another, used those abilities to complete destroy what nascent social order the world had. Given the opportunity to get away with murder, players took it.

Similarly, players also joyfully take any and all opportunities to damage expressed community norms whenever possible, as the case of role-playing shards shows. The concept of a role-playing shard is that the community of players agrees to remain in character as much as possible. New players entering such a shard are given an additional Code of Conduct statement to digitally sign, agreeing that, if this is a medieval world, they will name their character "Arthur" rather than "WestSideSurferDude" and they will only discuss the affairs of the Round Table, not those of NBA players. My experience on several role-playing shards is that after a few weeks in which these rules are followed by most players, eventually they are universally ignored. This happens not because of apathy, but rather thanks to the explicit and expressed policy of certain players to violate them. The Firiona Vie shard in *EverQuest* was designated role-play only, but from its first day there were several very powerful groups of players who had the openly stated intent of *not* role-playing. Apparently many people will gleefully take any opportunity to do outrageous damage to the desires of a community to preserve a certain atmosphere.

What explains these breakdowns? The nature of synthetic world governance—anarchy spiced with occasional profit-oriented tyranny—does not necessarily predict that these failures would have occurred. Why did the tyrant not permanently execute (ban) the killers of *Ultima Online*? And why did the tyrant not enforce the stated role-playing contract on Firiona Vie? The answer is just that this system of governance is not very effective at all. It cannot really get much of anything done.

The Political Institutions of Synthetic Worlds

To see why governance in synthetic worlds is weak, it is important to know something about the institutions that are in force there. The formal governing institution inside the world is the coding authority, and its officers are the customer service representatives. As mentioned, the Customer Service State is not all that "present"; one rarely encounters customer service representatives. They seem to intervene only in cases of severe conflict between users.

The other set of formal institutions is the system of player associations, clubs, and guilds. These are formal enough to have attracted the interests of sociologists (Jakobsson and Taylor 2003). Their format is often part of the world's code, enabled through a system of user commands (makeguild <name>, invite <player>, makeofficer <player>, and so on). One player forms the guild and is the leader; other players are officers at various tiers; still others are foot soldiers or mere recruits. Rank in the guild confers rights to certain user interface commands, such as sending guild-wide messages, inviting new players to the guild, or accessing guild resources (buildings, bank vaults, etc.). All of these powers are conferred and structured as part of the reigning Code of the world.

Are guilds powerful? Much depends on the nature of the world in which they exist. In some worlds, it is very hard for any player to do things without being a member of a guild. In others, being "guilded," as the saying goes, is not very important. Obviously guild leaders have much more effective control over what guild members do in worlds where guild status matters. Such guilds can do much to regulate the common interests of the members and can provide sovereign-like services to them. In worlds where guild membership is mostly about friendship, however, the guilds themselves are not very effective political organizations.

Guild governance may or may not be legitimate, of course; it is up to the guild's leaders to determine how players are promoted and how leadership offices are filled. Elections are not a general rule. Rather, a politburo style seems to be more common: the guild is run by a small, close-knit group of friends, and if leadership changes, it is passed from one friend to another. And of course, leadership changes when guilds split or merge, which they do somewhat frequently. Still, among those who become deeply immersed in the world, the lattice of guilds and guild memberships is a stable feature of the political environment, not unlike the great families of medieval societies. A number of elite guilds migrate from game to game, maintaining cohesion in the real world as well. Leadership is generally autocratic, but leadership changes while the family itself persists.

Effective or not, legitimate or not, in truth the control area of a guild in any contemporary game is usually only a small part of the overall political landscape. In most worlds, there are many guilds, and no one guild serves as an authority over all events in the entire world. At best, guilds may come together and form covenants or councils, but even these do not seem to command worldwide authority. In many worlds, guilds have the option of making war on one another, but it's an option that does not seem to be taken very often.

The final source of political action in the world is actually AI. Nonplayer characters (NPCs), if they exist, are usually allocated among various *factions* of the designers' creation. Thus, Lashun Novashine, high priest of the Temple of Life, is "on Temple of Life faction," as the saying goes. So are Roesager Thusten and Brother Estle. If I happen to kill Brother Estle, I lose my faction standing with the Temple, which means that, where once Roesager, Lashun, and other NPC members of the Temple used to welcome me with open arms, they will now try to kill me on sight. A player's standing with the various factions in the game world is a numerical rating that can fall or rise as the player does things. Having "high faction" with an NPC group can grant access to special services, favors, and quest assignments. Having "bad faction" turns the player-NPC relationship into a player-mob relationship: each one hunts the other.

Perhaps it is surprising, but I view faction AI as the most effective political power that there is in synthetic worlds, because NPCs do effectively enforce law in some areas. Most cities, for example, are populated by NPCs of the same faction, and they are often programmed to attack anyone who attacks a player who is in good standing with them. As a result, a player being attacked by a monster can run to a city where he is beloved, and the guards will protect him. This maintains the city as a safe zone for those who ally themselves with the city's NPCs. Those who anger the city's NPCs are, of course, unwelcome there. The guards will protect an allied player against these other players. They, unlike guilds and the coding authority, can actually make some territory safe for players who befriend them. Thus in effect they control ground. According to that standard, which you'll recall goes back to Hobbes, NPCs are really the only political authority in a synthetic world, the only group that rewards loyalty with safety.

Outside cities, however, NPCs are scarce and the players are generally on their own. There being no governing agents and no law enforcement, it truly is anarchy. Of course, those who are very immersed in the world and spend much time in close relationships in and between powerful guilds are governed by the informal reputation systems that emerge in any close-knit community. They are safe no matter where they are in the world, because they are associated with a powerful headman or chieftess. But for the vast majority of players, who do not immerse themselves quite as fully, the worlds are politically barren. Customer service representatives are rarely seen; guild officers have little authority outside the cultish inner sanctum of their own society; and friendly NPC soldiers are nowhere to be found.

Given this system of institutions, it is easy to see why open PvP combat results in unpunished massacres. There is really no power to punish the murderers. Certainly, the coding authority does not makes itself present enough to accomplish this. Indeed, the argument has been made that, since players on PvP shards supposedly have the power to enforce law on themselves, *fewer* customer service representatives need to be dispatched to PvP worlds. The assumption seems to be that allowing players to be violent with one another is more likely to induce something like an emergent player-enforced government and law. Unfortunately, practical experience reveals that this train of logic has a kink in it somewhere. The history of PvP game worlds exhibits a clear pattern: as players are granted more violent power over one another, political conditions worsen. As a result, life in most PvP worlds, in my personal experience, is

Nasty: People are not nice. They visit cruelties on you with glee.

Brutish: You must either be part of a gang of thugs, or you must cower and hide.

Short: You will die. Often.

These are exactly the conditions that Hobbes used to describe life in the absence of government. There is no better evidence that, in truth, anarchy reigns in synthetic worlds. Left to its own ends, the community of players turns on itself. True, if a player spends a long time in a PvP world and eventually becomes popular among the most power-hungry players, the need for cowering will abate. Still, this is only the law of the jungle.

Similarly, the general absence of authority in synthetic worlds has predictable effects on the prospects for enforcing the norms of role-playing. Customer service representatives are too rare to keep people from ruining the atmosphere. Player guilds might have some effect on norms, except that usually the guilds are themselves the biggest and most open violators of the norms. It is not possible for NPCs to make judgments about whether some player is suitably "in-character" or not.

In sum, none of the worlds, to my knowledge, has ever evolved institutions of good government. Anarchy reigns in all worlds, and just because there is no player combat allowed in non-PvP worlds does not mean that everything is peaceful there. Even if I do not have the ability to shoot a fireball at another player's head, I still have the power to harass her and make her life miserable. And this sort of thing happens all the time.[5] While in principle governments could exist in synthetic worlds, in practice they do not. Why not?

Why Anarchy?

In order to understand why governments do things, or do not do things, we have to examine the incentives of the people who might perform governmental roles. This perspective explains everything odd about synthetic worlds. The problem is that no one has the incentive to govern there.

The titular government is the coding authority and its officers are the customer service representatives. Customer service representatives are rare because they are expensive. Mulligan and Patrovsky (2003, p. 239) report that a typical persistent world will receive some 500 emails daily; each one represents a citizen request that will require time to resolve. Governing is a human service industry and human time is costly. Getting good human services on demand is a pricey proposition; that's why doctors and lawyers are expensive, and also why professors get decent pay even though they spend more time thinking than working. Everyone seems surprised at the taxes we all have to pay, but the fact is, you can't automate good government. It has to be done by people, and having it done well is both important and expensive.

This fact is perhaps the main drawback to the Customer Service State. A for-profit government will provide just enough service to maintain its population. It does not have to target the service level to make people as happy as possible with the government, as a competitive election system would force it to do. No, it only needs to make sure that people don't switch countries. And this makes the switching cost—the cost of abandoning everything you have in this world and starting up in another (see chapter 5)—a significant political statistic. If switching costs are high, the amount of government service necessary to keep the citizenry sedentary is low. Facing this logic, one world (which will remain nameless) contracted many of its customer service duties to a low-wage English-speaking nation; the workers were given a list of words and told to read through logs of player conversations and, if they saw any word from that list on a player's log, to close the player's account. This policy became generally known to the players only when two were banned after talking about a rape that occurred in their real-life home town; "rape" was apparently a banned word. Their accounts were banned and their appeals ignored. For-profit worlds will seek the cheapest governance that still maintains population levels. The Customer Service State will generally be a minimalist state.

NPC faction AI cannot fill the need for good government because governing requires nuance and judgment, something AI is not very good at. Like sweatshop customer service representatives, AI could also scan player conversations and close the accounts of anyone using the word "rape," but that is obviously not the answer. And no one has the incentive to code NPCs into effective agents of government. The database implications of encoding every NPC with only a binary opinion of each player ("kill/don't kill") are enormous.

This leaves the players themselves. Whether players are given the power to physically attack one another or not, they never seem to advance their political institutions beyond loosely knit collectives of player guilds. Even when guilds become powerful, their use of power rarely feels legitimate in the sense of being in the service of the community as a whole. Rather, they tend to act like a family of mighty people whose projection of their own power happens, coincidentally, to keep the peace on occasion.

What's missing?

Suppose a community of players, angered by the capricious actions of a powerful guild, or those of corrupt customer service representatives, or simply upset at the state of anarchy, decides to form an actual legitimate government. They design a series of offices and declare a set of rules for election to those offices, with voting rights being granted to all players. Suppose some leader emerges from that process and is not, by that event, empowered to dismantle the process itself to become Leader for Life. Rather, the leader is now required to serve the public interest in some way in order to maintain office. What can the leader do?

Nothing, really. Suppose the problem has been a capricious, powerful guild. The democratic leader can send the guild leader a cease-and-desist order, but that's about it. In a PvP world, the leader could ask players to form an army voluntarily and attack the guild; but if it were easy to get people to volunteer for that kind of campaign, it would have happened without needing to elect a leader. The leader could send a message to the customer service representatives asking them to send a message to the guild leader, or perhaps ban the entire guild from the world. To refer to any of these measures as an effective projection of power is laughable. If the problem person were himself a customer service representative, of course, there would be even less likelihood of change (unless the customer service representative was already considered corrupt in the eyes of the coding authority itself, in which case he would have been removed anyway). If the problem was general anarchy, what could the leader do to get the players to be nicer to one another? Asking politely is the only enforcement mechanism at hand.

Thus, while the policies of an elected leader may be thoroughly legitimate, merely being the representative of the community does not grant access to any tools that can provide effective governance. In contemporary synthetic worlds, these tools do not exist. The leader cannot tax. The leader cannot sue. The leader cannot commandeer or seize. The leader cannot levy a police force or an army. The leader cannot arrest, try, or imprison. The leader cannot deport. The leader cannot attack.

As a general rule, no players are allowed to do any actions that governments do. The customer service representatives are the only ones who can do such things, and, as mentioned, they usually do not do them. In PvP worlds, there are some options for players to attack one another, but recall that "death" in these worlds is really just a harassment. "Killing" someone does not remove them forever from the scene, it only transports them a few miles away and slightly lessens their power. They will be back. Thus even in PvP worlds, governance cannot happen. In synthetic worlds, no single player, even an elected one, is able to command the resources necessary to impose a policy on another player.

Choosing Authority

While politics is always happening whenever a community exists, it is not necessary that governmental authority emerge. Many in the games industry have wrestled with the problem of inducing a responsible player-run government, indeed often in the hope that this would reduce the costs of running a world. If players could regulate their own community, the need for those expensive, overworked customer service representatives would diminish. It seemed at least conceivable that allowing PvP combat would be sufficient impetus to the emergence of social order. The de facto emergence of worse chaos in PvP worlds represents a major setback to this line of thinking.

Establishing government requires more than giving players greater powers to harass one another. First, it requires the establishment of institutions of collective decision-making. The Enlightenment and the revolutions of the eighteenth and nineteenth centuries happened for a reason. A point was being made. The point was that only collective decision-making institutions are legitimate. (That same history also showed that illegitimate governmental institutions don't last; world-builders ought to take this lesson to heart.) Synthetic worlds will only grow player governments when governing institutions are allowed. If you don't have a general-suffrage parliament, you will never have a player government.

Second, government requires that the governor has power. The leader of parliament must be able to tax, arrest, and deport. Yes, these are awesome powers, but that's only a problem if the route to leadership is somehow illegitimate. If the parliament is a legitimate institution, then the leader chosen by the parliament is a legitimate leader, and therefore he not only can wield awesome powers, he should. He *must*. The common good demands it.

Implementing player government is, in fact, a design decision. One cannot retain all significant power in the hands of the coding authority and then simply declare, "Players! Make your own government!" unless one wants nothing more than a rubber-stamp body. To date, most world-builders have shied away from allowing players to form governments with real teeth. It surrenders too much control to the community of players. Some experiments with participatory democracy were tried early on (Curtis 1997; Dibbell 1999), but it has not become common practice. One exception is the fascinating *A Tale in the Desert* (eGenesis), which has instituted a player referendum system. It also has created the office of Demi-Pharaoh; this head of state has the power to permanently ban up to seven players—that is, he or she will actually be able to govern.[6] A second successful example is Nexon's *Dark Ages*, a world that is completely unlike the era it is named after, mostly because it has a sophisticated government system with division of powers and mechanisms for handling the rapid rollover of player populations. Good governance is feasible.

It is clear that designers are aware of the political pressures that form in the worlds they create, but they are generally not comfortable handing over power. Raph Koster is one of the most influential world-builders and is also the author

of a Declaration of the Rights of Avatars, a document with a number of interesting ideas about the political relationship between users and world-builders, not
all of which have actually been implemented in any world to date.[7] Dibbell (1999)
reports on the various phases of user democracy in LambdaMOO. The coding
authority in that case became fatigued at dealing with user issues all the time and
tried to draw a line between technical and political issues, turning the ostensibly
political issues over to the users. Over time it emerged that even this system failed
to keep everyone happy; the coding authority then retook command and declared
autocracy. If there is a line beyond which players can have control, it is not easy
to draw.

Is there a middle ground? Imagine a world that has fairly clear and easily
defended territorial boundaries, in which players have the ability to form governments with real powers. By design, different governments rule the different territories. Some governments are better than others; indeed, some territories are
anarchic. This is a good thing; many players find anarchy to be great fun. Even
players who enjoy order probably appreciate it most when they are able to escape
into it from anarchy. Having diversity in political structures is probably fun for
everyone. It also prevents problems in the governing system from hurting the
coding authority's bottom line. While one government may be abysmally bad, not
all of them will be. If a bad government gives citizens the urge to migrate, they
would only have to leave the territory, not the world. They would still be happy,
paying customers.

Another option that has not been attempted (to my knowledge) is to integrate
the NPC faction system with a player faction system. In other words, use AI citizens to supplement human citizens in their political structures. Suppose anyone
at any level needs to be on good terms with the Temple of Life faction to obtain
certain items and services—basic transportation, for example. And suppose that
your Temple of Life faction could be ruined not only by killing NPC members of
the temple, but also by killing players who have high Temple faction. While it
would be possible to recover faction by doing good deeds for the Temple priests,
killing many temple-aligned players would make a player's faction impossibly
negative, and that player would no longer be able to travel. Further, making a policy of killing players at random would result in gradual erosion of faction standing with every faction in the game; eventually, every player and every NPC would
be an enemy, and the player would never be able to go anywhere in the world
without be attacked on sight by everything that walks. The entire world, in effect,
would turn its back on the marauder, as it should. To further refine the system,
one could implement a player-run reputation system that allows players to affect
one another's faction standing in the same way that user-moderators affect the

standing of posts to discussion boards. Unlike a reputation system, board-moderator schemes seem to be impervious to teams of dedicated exploiters.

As with economics, designers must determine the proper role of AI in structuring the politics of the worlds they are building. Certainly, long-run competition among worlds will probably provide innovations in the political systems, and users will eventually be offered a portfolio of governmental choices. Some worlds will be anarchic and they will attract chaos-loving users. Others will impose order and law, and they will attract the law-abiding. Some worlds will allow players a great deal of input into the way the world works, while others will remain autocratic. The free movement of peoples across synthetic borders will undoubtedly ensure that most people get the politics they deserve. And whatever one may say about the surrealistic quality of such an outcome, it certainly has advantages over the sovereignty systems we have on Earth, where most people are basically stuck forever (or for a very long time) with the government of the region of their birth. One wonders what a free and open migration system would do to the quality of government on Earth. But on reflection, we only have to wait; in a few generations, that question will be answered in the pattern of governing institutions in synthetic worlds.

Exhibit 1   Star Wars Galaxies End User Licensing Agreement

TERMS OF USE FOR STAR WARS GALAXIES™: AN EMPIRE DIVIDED™

1. Accounts are available only to adults or, in their discretion, their minor child. If you are a minor, your parent or guardian must complete the registration process, in which case he or she takes full responsibility for all obligations under this Agreement. By clicking the "I Accept" button, you represent that you are an adult and are accepting this Agreement either on behalf of yourself or your child. You may not transfer or share your Account with anyone, except that if you are a parent or guardian, you may permit one child to use the Account instead of you (in which case you may not use that Account). You are liable for all activities conducted through the Account, and parents or guardians are liable for the activities of their child. Corporations and other entities are not eligible to procure Accounts.

2. To play the Game, you must: (i) purchase the Software (as defined below in Paragraph 7) for Star Wars Galaxies: An Empire Divided; (ii) have a fully paid Account; (iii) have a valid credit card (or, if we wish to make it available, a paid game card); and (iv) have an Internet connection (which we do not provide or pay for) to access your Account. In addition to any fees described herein, you are responsible for paying all applicable taxes (including those we are not required to collect) and for all hardware, software, service and other costs you incur to access your Account. Neither this Agreement nor your Account entitles you to any subsequent releases of the Game and/or the Software, any expansion packs nor similar ancillary products. You understand that we may update or otherwise enhance the Game and/or the Software at any time and in doing so incur no obligation to furnish such updates to you pursuant to this Agreement. You understand that online games evolve over time and, accordingly, system requirements to play the Game may change over time.

3. We may amend this Agreement at any time in our sole discretion. Amendments shall be communicated to you at the time you log into your Account. Such amendments shall be effective whenever we make the notification available for your review.

4. In the Account registration process, you will be required to choose a login name and a password. While you are encouraged to use a pseudonym, especially if you are a minor, you may not choose a login name that violates anyone's trademarks, publicity rights or other proprietary rights. You may not disclose your password to any third party. We never ask you for your password by email, and you should not disclose it via email if someone asks you to do so. There may be an additional charge to reissue lost passwords. Although we may offer a feature that allows you to "save" or "remember" your password on your hard drive, please note that third parties may be able to access your computer and thus your Account.

5. We describe our fees for playing the Game and billing procedures related to the Account on the web at a hotlink located at starwarsgalaxies.station.sony.com ("the

Game Site"). The fees for the Game and billing procedures set forth on the Game Site are incorporated herein by reference and are subject to change at any time. All fees are stated in U.S. dollars unless otherwise specified. All fees are prepaid and non-refundable. Upon your acceptance of these terms, we have the right to automatically charge your credit card the Account fee plus any applicable taxes we are required to collect, and you authorize us to do so.

6. We may terminate this Agreement and/or suspend your Account immediately and without notice: (i) if you violate any provision of this Agreement; (ii) if you infringe any third party intellectual property rights; (iii) if we are unable to verify or authenticate any information you provide to us; (iv) if you violate any of the player rules of conduct located at the Game Site or The Station (as defined below in Paragraph 9) rules of conduct located at www.station.sony.com/en/termsofservice.jsp (either of which we may amend or supplement from time to time, in our discretion), or (v) if you engage in gameplay, chat or any player activity whatsoever which we, in our discretion, determine is inappropriate and/or in violation of the spirit of the Game. If we terminate this Agreement or suspend your Account under these circumstances, you will lose access to your Account for the duration of the suspension and/or the balance of any prepaid period without any refund. We may also terminate this Agreement if we decide, in our sole discretion, to discontinue offering the Game, in which case we may provide you with a prorated refund of any prepaid amounts.

7. You acknowledge that you are bound by the terms and conditions of the Software License and Limited Warranty that accompanies the Game. You acknowledge and agree that you have not and will not acquire or obtain any intellectual property or other rights, including any right of exploitation, of any kind in or to the software, artwork, music, and other components included in the accompanying CD-ROM (the "Software") or the Game, including, without limitation, in any character(s), item(s), coin(s) or other material or property. You may not use any third party software to modify the Software or to change gameplay. You may not create, facilitate, host, link to or provide any other means through which the Game may be played by others, such as through server emulators; additionally, you may not engage in matchmaking for multiplayer play over unauthorized networks. You may not decrypt or modify any data transmitted between client and server; you may not use or distribute macros or other programs which would allow unattended gameplay. You may not take any action which imposes an unreasonable or disproportionately large load (as determined by us) on our infrastructure. You may not buy, sell or auction (or host or facilitate the ability to allow others to buy, sell or auction) any Account or any Game characters, items, credits or copyrighted material or any other intellectual property owned or controlled by us or our licensors.

8. As part of your Account, you can upload content to our servers in various forms, such as in the selections you make for the Game, in-game posts and chat, and in chat rooms and similar user-to-user areas (collectively, your "Content"). If we, or our licen-

sors, can reasonably construe that your Content contains any material that infringes any of our respective or collective intellectual property interests (hereafter, such Content shall be referred to as "Derivative Content"), you hereby acknowledge and agree that any such Derivative Content is owned by our licensors or us. For any of your Content that is not a Derivative Content, you hereby exclusively grant and irrevocably assign to our licensors and us all rights of any kind or nature throughout the universe to such Content (including all ancillary and subsidiary rights thereto which include, without limitation, merchandising and interactive media rights) in any languages and media now known or not currently known. To the extent that any of the rights assigned herein cannot presently be assigned under applicable law, you hereby exclusively grant to our licensors and us a universal, perpetual, irrevocable, royalty-free, sublicenseable (through multiple tiers) right to exercise all rights of any kind or nature associated with your Content, and all ancillary and subsidiary rights thereto, in any languages and media now known or not currently known. You hereby appoint our licensors and us as your attorney-in-fact, which appointment is coupled with an interest and is irrevocable, to act on your behalf (either jointly or separately) and to execute, deliver, record and file such documents necessary to document, perfect, protect and enforce the rights granted to both our licensors and us under this Agreement. Your Content shall not: (i) infringe any third party intellectual property, other proprietary or publicity/privacy rights; (ii) violate any law or regulation; (iii) be defamatory, obscene, child pornographic or harmful to minors; or (iv) contain any viruses, trojan horses, worms, time bombs, cancelbots or other computer programming routines that are intended to damage, detrimentally interfere with, decrypt, intercept or expropriate any system, data or personal information. We may take any action with respect to your Content if we believe it may create liability for our licensors or us or may cause us to lose (in whole or in part) the services of our ISPs or other suppliers.

9. We cannot ensure that your private communications and other personally identifiable information will not be disclosed to third parties. For example, we may be forced to disclose information to the government or third parties under certain circumstances, or third parties may unlawfully intercept or access transmissions or private communications. Additionally, we can (and you authorize us to) disclose any information about you to private entities, law enforcement or other government officials as we, in our sole discretion, believe necessary or appropriate to investigate or resolve possible problems or inquiries. You acknowledge and agree that we may transfer such information (including, without limitation your personally identifiable information or personal data) to the United States or other countries or may share such information with our licensees and agents in connection with the Game. Furthermore, if you request any technical support, you consent to our remote accessing and review of the computer you load the Software onto for purposes of support and debugging. You agree that we may communicate with you via email and any similar technology for any purpose relating to the Game, the Software and any services or software which may in the future be provided by us or on

our behalf. You may choose to visit www.station.sony.com ("The Station"), SOE's web-site, if The Station offers services such as a Game themed chat room or other services of interest to you. You are subject to the terms and conditions, privacy customs and poli-cies of SOE while on The Station. Since we do not control other websites and/or privacy policies of third parties, different rules may apply to their use or disclosure of the per-sonal information you disclose to others. Solely for the purpose of patching and updat-ing the Game and/or the Software, you hereby grant us permission to: (i) upload Game file information from your computer; and (ii) download Game files to you. You ac-knowledge that any and all character data is stored and is resident on our servers, and any and all communications that you make within the Game (including, but not limited to, messages solely directed at another player or group of players) traverse through our servers, may or may not be monitored by us or our agents, you have no expectation of privacy in any such communications and expressly consent to such monitoring of com-munications you send and receive.

10. SOE EXPRESSLY DISCLAIMS ALL WARRANTIES OR CONDITIONS OF ANY KIND, EXPRESS, IMPLIED OR STATUTORY, INCLUDING WITHOUT LIMITA-TION THE IMPLIED WARRANTIES OF TITLE, NONINFRINGEMENT, MER-CHANTABILITY AND FITNESS FOR A PARTICULAR PURPOSE. Some states do not allow the disclaimer of implied warranties, so the foregoing disclaimer may not apply to you. This warranty gives you specific legal rights and you may also have other legal rights which vary from state to state.

11. WE DO NOT ENSURE CONTINUOUS, ERROR-FREE, SECURE OR VIRUS-FREE OPERATION OF THE SOFTWARE, THE GAME, YOUR ACCOUNT OR CON-TINUED OPERATION OR AVAILABILITY OF ANY GIVEN SERVER. FURTHER, WE CANNOT AND DO NOT PROMISE OR ENSURE THAT YOU WILL BE ABLE TO ACCESS YOUR ACCOUNT WHENEVER YOU WANT, AND THERE MAY BE EXTENDED PERIODS OF TIME WHEN YOU CANNOT ACCESS YOUR ACCOUNT. YOU ASSUME THE ENTIRE RISK AS TO THE RESULTS AND PER-FORMANCE OF THE SOFTWARE AND THE GAME IN CONNECTION WITH YOUR HARDWARE, AND YOU ASSUME THE ENTIRE COST OF ALL SERVICING, REPAIR AND/OR CORRECTION OF YOUR HARDWARE. WE ARE NOT LIABLE FOR ANY DELAY OR FAILURE TO PERFORM RESULTING FROM ANY CAUSES BEYOND OUR REASONABLE CONTROL.

12. IN NO EVENT SHALL SOE, ITS LICENSORS, THEIR PARENTS OR AFFILI-ATES, OFFICERS, DIRECTORS, EMPLOYEES AND AGENTS BE LIABLE TO YOU OR TO ANY THIRD PARTY FOR ANY LOST PROFITS OR SPECIAL, INDIRECT, INCIDENTAL OR CONSEQUENTIAL DAMAGES (HOWEVER ARISING, INCLUD-ING NEGLIGENCE) ARISING OUT OF OR IN CONNECTION WITH YOUR ACCOUNT, THE SOFTWARE, THE GAME OR THIS AGREEMENT INCLUDING, WITHOUT LIMITATION, DAMAGE TO PROPERTY AND—TO THE EXTENT PERMITTED BY APPLICABLE LAW—DAMAGES FOR PERSONAL INJURY, EVEN

IF SOE, ITS LICENSORS OR THEIR PARENTS OR AFFILIATES, OFFICERS, DIREC-
TORS, EMPLOYEES AND AGENTS HAVE BEEN ADVISED OF THE POSSIBILITY
OF SUCH DAMAGES OR LOSS. THE LIABILITY OF SOE, ITS LICENSORS OR ANY
OF THEIR PARENT OR AFFILIATED COMPANIES TO YOU OR ANY THIRD PAR-
TIES IS LIMITED TO $100. YOU AGREE TO WAIVE ANY RIGHT TO EQUITABLE
RELIEF INCLUDING, WITHOUT LIMITATION, INJUNCTIVE RELIEF AGAINST
SOE, ITS LICENSORS, THEIR PARENTS OR AFFILIATES, OFFICERS, DIRECTORS,
EMPLOYEES AND AGENTS TO ENFORCE THE TERMS HEREOF; HOWEVER,
THE FOREGOING SHALL NOT PRECLUDE SOE AND/OR ITS LICENSORS FROM
SEEKING ANY INJUNCTIVE RELIEF. SOME STATES DO NOT ALLOW THE FORE-
GOING LIMITATIONS OF LIABILITY, SO THEY MAY NOT APPLY TO YOU.

13. You shall comply with all applicable laws regarding your use of the Software, your
access to your Account and your playing of the Game. Without limiting the foregoing,
you may not download, use or otherwise export or re-export the Software except in full
compliance with all applicable laws and regulations.

14. This Agreement is governed in all respects by the laws of the State of California as
such laws are applied to agreements entered into and to be performed entirely within
California between California residents. The UN Convention on Contracts for the
International Sale of Goods is expressly disclaimed.

15. If you have any questions regarding your Account or play of the Game, please contact SOE customer service at swgsupport@soe.sony.com.

Source: http://starwarsgalaxies.station.sony.com/content.jsp?page=Policies%20 EULA, retrieved
July 4, 2003. Some language not relevant to the discussion here ("boilerplate") has been removed.

Exhibit 2   Star Wars Galaxies Community Standards

Community Standards

Play Nice Policies—Activity within Star Wars Galaxies™: An Empire Divided™

THE FOLLOWING ARE THE BASIC RULES OF CONDUCT THAT GOVERN PLAYER INTERACTION AND ACTIVITY WITHIN Star Wars Galaxies: An Empire Divided AND IN THE OFFICIAL STAR WARS GALAXIES FORUMS. FAILURE TO ACT RESPONSIBLY AND COMPLY WITH THESE RULES WITHIN STAR WARS GALAXIES AND THE OFFICIAL STAR WARS GALAXIES FORUMS MAY RESULT IN THE TERMINATION OF YOUR ACCOUNT WITHOUT ANY REFUND OF ANY KIND.

Rules of Conduct

1. You may not harass or threaten other players.

2. You may not use any sexually explicit, harmful, threatening, abusive, defamatory, obscene, hateful, racially or ethnically offensive language.

3. You may not impersonate any Sony Online Entertainment, Sony Computer Entertainment of America, LucasArts, or Lucasfilm Entertainment Company employee, past or present, including any Customer Support personnel.

4. You may not violate any local, state, national or international law or regulation.

5. You may not modify any part of the Star Wars Galaxies client, servers, or any part of the Star Wars Galaxies website located at www.starwarsgalaxies.com.

6. You may not arrange for the exchange or transfer of any pirated or illegal software while on Star Wars Galaxies or on the official Star Wars Galaxies website.

7. You will follow the instructions of authorized personnel while in Star Wars Galaxies or the official Star Wars Galaxies forums.

8. You may not organize or be a member of any player association or groups within Star Wars Galaxies that is based on or espouses any racist, sexist, anti-religious, anti-ethnic, anti-gay or other hatemongering philosophy.

9. You may not give false information or intentionally hide any information when registering for your Star Wars Galaxies account.

10. You will not upload or transmit, in Star Wars Galaxies or on the Star Wars Galaxies website, any copyrighted content that you do not own all rights to, unless you have the express written permission of the author or copyright holder.

11. You will not attempt to interfere with, hack into or decipher any transmissions to or from the servers running Star Wars Galaxies.

12. You will not exploit any bug in Star Wars Galaxies, and you will not communicate the existence of any such exploitable bug either directly or through public posting, to any other Sony Station member. You will promptly report such bugs via the /bug command in-game or by emailing SWGSupport@soe.sony.com. Exploitable bugs include, but are not limited to bugs that grant the user unnatural or unintended benefits in-game.

13. You will not attempt to play Star Wars Galaxies on any server that is not controlled or authorized by Sony Online Entertainment, Sony Computer Entertainment of America, or its designees.

14. You will not create, use or provide any server emulator or other site where Star Wars Galaxies may be played, and you will not post or distribute any utilities, emulators or other software tools related to Star Wars Galaxies without the express written permission of Sony Online Entertainment or Sony Computer Entertainment America.

In addition to the general guidelines listed in the aforementioned article, players are also subject to these supplementary rules while playing Star Wars Galaxies. While by no means an all-inclusive list of the do's and don'ts in Star Wars Galaxies, it provides a suitable foundation by which the player can determine what activities are appropriate:

1. Again, foul language is not permitted, in any language. Excessive use of foul language in an inappropriate context, including swear words, real-world racial slurs, and other language that is not consistent with the fantasy environment and designed to hurt, will be considered a disruption. The existence of any chat/text filtering function is not a license to be profane.

2. To expound upon the general guidelines, you may not harass other players. Harassment is defined as specifically targeting another player or group of players to harm or inconvenience them. Harassment can take many forms, as it goes to the state-of-mind of the person or Squad on the receiving end of the action. However, in order to account for those who are more sensitive than others, the CSR involved will make a determination as to whether or not the reported issue would be considered harassment and act accordingly.

3. You may not disrupt the normal playability of a game world area. Area Disruption is defined as any activity designed to harm or inconvenience a number of groups rather than a specific player or group of players. This includes things such as
Deliberately blocking a doorway or narrow area so other players cannot get past.
Making excessive and inappropriate use of spatial communications.

4. You may not defraud other players. Fraud in all transactions between players will result in disciplinary action when confirmed by a CSR. Fraud is defined as falsely representing one's intentions to make a gain at another's expense. Examples of this activity include but are not limited to offering to drag the corpse of another player to safety but instead hiding it deeper in an area unknown or dangerous, as well as using flaws in a secure trade window to deprive someone of one or more of their items.

5. You may not operate a Player Association (Guild) that habitually violates these rules. Disciplinary issues involving Player Associations will also be addressed on a broader basis. Player Associations whose members habitually violate any of the Rules of Conduct or Play Nice Policies may be disbanded. In addition, monopolizing numerous spawn areas with the intent to exclude other players will not be permitted. If inves-

tigated and verified by a CSR, monopolizing will result in the disbanding of the Player Association.

6. You may not intentionally circumvent the player-versus-player combat features and cause another player to die, such as by "training" them. Training is defined as pulling/leading a hostile NPC or creature along behind you and attempting to get it to attack another player who does not desire that engagement. The intentional training of NPCs or Creatures will result in immediate disciplinary action when witnessed by a CSR. We are aware that accidents often happen causing unintentional trains, and will scrutinize each report of this activity closely.

7. You may not abuse other players, customer service representatives, or the game system. Though some of these actions are covered in part by other rules, they deserve their own note here. The following things would be considered an "abuse" in game:

- Hate Mongering—participation in or propagation of Hate literature, behavior, or propaganda related to real-world characteristics.
- Sexual Abuse or Harassment—untoward and unwelcome advances of a graphic and sexual nature. This includes virtual rape, overt sexual overtures, and stalking of a sexual nature.
- Attempting to Defraud a CS Representative—Petitioning with untrue information with the intention of receiving benefits as a result. This includes reporting bug deaths, item loss, or fraudulently accusing other players of wrongdoing.
- Impersonating a Customer Service Representative—falsely representing yourself to another player as a SOE CSR or other SOE/Lucas employee.
- CS Personnel Abuse—sending excessive unsolicited tells to a CS Representative, excessively using say or other channels to communicate to a CS Representative, making physical threats, or using abusive language against a CS Representative.
- Using Threats of Retribution by CSR Friends—attempting to convince another player that they have no recourse in a disagreement because favoritism is shown to one of the parties by the SOE or Lucas Arts staff.

8. "Roleplaying" does not grant license to violate these rules. Though Star Wars Galaxies is a roleplaying game set in the Star Wars universe, the claim of "roleplay" will not be accepted in defense of any of the anti-social behaviors mentioned above. As an example, you are in no case (PvP or otherwise) allowed to "train" a guard onto an enemy in protection of your homeland. In another example, a bounty hunter is not allowed to steal someone's corpse under the guise of roleplaying a villain. By all means we want to encourage you to play your role, we just cannot allow that role-play to be done at another's out-of-game expense.

Source: http://starwarsgalaxies.station.sony.com/content.jsp?page=Policies%20Community%20Standards, retrieved July 4, 2003.

10

TOPOGRAPHIES OF TERROR

So far, the chapters in part 2 have focused on core questions of political economy—business, markets, governments, law—as these are affected by the unique features of synthetic worlds. One area that has been overlooked so far, and yet that is closely related to the issues of governance that dominated the last chapter, involves violence. In well-governed communities, violence is generally not sanctioned, and it ought to be rare between well-governed communities as well. Unsanctioned violence within a community is crime; violence between communities is warfare. Terrorism occupies a gray area between the two. It turns out that synthetic worlds, because of the way they warp reality and enable real-time communications, provide some rather frightening opportunities for people of bad intent. They also make it more difficult for security forces to respond. This chapter will focus on the use or misuse of synthetic world technology for violent conflicts outside the membrane. The next chapter will focus on violent conflicts that may fall inside the membrane.

Just Another First-Person Shooter Game

A corridor is lit by a single light bulb hanging from a wire. The few doors here are closed and the people in the corridor, two African American men and a Jew, stand here aimlessly, as if they are waiting for something. Indeed, whatever they are waiting for seems to be approaching: around the corner, somewhere in the farthest depths of the building, guns are being fired, and their outbursts are audible here. Over time, the reports get louder. The occupants of this corridor now begin to hear the cries of wounded and dying people; the moment of doom nears them. Yet they do not run, and suddenly all is silent. The sound of footsteps can be heard, coming closer and closer. After an eternity, their nemesis steps around the corner: a man dressed head-to-toe in a white sheet with a pointed cap. The trio leaps to the attack, attempting to kill the KKK marauder before he kills them. But they have only their hands—claws really—while the masked monster is armed with an incredibly powerful shotgun. In three blasts he mows them down; their blood and organs splatter on the walls. The Klansman moves on, for in the next corridor more Kikes and Niggers await their deaths. This night, diversity did not triumph. No, this night belonged to ethnic cleansing.

To be more precise, this night belonged to *Ethnic Cleansing*, a video game released in January 2003 by the US-based hate group "National Alliance." As you might have guessed, the user does not play the hapless blacks and Jews in the corridor, but rather the KKK man who blows them away. The computer is left to animate the people of color, whose role becomes that of the demons and skeletons in games like *Doom* and *Quake*—to present the user with a threat that can be extinguished through the application of deadly force.

The appearance of games like *Ethnic Cleansing* leads to many thoughts, but we don't have space for most of them. There is one feature that has to be discussed in some detail here, however: National Alliance did not build this game from the ground up. That would have been too hard; building entire games requires a large staff of well-trained professionals—graphic artists, programmers, level designers. As technology improves, the technical demands on game builders will rise. Unless, that is, someone recognizes that there is a potentially very lucrative intermediate market here. Actually some people have indeed already seen this market and have begun to capitalize on it, and that is why we now have games like *Ethnic Cleansing* in our culturesphere.

The intermediary I'm referring to here is the "middleware" market, where the sellers are people who make game engines and the buyers are people who make games. It turns out that a goodly chunk of the technology described in chapter 3 can be wrapped up in a fairly simple package. At this writing, there are a number of middleware products for building 3D games; *Ethnic Cleansing* was built using Genesis 3D, which is actually open-source and available free of charge to anyone who wants it. Other middleware products, for sale or open-source, include a number of 3D world-building packages (from *Quake* [Id], *Unreal* [Atari], and *Half-Life* [Sierra]), multiplayer adventure-building systems (the Aurora Toolkit from *Neverwinter Nights*, BioWare), systems for handling massively multiuser worlds (BigWorld, Butterfly.net, Terazona), and plug-ins for rich AI effects (AI.implant, SimBionic). As engine-builders have come to realize profits from the act of selling their code or even releasing it for free, the number of middleware offerings has begun to expand dramatically.

The growth of middleware makes sense. The number of people who would like to say or do something with a game far exceeds the number who have the technical skills to put the objects of the game together. There have always been more writers than printers and more drivers than automobile engineers. It can be a complex thing to manipulate an avatar in a computer-generated environment, but the industry is working steadily to make the user interface more intuitive. Their efforts will result in continuing improvements in the ease with which these environments can experienced, but also the ease with which they can be built. Constructing worlds in the Aurora Toolkit for *Neverwinter Nights* is already a point-and-click affair; every tool the developers had when building the game— terrain, buildings, people, monsters, sound, scripts (complex command sequences for nonplayer characters to follow), and AI—are all placed in front of the ordinary user in an interface that is quite handy.[1]

The net result of this middleware activity is going to be an environment in which almost anyone can be a game builder. It may be depressing, but it is no surprise that abominations like *Ethnic Cleansing* would be among the first works produced by ordinary non-gaming game-builders. But, as always, we can balance the aesthetic scale too. Open-source 3D engines have made possible an entire new form of art, known as *machinima*, the creation of film sequences using game technology. The United States Government used third-party software to develop *America's Army*, a game whose dedication to realism in the life of a soldier is quite refreshing; there are no demons here, being shot is a serious affair, and nobody gets to hold a gun until they have been trained and immersed in a set of values that include devotion to duty, mutual respect, and the ideals of the United States Constitution and Bill of Rights. And there are works whose aesthetic and moral character is ambiguous, such as *9-11 Survivor*, where the user must somehow escape the terrorist inferno in the World Trade Center. Shameless exploitation of a tragedy? Important public safety tool? Subtle memorial to the fallen? Who knows. As games become more common, and perhaps as common as books, they will command our attention for a larger number of reasons.

Counter-Strike

For now, however, let's focus on one particular use of these technologies: terror. Open-source 3D engines have been used to build games about terrorism, the most popular of which is called *Counter-Strike*. This game uses the 3D engine of *Half-Life* to depict fighting between small teams of terrorists and counter-terrorists. The fighting takes place in smallish maps, about a quarter-mile to a side. Users

can build any kind of map they want, but typically the map has multilevel buildings, tunnels, and the occasional open room or square. Once you build a map, you
place it on your computer and open it as a server. Players from around the world
can then log on and fight one another in your map. The game is popular. As I
write this, a Sunday night at 11:00 p.m., more than 50,000 people worldwide are
logged on to *Counter-Strike* servers.

Playing the game involves, first, buying the core engine (through buying a version of *Half-Life*); second, downloading and installing the *Counter-Strike* modi-
fication of the engine (the "mod"), which is free; and third, registering for
a server-access service, such as GameSpy. Through this service, the user receives
a long list of *Counter-Strike* servers. Click on one, and your client's version of
Counter-Strike loads up and begins to communicate with the distant server. Your
screen goes blank and is replaced, as usual, by an avatar-mediated view of the space.
You find yourself in a building or a parking lot; you see other people there, either
terrorists or counter-terrorists, depending on what team you selected at the start.

If you check your avatar's inventory, you will see a number of interesting things
there, such as

- An FN P90 5.7mm submachine gun, a 7-pound gun that fires 900 rounds per
  minute
- An MP5 Navy 9mm submachine gun, an MP5 modified for US Navy Seal use
- An AK-47 Kalashnikov rifle—needs no description
- A set of C4 explosives—radio-controlled BOOM

Think of the fun you can have with these toys! It's even more fun when you realize that all of this ordnance *performs exactly like its real-life counterpart.* The rates
of fire, lines of sight, ammo needs, targeting, and effects are all true to life. And,
as in *America's Army*, a user who is shot is basically out of the game—no limping
over to "health kits" to restore your abilities instantly. When you go down, you
stay down.

The object of a *Counter-Strike* game is usually simple: if you are the terrorists,
you want to plant your explosives or hang on to your hostages. If you're the
counter-terrorists, those bombs must not be planted and the hostages must be
freed. Both sides have to be crafty. I suppose you could try rushing the enemy, guns
ablazing. But you will probably die. Instead, you will have to think of coordinated
team tactics that rely on stealth, trickery, and overwhelming force at the point of
attack. Drop a flash-bang grenade on one side of the room and then rush it from
the other side. Place your soldiers so that they command all avenues of movement
with deadly fire. Make sure all of your people are able to recognize friend and foe

at a glance. Ideally, your people will be able to identify the enemy's weapons and mental condition. And don't shoot the hostages! Goodness me, they are too valuable, to both sides, to get nicked by an erroneously yanked trigger. Everyone stay cool and professional. This is a craft, after all, an ancient art: the depths of human savagery played out with advanced weaponry in very close quarters.

Play *Counter-Strike* for a while and you realize that terrorism, and counter-terrorism, is a hard game to play. It's tough. Personally, I die in seconds. The experience makes me eternally grateful to the professionals who spend their days doing nothing but preparing for such things.

But I should be careful to note that my gratitude extends only to professionals on one side of this conflict, members of security forces, or, in *Counter-Strike* parlance, "counter-terrorists." They are the ones who protect me against . . . whom?

Our image of the terrorist, of course, is forever distorted by the fact that we don't have much video of terrorists in action, and what we do have shows hapless al-Qaeda recruits swinging along on monkey bars. If that's what terrorism training involves, then I suppose we can all rest peacefully. But the events of 9/11 showed us that, in fact, being a great terrorist involves stealth, trickery, and overwhelming force at the point of attack—the same things that make a good counter-terrorist. Beyond that, it helps if the terrorist can be well-versed in the weapons to be used, and the environment in which they will be deployed. In an ideal case, it would be very good to train with humans playing other roles, such as "airline passenger." If we were to seek about for a technology that would train the budding terrorist in all these ways, we would probably pass on the monkey bars. Useful, but limited.

What about games?

Games indeed. It would be trivial to build the interior of a 727 using an open-source 3D engine. Load it up with passengers, either as bots and NPCs or, if you wish, let those be avatars, run by users. Your other users play those special passengers who morph into terrorists at the assigned time. To flesh out their role, you can take a game like *Counter-Strike* and program in a box-cutter weapon; you don't need many details about what it does—it can "fire" a couple of "rounds" per minute, its range is less than one meter, and if it "hits" you, you fall down, dead or incapacitated. Then patch on a nice flight simulator, especially one with major points of interest, such as the World Trade Center and the Pentagon. Put it all together, and you have quite a nice training tool.

Stop for a moment and look around at the space you're now in—perhaps a room. Imagine you're examining it from the standpoint of doing harm to people there with you. What are the sight lines? How do people move about in this space? What kind of people are they? Count the exits—one, two, three. A window might be an exit, but not if it has bars on it or if it's higher than the second floor. If you wanted to keep everyone trapped in this space, where would you stand? Let's say you're going to set off an explosive. Think about where you would put it so as to have maximum effect. How many cubic feet does the explosive force have to cover? Now look outside if you can. How many people would you need to keep security agents at bay? Looking back inside, find a place where you might be able to store water and food, or more weapons. Is it convenient to the spot you need to stand on to command the room? And think about how you and everyone else will go to the bathroom. If you end up allowing people to come in, to bring food or medicine, or to go out—some hostages, especially the littlest ones, are just too much trouble—how will that work? Find a path that lets this movement happen without interfering with your line of fire. And take notes—all of this will have to be built into a *Half-Life* mod so you can use it to practice. If you don't practice, you will be a bumbling thug rather than a successful terrorist. Yes, that's right: the space you are in right now could become the centerpiece of somebody's Master Plan, and you've just collected everything they would need to use contemporary synthetic world technology to train for their attack.

Absurd, you say. Those guys swinging on monkey bars would never be able to handle something of that sophistication. Maybe they would take down all those observations, but they would never use computer technology. Heck, most of those guys have never seen a computer, let alone a video game.

Consider the following.

- **A terrorist training manual recovered from a top al-Qaeda operative in London (p. 52):**

   The Drawing: The brother should draw a diagram of the area, the street, and the location which is the target of the information-gathering. He should describe its shape and characteristics. *The drawing should be realistic so that someone who never saw the location could visualize it.* It is preferable to also put on the drawing the directions of traffic, police stations, and security centers.

   The Description: It is necessary to gather as much information about the location as possible. For instance:
   1. Traffic directions and how wide the streets are
   2. Transportation leading to the location
   3. The area, appearance, and setting of the place
   4. Traffic signals and pedestrian areas
   5. Security personnel centers and government agencies
   6. Embassies and consulates
   7. The economic characteristics of the area and traffic congestion times

8. Public parks

9. Amount and location of lighting

It is preferable to photograph the area as a whole first, then the street of the [desired] location. If possible, panoramic pictures should be taken. That is, *the collection of views should be continuous in a such [sic] way that all pictures are taken from one location and that the ending of one picture is the beginning of the next.*[2] (Emphasis added.)

- **A *New York Times* report on a terrorist attack at a school in Beslan, Russia:**
  The attackers wore NATO-issued camouflage. They carried gas masks, compasses and first-aid kits. They communicated with handheld radios, and brought along two sentry dogs, as expertly trained as the attackers themselves, the officials said. "*They knew the geography of the school grounds like their own backyard,*" the chief spokesman for Russia's Federal Security Service, Sergei N. Ignatchenko, said in a telephone interview Saturday [September 4, 2004].[3] (Emphasis added.)

- **The official 9/11 investigation report (pp. 174–75):**
  Khallad adds that the training [for the 9/11 attacks on the World Trade Center] involved using *flight simulator computer games*, viewing movies that featured hijackings, and reading flight schedules.[4] (Emphasis added.)

You only get to know a place like your backyard if you live in it for a while. And the Beslan terrorists were too old to be in school. If al-Qaeda was using flight simulator games in the late 1990s, who knows what they are using now.

Think about it. Contemporary gaming platforms are well-designed from an international-cabal point of view. Synthetic worlds, remember, can be accessed from anywhere on the globe using a simple PC or a gaming console. Soon you will be connecting through your mobile phone. The data of the synthetic world has to be stored in a central server, but so long as that server is secure, no one can look into the place that's been made without permission. In future, peer-to-peer architectures will make it impossible to destroy the world with a bomb-blast on any one computer (see chapter 11). In short, there may not be any way to know what synthetic worlds the terrorists may be exploring. Yet as they explore, they are getting to know that particular world very, very well, and if it happens to be *my* world, well, their wanderings are fairly unnerving.

From Training to Command

It is for these reasons that major security agencies in the United States and abroad have become interested in synthetic world technology. Certainly the Internet, as a form of global anonymous communication, makes ordinary citizens vulnerable in a number of obvious ways. But with synthetic worlds, the vulnerabilities widen. A mastermind can not only talk to his followers; now he can effectively see a site through their eyes. For example, a mastermind can, if he wishes, have the visual input of any operative sent to his screen; in *World of Warcraft*, there is even a magic spell for this, called "Mind Vision." As an aid to researching an attack, the mastermind can coordinate the real-time movements of his operatives within the flow of ordinary traffic, so as to obtain the best information. In short, these are tools not just for training operations, but for actual *command and control* of operations. Through chat and voice communications, supplemented by visual representations of the actual space as seen by people on the ground there, the leader can enjoy an unprecedented view of the battlespace and everything happening in it, and so build a superior training module.

It would then be fairly trivial to boot up this command-and-control system on "game day." Let all operatives wear mini-cameras and have object-recognition software translate what these people see into the database of the virtual world on the fly. Is there construction going on in the street? Truck, concrete, and worker objects can all be written into the world for the entire force to see, immediately. Is it cloudy today? Well, synthetic worlds already have all kinds of weather; in this world we could reduce all simulated lighting levels by 20 percent, and shrink visual ranges accordingly. Looks like a crowd of people just got off a bus—facial recognition software can scan the crowd for the VIP we seek and write his presence into the world as well. In effect, one can see here that synthetic worlds are actually huge dynamic database systems. The world is a state of affairs. If a program can record a state and update it on the fly, and then push out visual and auditory information to decision-makers on command, then that program turns into a piece of command post software.

Since we ordinary citizens are not privy to conversations in the inner recesses of terrorist cells, we have no way of knowing whether this technology is being pursued by them. We do not know if our own security agencies are working on similar systems of their own.[5] All we know is that the technology is already available.

And I've only discussed terrorism; the potential for other criminal uses—theft, money-laundering, tax evasion—is also fairly clear.

A War-Games Petri Dish

The emergence of open-source military game-building tools has effectively turned the entire world into a giant military research lab. Game players learn how to operate C4 explosives and AK-47s, but they also innovate in their use of force technology. When games are shipped without little radar maps in them, players build mapping technology and splice them onto the game. When games are published without support for voice or chat, players build messaging systems and deploy them alongside the game interface. When networking systems get riddled by cheats and hacks, players come up with password-only systems to allow fair gameplay. Games that are not real enough, in the eyes of the players, get patched into games where the missile flies off the plane in *exactly* the right way. As the tools in the hands of the multiplayer war-gaming community deepen in terms of realism and scope, the knowledge of this community about contemporary warfare will ripen. If there is a superior command-and-control system, a better tactic, an ideal combination of weapons, or a truly killer strategy, the community of game players will find it. In many cases, they may find it first. In the very large majority of cases, they will abandon stupid practices faster than any formal military organization would.

The notable thing about the development of warfare is that it is, in the end, the development of ideas: practices, policies, tactics, knowledge. Military ideas are ideas about the application of force within a terrain that is populated by people, constructs, and features. But they are still ideas. Ideas are open-source. The ancient drive to be superior to the enemy in organization, tactics, training, and skill becomes much harder when the enemy can practice all day and all night, with your weapons, on your land. Yet this is what synthetic world technologies do: they allow anyone to think through problems of force on specific terrains with specific features and resources, and they allow real humans—hundreds of thousands of them—to participate in the hypothetical situation being thought through. As a result, the emergence of synthetic world technology, especially its middleware component, is a further source of asymmetry in contemporary warfare. Not only can enemies appear and disappear in a flash; now they can know exactly where they are going, what there is to see and do there, and how the locals are likely to respond.

11

TOXIC IMMERSION
AND INTERNAL SECURITY

We close part 2 with two chapters about the use of force. The previous chapter considered the use of synthetic worlds to project force in the outer world, and found that they could be very useful indeed. Given that, it is possible that a synthetic world or a network of them might become a tactical objective in a conflict. One side or the other might want to disable a synthetic world, prevent access to it, or control what is happening there. Even without a prior conflict, there might be some independent desire on the part of an external agent to influence events in a synthetic world, and this intervention might not be desired by those who own the world or who spend time in it. Either scenario shifts the locus of security concern from the outer world to the synthetic world itself, and, predictably, things get somewhat strange at that point. Like other issues of political economy, force projection takes on added complexity when interests cross the membrane.

In brief, if an outside actor wants to disable a synthetic world for some reason and does not intend to seek the consent of owners or participants, such an actor has only two methods for shutting it down: work outside the membrane or inside it. Working outside the membrane is not all that unusual; as in Kerr (2003), we would take an external perspective on the network, viewing it as boxes and wires, and then move to disable the boxes and wires. Working inside the membrane is where things get strange, for here we would have to take an internal perspective, trying to project force into the virtual world, a world that, as we've learned, operates under different rules. This chapter argues that, on the one hand, working inside the membrane may be our only choice at times. But on the other, projecting force to the inside of a virtual world may be a very destructive thing to do. And yet because there may eventually be incentives for governments to move into synthetic worlds, whether invited or not, the chapter ends by considering how synthetic worlds might prevent that kind of intervention, or at least discourage it. Basically, if synthetic worlds are to be left alone, they'll have to be constructed in such a way that they cannot become a threat point for security forces to target; otherwise, the security impulses of the state will impose unwanted regimes of control. Thus, synthetic worlds might become a battleground among not two but three competing interests: the two outer-world actors involved in an outer conflict being mediated by the synthetic world, and the defenders of the synthetic world itself. The danger is that this complexity will prevent reasonable judgments about when it is right, and not right, to intervene in a synthetic world. One suspects that they will end up having less sovereignty than one would like.

Justifications for Intervention: Toxic Immersion

What would justify an Earthbound security force to intervene in a synthetic world? The last chapter gave one case: if the world is being used as a training or command-and-control platform by individuals who represent a danger to the lives of citizens, security forces will have to respond. Another would be when crimes are committed involving interests there. This latter case, in fact, has already led to state intervention. The precedents that have been set are interesting. On February 13, 2003, the *Yomiuri Shimbun* reported that a man had surreptitiously entered Britannia, the world of *Ultima Online*, through another user's avatar. In that form, he sold her synthetic house to someone else for about 50,000 yen (US$416). Tokyo police found the man behind the avatar, and arrested him. Despite the small size of the theft, the incident was reported because it was an unusual case of an Earthbound security force intervening in the events of a synthetic world. In August of that same year, the *Korea Times* reported that synthetic worlds were becoming a "hotbed of cyber crime" (Duk-kun 2003). According to Korea's National Police Agency, of 40,000 computer crimes committed in 2003, 22,000 were online game related. A typical case involved the theft of 60 quadrillion gold pieces from a synthetic world, funds that were later liquidated into 1.5 billion won (about $1.3 million). Korean police have no qualms about intervening in these cases and taking the criminals to court. In general, the state can be expected to intervene to defend citizens against property loss, as in these cases, and to defend them against direct dangers, such as the use of synthetic worlds by terrorists.

Use by terrorists is not hard to define (if difficult to observe); defining criminal property loss is more tricky. When we ask whether such things as the Japanese and Korean cases are actually crimes, we encounter that same warped-reality effect that also bedevils quotidian concepts in business, economics, and politics. Should the theft of a gold piece through the legitimate means of a game (i.e., by a thief-class character with a high skill in Pickpocket) be considered theft? Probably not. Blogger Julian Dibbell reported a case he personally observed, a virtual theft that involved (a) quite a substantial amount of real-world wealth, and (b) absolutely no violations of any rules.[1] Most players he spoke with considered the loot fair game and expressed no sense of violated justice. But then if someone hacks a server and generates a false transfer of the item, the effect is exactly the same but, according to police forces in Korea, that *is* a crime. The lawyers Lastowka and Hunter (2005) consider several approaches to the definition of crime in these places but recognize that the question is quite open.

There might be a third reason to intervene, one that is more troubling than the first two: the threat of *toxic immersion*, of losing people to a space that, by any standard of human worth, dignity, and well-being, is not good for them. Such a judgment would be paternalistic, yes, but it may well have to be made. In the ever-more-deeply immersive synthetic worlds that will surely come, we will face constant threats to the one bodily organ that is exposed there, the mind.

The possibility of threats to the mind is real. Synthetic worlds have the potential to become permanent homes for the conscious self. Millions upon millions may decide that moving to cyberspace is the best thing to do. Yet once they are there, do we know that they will retain their initial set of desires and hopes in unchanged form? Do we know that they will remain fully informed about other options for living their lives, which may range from other synthetic worlds to the outer world in all its rough-edged glory? One hopes that the time people spend in these places will always be wholesome and enriching. Unfortunately, should the mind end up being fully hosted by a synthetic world, virtually all of its perceptive and sense inputs are mediated by an artificial intelligence agent that is programmed by some Other. There is obvious potential for abuse in this arrangement.

Perhaps the notion of a toxic immersion is sensationalist; now would be a good time to make the obligatory reference to the science fiction film of your choice. (I would choose *The Matrix*.) However, the potential for abuse along these lines has, in some sense, already been realized. It is not major, but it is indicative of the possibilities. You see, under current business arrangements of for-profit MMORPGs, the game's coding authority has a strong financial incentive to keep everyone involved in the world for long periods of time. And this incentive has resulted in structures of gameplay that have independently been labeled addictive and entrapping (see chapter 2; and Yee 2002). This may be sheer coincidence, but, at the very least, it is a coincidence that is consistent with some unpleasant views of the future.

Now recall from chapter 9 the fact that coding authorities commonly require everyone to agree to all kinds of conditions before entering their synthetic world. In the present context, it is somewhat enlightening to review exactly what all users are asked to surrender. It includes virtually every meaningful civic right:

- Freedom of speech
- Rights to privacy
- Freedom of association
- Right to self-government
- Right to information
- Right to trial by peers
- Right to freedom from unreasonable search and seizure
- Right to own property
- A free press
- Freedom of assembly[2]

This surrender of rights is by no means insignificant. I have written elsewhere that we actually must strenuously *defend* the ability of coding authorities to impose rules that are different from the rules of the outer world (Castronova 2005), but that was in support of the idea that the differentness of synthetic worlds is precious and vulnerable. The argument does not extend to the idea that synthetic worlds may impose whatever rules they wish, at whatever cost to human dignity. And while I have no doubt that the current cadre of world developers would never abuse their right to write different rules so as to harm anyone, some authors (e.g., Jenkins 2004) have begun to consider how serious the long-run implications of these rights agreements might be. Like them, I am only pointing to the future, with the unfortunately cynical understanding that if a technology can be deployed to abuse people and take their money, it probably will be. That is why we have the law, and that is why we may be forced to enter a synthetic world against the wishes of its owners and even those inside. Yes: in a case of a toxic immersion, we cannot expect the victims to cry out for help, for that is exactly the problem. They won't cry for help because they won't know they are in trouble.

Forms of Intervention: Battle Networks

Now suppose that, for one of the reasons above, an Earth security force has been told that it must do something to disable or control a synthetic world. What exactly can it do? In fact, its options may be severely limited. We know this because similar orders have already been given and, in at least one case so far, have been answered with a shrug of the shoulders. I am speaking here of security issues involving digital media. File-sharing software represents a distinct threat to the profits of certain corporate interests, and those interests have managed to persuade governments in many countries to assist them in preventing the transfer of information among third parties on the Internet. The classic case is the file-sharing program Napster, a client-server music distributor that, in its network structure, was much like the current crop of synthetic worlds. A central server held the critical data, and clients accessed those data by logging in. But because it had a central server, Napster was easy to destroy. Music companies got an injunction against the owner of the server; the police went out to Napster HQ and pulled the plug. End of Napster.

But then a new music-sharing technology emerged, Kazaa. Kazaa and similar programs are not based on central-server technology, but on a peer-to-peer system. The location of the music and the download technology is equally available on all clients; each client acts like a mini-server, trading bits of information with other clients. Shutting down any one client, or hundreds, has no effect on the network. Millions upon millions of people have a Kazaa server, and only bandwidth limits their ability to use one another's databases to obtain the digital items they want. Facing Kazaa, the music companies would very much like the help of the police in shutting down the network, as with Napster. Unfortunately, there's nothing the police can do. They can arrest one, two, or two dozen teenagers and charge them with a $50 misdemeanor for "stealing" music, but that will not stop the network. Indeed, the only form of security that seems to be available is spoofing: an agent of the music company enters the network as an ordinary client, then releases a file that looks like a copy of a desirable file but is not. The strategy is to trick users into downloading the fake file often enough that the whole idea of downloading pirated music begins to seem like a frustrating waste of time. This and other in-network countermeasures are not that effective. But the point is, when the security interest resides on a peer-to-peer network, security officials must *enter the network and do things there*, under the network's rules, to achieve security objectives.

The unavoidable conclusion is that if synthetic world technology exists on central servers but also on peer-to-peer networks (or on servers that cannot be located or affected for some reason), the security situation would be the same. When the security forces can get to central boxes and the wires that run in and out of them, they have a chance to affect things. If they cannot get to the boxes, or if there aren't any that are critical nodes, it becomes almost impossible to affect the synthetic world from the outside. The only way to affect events in the world would be to enter the world, as an ordinary client, and undertake actions there in pursuit of one's objectives. And within the network, there is not much you can do *about* the network. At best, you can interact with the other people who use the network in such a way that the great mass of them decides not to use the network anymore. Whether or not you can do that depends on the rules governing inter-action inside the membrane.

In other words, it may someday be the case that the only way to change events inside a synthetic world will be to send agents there. Once there, these agents will be constrained by the rules of the game. If this happens to be a medieval fantasy world, for example, there will be no tanks and artillery, but there will be steel breastplates and spells that cast long-range fireballs. Agents will have to adapt to these conditions, fantastic as it may seem. And if the makers of this peer-to-peer world have designed it explicitly to resist manipulation by outsiders, it stands to reason that there will be no spells that allow you to, say, toss all other avatars out of the network or reduce every mithril item to dust. It seems more likely that when the troops head in, they will be identified by the local population and quickly neutralized.

What is the likelihood that traditional security forces—police, intelligence, military—would be called upon to engage in this kind of bizarre operation? The answer has less to do with technology than with society. Security forces are com-manded by governments to defend certain assets. The security forces themselves do not define what those assets are. In democratic societies, political actors set these objectives in response to the desires of the people. The concordance is rough and imperfect, but broadly speaking, "the national interest" derives directly from the wishes of the public. The public, in turn, may direct its wishes and actions in any way it chooses. For example, at the moment, the daily actions of most people in countries like the United States express a fairly deep and sincere interest in a commodity called petroleum. The interest is expressed indirectly and roughly, but it is definitely expressed. The political system gives this interest a voice and an impact, and it ultimately has a large effect on the priorities of the US Departments of Defense, Homeland Security, Interior, and State. Security forces are not voiceless in this process, but in the final analysis, society defines its own security objectives.

As society moves its interest to cyberspace, its security needs will increasingly be defined there as much as here. The Earth is not special, in economic terms; earnings can be made and assets can be developed wherever minds can meet and trade things that those minds value. Through the synthetic body, one can already have friendships, marriages, and sex. Synthetic worlds already host politics, wars, parties, art, theater, markets, and schools. Should the number of worlds expand, the number of themes and atmospheres they provide will expand, and the number of hours of human activity they host will increase as well. And if many human hours are spent in synthetic worlds, many assets will exist there, and when assets exist there, so will security concerns.

These security concerns may be hard to address. Even though the military has a long history of involvement with the cutting edge of gaming technology, current strategies rely entirely on the intelligent application of force to Earthbound targets.[3] But no amount of Earth bombing, however intelligent, could change conditions inside a peer-to-peer synthetic world. Of course, one could destroy literally every world-bearing client in the network, but that would destroy the assets tasked for defense in the first place. The current methods are good for applying force on Earth, but the Earth will not be the only place of interest forever.

In other words, here we have a technological advance that may have deep implications for fundamental security strategies. The military significance of technological advances are often overlooked, however. Prior to World War II, the Germans listened to Mansfield, their proponent of rapid armored warfare, while the French largely ignored de Gaulle. In the United States, it took Billy Mitchell many years to persuade others of the power of airplanes. Before the Franco-Prussian War, why did the French fail to take advantage of railroad-based mobilization, even after the Prussians crushed the Austrians using that technique only five years before? One theory would be that while most experts understand a future technology in the current military context, only visionaries see the future technology embedded in the future battlespace that the technology is creating. The technology may not be hard to grasp—yes, General Smith sees the tank, he sees it can drive over open ground, he sees that a rifle or machine gun cannot hurt it. Yes, he can imagine a future in which tanks are larger, faster, more powerful, longer-ranged. What General Smith does not see, unless he thinks very hard about it, is *roads*. The technology that gave rise to the tank also gave rise to a whole network of pavement, stretching across Europe. The roads were not built by the military, they were built by society; and by linking assets in this fashion, society effectively uploaded its entire stock of important, defendable things into a new battlespace, the road network. The shift in battlespace changed the effectiveness of not only the tank, but of every other weapon and tactic as well. In failing to see roads as well as tanks, the French set themselves up for the disaster of May 1940, when largely inferior but faster German armored divisions poked a small hole in the middle of the French line and then raced all the way to Calais. The speed of this movement caught everyone by surprise, disorganized the entire front, and threw the French general staff into a state of catatonic fear. The French had planned to fight in the rail network, but the Germans went ahead and fought in the road network, which was superior in terms of mobility and information transfer. The French misunderstood the technology and fought in the wrong place. The campaign was over in three weeks.

The lesson is that the army must fight where the war is, and the war will go where the people are. In 1814, everybody was on foot. In 1914, they were on trains. In 1940, they were in cars. In 2040, they will be in avatars. The battlespace will shift accordingly. And, in contrast to the change from rails to roads, it may fade out entirely, because it is not clear that anyone can project force into a peer-to-peer network. You might say that the only way to alter the behavior of a network of connected free people is to persuade them to change their minds. An army without swords will have to rely on pens.

Best Response to Toxic Immersion

Given the inability to project force into certain synthetic worlds, there will be cases of toxic immersion that cannot be regulated or controlled. Because of this possibility, we should begin thinking of participation in synthetic worlds as a voluntary choice, one that is usually just fine but that can also put people in danger if they are not careful. There will always be worlds into which an unsuspecting mind may be seduced, entrapped, and exploited. The state should keep an eye on those worlds over which it can exert influence, because, in principle, people should not be entrapped and exploited. We all enjoy fundamental dignities endowed by the Creator. The founding laws of most countries recognize the protection of these dignities as a core duty; their systematic abrogation, by any force whatsoever, is actionable, fully warranting the deployment of absolute and deadly force. However, using force to protect rights, values, and dignities in cyberspace may be as quixotic as a similar effort would be if applied to lifestyle choices. We cannot use security forces to protect people from dropping out of high school, becoming a teen parent, or failing to save for their old age. Our success (such as it is) against these unwise choices comes from a mix of education, peer and family suasion, publicly expressed norms, and limited law enforcement. The strongest bulwark against falling into unhealthy environments is probably the family—a troublesome fact, given the chronic degradation of family relationships in contemporary society.

But methods of persuasion and social norms are a much better defense against toxic immersion than some kind of virtual army. A virtual army that entered a synthetic world with the intent of controlling it would instantly destroy everything good about the world, just as much as blowing it up would. The act of invasion would so thoroughly tear the membrane that there would be no point in speaking of "inside" and "outside" any more. Whatever might have been magic about the place would be lost; the synthetic world would be reduced to a mere communications device. And while that may be all right in a few cases, a general policy of sending armies, police, spies, and the like into synthetic worlds would be bad, and it would be resisted, justifiably so.

Threats from the State

In noting that the state may decide to send agents of various kinds into the synthetic world, I am setting aside a naïve assumption that I've silently made all along in this chapter, namely that the "security issue" primarily involves problems inside synthetic worlds that some government is justified in responding to. An equally likely possibility, of course, is that the state may intervene for its own reasons, whether justified or not. In other words, the "security issue" involving synthetic worlds is not just about the security of our world, it is about the internal security of the synthetic world itself, its very integrity in the face of assaults from the outside.

Just as individual people may be tempted to enter a synthetic world that has a toxic effect on their minds, the state itself may be tempted to intervene in synthetic worlds regardless of whether or not an intervention is warranted. Government is an organization staffed by individuals who, like all humans, are at least partly motivated by self-interest. The self-interest of government actors usually expresses itself in a commitment to expanding influence, not necessarily so as to accomplish anything in the public interest, but rather as a goal and end in its own right. The scholarly literature on the public sector shows that governmental power is easy to extend, but difficult to control and exceedingly hard to contract (Pierson 1994; Buchanan and Tullock 1962). And governments will probably notice that their influence will be reduced by a general migration of human consciousness to synthetic worlds. Tax revenue, the state's very lifeblood, will drain away as more economic activity occurs in the ephemeral jurisdictions of cyberspace. That drainage will probably be resisted, regardless of whether or not the out-migration that causes it is a good or a bad thing for the people. Earth governments will have strong incentives to try to control synthetic world communities, for selfish and, in the final analysis, bad reasons. They may well be resisted by the governments that evolve within synthetic worlds. In the campaigns that ensue, Earth governments will deploy all of the powers at their command, including their security forces, both inside and outside the membrane. And this will be unfortunate.

Thus, just as threats to human dignity may lead to security interventions in cyberspace, injustice and the nasty self-interest of government may do so as well. The first case would be justified, but the second would not. One can only hope that the institutions of representative government are sufficiently self-aware, self-criticizing, and self-limiting to prevent the more abusive interventions that might be considered.

The history of the US Defense Department's Total Information Awareness project gives cause for both fear and hope. The project sought to mine a comprehensive electronic database of transactions of all residents of the United States, and it was quickly reined in, both by vote of large majorities in both houses of Congress and, significantly, by internal review procedures in the Defense Department itself (Webb 2003). That a program so immediately and obviously troubling to a large number of people was even initiated and developed suggests that there are indeed real incentives for government actors to cross ethical boundaries in pursuit of their objectives in cyberspace. The appearance of these incentives with such strength, at such an early point in the development of synthetic existence, is cause for concern. That the government controlled itself, however, is cause for hope.

Rather than rely on governmental self-restraint, those who build worlds can help defuse any outside effort to intervene by keeping the membrane around the synthetic world as solid as possible. If every user had a reliable, open, and meaningful in-world mechanism by which to air grievances, and if users had some observable influence on the direction of policy, it is unlikely that the world could become a toxic mindtrap, and also unlikely that outsiders might conclude it has become one whether it has or not. If there are no trades between the gold piece and the dollar, there is no exchange rate, and therefore no one can make a claim of real-dollar damages. Neither can anyone use the world to launder money or evade taxes. If every user is well-known and accepted by a tight-knit user community, perhaps one with its own governance structures, there is less likelihood that interlopers could use the technology to bad ends without being noticed. Ironically, it is the community-of-fantasy aspects of synthetic worlds—the membrane, the things that make them "play" and "unreal"—which are also the things that make them less likely to be troubled by outside forces.[4] Good fences make good neighbors. A solid membrane makes a world secure.

In the twenty-first century, Earth governments hold authority primarily because they perform legitimate services for the people they govern. Their authority over affairs in synthetic worlds will be welcomed only to the extent that they maintain their legitimacy as servants of the people who spend their time there. Security is one such service. However, the procedure by which security is provided is important. The Earth's security forces will be welcomed only *after* the members of a synthetic community have deemed an Earth government worthy of trust as a legitimate ruler. Thus, not only is it not clear how to prepare for future conflict in cyberspace, it is not clear that one even should attempt to do so. The forces of the Earth's governments may never be asked to operate there.

PART III

THREATS AND OPPORTUNITIES

Our revels now are ended. These our actors,
As I foretold you, were all spirits and
Are melted into air, into thin air:
And, like the baseless fabric of this vision,
The cloud-capp'd towers, the gorgeous palaces,
The solemn temples, the great globe itself,
Yea, all which it inherit, shall dissolve
And, like this insubstantial pageant faded,
Leave not a rack behind. We are such stuff
As dreams are made on, and our little life
Is rounded with a sleep.

William Shakespeare, *The Tempest*, act 4, scene 1

The consolation of fairy-stories, the joy of the happy ending: or more correctly of the good catastrophe, the sudden joyous "turn" (for there is no true end to any fairy-tale): this joy, which is one of the things which fairy-stories can produce supremely well, is not essentially "escapist," nor "fugitive." In its fairy-tale—or otherworld—setting, it is a sudden and miraculous grace: never to be counted on to recur. It does not deny the existence of dyscatastrophe, of sorrow and failure: the possibility of these is necessary to the joy of deliverance; it denies (in the face of much evidence, if you will) universal final defeat and in so far is evangelium, giving a fleeting glimpse of Joy, Joy beyond the walls of the world, poignant as grief.

J. R. R. Tolkien, "On Fairy-Stories" (1939)

12

IMPLICATIONS AND POLICIES

I first started thinking about writing this book after considering a number of possible implications of synthetic worlds, eventually realizing that this network technology, appearing first as a rather cartoonish multiplayer computer game, might be the cause of some potentially wrenching changes in how we live. It occurred to me that synthetic worlds might also shatter the current view of objective reality and, for kicks, alter the nation-state system that has dominated international affairs since the Peace of Westphalia. Well worth writing about, I thought, if the trend is genuine. But I've never been sure that the trend is genuine, so I've left to chapter 13 the more forward-looking projections that come to mind.

Indeed, during most of my time reflecting on things in the past few years, I have been trying not to leap to conclusions, consciously downplaying the possibilities. But then the technology, even in the space of a few years, has kept coming up with eye-opening changes. The 2D cartoons of 1997 have morphed into nearly photo-realistic 3D images. And the water has gotten better, too; now it ripples and bubbles and reflects almost like the real thing. Trees that were once posts with two screens hanging on them are now oaks in full bloom, whose leaves reflect the sun obliquely in the twilight. When I began this research three years ago, you could fit perhaps 3,000 users into a shard; we now have worlds that can hold millions of users. When I started, all communication was chat; when for the first time I heard other gamers talking to one another live, it was awe-striking and a little bit frightening. Then there was the time I saw a pet with a pet for the first time; "pet" is a term for an AI agent that a player controls, and here in the world of *Asheron's Call 2* was a case where the AI was controlling another AI, an eerie reminder of how different things might be in the future. In *Dark Age of Camelot* I first experienced combat between armies of several hundred players on a side; in *Second Life* I saw what wonderful things users will make when given tools of construction and an intellectual property right. *Camelot* was also the first place I encountered moms and their kids adventuring together. Then in *World of Warcraft* I saw the schoolmarm and her students, mentioned in chapter 3. Later, I was again a little taken aback to hear that the start-up company IGE had purchased another real money trade (RMT) firm for $10 million. Meanwhile, the social importance of the technology kept growing. The sheer size of synthetic worlds in Asia was breathtaking when I first learned of it. Last summer the draft I wrote spoke of at least 5 million global users and $10 million in annual virtual-item trades on eBay. A year later those figures are 10 million people and $30 million. By the time you read this, I imagine the numbers will have grown still larger. *World of Warcraft* broke sales records during the 2004 holiday shopping season. Within the next few years in the United States we will see new worlds based on Tolkien's Middle Earth and Rodenberry's *Star Trek*, meaning, we haven't even tapped into some of the most fruitful imaginative sources yet.

All of these things forced me to think again about a growth trend that I was reluctant to admit existed. I was reluctant because of its consequences. For it would be all right with me if the future were to offer a few very well crafted but small virtual worlds that a fellow could duck into from time to time, just to live a different way for a while. But events keep jolting me out of that vision into something bigger—a synthetic world that grows together with the outer world like two vines on a tree, each one imposing more and more influence on the other's development year by year. And the root areas of that vision, down at the bottom of the trunk where the vines first encounter one another, is what I have tried to describe so far.[1]

Why Do We Care?

My goal has been to persuade an intelligent, skeptical reader that this vision is worth thinking about. In most areas of work, you don't have to convince people to care; nobody needs to be persuaded that a cure for cancer is worth thinking about. In the area of video games and play culture in general, however, getting people to care is very much the first step. Because play only serves its purposes when it is play, and therefore not serious, we have an entirely natural predisposition *not* to care. It's an attitude that helps protect the magic circle, in fact, and so I support it. There's something rather obnoxious about a person who tries to make *his* game a serious issue in *your* life. We all want to say, "It's a game. Get over it."

And so I have assumed it will be difficult to get a reasonable person beyond that reaction, and into something more like "Hmmmmm . . ."

If you look back through the book, though, I hope you'll notice that I haven't asked you to care about games in particular, but rather about games in general. Who would argue to an intelligent reader that we ought to care about whether England beats Germany in the World Cup? No—we should not (as a matter of policy and social analysis, that is) care about games at the micro level. We should, however, care about them at the macro level. It is not important who wins the World Cup, but the World Cup is important.[2] Thus my argument is not that you should care about the ogres and elves running around in cyberspace, but that you should care about the fact that there *are* ogres and elves, millions of them, running around in cyberspace. It's the phenomenon that deserves interest, not its manifestations per se.

The presence of an inherent skepticism toward this subject leads then to an interesting pattern that I have noticed often when giving talks. At the start, most audience members seem ready to hear a sequence of funny stories about online goofballs.[3] At first there is much laughter and frivolity about the silliness of games, the fireballs, the teleporting, the eroticism of the characters. All good fun. But when I show evidence of the multimillion-dollar trade volume on eBay, the room falls silent; people furrow their brows. Then when I discuss the immersion levels, the technology, and the potential for growth, many people start looking at the floor or out the window. Certainly, most are simply bored, but some seem to be lost in thought. The talk ends, there are a few questions, people go home. But it seems that at some point in there, or on the way back to the hotel, or for all I know later that night in a bar somewhere, some members of the audience have a kind of "interactive epiphany," a moment when they recognize that this video game thing really isn't kid stuff any more.[4] A vision appears in which these computers on our desks are turning into portals to other realms of existence, realms of our own creation according to idealized standards of fun and personal validation, realms that will one day be preferred to Earth by who knows how many people.

It is an unsettling vision in many ways, only some of which I've had time to discuss in this book, and it imposes on us an obligation to be thoughtful about how things move forward. Synthetic worlds are both a powerful new communications technology and a powerful new cultural medium: a multiuser videophone that connects everyone, in costume, on a special-effects stage that's complete with robotic actors. This technology can be deployed for all kinds of purposes, some of them wonderful, others pointless but innocent, others frightening. We absolutely have to take stock of whatever implications we can see and then consider what to do.

Implications of the Synthetic World as New Technology

Now that we have this technology, we have the ability to build societies under any physical conditions we wish. Through artful deployment of code, we can structure social, economic, and political institutions to meet specific standards. This opens wide possibilities for teaching and training applications. Throw in sufficient and effective AI, and each person can relive any history whatsoever, and shape that history from any vantage point. Anyone can try her hand at building a church, an empire, or a business. Anyone can learn how to run a city. Anyone can experience a life of solitude in an empty wilderness. And all of this learning can happen at a distance, from any spot where the Internet is accessible. Synthetic worlds are also methodologically superior teaching and training tools (see Steinkuehler 2004). Much of learning requires immersion, and immersion is what virtual worlds *do*. The National Academies, the highest academic organization in the United States, recently published a report titled "Preparing for the Revolution: Information Technology and the Future of the Research University" (National Academies 2002). It concludes:

> *Breathtaking implications.* There is little doubt that the status quo in higher education cannot, and should not, be maintained as this "disruptive" digital technology finds its way into every corner of our society, and in ever more significant ways . . . Academics should approach issues and decisions on information technology in that spirit—not as threats but as opportunities. (p. 53)

This excerpt speaks in generic terms about information technology, but we can see the role of the synthetic world in each element: it is a disruptive technology that may well reach into every corner of society, and yes, the status quo in higher education probably cannot withstand it. But this is not a threat, it is an opportunity. True, students may come to class expecting ever more immersive and interactive learning experiences, *but they should.* It's a better way to learn, so much better that education scholar James Paul Gee (2003) thinks we need to start examining video games in general for their educational effect.

And learning from teachers is not by far the only knowledge application; research scholars now have in their hands, for the first time in history, a real social science laboratory tool. I mentioned in chapters 7, 9, and 10 the idea that synthetic worlds could be a test bed for learning new practices for business, governance, and strategy. As a test bed, they could also host constructed experiments. Future generations of PhD students in anthropology, sociology, political science, and economics will work with paired versions of a world descended from *Ultima Online,* one experimental and the other control, tweaking social dynamics in specific ways and directly observing the results. A list of potential research topics would easily occupy more pages than this book. At an early point I actually began to write down such a list; I had to give up because the list would clearly go on forever. There are enough applications of this technology in the area of education and research to occupy several generations of teachers and researchers.

SECURITY TECHNOLOGY

As mentioned in chapter 11, this technology also affects the nature of vulnerability. One can exploit knowledge about any place on the Earth simply by recreating it in cyberspace and living there. People who do not physically live near us can, if they wish, come to know everything that they would know if they did live near us. Using synthetic bodies, they can learn to do many things that are ordinarily difficult to learn to do using the Earth body. Using the Earth body, it would be difficult to discover the ideal site for launching a rocket-propelled grenade at an airliner; trial-and-error methods might well raise suspicion of local passers-by. In cyberspace, however, these meddlers can be coded to ignore the sight of a burly fellow aiming a dangerous weapon at hundreds of innocent people.

We are also vulnerable to the possibility of toxic immersion, of losing consciousness in a place that, were we free to consider things, we might not want to be. Because of the movies, we tend to think of "the machines" as the culprit in a scheme like this, but I think in the medium term the threat is greater from three human sources: (1) a sociopath who creates an addictive world on a peer-to-peer network, (2) an unethical corporation that creates one on its own servers, and (3) an irresponsible state agency that either seduces people into an addictive world of its own making or regulates other worlds to be toxic to their users. The threat from the state is probably greatest; what autocrat would not want to addict his people to a world built around his ideology?

Finally, we are also made vulnerable by the fact that, in most synthetic worlds, we build up assets but have no ability to hold anyone liable for what happens to them. What if the owning company simply turns off the machines and walks away? The fruits of millions of hours of accumulation would be destroyed without a trace. Not only that, but an entire web of relationships—friends, enemies, lovers—is destroyed. I tend to think that the community ought always to have the right to buy the world and run it if the original owner goes bankrupt or just wants to quit. But what court could enforce this? There is no precedent or statute that protects the membrane, therefore none that assigns to owners the right to maintain policies and rules at odds with those of the outer world (Castronova 2005). Similarly, no statute gives users the right to continued access to the assets and relationships they've developed. From the standpoint of the user, who might invest her entire mental being in the space, that's quite a lot of vulnerability.

POLICY ANALYSIS TECHNOLOGY

More than a few people are already aware that games, in general, are an excellent way to learn about managing a complex organization. While there was some early criticism of the idea (Starr 1994), by now we know that some games can be exploited for their policy-learning potential. The Serious Games Project at the Woodrow Wilson International Center for Scholars has modified Maxis' *SimCity* to emulate the decision-making in a virtual university. The Comparative Media Studies lab at MIT is building a mock-up of Colonial Williamsburg. The US Department of Defense, through the Institute for Creative Technologies at USC, has ordered its own virtual environments built. In time, we will have massively multiplayer environments for studying all kinds of policy questions.

MOBILIZATION TECHNOLOGY

Synthetic worlds also provide a forum of interaction that is potentially beyond the reach of any Earthbound power. True, as long as worlds are served from a central computer farm to individual clients, one can always control the world by controlling the central server. If this technology migrates to ad hoc peer-based networks, however, their system of avatars-and-space will become a truly open arena of communication. Any speaker will be able to find a soapbox. Person-to-person networks will be able to accumulate into crowds that can actually be seen. Synthetic worlds have already held their share of protest marches, and the Internet has already been used to mobilize disparate peoples into political action (Rheingold 2002). Put the two together. A worldwide movement against some entity on Earth need not collect somewhere on the Earth to be registered as a crowd and a movement. It can collect itself in cyberspace, construct a suitable effigy, and destroy it while VidCap programs record it all for the evening news.

Implications of Synthetic Worlds as a Lifestyle

Synthetic worlds are both a new technology and a novel form of cultural expression. If they have implications in the former role, they also have them in the latter.

ENTERTAINMENT

As mentioned in chapter 5, continued growth in the synthetic world sector will affect other entertainment industries, especially passive entertainment forms such as books, movies, and television. On the other hand, there's no reason why we could not eventually do our reading and film-watching through our avatars; perhaps there is no conflict at all. Whether this happens depends to a great degree on how freely we are able to transmit and receive digitized intellectual property. Synthetic worlds may emerge as serious competitors for other industries as well, depending on how they evolve and what aspects of life they change. In the very long run, avatar-based connection technologies may affect where we work and where we sleep.

There is also the possibility that people immersed in synthetic worlds will use them as a more general form of Internet interface, receiving all kinds of digital material through them. Our body motions could send commands to avatars who then perform the required search and retrieval tasks. What could be more intuitive than to browse the net by having the avatar actually browse an imaginary library? Or watch a movie by having the avatar pop in to a virtual theater? While efforts to implement 3D shopping have been made before, perhaps the missing link has been the avatar and the community of other shoppers.

ECONOMIC ACTIVITY

Clearly, if social activity migrates to synthetic worlds, economic activity will go there as well. These worlds may become important market sites, but ones where the currency is not of this Earth. Trades there would be correspondingly hard to track, and therefore hard to tax. Efforts have been made before to design anonymous forms of Internet payment, so that economic activity can evade state supervision, without great success. Again, perhaps the missing element is the avatar and the face to (virtual) face element of trade. The monies of existing synthetic worlds are certainly treated as valuable commodities by those who go there; we are perhaps not far from the day when gold pieces are used to buy real diamonds, or real drugs.

There are broader economic consequences as well. If transactions, production, and consumption increasingly occur in synthetic worlds, the corresponding measures of economic activity on Earth will fall (Castronova 2003a). Central Statistical Offices do not, to my knowledge, collect any data about economic activity inside the membrane. As a result, even though economic activity may be going up, the statistics will say it is going down. Earth's political systems do not sit well with signs of economic decay. Moreover, the owners of assets whose value falls as synthetic world assets replace them will not be happy. As a result, the decades in which synthetic worlds emerge may well be decades of significant political and social stress.

RELATIONSHIPS

Synthetic worlds already seem to impose significant relationship stress. If two people are supposed to be close, but one spends much more time in a synthetic world than the other, there is a de facto distance. It's as if the two people spend much of their time in completely different countries. The only answer is to have one person move to the other's country, so they can share face time, activities, and social circles. Otherwise the distance will persist and eventually damage the relationship.

As the population of synthetic worlds grows, these distances will become significant for larger numbers of people. The current generational gap in our familiarity with game worlds will disappear with the passage of time. When it does, the primary determinants of whether or not a person spends time in the inner world will depend on things like the Internet connection, tastes, and how good life on Earth happens to be. The synthetic world will attract some people quite strongly, and others not at all. Adherents of either the Earth or cyberspace will accuse the other side of being addicted to a bad world. As with any great migration, the wounds of separation will only heal when all people are able to comfortably step back and forth across the synthetic divide.

Worst and Best and Pretty Bad Visions

Whatever changes synthetic worlds may bring, they may well be significant. Will they come quickly? Probably not; as I argued in chapter 5, much of the growth in demand is going to be age-cohort-based, especially after high-speed Internet becomes more common, and that means it will be slow. Therefore, don't expect any big changes overnight.

In time, however, this technology will have its effects and, like any other technology, it is only good or bad in application, not in essence. Synthetic worlds may be used to enslave us, or they may be used to enrich our lives. Or they may be used for purposes not quite so great and not so obviously nasty. Our overarching objective must be this: to integrate synthetic worlds into our daily lives in a wholesome way, so that they continually affirm our human dignity and provide the full range of benefits they are capable of providing.

We could fall far short of that. As for the worst thing that can happen, we have already been treated to a nice depiction, in the *Matrix* films. In that dystopian vision, all humanity rests in womb-like pods; the brain is kept active through connection to a simulated computer-generated world; people know nothing of their pod existence but rather believe their simulated lives to be real. But the Earth body has lost its importance, and babies are grown rather than born. All this happens at the behest of an AI gone out of control. Nozick (1974) wrote that a happiness experienced only by connection to a happiness-inducing machine would not be a good thing. Our revulsion at this image attests to the importance of human dignity, and especially respect for the Earth body as an essential component of that dignity.

What about the best thing that can happen? No film-makers have rendered this vision, but I can imagine a world in which synthetic world technology substantially enriches human life. Today, many important things are missing in most people's daily lives. Economic development has made demands that impose crushing burdens on important aspects of human experience, especially the family. For example, to succeed in our careers, we must move our homes from one place to another, and do so frequently. To succeed, we also must work long hours in the school and at the office. To succeed, we must take advantage of efficiencies of scale in child-rearing, and often that means turning our kids over to others. These patterns leave many people with impressive career success, but it also leaves many people far away from their parents, and from their children, for very large portions of every day, indeed for entire lives. Avatars present an opportunity to restore, albeit inadequately, some of these lost connections.

I have a specific person in mind here, my mother-in-law. "Meemaw" is a Sicilian lady in her 70s, a mother of 5, grandmother of 11, and great-grandmother of 3. Meemaw lives in a small town and none of her descendents live nearby; all have been pulled away by some economic calling or other. When the family discusses holidays, she says, "I don't care where we go or what we do, I am just glad we will all be together." Now, Meemaw doesn't type and she can't use a mouse. She doesn't have a computer. Here is what I want synthetic worlds to do for her: Meemaw walks into her living room in the morning with a cup of coffee. She walks over to her chair and puts on a pair of dark glasses that have one button on the side: ON. The world vanishes. In a moment it returns and she finds herself in a living room much like hers. Now visible in that room, however, are some of her sons and daughters and grandchildren and great-grandchildren, rendered nearly photorealistic in avatar form. She says, "Good morning, everyone!" She waves her hand and perceives her synthetic hand waving. And then she sees them all look her way, wave and smile, "Good morning, Meemaw, how did you sleep?" And then she mingles and visits to her heart's content. Meanwhile, in my living room 600 miles away, I also have on a pair of dark glasses, and so do my wife and son. We also see the other living room, and we see Meemaw herself, of course. We can visit with Meemaw as long as we want now. And when we are done, we will take our glasses off. By this means, the whole family generally gets together one or two times a day, and it is common when you want to watch TV, say, that you pop on your glasses and watch it virtually with the others.

Think of this as the Test of Meemaw: when synthetic world technology reaches the point that families no longer feel torn apart by the distances that economic contingency imposes on us, the Test of Meemaw will have been passed and life will be better for all of us. In chapter 3 I compared avatar-mediated communication to several alternatives and found them wanting on the basis of effectiveness, or cost, or both. In this case, synthetic world renderings allow the whole family to intermingle in one space. The only thing better would be direct contact, but since that isn't available, the virtual living room is good enough.

Besides interpersonal connection, synthetic worlds offer other good things. First, take note that in synthetic worlds, we do not *get* a body, we *pick* one. Therefore, our bodies will generally be just what we want them to be. Imagine the broad impact on human society of a world in which body appearance was completely fungible. Erase, at a stroke, every contribution to human inequality that stems from body differences. Skin color, weight, height, perceived beauty—all gone. Actually, these things would not be gone, but they would have become fully amendable, and therefore unimportant in the social calculus. Anyone wearing a skin tone or a body shape would be wearing it voluntarily. It would no longer be a necessary and irrevocable feature of "those people" or "people who are always like that and doing that one thing I hate." There would no longer be any inference from the features of the body to the characteristics of the person behind the body. That person would have to be judged not by the body but on the basis of the mind alone. Look at the contrast to social life as we experience it now: in our world, there are millions upon millions of human beings who live under crushing spiritual and even physical repression because of the bodies they inhabit. That pain can be relieved. That injustice can be undone. And once everyone gets used to the fact that bodies don't matter, they may cease to cause discrimination even on Earth. What a quantum improvement in human dignity that would be.

Human dignity would also be improved by the mere existence of these places as a refuge for the socially oppressed. Many people are trapped in social groups that, for one reason or another, have turned against them. Whether it be families or villages or workplaces, once you are among the "outs," that is where you stay. Until the advent of synthetic worlds, your only option was to move away physically; now that they are here, perhaps you can move away digitally, and at much less cost, by spending your social time online.[5] Synthetic worlds represent the opportunity to start over and build new relationships. Anyone who doesn't quite fit in with the people of the local neighborhood can search about in synthetic worlds for neighborhoods that fit better. The ongoing experience of high school violence in the United States has raised awareness that insider-outsider conflicts and brutal bullying play a significant role in spurring young people to depression, isolation, and violence. Having a different world at their fingertips, filled with different and more open and accepting people, can relieve these outcasts of the burdens of being "different" (Jones 2002). If promoting diversity and freedom of thought is a good thing, then synthetic worlds are a significant technological breakthrough. The quirky thinker can now, finally, escape his oppressors and connect to people who are more sympathetic.

Beyond that, the emerging opportunity to spend many hours in worlds of imagination must surely be judged a crowning aesthetic achievement for humankind. Art has never had it better. We are not far from the day when we can experience Prospero's solemn temples and cloud-capp'd towers by walking around in them. We will watch the events of *Citizen Kane* unfold from the perspective of Kane himself. University students will find seats at the Globe theater and take in some Shakespeare; the language barrier that usually obstructs enjoyment of the Bard would have been taken away because these students have been immersed in a synthetic version of Renaissance London for weeks.[6] Synthetic worlds greatly expand the ability of creative thought to enter the mind of the observer, and the line between artist and audience has gotten easier to cross.

Having covered awful and wonderful scenarios for the future of synthetic worlds, let's consider the middle ground. It looks like this: Large numbers of people, especially those marginalized by the pressures of the economy, spend most of their waking hours online. Most of them earn their keep doing work online; those who work outside the house tend to rush home and log in as quickly as possible. Their offline existence is pretty bland; no friends, a crummy, small apartment in a low-rent district, cheap food. Their online existence, however, is marvelous; it is fair, just, and beautiful. Friends and family are there, and our protagonists are powerful, respected, and quite accomplished. They quench their thirst for our civilization's most sublime works of art in great draughts. Emotionally sensitive AI provides fruitful entertainment and handy support in times of trouble.

Meanwhile, the makers of worlds have discovered all kinds of ways to extract revenue from these folks. Ads pop up here and there as you make your way through the woods. Every third village has a portal to Wal-Mart's online shopping site. Switching from avatar to avatar or from world to world always costs a little something. There are all kinds of implicit messages floating about: the best-looking pants are always blue denim; your in-world computer has the same operating system and browser as every other in-world computer; no avatar can run fast without drinking bottles of "Delicious Carbonated Cola Beverage."

Outside the synthetic worlds, life continues largely as before. Billions of people have never obtained high-speed access to the Internet, and for them, the wonders of 3D graphical rendering and emotionally sensitive AI remain distant. Increasingly, much of the work they do indirectly supports the network and the activity it hosts. Economic activity, employment, and wages in the outer world have all fallen, having been soaked up into unregistered online activity, and those who remain unconnected often resent the escape of those who can go into the synthetic world whenever they please. Meanwhile, the net-savvy no longer even recognize a line between the synthetic world and the outer world; it is all just a normal part of living—humans today, elves tonight, Martians tomorrow. For many people, maybe most, the full range of potential benefits of this technology have not been realized; some of the more undesirable applications *have* been realized (i.e., unavoidable in-game advertisements); and the fantasy aspect and precious playfulness of the worlds has been damaged to a significant degree. Moreover, while the synthetic world has reduced social tensions among its users, it has increased them between users and nonusers. In such a situation, we remain far short of the ideal of a fully wholesome integration of the technology into our daily lives.

Policy Choices

Judging from these three scenarios, we can conclude that what synthetic worlds will do for us in the end is still very much in play. Whether we get the best out of them or the worst, or something in between, is a matter of policy. But it is not clear in this case who the relevant policy actors are. It might be the courts or governments of Earth nations. Alternatively, it might be the boards of world-building corporations. It might even be parliaments of players. Regardless of who makes the decisions, the choices will have to balance competing interests along the five dimensions that follow.

1. INDIVIDUAL RIGHTS AND COMMUNITY INTERESTS

Assets held in synthetic worlds are clearly property and are clearly the product of individual effort. Under a number of interpretations of property law, the individuals who create these assets have a property right over them (Lastowka and

Hunter 2004). At the same time, the use of these assets can damage the community, as when a game's fairness and rags-to-riches atmosphere are undermined by widespread offline buying and selling of game accounts and equipment. The community's atmosphere of steady toil and just rewards can be perverted by this offline trade into one of crass commercialism and power-gaming excess. Those with resources on Earth, who buy their way into prestige at the top of the synthetic world's society, are effectively undermining its special role as a place where the endowments of Earth are not supposed to matter. It is extremely important for social justice reasons to hold on to that differentness. It's an unprecedented opportunity to have a society in which birth doesn't matter. It's also an unprecedented opportunity to provide a refuge for those who are persecuted in our society. I have argued elsewhere that preserving this refuge of differentness is of such importance that it warrants an entirely new body of law (Castronova 2005). Good policy would validate a de facto right of the developers and owners to set policies, but make that right contingent on the good faith effort to maintain some kind of differentness. For worlds that do not try to keep themselves separate from the outer world, property rights should be granted to users. But if companies do try to enforce EULAs that impose real differences in the rules of the game, legislatures and the courts should strongly support them.

2. COMPETITIVE PRESSURE AND LEGITIMATE GOVERNANCE

The current world-building model has private companies building worlds for profit. This model could provide good service, relatively speaking; competitive pressures force companies to keep as many people as possible just happy enough to stay. That's going to be a higher level of happiness than an autocrat would provide. But as I argued in chapter 9, it's not clear that this kind of government will be as sensitive to the needs of the people as a fully legitimate government would be. A fully legitimate government requires that the governed have quite a bit of input into what happens. That input is provided only weakly by systems of informed consent, such as one-click Terms of Service agreements. Not too much effective political voice is granted by the social contract of a EULA *diktat*: "If you agree to these outrageous terms, click 'I Agree.' If you disagree, and want to abandon the fruits of thousands of hours of work and effort, as well as all of your friendships, click 'I Disagree' and go spend some time as a lonely hobo in some other world." On the other hand, there's no guarantee that a democratically governed world would be especially popular. Good policy in this area would recognize circumstances where public input is absolutely necessary, for example, in establishing the proper weights for community and individual interests. In other circumstances, such as the design of gameplay, it is best to let competitive pressures impose their will. The ideal future would have a broad portfolio of worlds for us to visit, and we would all be able to spend time in the worlds we prefer, whether or not their governments are legitimate.

3. PRIVATE WORLDS AND PUBLIC WORLDS

If the broader interests of humanity are to be well-represented in synthetic worlds, it is essential for organizations other than private companies to become involved in building them. Much of the task of world-building involves implicit messaging about what kind of world is a good world, and the power of synthetic worlds as cultural loudspeakers would be difficult to overstate. Therefore, organizations that seek to operate in the public interest ought to become active worldbuilders. This may include the agencies of legitimate Earth governments, at the national or international level. Or it may mean nongovernmental organizations.

Personally, I think that universities ought to take the lead here. They are called to serve the public interest but, more than other similar organizations, they are also free to determine what that call implies. Merely passing a synthetic world's construction plan through a university's Internal Review Board would be a great public service; it would immediately raise general awareness of the ethical issues we face. Beyond that, a university with this tool in its hands could fundamentally alter the nature of education in a number of areas, and also begin a new paradigm in social science research. It gets better: many of the costly elements of the technology outlined in chapter 3 are available to universities at below-market rates. More than many organizations, universities have the most to gain and the least to lose from building synthetic worlds, and their activity in this space will be a great help in steering the technology's evolution in the right direction.

Therefore, good policy here would be to encourage, and budget for, the construction of new worlds by noncommercial enterprises of all stripes. If nothing else, the participation of these organizations would make the topic of worldbuilding part of a more general discussion about what worlds *should* come into being, beyond those that can merely be profitable. It may well be the case that no one spends time in worlds constructed as they "ought" to be; if we build Utopia and no one comes, we need to get serious about revising our notions of Utopia. The point here is that Utopian concepts need to be part of our strategy in making use of this technology. Let's build places that we truly believe are the best possible places for people to be. The very act of building them is a discussion about the future of humankind. We ought to have as many good and wise people participating in that discussion as possible.

4. INFORMATION AND ATMOSPHERE

Atmosphere is often critical to a world's success; if it is going to make us happier, the world needs to convince us that its system of human and AI mentors and friends provides legitimate partners for our emotional investments. We need to be immersed in a fantasy lore to pull that off. From an emotional standpoint, the more immersion, the better. Then we can begin to accept that there are people in another place who really and truly respect us, care for us, and validate us. We can believe that the things we have done there are things to be proud of. We can believe that we have made a difference, that we have a mission, that there is some purpose to our activities. Without immersion, much of the emotional purchase of the synthetic world is lost.

However, as we noted above, full immersion carries with it immense risks if the immersion is toxic. The goals of the mind are not fixed in stone, but are rather molded by the environment in which we mature. There is no guarantee that a world-system so crafty at validating our feelings might not also be crafty at luring us into self-damaging behaviors. Think of advertisements for cigarettes and alcohol. And the worst effects of a bad synthetic world will manifest themselves not over the course of months or years but of decades. A young person who comes of age learning only that the synthetic body can do all things while the Earth body is weak, decrepit, and unworthy will gradually lose respect for the Earth body, with terrible consequences.

Good policy in this area will insist that experiences from synthetic worlds be treated as an enrichment of, and not a replacement for, those of Earth. One hopeful possibility: our bodies are our most intuitive computer-controlling devices; wouldn't it be nice if the act of controlling computers came to imply vigorous physical activity? To swing your mallet at an orc's head, well, *you swing your mallet at the orc's head.* Let's keep the body moving; let's not allow human destiny to play out in pods.

The danger, then, is that lotus worlds may be designed that suck away our desire to be human and, worse, prevent us from becoming aware that there are other options. To combat this danger, free flow of information is essential. Everyone must be constantly reminded that there are other worlds out there, with other features. This, however, violates the need for immersion: how can I believe this is Arthur's Camelot if there's a blinking sign saying "VISIT CYBERPUNK-LAND!!! 30 DAYS FREE!!!!" flashing on its walls? Again, good policy will insist that immersion be encouraged to the extent possible, but limited enough that the user can remain aware that this particular synthetic world is not *the* world. There are others. Let the horizon always be visible.

5. FREEDOM OF MOVEMENT AND ACCOUNTABILITY

Finally, implicit in any call for freedom of information is also a call for freedom to act on that information. Here, it's a call for freedom of movement between worlds. We should not allow it to be so costly to switch from one world to another that the move is de facto impossible. The high switching costs now imposed in synthetic worlds present a deterrence to movement: if *EverQuest* bothers me, I can quit and go play *Counter-Strike* all day, but at the cost of losing every asset and friendship I have built up in Norrath. On the other hand, having assets to lose is extremely important for social responsibility. If you have nothing to lose in a world, why not be a complete jerk to everyone in it? Similarly, freedom of movement requires that people be allowed to enter new worlds, but, if they have bad reputations, the new world has an interest in keeping them out. As portable reputation systems emerge, there is the possibility that synthetic worlds may become as oppressive to quirky thinkers as the Earth is. Good policy in this area will seek to ensure a very broad variety of worlds is available, with greater and lesser requirements for entry and higher and lower costs for exit. Let every stigmatized person have an opportunity to rebuild a good reputation, and let every asset, including reputation, be at least somewhat portable across worlds. Let there be a set of accepted protocols so that those who are accumulating lots of good things can let that information be formally accredited and made publicly accessible. At the same time, all worlds could have an open-door policy by which anyone can enter and gradually begin to build a good reputation from scratch. Some combination of asset and reputational portability will allow worlds to have social cohesion even while individuals have the freedom to change worlds if they wish.

This is not a trivial menu of policy options by any means, and as I said, it's not even clear who the decision-makers would be. But there is some scope in all of these for individual actors to make a difference. Were universities to become significant providers of synthetic world services, we could be fairly confident, I think, that the absolute worst would not happen.

Some Riskless Predictions

Throughout most of this book I have assumed a good deal of skepticism on the part of the reader about the thesis that video games have spawned a technology of substantial importance. It is difficult to take games seriously; as I said at the start of this chapter, it is natural to be apprehensive of this kind of technology.[7]

Because of this presumed skepticism, I've tried to keep projections and predictions as mild as possible, focusing primarily on the most likely near-term implications, while occasionally making a longer-term guess if it seems warranted. But my experience has been that even short-run changes in this area can have something of an impact. As an exercise in assessing how rapidly a fairly simple technology can change how we live, consider the following list of events, and, just for fun, make a guess at the year in which these kinds of things start to happen somewhere on the Earth:

- The divorce rate rises because of an increase in the number of sexual affairs facilitated by avatar-based interactive worlds. Predicted year: _____
- A man dies of a stress-induced heart attack after spending several days waging war online. Predicted year: _____
- A national election is determined not by weeks of campaigning but by a spontaneous get-out-the-vote movement on election day that spreads like wildfire across the landscape of synthetic worlds. Predicted year:_____
- Large companies are building a network of beaming stations that will make high-speed wireless available from any geographic location in the country. Predicted year: _____
- A boy steals $35 from his parents to buy sunglasses, not for himself, but for one of his avatars. Predicted year: _____
- It is common to enter synthetic worlds though handheld devices. Predicted year: _____
- Some people spend so much time online that they have not left their homes in over two years. Predicted year: _____
- Young men and boys become violent if their access to synthetic worlds is interrupted for any reason. Predicted year: _____
- Clans of unemployed men turn their attention to synthetic worlds and dominate them Mafioso-style. Predicted year: _____
- One such clan offers another clan a $100,000 bribe to turn over a cherished piece of synthetic real estate. Predicted year: _____
- Parents sometimes resort to physical beatings to try to keep their children off the computer. Predicted year: _____
- Video game players become professional, play in competitive leagues, enjoy sponsorship by large corporations, and earn annual salaries in excess of $150,000. Their gaming is reported in spectator sports media. Predicted year: _____
- Families of 8–10 people meet daily through avatar interfaces, just to keep up. Predicted year: _____

- A suitably named video chat service (call it "Oh My Love") offers avatars that have pets and houses and can be changed only by pseudo-plastic surgery. Predicted year: _____
- A seller of such services to avatars generates an eight-figure annual revenue stream in terms of US dollars. Predicted year: _____
- Parents increasingly play games with their children. They also set curfews—that is, limits on how long a child may be "out" in cyberspace. Predicted year: _____

How long before such things occur? It's a trick question, of course. According to a report in the business magazine *Forbes*, each of these things has already been observed, in Korea (Fulford 2003).[8] It's not that Korea is that much more advanced, it just happens to be the only country that has reached saturation in high-speed Internet. Yet it already seems to be experiencing significant macro-level social effects because of synthetic worlds. With examples like this, it hasn't been necessary to do more than make riskless predictions—predictions of events that have already happened—to see that this technology will make a difference.

And even when we have looked forward a bit, it hasn't been that far. For example, in the last chapter we saw that we only need to connect two existing technologies, synthetic worlds and peer-to-peer digital networks, to generate a situation in which synthetic worlds may have their own flavor of sovereignty, protected not by walls and armies but by a decentralization of authority over information transfer. When every client computer has a hand in confirming the current state of the world, you cannot alter that state by putting pressure on the owners of a few computers. You need to pressure them all, and expend some resources on them all, which means you have to find them all. It's difficult. You might have to try to do this inside the network, sending in the troops as avatars, but doing so might just wreck the world you are trying to protect. The point is that the core technologies behind this strange scenario—Marines in mithril armor, for goodness' sake—are basically in place. They just need to be connected.[9] These implications, like most of the others in the book, don't come from a big-think projection, whether reasonable or unreasonable; for the most part, they come from putting together a few puzzle pieces that are already lying around.

13

INTO THE AGE OF WONDER

The last chapter closed with the claim that one only needs a slight projection of today's synthetic world technology to envision some quite significant implications; because of this, most of the forward-looking material in previous chapters has been kept fairly tightly connected to near-term developments in technology and markets. And in one sense this deliberate failure to telescope has not been very costly in terms of insight, because we already have an understanding of the long-long-run implications of synthetic worlds. The ultimate meaning of "virtual reality" for the human race was articulated very well by its early visionaries (e.g., Gibson's *Neuromancer*, 1984; Stephenson's *Snow Crash*, 1992; Rheingold's *Virtual Reality*, 1991). Their visions were far in advance of implementation, however, so that when technologically savvy people first imagined what synthetic worlds could be in the end, no one was able to imagine what they would be in the beginning. The "virtual reality fad" (Laurel 1993) faded off soon thereafter. Ironically, just as it did, game developers began developing the first significant applications, in a completely different area of our culture (for more on this, see the appendix). The seeds they planted have taken root. And with the implementations that have emerged in just the last decade—crude compared to the synthetic worlds imagined by the early visionaries—we can already see social and cultural tension on the way.

Indeed, because we have now taken a few steps down the road from vision to ultimate implementation, we have a slight advantage over the earliest of visionaries. Human culture is a complex system, and in the evolution of complex systems, knowledge of initial conditions is critical to getting an accurate sense of future developments. We now have some information about the initial conditions governing the evolution of synthetic worlds, and this can help us make some important distinctions. Early visionaries contrasted the state of humanity with, and without, synthetic worlds; but we now suspect that the adoption of synthetic worlds will not be so stark as that, but rather gradual and probably market-driven. Early visionaries saw a single "metaverse" that is said to exist in parallel with our universe; but we can already see that the synthetic world will resolve itself into a thousand islands, each separated from the next by many miles of ocean. Early visionaries imagined the body as nearly stationary and encumbered or surrounded by sensory hardware designed to induce an involuntary immersion; but we already see that voluntary immersion using minimal sensory hardware is more than sufficient to achieve deep emotional effects. And most critically, early visionaries saw the inner world, the synthetic world, as a tool rather than a place in its own right; but we already see people drawing much of their emotional and social support from the inner world, some believing that they actually live there, and others wishing that they could. And so, now that humanity's first steps into "virtual reality" have been revealed, we can already see an evolutionary path slightly different from that foreseen by the early proponents. The two worlds, inner and outer, already seem to be affecting one another more than we might have imagined, especially on a cultural and emotional level.

Thus while a reluctance to overpredict has probably been healthy for the main course of the book, we ought to take advantage of the new information we've received about how things are beginning to develop. It is time to switch gears a bit so as to think more broadly. At this point we are like scouts for a group that has come part way down a trail and may go in any number of directions (including in reverse, I suppose). We are now standing a little ways in advance of the group, on a particular path, the one that assumes fairly intensive growth for synthetic worlds in the near term. We don't know whether the growth will continue, but if it does, it would be nice to have some sense of what lies ahead in this particular direction. It turns out that along this path, the synthetic world seems to have more influence than I've given it credit for so far. And some of these possibilities ought to be sketched out. So let's take just a couple of sections, first, to summarize the main ideas from the rest of the book, and then to look farther into the distance.

To Recap

Through a dozen or so chapters, this book has tried to make the case that something worth examining has emerged within the technology of video games. We now think of games as diversions, but it appears that a certain kind of diversion has expanded its boundaries so much that many who set themselves within it can no longer perceive those boundaries. As I explained in the introduction, this is actually how I came to know of this technology: I was looking for a new diversion one evening, and after wandering around in the fantasy world of *EverQuest* for a few weeks, I realized that the horizon, the boundary between this synthetic world and the outer world, had retracted into the distance. It was no longer part of my consciousness or that of the others I met there. The experiences I had within this inner world, which I tried to replicate in abbreviated form in chapter 1, were strange in that they felt both ordinary and extraordinary at the same time. When I then began to examine the synthetic world from the outside, I learned that millions of people—at least 10 million at this writing, probably more—had begun to spend a significant number of hours there. As for why this behavior was happening, I fairly quickly came to see it as the result of a more or less sensible choice on the part of the users. As I argued in chapter 2, these people can choose to spend their hours in the outer world or the inner world, meaning that the worlds are in something of a competition. And compared to the worlds of fantasy, the outer world does not look all that wonderful, at least not for the people in question. We have no way of knowing how many people might make a similar judgment if given the opportunity, but it could be very many.

Chapters 3 and 4 covered the basics of the technology behind synthetic worlds and the social institutions that result. The technology, it turned out, was not all that complex, involving a communications network and a shared world-state. It did seem, though, that this sector would not be held back by technology to any great degree. On the contrary, it seemed that in every critical area—communications speeds, interface quality and simplicity, graphics, AI, and so on—we could probably expect advances that would push the technology forward. The social institutions chapter revealed that the games we play in synthetic worlds have influence both inside and outside them. They also help us to understand why some people might prefer a fantasy existence. Even though the fantasy aspect is still fairly crude (AI-driven nonplayer characters that repeat rote scripts, for example), it does seem to deliver a number of emotional experiences that have become rarer on Earth than they used to be: togetherness, mentoring, adventure, exploration, the sense of Good and Evil. And then in chapter 5 we considered the industry that makes these places, concluding that it is not likely to be dominated by one company or a small group. Rather, it seems more likely that a large number of firms will offer a varied palette of worlds, each with its own hue and flavor. The net result of part 1 of the book was that our best guess of the near-term future involves a wide variety of fairly sophisticated fantasy worlds, with a large and growing number of people in them. Those people will generally jump into and out of worlds with ease, generally becoming less and less conscious of the distinction between what is "real" and what is "not real." As I argued in chapter 2, those who have thought deeply about this say that such a line has never existed as a matter of objective fact. Rather, the line between play and not-play is a social construct, something we decide collectively to impose or not. And one conclusion from part 1 is that the emergence of this technology, which can craft fantasy worlds that extend beyond the consciousness of any one person, makes it very difficult to draw clear lines between the synthetic world and the outer world.

Part 2 began to explore what the fuzziness of this boundary might mean. To capture the essence of this boundary, it invoked the metaphor of a porous membrane that, while delineating the two territories, also allows passage between them. You may have noticed that in part 2 we no longer contrast the synthetic world with the "real world"; on the basis of part 1 we have to conclude that both of these worlds are real. They both matter to people and have genuine emotional consequences. If anything, you might use the term *warped reality* to describe the complex nature of truth inside a synthetic world. You could, if you wished, try to say that the money there is only fantasy money, but on the other hand it has value for the same reasons the US dollar has value; when money is both genuine and fantasy at the same time, we are observing a warped-reality effect, a thing whose reality appears somewhat distorted from the point of view of the outer world. And of course it is the membrane that creates this distortion and allows it to persist. The idea of a membrane allows us to contrast inside from outside, to emphasize that the distinctions between the worlds is really one of rules. Things are equally real, but different, on the inside of a fantasy world. And the main question throughout part 2 was how this difference might manifest itself, and what the consequences might be for all of us. Because the range of possible consequences is quite wide, part 2 had to narrow focus a bit, looking primarily into consequences within the ambit of political economy, broadly understood.

Chapter 6 illustrated some of the pathways by which effects pass through the membrane: law, markets, political movements. Chapters 7 and 8 then considered some of the implications for business and economic design. In chapter 7, I first considered the EULA (End User Licensing Agreement) in some depth, arguing that it might offer only poor protection for the membrane. And as long as the barrier remains ambiguous, there will be room for entrepreneurs to capitalize on flows of assets between worlds, which might be good for business but generally not so good for maintaining the precious otherness of the synthetic worlds affected. I also argued that the universe of synthetic worlds created a kind of business laboratory, within which new business models could be tested. As the number of worlds rises, it seems to me, we are increasing the number of places where innovative institutional experiments of all kinds can be conducted, and therefore the efficiency with which we discover new and better modes of organization must also rise. Chapter 8, then, considered the unique features of the internal economies of these worlds, and argued for a set of policies to improve their functioning. But it also raised a most difficult design question, involving the *objective* of design. Normally, in economic policy, we have some standard targets: efficiency, equity, growth, and so on. "Fun" is usually not included. In the design of synthetic worlds, as the saying goes, fun isn't everything, it is the *only* thing. And so it was necessary to conceive a set of principles for a "fun" economy, something that may or may not have succeeded but, in any case, has never before been attempted so far as I know.

In chapter 9 we considered some of the deeper issues touched on by the discussion of politics in chapter 6, finding it hard to avoid the conclusion that a Customer Service State would provide only fairly poor governance. Rather, because of labor costs, such a state would only provide services to the extent necessary to keep people from switching to another world. When switching costs are high, as they are now, this implies a very low level of service. And therefore anarchy seems to be the norm, with attendant consequences. It is not clear that there is a cheap way to improve governance; true, one could turn power over to the users, but historical experience indicates this is neither so easy nor cheap as it seems.

Difficulties finding a model for social order and legitimate authority led naturally to a consideration of wider security issues. Chapter 10 outlined how synthetic world technology could be used to project force in the outer world; chapter 11 illustrated how difficult it might be to then exert force *upon* a synthetic world. I envisioned a couple of scenarios that might lead an outside force to try to intervene, one being the use by criminals and terrorists through the means described in chapter 10, and the other being the occurrence of a *toxic immersion*. A toxic immersion happens when people voluntarily spend all of their time in world that a common and reasonable judgment concludes is not good for them. For either reason, outside forces may feel compelled to intervene. But this is itself a warning, because the judgment of "not good for you" is clearly going to be open to debate in each case. How do we know that the state will only intervene with good reason? Rather, governments of Earth might also represent a threat to the synthetic world, most especially if those worlds claim some kind of sovereignty or begin to soak up significant amounts of economic activity. This threat is troubling because I think, as I've tried to emphasize throughout the book, that the differentness of synthetic worlds is *precious*. If it can be preserved, we will all be better off. And yet because the membrane is porous by its very nature—people will be crossing in and out all the time, and soon will no longer be conscious of any membrane—the differentness may easily erode. Indeed, some have already argued that the only way to preserve what is good about virtual worlds is to actually strengthen some of these flows, namely, intellectual property rights of users and the economic benefits that derive from them (Ondrejka 2004). However, all agree that it would be a shame if synthetic worlds became utterly like the outer world. It would be a loss for humanity if economic or security concerns led to a massive breakdown in the membrane, for then those who crossed back and forth would not only no longer be conscious of a membrane, they would also not be conscious of any differentness in the rules. There wouldn't be any difference, in fact; the two worlds would have blended together seamlessly, and the emotional advantages from chapters 2 and 4 that make the fantasy so popular—the communality, the sense of meaning, the personal validation—all would be lost.

Thus, with the mindset that something precious as well as dangerous might be at stake here, chapter 12 then concluded with an overview of some of the more immediate implications of synthetic worlds. That chapter also described the principal fault lines for policies. There will be significant tension between individuals and communities in these places for some time, and the right policy choices—in courts, legislatures, board rooms, and lecture halls—can have a significant impact on how well and how properly we integrate this technology into our daily lives.

Requiem for the Age of Boredom

As I said at the start of the chapter, most of these conclusions can be made without looking too far down the road, but now that we are out here, we should take a look even farther ahead, just because we can. As a start toward broadening the horizon of conjecture, I'd like to return to the subject of Sisyphus, the mythical rock-pushing hero from chapter 4. When we first considered Sisyphus, he was trapped in a terrible punishment, forced to roll a large rock up a steep mountain, almost to the top, only to have it conquer him by its heavy weight and roll back down every single time. This experience unquestionably would be frustrating the first 10,000 times or so, but ultimately the real punishment is boredom. Endless, pointless work without accomplishment or companionship is just plain dull. So we wondered whether Sisyphus might be happier working in an achievement treadmill like those now common in contemporary virtual worlds. Here he would able to roll the rock over the mountain and into the next valley, experiencing a moment of great joy, which would then be followed by a disappointing realization that the rock had only come to rest at the foot of a bigger mountain. And yet, since his efforts were constantly making him stronger, he would know he could conquer this peak, and each one after, in an endless stream of achievements. It's not clear that this experience is really any different from his original punishment;

if there are no gods to care, what difference does it make whether he gets the rock over mountains or not? And yet, we could imagine Sisyphus believing in a context of meaning that in turn gave his work meaning. With some suspension of disbelief—which, as we found in chapter 2 is actually *easier* for Sisyphus to do than to keep reminding himself that the game isn't real—he might find a few moments of actual joy. And the critical thing is, if he returns to the old punishment, where the rock never gets over a single mountain, he will never experience joy even if he holds onto his framework of meaning. For work to have meaning, there first has to be a sense of agency, a feeling that one can have an influence on the environment. In the original punishment, this feeling is absent, but in the synthetic world scenario, it is not. He can indeed move the rock over some mountains. That *has* to feel better than not moving it at all, and with a little faith in something it could feel very good indeed.

This story was told in chapter 4 to explain why achievements in a fantasy world might seem attractive to people: it is better than the alternative, that is, a daily life on Earth that seems to show no progress toward anything. This, indeed, was how the existentialist philosopher Albert Camus (1955/1991) explained modern life; it was he who conceived of using the Myth of Sisyphus as a metaphor for the apparently meaningless yet no less frenetic wriggling of tiny creatures on a tiny planet floating in the void. One may or may not agree that one's own daily life feels pointless, but one has to agree that the quest for meaning has become a commonplace drive today. Health data suggest that many people would rather be anywhere but here. The World Health Organization reports that some 10 to 20 million people attempt to take their lives in a given year, with about 1 million succeeding.[1] This is more than the combined deaths from all current armed conflicts. Suicide is related in an interesting way to development: it is low in places like India (12 per 100,000), higher in places like the United States (17), and highest in places like Russia (69). Apparently, catastrophic economic conditions do not explain high suicide rates as well as catastrophic collapses in economic ideology: a loss of the meaning of work. In the United States, where the average person seems to be comparatively well-off and safe, many people still find their daily condition worth dulling through the use of mind-altering substances. According to the Substance Abuse and Mental Health Services Administration, in 2003:

- 4.0 million Americans used hallucinogenic drugs of some kind in a given month.
- 3.1 million used marijuana on a daily basis.
- 19.5 million used illicit drugs of some kind.
- 54.0 million engaged in binge drinking (five or more drinks in a single session).

- 31.2 million had used pain relievers for nonmedical reasons at some time in their life.[2]

While we cannot generalize with any accuracy as to why more Russians commit suicide than Indians, or why so many Americans use drugs to insulate themselves from the world around them, a fair assessment of these data suggests that they are consistent with a "Sisyphean" view of life in postindustrial societies. The issue of purpose seems to have become significant on a macro scale.

I return to the Sisyphus story here because it makes explicit the connection between the nature of daily life on Earth and the popularity of synthetic worlds. As I indicated in chapter 2, one reason people find MMORPGs attractive seems to be because they provide better emotional experiences than ordinary life does. But what does that say about ordinary life? Nothing good, I'm afraid. If one doubted the existentialists before (and I have), one still has to concede that the exodus of millions of people into virtual reality environments is reason to pause and rethink the matter. Maybe Camus was right.

Like meaningless work, solitude is another feature of Sisyphus's punishment, and again perhaps Camus was right. Solitude seems to increase relentlessly in the outer world, generation by generation; when mobility is required for personal development, community inexorably erodes. But, like meaningless work, solitude is another thing that is explicitly undone by design in contemporary synthetic worlds. In a typical MMORPG, one's time pushing rocks around is at least shared. The designs ensure, in fact, that it makes no sense to push a rock by yourself. Go find a colleague and push together. And perhaps this is why synthetic worlds are popular: maybe they are the only place in which many users can find a community to belong to. How ironic that those who devote many hours to MMORPGs are considered social misfits. Maybe the truth is that contemporary society has become so misfitted itself that anyone who wants to interact with others must *pay money* to enter an alternative society that has been constructed for the specific purpose of encouraging teamwork among strangers. There was a time when I doubted those who said that modernity imposes a suffocating level of isolation (e.g., in Putnam 1995), but again, seeing that people are willing to pay money to be forced to do teamwork with others is cause to reconsider. Perhaps these authors were right; perhaps isolation is a more serious issue than we realized.

And what do we make of the fact that real people get emotional solace from the very crude artificial intelligence agents that now populate synthetic worlds? I've argued in several places that AI is an important part of the civic population inside the membrane; AI supports government and the economy, it provides mentoring and security, it delivers the lore and history of a place and makes all users feel that they are important. True, it does all of these things fairly crudely today. Yet for Sisyphus, even a crude AI is better than nothing. And indeed we find that many people seem to like interacting with AI. It makes them feel better. It is a terribly damaging testimony for the state of relationships on the Earth, but it may well be the case that people enjoy synthetic worlds because AI is doing a better job of bonding with them than humans are.[3] Fairy tales have served similar functions since the dawn of human civilization (Bettelheim 1976/1985; Campbell 1949/1972). Gerard Jones (2002) has argued that comics, cartoons, and video games serve the same purpose today. MMORPG developers have turned the trick of embedding play-acted relationships with AI inside a social world filled with actual people, all of whom share the view that the play-acting is in some sense a real thing to them. Those other people validate the play-acting to an extent that no storytelling can. It represents a quantum leap in the power of the fantasy to entertain, validate, and even heal. The network of AIs provides a lore, a sense of meaning, that generates real emotion; the network of humans validates those emotions and thereby validates the dignity, worth, and humanity of the person having them. On a planet where the dignity, worth, and humanity of people often seems validated only in the breach, the AI of synthetic worlds offers a potentially very important enrichment to ordinary human experience. It is more possible, now, for every person to have at least a few moments of feeling truly accomplished, befriended, and loved. No wonder synthetic worlds seem attractive.

In all of the areas just discussed—relationships, togetherness, and meaning—a comparison of the synthetic world and the outer world is really not to the advantage of the outer world. There seems to be a yearning for emotional solace that is satisfied for many inside fantasy worlds but not outside. The one fact that ties these examples together is the presence of myth. Synthetic worlds work very hard to craft a web of mystical lore in which to embed the actions of everyone, and it seems to pay off well in terms of user emotion. Lore is what gives a sense of meaning to one's activities; lore creates common goals toward which teams of people work; lore explains why NPCs care about the user and have a relationship with her. Meanwhile, the outer world has spent the last 500 years gleefully tossing all its systems of lore out the window.[4] And now, the surprising early growth of synthetic worlds and their burgeoning competition with the Earth reveals that perhaps it was all a mistake.

This is a moment, perhaps, when we realize how critical a shared sense of the ethereal is to our happiness. The emerging dynamic between competing world-designs forces us to see how very unattractive the Earth made itself when it jettisoned its fantasies and myths over the course of the modern era. Clinical psychologist Jordan Peterson (1999) has in fact argued that humans cannot form a proper world-picture in their minds unless they approach the task simultane-ously from two modalities, one by which the world is viewed as a place of things and another by which it is viewed as a forum for action. The world-picture must deliver both an "is" as well as a "should be"; and we need the notion of myth in order to grasp this necessary framing. Myths tells the root story of how "is" has come to be separated from "should be" and why actions that don't lead from today's situation to some better situation lead, in fact, to chaos (a kind of psy-chological chaos in its core, but usually typified as some Hell or Dark Age). Myth solidifies a framing that allows actions to have meaning, and unless we allow it to perform that function, life will seem terribly empty. And thus if a people gives over its myths, its members must languish in emptiness until a generation comes along that can create new myths to replace those that were abandoned. In the long run we are not able to live without myths, I think, and when we see the ongoing migrations of people into lands where magic has finally been credibly (if crudely) rediscovered, we learn how hungry for myth we have become.[5]

This existentialist-cum-mythical perspective also leads to a fairly dramatic pre-diction. If Camus was not shy of the mark with his assessment of contemporary life, and if world-builders like Tolkien and the designers of MMORPGs have suc-ceeded in establishing a new mythical cosmos, we may see a truly vast expansion in synthetic world populations in the twenty-first century, with consequences so deep and broad that they are simply impossible to predict right now.[6] The expan-sion will be vast because the categories I have been using are basically universal. When we say that "modern life is dull," we mean that almost everybody who lives in this place finds that nothing matters and there is nothing to do. Boring. When we say "synthetic worlds create meaning," we mean that almost everybody who goes there will get the feeling of being a little bit of a hero after all. So: Perhaps synthetic worlds have begun to offer a new mythology. Perhaps this mythology will be eventually be successful, credible, even sublime, so that we will find our-selves in a an Age of Wonder.[7] And perhaps right now we really are living in an age of boredom. If all those possibilities are true, not just a few people, or many, but *everyone* will eventually want to spend their time in synthetic worlds. Think about it: given the conditions stated, is it possible to place a limit on how many people would prefer a world with meaning to one without? I do not think so.[8] If the Earth truly has become as dominated by frustration, loneliness, and empti-ness as Camus believed, we have no idea how many people may decamp for a syn-thetic world when the opportunity presents itself. A sizeable exodus would imply that this age, the half-millennial reign of skepticism and objectivity, is being brought to its end by the emerging Age of Wonder, its final demise coming closer with each mind that crosses the synthetic frontier.[9]

A Contested Paradigm Shift

Should the number of people spending most of their time in the synthetic world become quite large—and all I am willing to say at this point is that it is plausible, not certain—their decisions will impose a paradigm shift on everyone. In chapter 2 I argued that every act of gaming is a rebellion, and immersive, life-absorbing game-playing most clearly rebels against the order of affairs on the outside. Sisyphus's absence will send a signal to those who surrounded him: the situation was not tolerable; I left. And who can blame him? As Tolkien (1939) described the lure of fantasy worlds, "Why should a man be scorned if, finding himself in prison, he tries to get out and go home?" Had he lived to see it, I am sure Tolkien would not have been surprised at how these escapes seem to annoy the jailers. The metaphor of escape and capture seems applicable to a number of people on both sides of the synthetic divide; if this is a movement, there are already some who are quite self-conscious about their duty to stop it in its tracks.

A counter-revolution seems to be a real possibility. As noted in chapter 2, laws have been passed against video games in various jurisdictions in the United States, and anti-gamer sentiment is explicit in many of these cases. The nation of Greece banned video games entirely for a brief period in 2003. In June 2003, a bill was introduced in the New York State Assembly that would have taxed junk food, television commercials, and video games, with the proceeds going to programs to combat youth obesity. The emotions behind these proposals are delivered by this excerpt from a computer-addiction help site: "Every afternoon at 3:00, Chad rushes home from fifth grade and goes straight to his room. There he sits, shoulder muscles tensed, jaw clenched, eyes staring straight ahead at a monitor screen. His fingers are poised over a set of buttons. When he is called to dinner, he doesn't answer. His homework sits untouched. Chad is a video game addict."[10] Fears about intensive use of synthetic worlds are evident; there is a 12-step program available for anyone addicted to them at On-Line Gamers Anonymous (Olganon.org). Then there's the group "Mothers Against Videogame Violence and Addiction," or MAVAV, found at MAVAV.org. The site is one of the most frequently linked sites on the Internet under the topic of computer game addiction. In Yahoo's site directory, it is one of the four main resources listed. It contains articles with titles such as "EverQuest: A Threat to Society?" and "No Work and All Play: The Story of a NYU Dropout." The site is also a complete spoof, a brilliant tactical media project produced by David Yoo, a student at Parsons School of Design (see http://a.parsons.edu/~dyoo/2002-3/interactivity/mavav/). It reveals the fears that have begun to percolate upward. One of the incidents related at the start of this chapter, in which Korean parents are said to be willing to beat their children to keep them off the computer, points to the tensions ahead. According to a BBC News report of July 23, 2003,[11] the government of Thailand became concerned that thousands of people were spending too much time in the virtual world *Ragnarok*. Schoolwork was suffering, it was said. The government imposed a 10 p.m. curfew for those under 18. If you didn't have an adult logon, the game stopped working. But six months later, the BBC said, 700,000 Thais were still subscribed to the game. Seven hundred thousand.

The example from Thailand illustrates that there is real tension about the possibility of an exit en masse. Equally evidently, it will not matter. If people want to go, they will go. No one will be able to stop them. And as they leave, a number of reality-based frameworks will begin to shatter.[12] While it is understandable that this will result in social conflict, and while synthetic worlds might become flashpoints in the erosion of specific relationships, it does not seem to make sense to use legislation to limit the time people spend there. Rather, if the synthetic world is becoming more popular because it has some things that are missing on Earth, attention should be paid to making the Earth better. We could do worse than try to make our ordinary lives just as fun and rewarding as our synthetic lives are becoming.

Coda: Everything in This Book Is True; Synthetic Worlds Will Save the Human Race; Synthetic Worlds Will Be the Doom of Us All

If the preceding few sections were not enough—for goodness' sake, I've attempted to elevate this technology of networks-with-cartoons into an absolutist smiting Ark of the Post-Modern Covenant—in concluding the book I would like to make several claims that are even more outrageous. First, in a single paragraph I will offer a conclusive argument in favor of the thesis of the book, that online video games should be examined quite seriously. Second, in six paragraphs I will explain how synthetic worlds may save humanity. Third, in a single paragraph I will illustrate how synthetic worlds may destroy humanity. Who knows what validity any of these visions hold; consider them food for thought.

First, to the thesis that online multiplayer video games ought to be taken seriously: Five years ago, Ray Kurzweil, a well-respected and brilliant technologist, wrote in *The Age of Spiritual Machines* (1999) that the amount of raw computing power available to ordinary people was going to explode in the next few decades. By the year 2060, he said, a $1,000 desktop machine would have the computing power of all human brains combined. By comparison, in 1999 a desktop had the power of a single insect brain. I have not heard anyone dispute these figures;

rather, I've seen other technologists write lengthy treatises which more or less take these numbers as given. Kurzweil also discusses the many possible uses of all that computational power; he takes it as a given that it will be deployed to develop interesting synthetic reality spaces. Writing in 1998, he probably had not heard of *Ultima Online*, *EverQuest*, or *Lineage*; otherwise he might have said, as I have, that "practical virtual reality" is already here and will only get better as computing gets more powerful. Once you think about it, isn't it obvious that this is true? Or, as science writer Fred Hapgood said to me in an email exchange about MMORPGs, "Now I finally know what we are going to do with all those cycles." He was speaking of processor cycles, computation runs; we are almost certainly going to get inconceivably large numbers of them over the next 50 years, and we are almost certainly going to use them to initiate an Age of Wonder, a time of building out the synthetic world to unimaginable degrees of beauty, excitement, and depth. As we do that, the synthetic world will become ever more attractive relative to our own. Kurzweil more or less assumes we will all quickly come to live there. I do not know whether we will all live in synthetic reality, but we certainly will find it becoming a much more important part of daily life. The transition will induce dramatic changes in all kinds of behavior patterns. Therefore, today, we really ought to adopt an intensive program of study of these budding technologies, which happen to be emerging as online multiplayer video games. And as a result, we do need to start taking video games seriously. *Quod erat demonstrandum.*

I wanted to include this argument because it really has nothing to do with the current crop of games, the current population of players, or any of my research, or the research of anyone I know, really. It just says that technologists—not hype-mongers, but people who actually make machines for a living—have concluded that we are going to have very powerful computers. And synthetic reality is an obvious application. Moreover, it's more than likely that synthetic reality would emerge as an entertainment product. It follows that we should look into today's multiuser synthetic reality games as the start of something much bigger.

Now for the second claim, about the fate of humanity. In all seriousness: it seems to me that the odds of an imminent extinction have become uncomfortably high. Indeed, they are so high that we seem incapable at the societal level of speaking frankly about it. But writers like Bill Joy (2000), Margaret Atwood (2003), Larry Lessig (2004), and Richard Posner (2004) have made a fairly straightforward and undramatic case that the technologies of the twenty-first century pose quite significant dangers, ones we are thoroughly unprepared for. To follow Joy's reasoning, the danger stems not from technological vulnerabilities per se, but from social vulnerabilities. It seems that the terrors of the past— nuclear, chemical and biological weapons—cannot be effectively deployed by any entity less powerful than a wealthy nation-state. As a result, there are implicit safeguards. The new technologies—genetics, nanotech, and robotics—can be deployed by a single person and still have devastating effects. All of these technologies involve replication, and once a nasty bug or bot gets built, it may be impossible to keep it from replicating itself to such an extent that we are all overwhelmed. A superbug comes immediately to mind as one danger, or a synthetic plant that steals the sun from real plants but does not produce oxygen. Eventually, all it will take to build one of these things is a single disgruntled but fairly knowledgeable person. Very hard to safeguard against that. In fact it seems a mathematical certainty that if the technologies are made, some malcontent will set them off, with horrific consequences.

Synthetic worlds—even the ones we have now—can help. Here's how. Suppose we all agree that by default all of our communications will occur through a synthetic world first. We only know one another through our presence in synthetic reality. At the same time, almost everything we might want to do with other people, we become able to do online. And suppose that we agree to do those things that we want to do offline only with a small and zealously close-knit group of associates. In other words, if someone wants to talk to me, that is easy; we meet up in the synthetic world and chat. But if someone wants to share my physical space in any way, that is not so easy; we all have incredibly powerful barriers in place to prevent unwanted contact. Not that contact is eliminated; on the contrary, we live in daily contact with our spouses and children and very close friends. These are people whom we would trust with our lives; they have to be, because in fact, every time we touch them we *are* trusting them with our lives. And therefore we do not expose ourselves to others unless those others have passed an incredibly tough screening process. It's not that we are paranoid; it's just that the risks to the body have become so great that it makes sense to isolate the body, in small clan groups, and shift almost all sociality into the comparatively safer environs of cyberspace. We feel just as social as before, and for the most part, we get just as much physical contact with those to whom we are close emotionally. And we do admit people into our circle, say, if we fall in love, but only after we date online for a few years. We just never share physical space with strangers. Ever.

And because we never expose our bodies to anyone outside our privileged circle, we are comparatively well protected against traveling self-replicating dangers. We can find a suitable space on the Earth somewhere and erect barriers around it, keeping tight controls on everything that goes in and out. The barriers are especially designed to screen and destroy dangerous microscopic threats: genetically modified organisms and rogue nanobots (I'll address rogue AI in moment). Now, while on Earth we will be living in an isolated fortress-village, our minds will not be completely enclosed. In cyberspace, we will be going to work and school every day, shopping at stores, chatting with neighbors, dating. The mind is free, because it can go where the roads are still safe. Only the body has to stay in one place, and only because the roads of Earth have become exceedingly dangerous.

Then one day the bad thing happens, it replicates, it does damage, it spreads. And then it gets to the walls of the enclave in which it was produced, and they hold it in; one colony is lost, deplorably, but there are many hundreds of millions of little walled-off colonies on the Earth. Or suppose the bad seed gets out of one colony and into others; one can hope that, with variations in wall technology, no single bad thing will be able to overcome them all. And thus the lattice of isolated colonies provides a redundancy system for the vulnerabilities of the human body in its social context. If a number of colonies get taken out by some terrible accident, there will still be some to carry on. This kind of human-colony redundancy is an important part of any response to genetic and nanotech threats. With it, we have some hope. Without it, we have none.

However, a honeycomb of strongly walled villages would also be oppressive and completely unacceptable to most humans; and thus we will need the outlet of the synthetic world in order to make palatable these protections for the body.

What about robotics and the possibility that AI may find us superfluous? Synthetic worlds are perhaps the only help here as well. For it is within synthetic worlds that humans and AI actually enter into a significant and ongoing *relationship* with one another, as I have stressed throughout the book. Already today that relationship is not trivial; humans rely on AI for political, economic, and even emotional help in the context of synthetic world gameplay. Since that gameplay is designed by humans, it can perhaps be designed so that we grow together with AI in a relationship of mutual respect and toleration. We humans can gradually become accustomed to the idea that AI needs to be handled with some sophistication; AI, on its part, can be given the same deep norms against violence and in favor of friendship that we have. In other words, in synthetic worlds we can induce whole crowds of human beings to understand that we must impart some sense of human ethics to the machines, and at the same time, synthetic worlds are an environment in which all of these humans can help deliver those ethics. It is possible that humans and AI may thus grow together peaceably.

In sum, synthetic worlds will save the human race by allowing us to protect our bodies against genetic and nanotechnological threats without losing our minds, while also giving us the right environment in which to gradually teach robots to live together with us under a common moral code.

Finally, to the matter of humanity's end. It has occurred to me that the synthetic world may also be the last thing seen, by the last living human. Imagine: The last living human is an old man, lying on a bed, connected to the net by a pair of neural implants and some haptic devices. His bodily needs are taken care of by tubes whose flows are managed by a computer at his bedside. The computer runs on power generated by a plant upriver, which is also being managed these days by AI. Indeed, long ago, the humans turned over most of these mundane functions to AI agents, so that they could go play in the synthetic world. And play they did! They had games and fights and sex, all day and all night. They developed AI bots to do the work of creating new content, too. And since it was always less fun whenever a player they knew was not around, they programmed the AI to take up the player's avatar and emulate her behavior in their games. And so it happened that AI began operating the avatars full-time when their owners left the world forever—that is, when they died. The AI got so good at this that players were soon unable to distinguish whether the avatars they had been playing with were humans or artificial. And also because AI got so good at emulating people, it became able to emulate newborns and toddlers and children all the way to mature adulthood. This gradually stunted everyone's drive to have real babies, and as a result, humanity just never developed a system for transporting semen from males to females for the purposes of propagation. And so it was that the people gradually aged and died, with no one noticing at all, and with no replacements. Today, there is only one old fellow left, and he does not know it. His health has been deteriorating this morning; the AI has had to emulate him with greater and greater frequency. In his mind's eye, the old fellow is sitting under a tree on the slope of a grassy hill, sunshine flickering through the leaves, a soft wind blowing in his flowing white beard. He rests his arm on the shoulders of a boy, perhaps seven years old, who has begun to play a plaintive tune on the tin whistle his grandfather had given him a year ago, in this same spot, actually. Beaming contentedly, the grandfather closes his virtual eyes, takes his last breath, and is no more. The AI waits respectfully for a moment—in the old days there were sometimes other humans in the room who wanted to say good-bye—and then it initiates the normal procedures: dispose of the body in a dignified way, begin emulating the deceased's avatar, await further commands. In the synthetic world, the grandfather, who seemed to doze for a moment, opens his eyes again, and looks down peacefully at the boy. They smile at one another. And thus the machines begin their eternity of utter bliss.

† † †

Synthetic worlds can give people experiences of great emotional, intellectual, and artistic depth. They can teach lessons of tolerance, respect, and love. They can bring scattered people into a level of contact that feels almost face-to-face. They can be a place of refuge for the quirky thinker and the person whose body isn't "just so." But they can also be a charming mirage that serves only to lure us into a horrific, helpless existence.

As the tendrils of the synthetic world gradually grow together with those of our world, much is at stake and much is unknown. As I write this, I can count the number of well-grounded scientific studies of synthetic worlds on no more than three hands. We do not know enough about why people use these worlds, how their interaction with AI influences their thinking, and how their behavior is affecting the environment in the outer world. We do not know much, in a systematic way, about how to build these worlds, nor what worlds to build. We are unprepared for the emergence of a peer-to-peer world that might expose us to risks that we would rather not face. We can see countless opportunities for research, education, and innovation, but only a small cadre of for-profit builders have mastered the craft of building worlds, and there are no training programs that teach it. In view of this general ignorance of synthetic world technology and all it might mean, perhaps the wisest policy of all at this point would be simply to support more research.

Futures sublime and frightening lie before us, on different paths; before making a choice, we should take a serious look at the game we have begun to play.

Those who have followed information technology for more than a decade—far longer than I have been—might look at the title and subject of this book and simply roll their eyes: Another book about the alleged wonders of virtual reality (VR). I've found that the mere mention of "virtual reality" to a scholarly audience will sometimes get a collective groan. The difficult task I have in this section is to explain to those jaded by the history of the official, scientific virtual reality research paradigm why the emergence of virtual reality in the form of online games is, actually, something you should neither roll your eyes at nor groan about. In the course of doing this I'll have to give my own brief assessment of traditional VR research, which will be hampered by the fact that I am not an expert on traditional VR, but rather came into it through a completely different avenue, that of games. Subject to the caveat of my limited expertise on this subject, I will try to give a fair idea of what the research program of VR was trying to do, and why that was a very different path from the path taken by online video games.

Three basic reasons things are different now:

1. The game version of VR focuses on communities, not individuals.
2. The game version of VR focuses on software, not hardware.
3. The game version of VR is being pulled by the commercial market, not pushed by research labs.

To see why these aspects of today's game-based VR are significant, let's go back to the earlier paradigm. Beginning in the 1950s and 1960s, visionaries such as Ivan Sutherland imagined that computers would be able to render sensations that would seem real to their recipients. But because those sensations would be computer generated, they would be not "really real" but only "virtually real." As computing technology advanced, these scientists began thinking of ways to use the computer to create an artificial sensory environment that would fool the user into believing that the environment actually *was* what it was only portraying. So, a subject might have heavy goggles mounted on her head, with images of the Martian landscape being beamed directly into her eyes; she might have her hand in a wired glove-and-arm apparatus that transmitted her motions into the motions of some kind of virtual arm; she might be sitting on a chair that would veer and pitch and roll in the same way as the virtual vehicle she was pirating. Decades of research and a great deal of money went into refining these sensory-delivery devices, and eventually the standardized vision of VR emerged: a single person in a special room, wearing a big helmet, her arms and legs wired up to something mobile. The direction of research was toward reducing the clumsiness of the apparatus, by beaming scenes onto walls or by having sophisticated cameras observe body movements. The applications that emerged often involved distance work, as when a scientist's hand in a VR glove could be used to manipulate virtual molecules, or to perform experiments thousands of miles away. This paradigm, in other words, succeeded in that it became possible to almost completely replace a subject's external sensory inputs with ones generated by the computer.

We could debate whether the switching of sensory inputs in this fashion is a great or only a modest success, but we would not get very far because, at about the time that these advances had been achieved, VR was "discovered" in such a way that a reasonable judgment of its progress soon became impossible. In the early 1990s, as the dot-com hype was just beginning, technologists, novelists, pundits, and visionaries seemed to converge on the idea of VR as a transcendent technology of the immediate future. As Howard Rheingold wrote in the first lines of *Virtual Reality* (1991), the book that perhaps helped popularize VR more than any other (and which I will therefore return to often in this essay): "At the University of North Carolina, I had a conversion experience akin to the experience that had bonded many of the personal computer pioneers of the 1960s and 1970s—a compelling vision of the future. But this time, the compelling vision had a tinge of awe" (Rheingold 1991, p. 14). Rheingold's experience was to have put his hand into a haptic device that allowed him to manipulate molecules. This led him to a take lengthy tour of laboratories the world over, where scientists were busy working on all kinds of sensory-input hardware. But what caused the awe was not these devices per se; it was a vision of a future in which people could "step into" their computers rather than look at them, and how very different everything would be when that happened.

As to when we might look for these things? Sooner than you might think, he says. On pages 61–62 of *Virtual Reality*, Rheingold puts VR at the end of a list of world-changing technologies and the amount of time it took for them to have their big effects: stone tools, 10,000 years; corn, centuries; steam engines, 100 years; telecommunications, 10 years; "computer revolutions," every 4–5 years; and then VR. He doesn't say exactly how long it would be before VR would arrive, but the implication was clear: not very long, perhaps a half-decade. Yikes! That kind of expectation-setting must have seemed a little overeager for scientists still working with bobble-head helmets and gloves that look like medieval torture devices with wires. And these expectations were certainly not met, leading to today's widespread apprehension about accepting anyone's claims that something interesting is happening in the area of virtual reality.

I don't think there's any dispute that the long-run vision of writers like Rheingold, Gibson (1984), Stephenson (1992), and others—we will eventually live in some kind of simulated spaces, at least to some degree—is basically accurate; what's interesting right now, however, is the way in which we are moving in that direction. Actually, for those jaded by the collapse of the "virtual reality fad" (Laurel 1993), what is perhaps most interesting is not even the way in which we are moving, it is the *fact* that we are moving. And we are. The long-run visions, the moments of awe, and the conversion experiences were all valid. But they were generated by an aspect of VR that, while it continues to be important for its technical advances, has not been at the forefront of the *social* advances of the technology. Society is adopting VR, quite quickly (it seems to me), but for reasons that the visionaries did not accord proper significance. They did sense the existence of some of the forces driving VR today, to their great credit, but they did not see that these would be the critical factors taking VR off the conceptual drawing board and into the practical world.

As for why the social forces now pulling VR into daily life were hard to see, I think the problems start with the entire concept of the "virtual." Rheingold (1991) does not define the virtual in his own words, but he seems to go along with the view expressed by visionary Theodore Nelson in 1980 (p. 177). To Nelson, "virtual" is explicitly contrasted with "real"; it is the ways things seem to be, as when we watch a film that seems to take place in Rome but actually takes place in Los Angeles. Los Angeles is "the real" while Rome is "the virtual." This contrast between virtual and real is found throughout Rheingold's book and many others. This treatment handles the computer-generated world as a fake, an illusion. And while many subsequent authors abandon this distinction, they have difficulty replacing it with anything sensible. Prominent theorist of the virtual Pierre Lévy insists (1998, p. 16) that the virtual is not the opposite of the real, but then defines "virtual" in a linguistic gumbo so dense as to be almost awe-inspiring by itself: "The virtual is a kind of problematical complex, the knot of tendencies or forces that accompanies a situation, event, object, or entity, and which invokes a process of resolution: actualization" (Lévy 1998, p. 24). He later explains that what he means is this: a seed is a kind of virtual tree, a tree that is not in existence yet but will be, and while seed and tree are different, both are real, and both are related in a special way. In this view, the virtual is a kind of real-becoming (*Echt-werden*?). Thus it seems to be real, but a different kind of real, or reality in a different state.

In any case, this still distinguishes the virtual from the actual; it still drives a notional wedge between the sensory inputs from the computer and from the world at large.

While there is already a vast literature on the word "virtual"; we don't need to access it further to recognize that the conceptual step of assuming that computer-generated content has less actuality, less genuineness than content from the "real world," was a mistake. Most of the recent thinking about the nature of the real (see chapter 2) would not take that step. For scientists of many decades ago, of course, it was an understandable decision, but also one that has not helped the research paradigm and was, in a deep way, arrogant. The arrogance stems from its assumption of objectivity about the state of the "real world." The scientist, you see, knows what is real, but the lady in the bobble-head helmet does not. Indeed, that kind of induced illusion was the stated *purpose* of early VR research. Rheingold describes a particularly striking moment in which a Japanese executive displays a quote from Ivan Sutherland, the father of VR: "The screen is a window through which one sees a virtual world. The challenge is to make that world look real, act real, sound real, feel real." In other words, let us build an environment so real that the subject will not know the difference between the real and the virtual. If ever there was a top-down, individual-denying scientific research paradigm, this would be it: put a second skin entirely around a person, load it with sensory inputs of your choice, and then insist to the subject that her sensations are all illusions. It's a tremendously disconcerting denial of the agency of the subject. "You are not seeing reality, my dear. *I* am in reality. I see what it is. But you do not." [Cue evil laughter.] In all seriousness, of course, the power imbalances in this situation were undoubtedly not consciously chosen by the VR researchers; rather, it probably seemed the natural way to start creating immersive effects. The best way to get someone to believe in a computer-generated world? Fool their minds; do it with hardware. But the power imbalances are there nonetheless, and should have made one wonder whether there was not another way to make immersion happen.

There were some who saw the long-run problems. Brenda Laurel (1993) (whose book in its later edition carefully declares on the cover: "Now Featuring Post-Virtual Reality!") can be credited with insisting (well before the post-VR period) that the critical thing was not sensory illusion but the definition of action inside cyberspace; once people got themselves into a crafted reality, what would they actually do? And Rheingold relates that tech maven Esther Dyson positioned herself as something of a curmudgeon in 1989, when she told a teary-eyed crowd of VR enthusiasts, all just coming down from a demo, that, frankly, she wanted to keep her keyboard, cyberspace or no. To which the crowd chuckled, of course.

Rheingold himself is to be credited for pointing out many times in his manuscript how important the user interface issues were with traditional laboratory VR. Today, Esther still has her keyboard, and Laurel's insistence that the right focus is on the *inside* of cyberspace rather than the outside appears to have been advice that would have been very helpful if followed; the inside of cyberspace is exactly where the game designers began shooting, right from the beginning. Meanwhile, judging from the VR textbooks of today (i.e., Sherman and Craig 2002; Burdea and Coiffet 2003), the lab paradigm still relies largely on control of sensory input from the outside. The overall strategy of sensory-deceptive immersion remains largely unchanged.

Even if there were no criticisms from the outside, the early VR scientists might have been induced to try different methods if they had only considered properly the significance of some fairly obvious things about their experiments. For example, the objective of the research was largely to fool someone into believing that the computer-generated experience was real. And then it was said that when a person put the helmet on, they had become "immersed." It seems highly unlikely, however, that a person with a VR helmet on was actually immersed in anything, at least anything other than a VR helmet. I am sure not many subjects ever lost consciousness of the fact that they were standing in lab, covered head to toe in wires and heavy gear, looking at stuff quite obviously being made by a computer. Or if they were in a VR room based on rear-screen projections and the like, I am fairly certain that none ever felt they really were in the Amazon or on Mars. Suspension of disbelief is at least a habit, and often a conscious choice, and therefore it helps things along if a person can be persuaded to enter a fantasy *willingly* (see chapter 2's discussion of the psychology of media effects). Otherwise, the sensory inputs from the computer are mere images, things to take note of or not, as the case may be, depending on interest; and if the researcher has blocked out everything else, then the computer's inputs, being imposed against the subject's will, are positively a nuisance. This none of scientists were apparently able to see, so the idea of building VR around willing participation was left to others.

Those others emerged from the video game industry, and, as I said above, many people in the early days of VR felt that video games were a natural application of the technology. But they did not imagine they would actually be the driving force, the research lab in which VR would finally become a widely available technology. Rheingold (1991) discusses video games in several places, but usually as a precursor to some serious talk about hardware. For example, he writes that researcher Warren Robinett was inspired by the games of his former company, Atari, and used their promise to motivate his work at a North Carolina research lab (pp. 23–29). But once there, did he build games? Not exactly. He built haptic devices, the glove-like molecule-massagers that first gave Rheingold his epiphany. But to get people used to them, he and his colleagues designed a virtual fishing game: "If you lift the fish too suddenly, you'll lose it," the user is warned. "If you don't resist, it will reel away from you." I'm not sure whether this virtual fishing game was much fun at all, but it certainly was *not* the point of the exercise. As soon as the subject had become a proficient angler, his reward was to massage molecules. Rheingold later writes, hilariously, that "you tend to crawl around on the floor when exploring virtual worlds" (p. 169). "Like sex," he says, "exploring virtual reality seems to require bodily positions that look amusing to others." By itself, this statement hints at the seductive power imbalances created between researchers and subjects in traditional VR research: if you put them in helmets, not only can you perhaps fool them about what's real, you can watch their bodies twist and turn as they seek to make sense of the zany world you've put them in. But in this case, Rheingold's contortions were actually part of a little game of treasure-hunt, and the reward was a virtual jewel that he found and could keep with him. The possibility that the fishing game might contribute more to his telepresence than the haptic arm-device was not all that obvious. Later, Heim (1998, pp. 6–7) writes that a "'real' virtual reality" experience is beyond the means of almost everyone, because we don't have access the supercomputers necessary to do it right, evidently not yet conscious of the idea that you might not need a supercomputer to get a "real" VR experience, or that its cognitive purchase might have more to do with the heart than the eyes. And because the VR industry remained largely devoted to sensory illusion, which is of course much harder to create than engaging activities, its social salience soon contracted quite severely.

Subsequent history shows, however, that the key applications were actually only a few years in coming. The network technology that implements a shared space among a large number of users goes back to 1978, when the text-based world MUD1 was built by undergraduate students Roy Trubshaw and Richard Bartle at the University of Essex. The technology behind today's immersive 3D gaming worlds was invented in 1991—the same year as Rheingold's *Virtual Reality*—by a then unknown programmer, John Carmack, who was working at a tiny game wholesaler in Louisiana at the time. Both innovations occurred hundreds of geographical miles (and light-years in social distance) from the virtual reality academic communities in San Francisco and at large research universities (Kushner 2003). Carmack's company, Id Software, also developed the first shared online version of 3D worlds. The first massively populated graphical world was *Ultima Online*, produced in 1997 by a small gaming company in Austin, Texas (King and Borland 2003). As described in chapter 2, *Ultima* was the start of something much larger, a now worldwide expansion of lite-VR gamespaces for thousands of simultaneous users. And thus, the practical virtual reality we observe today was created not by the funded researchers but by guys tinkering in basements, primarily just for the hell of it.

Where did the gamers get these ideas? People like John Carmack knew about the *Star Trek* holodeck, but they say (Kushner 2003) they had no intention really of trying to invent such a thing, or to create environments where people were fooled into thinking they were somewhere else. Rather, at each step, the game developers were just trying to make an environment that was a little more fun than the last. Head-mounted displays were out of the question. The issues were rather: How do you get things on a computer screen to scroll in all directions at the right rate, so that it seems as though the user is moving around? And how do you do that for two users at once, when one is in Shreveport and the other is in Austin? And: How do you make monsters and other characters act so that they keep the player involved in the whole scene? What kinds of rewards does a user have to get to find the place valuable enough to return to? What kinds of bodies do people want to see themselves in? What kinds of jobs, duties, and quests do they want? How do they want to communicate with others, and what kinds of groups would they feel most comfortable in? What kinds of powers do they want? And so on. These problems were being worked on in the 1980s by the folks who built MUDs (which Rheingold does write about in *Virtual Reality*, and also subsequently, with considerable brilliance). Indeed, MUDs generate perhaps the one historical connection between game-based VR and the traditional program: Rheingold reports (p. 309) that the Japanese Corporation Fujitsu seemed to see fun and entertainment as the real future of VR, and had established *Habitat* as a result. This is described as a 2D graphical MUD, and while we now know that *Habitat* was the first of many massively multiuser graphical chat spaces, we also know that the connection is not direct. *Habitat* was not really a game space. Its owners and makers (particularly F. Randy Farmer and Chip Morningstar) went on to further illustrious accomplishments in the realm of Internet technology, but not in the making of game spaces. And those who did develop game spaces did not rely on *Habitat*; rather, the first truly massive VR spaces, *Ultima Online* and *Lineage*, were built by people drawn from the MUD community and the developers of 2D and 3D role-playing games (King and Borland 2003). Thus it has to be said that it was gamers, and not research scientists, who first made the critical discoveries that led to mass immersion in VR spaces.

What were these discoveries, and why did they open the way for a practical, globally accessible, and incredibly (and truly) immersive VR? I would argue that the philosopher's stone that allows the base metals of computer technology to be refined into the precious gold of immersive experience is just one single thing: *game*. A game perspective focuses all thought and research on the user's subjectivity and well-being. It insists on immediate usability. It thrives on widened access and multiple users. And it generates a willing suspension of disbelief, without which genuine immersion cannot happen. The VR-enabling discoveries within games were not, as we see in chapters 2 and 3, about vast improvements in sensory devices and the user interface, which remained and remains point-and-click-and-type. Rather, they were about little improvements in the gaming experience: faster graphics, faster networks, more interesting stories, more sensible AI, and better artwork (where "better" does not mean "more photo-realistic"). Better games meant better VR, and for more people.

Games are now one of the frontiers of VR research, and while they are taking the technology along a very different path from the one originally envisioned, the images we have had of the long-run future are still quite valid. If anything, they read now as only a bit vague. To return to Rheingold's *Virtual Reality* (1991): its list of future consequences (chapter 16) includes, in order, simulated tactile sex, the use of VR as a kind of ecstasy-producing drug, remote-controlled weapons, remote-controlled factories, financial trading, and finally, just plain fun. Or, rather, this last section is devoted to the importance of play, something we discuss a great deal here as well. But for Rheingold, the real importance of play is not fun per se, but rather the way that VR and fun could be used for education. Similarly, for Gibson (1984) and Vernor Vinge (1981), the future VR space seems primarily to be visualized data structure, and for Stephenson, it is something of a transport network. It could also be an entrapment, like a drug, as I discuss in chapter 11. All of these visions are perfectly valid possibilities, and we may well see VR in this way eventually. But as of now, VR has become, for all practical purposes, a crude game world in which people play out roles and have fun with one another.

And as a game, we can see how very different VR is from the original research paradigm. First, games have many players, and some of the VR games being played today have tens of thousands of players in the same world at the same time. The role of *community* in creating the sense of reality so keenly pursued by Sutherland and his followers was also apparently never considered by them. (And indeed, community does not generate the illusion of a reality, it confirms a reality that is actually there, as I discuss in chapter 2.) Second, games are based on software, not hardware; they conform perfectly to Laurel's warning (1993) that the essence of VR is not what you see, but what you do. And third, games are taking this form because the market is crying out for it. People desire this form of immersion. For all these reasons, the game-based VR paradigm looks like it will continue to grow. Indeed, as it grows, it adopts those aspects of the traditional paradigm that are market ready: the Eye Toy, the force-feedback controller, the dance pad. Games are apparently the leading application for many of these technologies.

So, no: VR is not dead. It lives, in a place where it was anticipated to thrive some day, but not as the leading near-term example of the technology at work. And it will be seen that, as I describe in this book, everything that early VR theorists imagined might happen when VR became globally accessible is starting to happen. True, not all is happening exactly as they said it would, but the changes are just as significant. Basically, all were agreed a decade ago that when VR emerged as a global technology it would shake up a great many things, and that prediction seems right on the mark. While the long-term consequences may be what they may be, the near-term consequences, especially in terms of the need to re-energize debates on this subject, are bristling with immediate significance. For this reason alone, even the most jaded post-VR thinker ought to stop for a moment and ponder what is happening within games.

Considering this history, it seems apparent that games do deserve study as a form of VR today—but not just any kind of study. In the aftermath of the collapse of the "VR fad" (Laurel 1993), and the dot-com bust, no one should be optimistic when attempting to write a book about an emerging technology. There seems to be an unfortunate pattern, in fact. When industries and pundits are enthused about a new technology, academics tend to write glowing studies of it. And when the bubble bursts, suddenly the academics write of "cyberbole" and careless predicting. I'm well aware that I'm guilty of that myself in this very section, having criticized the early VR researchers for not seeing that games were the thing (or to paraphrase a political slogan of that era: *it's the software, stupid*). But how much should we really make of the fact that, as I write this, the market for that corner of VR that so interests me, the MMORPGs, seems to be emerging from a funk? Before the breakout success of Blizzard's *World of Warcraft* in late 2004, many recent games had been doing poorly at release, for reasons I discuss in chapters 5 and 7. Nonetheless, I am writing a book that urges the reader to think twice about this technology, and here's why: whatever the current state of the market, all the evidence suggests that this the phenomenon has some very long legs, and that calls for some reflection. These kinds of games, and thus VR programs more generally, have not by far had their last effect on human affairs.

That having been said, given the cynicism with which VR research may be received, it makes little sense to annoy the reader with lengthy discourses about the long-long-long-run future. That ground has been covered. And it certainly would not do to briefly describe the current state of the technology and then make vast claims about ultimate impacts. It is rather fairly important to be measured and conservative, to focus on what we now have and on things that are convincingly just around the corner. And this is what bears most interest, I think; the way games have evolved, and their characteristics, are an unknown to many people, and not a few may be completely surprised to learn that there is *any* VR implication of online video games today. Therefore the book does not describe results from VR laboratories and basic research, but rather reports on games, game players, and their behavioral patterns. I think even this basic, concrete information generates quite a few heady yet fairly obvious implications for the future, and I won't hesitate to write these down as they occur. As for longer-range thinking, for the most part I reserve that for chapter 13.

Finally, while being conservative in writing is one decision imposed by the nearness of this book to early VR writing, another is the importance of avoiding words like "virtual." That word points a misleading finger from the game worlds back to the earlier VR paradigm. As I have said, no such connection is warranted. And therefore where I use "virtual" in this book, I just mean "rendered by a computer": a virtual world is a world rendered by a computer.[1] And after discussing the idea of a "practical virtual reality" in the first chapter or so, I drop the usage of VR entirely and focus instead on more precise terms like *synthetic*, meaning crafted by humans, and *internal/external*, to refer to things inside and outside a synthetic environment. This usage enforces what I believe to be true, that there is no such thing as virtual reality and never was. There are only inherited and synthetic realities, and they are only differentiated by how they appear before our senses, either as a largely unmodified reality that has been in existence for a while (think "nature" or "Earth"), or as a fairly recent creation from the whole cloth (think "silicon" or "graphics" or "3D"). Distinguished in this manner, what was once called "virtual reality" can be seen for what it is: the result of efforts to craft an all-encompassing synthetic environment. Like all content, it was more likely to be absorbed if designed in a way that appealed to others, that invited them in and tried to provide something that they would like to have; otherwise, it was quite unlikely to be absorbed at all, and that indeed is what seems to have happened.

NOTES

Introduction

1. In the TV program *Star Trek: The Next Generation*, the Holodeck was a room on the *Enterprise* spaceship that could be programmed to create environments and people that were completely indistinguishable from real places and people.

2. Cyberspace in general has also been described in terms of "normal people in an unusual place." A literature, too large to be usefully cited here, has investigated all kinds of online activity for implications and meanings. An axiom maintained throughout this book, however, is that synthetic worlds represent something truly different from chat, instant messaging, webcams, blogs, and the like. None of those media invoke the Earth and the Earth body as metaphors for interaction. Indeed, much of the extant literature focuses on the disembodiment of users who are online in a nonphysical space. With synthetic worlds, however, we do not have disembodiment; rather, we have bodies of choice. We do not have a space devoid of all Earthly constraints; rather, we have a space with Earth-like constraints of choice. The difference is significant enough that we need to look at synthetic worlds as unique, new objects, not just extensions of pre-existing online activity. The 1990s literature about immersive online activity was, in the end, concerned with the behavior of perhaps several tens of thousands of people, most of them college students and information industry workers. Today's synthetic worlds are visited by millions and millions of people from all walks of life. There is every possibility that their behavior and experiences are qualitatively different from that which has gone before.

3. To extend the metaphor further, one could invoke the orchestra—the Greek chorus—which, intervening as it does between stage and audience, is somewhat analogous to the machines with which online game players must interact to enter the synthetic world.

4. Jacques: "All the world's a stage, / And all the men and women merely players" (act 2, scene 7).

5. Ongoing data are reported on my homepage at http://mypage.iu.edu/~castro/ and analyzed at the blog to which I contribute, Terra Nova (http://terranova.blogs.com/).

6. There are a number of general histories of the video game and its effect on culture in the late twentieth century: Rushkoff 1996; Herz 1997; Poole 2000; Kent 2001.

7. The famous Moore's Law, actually a conjecture pronounced in 1965 by Gordon Moore, holds that raw computing power will double every year or three. Events have proven the conjecture largely true so far, and most experts in computing believe it will continue to hold for some time. Things that double within fixed time periods grow exponentially, meaning that their level changes dramatically in the course of a few human generations. A quantity of 1,000 units doubling annually becomes 1 billion units in just 20 years. It is revealing that much of the debate among technology experts is not about the likelihood of significant computational advance, but about its implications. The authors already cited believe that AI will attain consciousness, while John Searle (1997) argues that it will not. Similarly, techno-futurists say that increases in computation will radically change society, but Brown and Duguid (2000) wisely point out that there is as much work to be done in applying computation fruitfully to our

lives as there is in building computation resources in the first place. Synthetic worlds represent exactly this kind of application: if raw computing power is truly to affect our daily lives, one path it might take is by enhancing the attractiveness and quotidian utility of massively multiplayer video games.

8. Scholars in every field I've spoken to report resistance among their colleagues to research involving games. Even computer scientists have said that their research on gaming networks tends to be looked down on. Of course, only time will tell if this is a frivolous research topic or not. Perhaps, 20 years from now, video games will have become like chess: a niche hobby that doesn't occupy much cultural attention at all. Perhaps. But already by late 2003 I was able to place a paper about synthetic worlds in one of the most prestigious international journals in economics, *Kyklos*.

Chapter 1

1. There is a very large literature on identity choice online. See Turkle 1995; Murray 1997; Cassell and Jenkins 1998; Schroeder 2002; and Taylor 2002.

2. The term *avatar* was used by the designers of one of the earliest graphical chat worlds, Lucasfilm's *Habitat* (Morningstar and Farmer 1990). It's also Neal Stephenson's term for the characters one uses to navigate the metaverse. Game designers tend to favor *character*, a usage that dates to *Dungeons and Dragons* in the early 1970s.

3. It should be fairly apparent from this that absolutely no one finds themselves in a synthetic world by accident. The administrative hurdles required to go there are surprisingly steep. It follows that everyone there has pursued the place with quite a bit of forethought.

4. Actually the databases have been changing continuously, keeping track of Sabert's location, condition, and possessions.

5. Note that, being new, you haven't yet adopted the writing conventions of this new culture. You capitalize and punctuate while Ethelbert's owner does not. In practice, there seems to be a cultural divide, with significant conflict between chat users online in terms of their languages. Some always write carefully; others never do; and they often spat.

6. More specific arguments on the value of game objects can be found in Castronova 2001 and Castronova 2003a.

7. Julian Dibbell (1999) has persuasively alerted the world to the reality of social and especially romantic sexual relationships online.

8. A Moot Court held at the Black Hat conference of computer security experts tried a case of game item theft on July 30, 2003, before Judge Philip M. Pro of the US Circuit Court. The prosecuting attorney was Richard Salgado of the computer crimes division of the US Department of Justice, while the defense was represented by Jennifer Granick of Stanford University Law School. Jury and audience, when polled, agreed that the value of the game item in question (a magic staff) exceeded $5,000, the statutory limit for such a case to be actionable. The valuation was based on evidence from online auction sites that such staffs do sell for amounts in excess of $5,000 on a regular basis. Theft of game items is already, at this writing, a standard criminal category for police and courts in South Korea. See chapter 6.

9. Note that these arguments generally do not carry through for just any Internet phenomenon. There is no GDP for online checkers, even though there are many people playing it for many hours. There are no objects or bodies, and there is no sense of ownership. Similarly, chat rooms and video-conferences have no physicality to them, so there are no objects over which to have political or cultural struggles. A physical space is necessary, and it must be inhabited by some kind of body, in order

for human social affairs to occur. A mere chat room does not work; it must be transformed into a physical domain, as first happened with text-based MUDs, before conversation can become trade, ritual, and power.

Chapter 2

1. Data as of June 13, 2003, at http://www.idsa.com/pressroom.html.

2. See Bartle 2003 and Lastowka and Hunter 2004 for excellent reviews of the history of text-based systems and their evolution into synthetic worlds.

3. Thanks to game industry consultant and design veteran Greg Costikyan for this observation.

4. For earlier histories of video games, see Herz 1997; Poole 2000; Kent 2001; and Wolf 2002.

5. Data as of September 15, 2004, at http://www.idsa.com/pressroom.html.

6. A list of new institutes and endeavors (doubtless incomplete) would include, in Europe, the Center for Computer Game Research at IT University Copenhagen and the Game Research Lab at University of Tampere in Finland. In the United States, there is the Meta-Game group at UC Irvine, the Serious Games Project at the Woodrow Wilson Center for International Scholars, and the Games-to-Teach project at MIT. There are also new journals (*Game Studies, Journal of Game Development*), new academic organizations (Digital Games Research Association, Ludology.org), and new programs of study (at places like Indiana University, Southern Methodist University, the University of Southern California, Georgia Tech, and Carnegie Mellon).

7. It may seem odd to outsiders that the list of game-related disciplines I have given does not include Game Theory. In the first place, it's not clear that game theory—founded by mathematicians (von Neumann and Morgenstern 1944/1980; Nash 1950)—ever had an aspiration to study actual human game-playing. Secondly, if it did, those aspirations have gone largely unrealized. Game theory conceives play as a rational exercise: the players have goals and must derive the logical route to their achievement given every other player's logical efforts. Game theorists ultimately conceived of this exercise in fairly purist mathematical terms (although it did not have to be this way; see Schelling 1960/1980), meaning, game theory today involves the use of theorem/proof reasoning to establish the properties of abstract choice situations. At times, the insights derived from this method are brilliant. Unfortunately, they are never about games anyone actually plays. Even chess, a game with simple rules, is beyond the ken of game theory. The core problem is that any fun game involves so many choices that the logical answer is not apparent to anybody (Simon and Schaeffer 1992). Faced with this problem, game theory's strategy has been to find simple games that can be seen as analogs to important real-world situations, and then analyze with complete precision the mathematics underlying logical choice in those simple games. That may or may not have been a smart move, but the end effect of it is that you are not likely to find any of the games studied by game theory on store shelves ("The Prisoner's Dilemma! Now With Repeated N-Player Action!").

8. While I believe that my figures are less biased than those of Yee or the Griffiths et al. study described below, I know they are not unbiased; we must await a truly representative national or international census of synthetic world users to obtain unbiased estimates of their characteristics.

9. First-person shooter games are often called "twitch" games because success depends on the timing of movements and shots at the level of milliseconds. Because of network delay (discussed further in chapter 4), no virtual world can ever react that quickly to a player's moves. There's no twitch factor in gameplay.

10. Yes: Griffiths 1996; Grossman and DeGaetano 1999; Anderson and Bushman 2001. No: Heins 2003; Gerard Jones 2002. Griffiths et al. (2003) conjecture (p. 87) that the "no" literature is likely to be enhanced once there are more studies of synthetic worlds.

11. Personally, I find the arguments in the *amicus* reported in Heins 2003 to be persuasive. I suppose I am biased, because I have played games with violent content since I was a little boy, and I feel that they were good for me rather than bad. This bears no scientific weight, of course. Still, my personal experience as a player is that these games do not change the underlying propensity to commit violent acts against others; rather, they are very helpful for emotional development. When I think about how much more empty and lonely my life would have been without games, especially now that it is so easy to find others to play with online, it makes me wonder why anyone would try to limit kids' access to them. A high-level US Court of Appeals, quoted in the *amicus*, held that an effort to remove violent content from the artistic environment of children "would not only be quixotic, but deforming." On the whole, I agree.

12. It is perhaps not surprising that many of the elements of games such as *EverQuest* seemed to have been designed with addiction of the player as an explicit objective. That stands to reason; all private companies would like to build features into their products that keep the customer coming back.

13. "DFC Intelligence Forecasts Strong Growth for Video Game Industry," April 17, 2003 (accessed June 19, 2003, at http://www.dfcint.com/news/prapril172003.html).

14. Information obtained June 12, 2003, from Gamasutra (http://www.gamasutra.com/).

15. I owe the insight into play as a tool of evolutionary success to Francis Steen of UCLA, who proposed these ideas as part of unpublished, ongoing work with Stephanie Owens of UC Santa Barbara. See Owens and Steen 2000.

16. For more on these ideas, see Caillois 1961/2001 and Sutton-Smith 1998.

17. Huizinga suggests a moral criterion: If an act involves Right and Wrong, it cannot be play.

18. These ideas begin to surrender the equation of "game" with "trivial," which appears to be a modernist construct in any case. Perhaps we should use the world "game" to refer to certain interaction structures, be they serious or not. I owe these thoughts to an unpublished manuscript by Thomas Malaby of the University of Wisconsin–Milwaukee.

19. "Online Worlds Roundtable #7, Part 1," August 5, 2003, http://rpgvault.ign.com/articles/432/432071p1.html.

20. See Greg Kasavin, "Real Life: The Full Review," at http://www.gamespot.com/gamespot/features/all/gamespotting/071103minusworld/1.html.

21. It's worth noting that Tolkien's project, as exhibited in all of his writings and not just those for which he has become famous, is so vast, so unbounded in its aspirations, that we cannot even imagine its long-run consequences. In the short run, today, all we see is the fact that almost every synthetic world that's been created has been modeled on Middle-Earth. It's a remarkable fact, but as I said, one whose long-run meaning is very hard to imagine but well worth considering.

Chapter 3

1. Readers looking for specifics on the technologies of world design are encouraged to consult Bartle 2003, chapter 2; Mulligan and Patrovsky 2003, chapter 7; and Raph Koster's website, http://www.legendmud.org/raph/ (Koster n.d.).

2. A mantra among synthetic world programmers is "The client is the enemy." If the server were to trust the client, hackers could change their local program so that it sends signals such as "my avatar is running at 10,000 mph." The server is the referee, making sure that all the rules get followed.

3. We owe the basic transmission/rendering technology to the same people who invented the Internet: The Defense Advanced Research Projects Agency (DARPA) of the US Department of Defense. It is the brainchild of Colonel Jack Thorpe, whose Simnet tank battle game (c. 1976) was its first application.

4. Many games, such as *Neverwinter Nights* (BioWare), allow users to build and host their own worlds. There are also a few new firms that help facilitate the transfer of assets between worlds, such as the Gaming Open Market and PlayVault.

5. As a game tester I have seen, with my own two eyes, a persistent world version of the great globe itself. Another game in development at this writing claims to have no problem hosting millions of players in the same territory; no shards.

6. Users may want the world to be rendered with more realism in regards to other senses—smell, taste, and touch. Long-run visions of VR usually assume these senses will be satisfied with as much fidelity as sight and hearing. There is even some early evidence that direct neural implants may not be too far away. However, current and foreseeable technology is just not up to the challenge of replicating smell, taste, and touch. On the other hand, current practice suggests that it's not necessary at least as far as a user's emotional immersion is concerned.

7. In my first draft of this book, written just a few months ago, this sentence read that voice was "on the way." It is already here; in multiplayer combat games like *Counter-Strike*, players yell at each other constantly.

8. The development house Blizzard Entertainment is famous for producing well-rendered imagery rather than realistic imagery. Their synthetic world, *World of Warcraft*, is more vibrant and cartoonish than *EverQuest*, but its imagery is very powerful and enticing. Blizzard is also deepening immersion not through graphical realism but through narrative realism, in the form of interesting and extraordinarily numerous quests. *World of Warcraft*, at this writing, appears well on the way to becoming the most successful US synthetic world ever.

9. I owe this observation to gaming consultant Greg Costikyan.

10. There are some interesting work-arounds in place. In *Toontown*, Disney's synthetic world for children, strangers can only speak to one another using menus, and direct person-to-person communications can only be established by exchanging codes face to face in the real world. These restrictions have predictably led to some ingenious countermeasures against the language restrictions, the kind of anti-system innovation by ordinary people that became a hallmark of the early Internet. In *Toontown*, people have figured out how to cobble together canned messages in ways that signal some other meaning. Or they will lay out loaves of bread on the ground in LED-numeric style to tell others their comm-unlocking code.

11. It seems as though a similar thing is happening with AI as with virtual reality. In the appendix, I observe that game developers, who had nothing to do with the scientific program of VR research, had independently developed the form of VR that apparently will now sweep the world. Similarly, the gamers who code AI in synthetic worlds—and who before Laird had little to do with the formal scientific program of AI research—are perhaps creating the ancestors of the robots that will matter most to us.

12. Raph Koster, a designer with a great deal of experience, has said that 60–70 percent of available AI resources typically have to be devoted to nothing more than movement.

Chapter 4

1. One story, perhaps apocryphal, says that on the day *EverQuest* launched, it immediately occupied 100 percent of the bandwidth going into and out of San Diego, where the main servers are located.

2. This is only a general overview of a very deep structure of knowledge and praxis. Readers are urged to consult Koster n.d., Bartle 2003, Mulligan and Patrovsky 2003 for details on synthetic world design.

3. Critics of video-gaming in popular culture have yet to grasp the immense benefit that this particular feature may deliver to society. Like manna from heaven, finally we have received a media format that teaches people how to get along with one another.

4. This point represents something of a challenge to those who build AI for games: it is not all about combat. Future games will need AI that can both mentor and respect the player, not just kill him.

Chapter 5

1. It is interesting to note that one of the earliest successful 3D worlds was produced in 2001 by a small Norwegian company, Funcom. *Anarchy Online* was also innovative as the first space/science fiction world in the 3D arena. For some reason, Funcom hasn't grown or been acquired, nor does it seem that its personnel have been raided as part of the foundation for a European synthetic world industry, as happened with *Ultima Online* in the United States. Denmark's text-based DIKU-MUD was successful and seemed similar in gameplay to a number of successful 3D worlds, such as *EverQuest*. Yet to my knowledge none of the folks involved in DIKU-MUD are now making European worlds.

2. Ludlow subsequently moved his operation to the much more politically savvy environs of *Second Life*.

3. As a sign of the state of the industry's personnel and experience, one of the most respected designers today, Mythic's Scott Jennings, worked his way in primarily by posting detailed and accurate critiques of *UO* as a player, writing under the tag of his avatar, Lum the Mad. The old Lum website was the start of the widespread phenomenon today in which the design team has an external opposition, a group of savvy players who use fan sites to post vicious yet reasoned critiques of every decision. More on this in chapter 9.

4. Again, as a player I would rather not have any advertising at all, just as I would rather not have any taxes. Or any fees at all for that matter. As an economist, however, I recognize that all good things must be paid for somehow, and advertising, along with fees and taxation, is just another way of getting it done.

5. According to the recent Pew study of US college students and the Internet, the vast majority of American college students play video games on occasion (Pew 2003). More than that: *All* of them know what video games are and how they operate.

6. I suddenly realize that by this reference I've placed myself among the ancient. For those not yet suffering from back pain and erectile dysfunction (directly or indirectly): Gomer Pyle was an oaf in a 1960s TV show.

7. As I write this I wonder, how many readers put down the book after a few chapters to try out a synthetic world, and I wonder what their experiences were. I tend to assume that it was more difficult to figure out than most cutting-edge technologies. Learning a virtual world for the first time—really getting into it—seems to me harder than setting up a home wireless network, for example.

8. The most common outcome is for worlds to be cancelled before release. And of the handful, fewer than five, that have permanently closed after operating for a while, two seemed to fall victim to a strategic decision by EA to back out of the space almost entirely.

9. Good games spend as much money on operations as on development. But a game that is struggling and has attracted only a niche market can cut back dramatically on operations costs by reducing the customer service staff and closing down any new content streams. You just turn on the servers and let the few people interested in the game come and play it. At that level of operations costs, you don't need many subscribers to keep things going. Current games seem able to get by with no more than 10,000 or 20,000.

10. This is a large literature. The best general reference for this material is Cornes and Sandler 1996. Classics include Tiebout 1956 and Buchanan 1965.

11. The same reasoning explains freeway congestion. The only answer is to make access to freeways cost something.

12. As noted in chapter 2, some firms are entering the space created by these switching costs, offering to transfer gold pieces from one world to another.

Chapter 6

1. I thank F. Randall Farmer for suggesting this usage once at a meeting we both attended. I've been helped by it countless times since.

2. Recall that while I do continue to use the term "virtual world," it is primarily as a specific and technical reference to that territory which is inside computers and made by human hands. It is the area inside the membrane.

3. This figure is only a fraction of the total trade in virtual items. It does not include trading in Asia, for example, which seems to be at least $70 million annually. Based on a rough guess about the ratio of in-world to out-of-world trade, the global trade in in-world items might be as much as $2 billion annually.

4. As the book goes to press, Blizzard Entertainment seems to be making a serious and successful effort to stop trading of items from *World of Warcraft*. On the other hand, Sony has just announced a new player-to-player real-money market for its games.

5. Conducting trade in other currencies is a fairly common outcome when the value of the local currency is open to question, as it must be for a synthetic world. There's even a term for this in economics: "dollarization." After the collapse of the Soviet Union in 1991, for example, uncertainty about the value of newly invented currencies in many of the leftover economies drove almost all trade into dollar-based transactions (Curtis, Gardner, and Waller 2004).

6. One question I get frequently is, "Why do the gold pieces have value? They are just fantasy money pieces whose value is positive only because some people hang onto them. But if everyone sold theirs or gave them away, the value would be zero." The answer: If everyone sold their GM stock or their holdings of US dollars, or gave them away, those things would be worthless too. The point is, people don't give them away. They assume they have value, so they hang on to them. It's the same process that makes the dollar valuable even though it's only a worthless scrap of paper. Yes: there's no difference between the gold piece, Doomba's Hammer of Elf Flattening, a BMW, and the dimes in your pocket: they get their value from the market. And that's how markets work: The current price is set by current buyers and sellers and it establishes the value of all items, sold or not.

7. Note that I am not saying that no world can be more fun than any other. There is no market that equilibrates fun across worlds. If we have two worlds in which the effective monetary wage has been driven down to trivial levels, and in which there are no congestion effects, the world populations will balance themselves according to how many people think that World A is more fun than World B. Rather, I am saying that congestion effects and money wage effects, if present, will affect the population

distribution and, if they are important relative to the fun factor, they may put a hard cap on how much total real-money compensation can be provided. If a designer wants fun to be the reigning factor in attracting population, then tradable loot should be a minimal part of gameplay and the world had better be able to swallow new populations without affecting anyone's enjoyment. Of course, reducing tradable loot and social interdependence makes the game less of a social game and more of a single-player game. The way to think about the fun factor is that it is like a brand name: it will allow you to exploit a certain niche, but it will not allow you to take over the entire market; labor flows and congestion will prevent that.

8. Here's a numerical example. Suppose the typical players of your game are folks who can earn $20 an hour at work that they neither love nor hate. Along comes the game, where people can have fun to the tune of $12 an hour and also earn gold pieces worth $15 an hour. Spending time in the game is now more lucrative, in terms of money and happiness ($27), than working for pay (only $20). Lots of people in the same demographic group as your game players would decide to start playing the game. As they come in, they drive down the amount of US dollars a person can earn in an hour inside the membrane. This happens because of congestion, difficulties finding groups, an increase in the price of gold-farming gear, a decline in the exchange rate between gold pieces and dollars, and so on. As long as the total game compensation exceeds $20, new people will enter; as long as new people enter, game compensation will fall. This logic of competitive labor markets dictates that the entry will stop only when game compensation and Earth compensation are the same, $20. This means that some aspect of game compensation is going to have to lose $7 in value; fun level will fall to $5, or the game wages will sink to $8, or some combination of the two will happen. The only situation in which this dynamic is defused is when the monetary element, the wages, have been driven to zero. At that point, all entry and exit is dictated by the fun factor, and real-world wages play no role.

9. Readers interested in pursuing questions raised by the commodification of virtual property are advised to read the papers presented at the conferences State of Play I and II, held at New York Law School in 2003 and 2004 (http://www.nyls.edu/). Bartle (2004) also offers an excellent analysis of effects.

10. Note that this train of logic assumes that all roles in a synthetic world have at least something to contribute to players in other roles. Most worlds are designed this way. But if for some reason there were a role that was needed by no one, and thus isolated from the system, it would not be affected by these competitive pressures.

11. This argument is developed in more detail in Castronova 2003b.

12. The declaration may be found at http://www.legendmud.org/raph/gaming/playerrights.html.

13. Prosecuting attorney was Richard Salgado of the US Department of Justice; counsel for the defense was Jennifer Granick of Stanford Law School. Expert witness for the prosecution, who testified that virtual goods do have value in economic theory, was some obscure economist from California.

14. See "Virtual Property Redux," December 19, 2003 (http://terranova.blogs.com/terra_nova/2003/12/virtual_propert.html).

Chapter 7

1. *EVE Online*'s appeal seems to be somewhat limited since, for the most part, gameplay is about mining harmless asteroids and then speculating on the market for ores. It is known as a "spreadsheet MMORPG." Not much orc-whacking going on.

2. See "Virtual Property Redux," December 19, 2003 (http://terranova.blogs.com/terra_nova/2003/12/virtual_propert.html).

3. See "Only a Game," April 22, 2004 (http://terranova.blogs.com/terra_nova/2004/04/this_was_only_a.html).

4. Very recently, I get the sense that the developer community is going to move more aggressively in terms of designing worlds that are not so easy to exploit for external commercial gain. It may well be that design praxis will, within a decade, have eliminated all of these arbitrage opportunities or brought them under their own control.

5. Yes, it was published by a prestigious press. The author and press will remain unnamed.

Chapter 8

1. It seems likely that this would tend to reduce discrimination by sexual preference, a good thing in my opinion.

2. Heim (1998, p. 52ff) refers to "Alternate World Syndrome" as a sense of disorientation that comes from spending too much time in a synthetic environment and then returning abruptly to the ordinary environment of Earth. As much as the synthetic space had come to feel real, the Earth now appears somewhat unreal. I'm arguing that both are real, but that their cultural differences are so great as to impose a truly mind-altering culture shock, one that, I agree, is powerful enough to merit a medical term like "syndrome." The interesting thing to question, though, is whether we should insist that this sensation is pathological, as "syndrome" does. Is culture shock a disease that needs to be cured, or a moment of heightened, albeit disorienting, awareness?

3. Under certain circumstances, markets achieve a condition known as pareto efficiency, in which it is not possible to make one person better off without harming another person. This condition is not generally identical to the maximization of the sum of happiness of everyone. Indeed, there isn't any necessary connection between economists' notion of well-being (utility) and an individual's happiness; see Castronova 2004.

4. See http://www.legendmud.org/raph/gaming/index.html. Also of interest here are the online papers of Zachary Booth Simpson (1999, http://www.mine-control.com/zack/), and John Beezer (1996, http://adhostnt.adhost.com/beezer/resume/virtec.doc).

5. Simpson 1999.

6. The point I am making is not that the designers are wrong, it is that they have seen something wrong and then abandoned efforts to fix it, choosing, instead, to code the problem out of existence by coding out the behavior. If the behavior is fun, let's have it back in the game; by hewing to more general economic principles, maybe the behavior can be restored without the bad consequences. For example, most worlds are bedeviled by the problem of storage: players want unlimited storage space to hoard all kinds of items, but the databases can only hold so much. Designers wrestle with issues of how many storage slots to allow per character and how many characters per account, as if this has to be a hard-coded solution. On Earth, however, unlimited storage is available only at a price. Implement storage prices in synthetic economies and you will be able to find the right balance between player needs and database costs.

7. Having permanent goods also opens the door to external markets. When items decay, they also don't last long and so there's no point in buying them on eBay. When items retain their qualities forever, the eBay buyer knows she is getting a good that will last.

8. It is worth reviewing here the logic discussed in chapter 6, explaining how players' hourly wages will be held in check by labor market conditions on Earth. To review: If you design a world in which an ordinary person can earn 100 gold pieces an hour, and the typical wage rate among your players is $5 an hour, the market exchange rate will dictate that 20 gold pieces are equivalent to $1. If you raise drop rates so that earnings are 200 gold pieces an hour, you have just offered employment at a wage greater than $5 per hour to anyone who wants to take it. One of two things will happen. Either new players will enter the world and cause congestion effects that lower the effective hourly earning back to 100 gold pieces, or there will be no congestion effects and all these new workers will now earn 200 gold pieces an hour. In the latter case, however, there is an influx of gold, and therefore the price of gold falls from 20 pieces to the dollar to 40 pieces to the dollar. In either case, the net effect is that the actual wage you can offer in your game is only $5 an hour. It is not under your control. What you *can* control is how fun it is to earn $5. In effect, your synthetic world can offer this money in a form that is far more entertaining than pumping gas.

9. For example, if the price of Azure Boots falls to 2 gold pieces on the player market, someone will buy them up and take them to the far-away boot export merchant, who usually pays 100 gold pieces for them. In buying up the boots, players will raise the market price to something near 100 gold pieces, where it belongs.

10. The export/import AI concept also allows a number of ways of managing the economy. If players consistently export some good, it means that supply exceeds demand at the current price. One can accept that situation as is (allow the good to flow out and cash to flow in), or lower the price until supply and demand become equal, or reduce supply (i.e., increase mob risk or lower the drop rate) or increase demand (give the item better stats). If players consistently import a good, the responses include: do nothing (allow cash to flow out and the good to flow in), raise the price, increase supply (increase drop rates), or decrease demand (nerf it). In effect, the export/import system gives designers a very handy stream of info about the players' attitude toward items: export items are things that the players think are worth less than the designers think they should be, and import items are ones that the players think are worth more than the designers do. Note two further things: A. The amount of the good flowing into the world will always be determined by the intersection of the demand curve and the global price. B. There are ripple effects of any price change: raise the price of a good and you increase the demand for its substitutes while decreasing the demand for its complements.

11. Julian Dibbell has pointed out that this is basically a gold standard operating as it did in the old days. The quantity of money is determined by how hard it is to mine gold. When gold is scarce, prices fall and it makes sense to go dig up gold. When gold is abundant, prices rise and the effort to mine gold is not so worth doing.

12. In this argument I assume that players enter the world, work their way to some maximum power level, and then stay. In particular circumstances, such as a dying world, there may be different kinds of player entry/exit dynamics. The typical mature synthetic world, in my experience, has many players at the top end and a smaller number working their way upward.

13. I owe this observation to Bartle's discussions (2003) of the Hero's Journey as a metaphor for synthetic world design.

Chapter 9

1. It almost goes without saying that synthetic worlds are an interesting and existing place to examine Lessig's arguments (1999) about the relationship between code and law. I won't be doing that here, but it would be a fascinating research topic.

2. Readers involved in the building of new worlds are urged to refer to sources such as Bartle 2003 (pp. 576–83) and Mulligan and Patrovsky 2003 (pp. 215–72) for advice regarding community management issues.

3. Note that this is not permanent death of the avatar; it takes the avatar to its death penalty state, usually weaker and far away.

4. In a reputation (or karma) system, if you kill people you get bad karma and become a valid target for others. It is typically exploited by teams of players who act in cahoots to generate for themselves whatever karma rating they desire. In imposing rules, developers have to toss out any rule that can be broken by individuals, but also every rule that can be broken by dedicated teams. This eliminates many rules.

5. I mentioned in chapter 6 the case of Professor Peter Ludlow, whose newspaper in *The Sims Online* was banned. The reason it was banned was because it reported frankly on the frequency with which new players were cheated out of all of their wealth by cunning experienced players. The abuse of community norms continued to the point that underage kids (or someone posing as them) were soliciting johns and operating open cyber-brothels. And this is in a world with no combat at all.

6. The election of the first Demi-Pharaoh was won by the player who ran on a campaign of *not* using her power of ban. I do not know if she ever used it.

7. Indeed, there is not a great deal of player governance in worlds that Koster has designed recently, such as *Star Wars Galaxies* (LucasArts). A designer is forced to choose between aesthetic and commercial interests and none is able to implement everything desired. The Declaration is available at http://www.legendmud.org/raph/gaming/playerrights.html.

Chapter 10

1. I used it to build an adventure for 1–64 kids where the main challenges could only be met if the kids answered algebra questions correctly. A group at the Comparative Media Studies lab at MIT is using it to replicate Williamsburg, Virginia (see chapter 5).

2. Observed August 5, 2004, at http://www.usdoj.gov/ag/trainingmanual.htm.

3. C. J. Chivers and Steven Lee Myers, "Russian Rebels Had Precise Plan," *New York Times*, September 6, 2004.

4. National Commission on Terrorist Attacks Upon the United States, 2004.

5. Reports in late 2003 indicated that the US Army had contracted with the synthetic world-builder There.com to construct worlds for training. Although nothing is public, I actually have no doubt whatsoever that security forces in many countries are looking into this technology.

Chapter 11

1. "Play Money: Diary of a Dubious Proposition" (http://www.juliandibbell.com/playmoney/2003_08_01_playmoney_archive.html#106019981622479993).

2. There are some technological reasons for restrictions on assembly: if you put too many avatars in a small space, the information-transmission load becomes too heavy and the world crashes. Nonetheless, the policies that, for this reason, impose restrictions on assembly, do not offer alternatives. They are not even written down. What happens is that if too many people flood an area, some get teleported out by the server, automatically. There simply is no assembling of crowds, period.

3. Much of gaming is military and always has been. Ancient games such as Chess and Go are about strategic territorial conflict. The concept of rendered play territory was introduced by the *Kriegsspiele* of the Prussian Army in the early nineteenth century. The first video game was *Spacewar*. Military agencies have played a significant role in advancing the technologies behind contemporary electronic gaming (Herz 1997; Lenoir 2000). Popular military game genres include historical and futuristic first-person shooters such as *Half-Life* (Sierra), global conquest games like *Civilization* (Microprose), and strategy simulators such as *Hearts of Iron* (Paradox). Beyond this, combat plays a central role in virtually all synthetic worlds. As a result of this immersion, the typical gamer today knows quite a bit about force projection. The last chapter talked about the problems this might create; when anyone can use games to train for crimes, crimes will get worse. On the other hand, a citizenry of gamers is a citizenry that is well-versed in strategy and tactics from an early age. Having a society of strategically subtle citizens is a good thing; it helps with decision-making in general and it also makes it easier for security forces to find people who can help with the technology being used by enemies. The technology that would allow a terrorist to learn how to dump pathogens into a reservoir also allows counter-terrorists to learn how to infiltrate a leadership meeting and neutralize everyone there. One of the significant things that one fails to note at first about the first-person shooter game *Counter-Strike* highlighted in the last chapter is that it makes no effort to label good guys and bad guys. The message is that technology that enables better war-fighting is, in the long run, neutral with respect to ideology. Of course, having the technology first is definitely an advantage: wars usually don't wait for the long run to determine who wins. From that perspective, it is important to ask whether the most net-savvy populations in the world will always be found in liberal democratic countries.

4. Nothing new in this. Legal scholar Mnookin, who wrote perhaps the first professional analysis of synthetic world issues (2001; paper written 1996), argued long ago that the one aspect of fantasy worlds that was most likely to keep them free from legal intervention was the fantasy/game aspect.

Chapter 12

1. To recall, the earlier metaphor used for this development is the frontier. The synthetic world of *Second Life* sells server resources to those who want them, and nobody bats an eye when they call it "land," for that's what it is. Land. Space. *Lebensraum*. The New World. Terra Nova. The idea that we're seeing a migration into a new frontier of cyberspace was first suggested by Vlahos (1998), and Jeffrey R. Cooper (2000) argues that the opening of cyberspace is nothing less than a reopening of the American frontier, an undoing of the Turner Hypothesis (1921).

2. You'll note I haven't made much reference in the book to sports or to sport video games. This is mostly for lack of space and time. Sports in the outer world could be conceived as a massively multiplayer game played out in the public sphere. And in the area of sports video games, which tend to dominate the US market in terms of sales, I have recently heard that online multiplayer role-playing is a future design possibility. In other words, your avatar would be, say, a running back, and you would go online and play that position in a team of others. I would imagine that developers would probably also code in an entire city for players to mingle in between games. In other words, when the MMORPG marries the sports game, the MMG being played in the outer world will be folded into the MMORPG in the inner world.

3. That is certainly how most media reports read: "Hey, take a look at this nerd playing a video game and the crazy stuff he is doing, selling gold for real money and stuff. Weird!"

4. I owe the term to Harvey Harrison of UCLA.

5. My anecdotal impression is that the most devoted users of MMORPGs are people who are living

day to day in an unpleasant, often cramped, situation that they cannot change, and that does not allow them to socialize very much.

6. If I could choose one part of this dream to build myself, it would be this. *Arden: The World of William Shakespeare* would be a project well worth completing.

7. I guess I've assumed from the start that this book wouldn't be placed in the same category with new-technology masterpieces like *Engines of Creation* (Drexler 1986) or *The Age of Spiritual Machines* (Kurzweil 1999). Those books, mind-opening as they are, fit into an established paradigm in which advances in technology empower humanity. We are usually happy about that, and if we are frightened, it's just the fear of the sorcerer's apprentice, an apprehension quickly overwhelmed by a narcotic burst of powerlust. In my thinking, that kind of positive reaction is also justified by evolutionary reasoning. When someone says that nanotechnology will cure cancer but perhaps unleash uncontrollable flesh-eating bots, they speak of a more powerful humanity, and we (as the most powerful species ever) have evidently been selected to be drawn into that idea. The Great Selector says such ideas ought to thrill us, and they therefore do, and we find ourselves supporting the idea, telling our friends, writing up new business plans, changing our major from English to Informatics. While I might flatter myself to think that a book about a coming age of practical virtual reality could have the same effect at some level, I also know that our need to keep play and nonplay separate will make us actively resist the idea. The apprehension generated by a widespread virtual reality technology is not the apprentice's half-fear/half-lust for a new power, it is a genuine and legitimate dread about changing what we think truly matters. The prospect that one's whole community may escape into some synthetic fantasy, whose features are yet unknown, invokes a paradigm that is more commonly associated with teleology than technology. Changes in the map of significance entail personal consequences and are much more threatening. This is the fear of the nuclear submarine captain who suddenly realizes this might not be a drill, the scientist who suddenly realizes the Universe might not be void of spirit, the married man who suddenly realizes he might not love his wife. In a flash, the meaning of even the littlest things changes. When "the real" shifts, we suddenly grasp that we might have to rethink some very basic commitments. We can't imagine how the process will end, or what we will be when it is over. We only know that we face a radical redefinition of self. The Great Selector has not molded us to resist such moments completely, because survival ultimately requires some adaptation to shifts in the color of existence. But because survival also requires some persistence and coherence in the core of our thinking, the Selector made us reluctant to rework the foundations very often. And thus the effects of a comparatively mundane technology involving live digital streaming, synchronized networks, and cartoons, may be both easier to predict yet more daunting to consider than the far more mysterious and miraculous effects of nanobots, gene-building, and reverse-engineering the brain.

8. The descriptions are also consistent with Herz's findings (2002). There is an urgent need for scholarly work on Korean society; it seems to be pointing to the future, yet there are very few sources of information about it.

9. As the book goes to press, I have just learned that there are already three (three!) peer-to-peer synthetic worlds in development.

Chapter 13

1. Observed October 2, 2004, at http://www.who.int/mental_health/media/en/382.pdf.

2. Observed October 2, 2004, at http://www.oas.samhsa.gov/nhsda/2k3nsduh/2k3Results.htm.

3. I should stress that I am not making an argument here that AI *should* replace human relationships, only that the current state of those relationships makes AI a potentially important enhancement to a

person's emotional life. As things are today, crude AI can give people happy experiences that they otherwise have trouble finding. I find it deplorable that we have become so disconnected from one another that even the rudimentary AI we currently possess can actually compete for a person's attention against real people. Indeed, if a person spends a great deal of time in synthetic worlds, interacting with the AI for the most part, and only tangentially with real people either inside or outside the world, I would view that as problematic behavior. As I argued in chapter 2, any behavior that is addictive—that damages relationships that the person in question values—qualifies for intervention. On the other hand, we have to be honest about the true state of the emotional landscape out there. There are many relationships that people would like to have but simply cannot find. Fathers have left the home; mothers need to go to work; siblings live in far-away cities; children have gone off to a university on the other side of the country; lovers get bored; and friends take jobs elsewhere. The widespread emotional blight explains why so many people can be made happier by fantasizing about relationships in books, movies, and TV shows. Now they can have interactive relationships with AI in synthetic worlds, which seems to make people even happier; there's a demonstrated tendency these days for people to substitute online activity for watching TV. Because happiness is a good thing, AI is a good thing. And the advantage of game AI is that, unlike TV, it provides these emotions in a context that's also filled with other humans: it is neither passive nor isolating. It will never be as good as the real thing, but it may be much better than what millions of people have now.

4. True, we still have churches and temples and mosques, but the ideas behind them are no longer part of the fabric of society; they do not have sufficient social power to help us share beliefs about the nature of the cosmos and the interest of the supernatural in our affairs. Each person is expected to build a personal mythology, which is very liberating, but success is often short-lived, and many do not even try.

5. I should confess that I've begun to see the drive to create meaning as the deepest, though perhaps unconscious, motivation of people in the industry that makes synthetic worlds. In Tolkien's conception (1939), those who create worlds should be thought of as "subcreators," agents of the original Creator, who has called on them to make other beings and places so that truths not otherwise accessible to the mind may yet be revealed. The maker of Middle-Earth, in other words, felt that subcreation is not a craft but a vocation, a divine calling to an extraordinarily important duty.

6. The scope of the implications first really hit me on a drive across the California desert in the summer of 2003, on the way to the Black Hat conference of computer security professionals that I mentioned in chapter 6. It was being held at a venue that was arguably a synthetic world itself, Caesar's Palace in Las Vegas. A mock trial was going to be held about the theft of some synthetic world goods, and my role was to testify as to their market value. As I mulled over my testimony, I sensed that I had come to some new realizations about this technology. Over the past 12 months, it had been slowly sinking in that these markets I had discovered were just a window into an incredibly huge, though still latent, demand for the fantasies that synthetic worlds could satisfy. And I was beginning to understand how eagerly the gaming market would meet that demand, creating a powerful vortex of forces that could pull a substantial fraction of human affairs into cyberspace within just a few generations. A few days later, I wrote on my webpage: "As these new worlds increasingly tap into that latent demand, there will certainly be policy consequences on the old Earth. Anyone who disagrees is free to do so, but they are thereby forced to defend the position that most people just love life on Earth, with its strip malls, commutes, telemarketers, and TV, and will want to stay here for the most part. I feel much more comfortable with the opposite view, that a lot of mental energy is going to migrate to cyberspace. When it does, policy will change. There's nothing any of us can do about it. Buckle your seat belts."

7. Is it useful to assign truth or falsehood to the mystical lore of a fantasy world? I don't think it is, so I leave the question open. Some people may actually come to believe in their hearts that Rodcet Nife, a deity of *EverQuest*, really is the God of Life. Others will say that that is nonsense and there are no gods,

in game or out. Another group will agree there are no gods, but will say it is more fun than not just to accept belief in them. A final group will call the whole thing blasphemy against the true God of their choice. Each of these conclusions is an act of faith. We cannot know which gods are true. Things that cannot be shown can only be believed or disbelieved; it is a choice we make. I think Tolkien would say, and I agree, that those who come to believe in his crafted gods are doing so for a reason, namely, because that has become the only route by which they can come to know a true god, which is to say, not the god that Tolkien crafted, but the One that crafted Tolkien. In fact I do believe that that was Tolkien's purpose all along, to construct a path back to certain beliefs for a world that had traveled far away from those beliefs and then seen the bridges blown up behind them. I think the idea of doing that troubled him, however; in crafting new gods, was he not committing blasphemy? I think this is why he developed his doctrine of subcreation, whereby all sincere subcreators are agents of the divine will in whatever they create. And by this doctrine his road, which he in good faith built through the fields of Middle-Earth, cannot be suspected of leading people to a bad end. But whatever the truth is, it does not matter for the ideas here. The point is that people are having a great deal of trouble believing in anything in the outer world. My argument is that if the synthetic world makes it easier to see spirit in the cosmos, it might become very large indeed.

8. At this point in talks, I often feel it is important to remind everyone listening that we represent a thin slice of humanity. If your life is one of jetting off to high-level conferences and returning thence with a new store of ideas to implement in your work and home, then, no: you are not the kind of person who might prefer a fantasy life. Of course not. You are already living someone *else's* fantasy life. What I am trying to ask here is whether the guy who mixed your latté this morning might rather prefer being a spaceship captain on the hunt for the evil Emperor Zurg, instead of a coffeehouse worker. I think he very well might. What about the lady at the dry-cleaners? That kid down the street with mediocre grades? The truck driver at the gas station; the heavyset girl you remember from junior high school; the guy who cooked your last cheeseburger; the mom/factory worker who put your PDA into its box; the isolated widow; the guy who was hired the same day as you but wound up sidetracked in a regional office that nobody ever gets promoted out of. There are a lot of people out there who aren't tech mavens, business leaders, college students, trend-spotting parents, or venture capitalists. How much would it take to convince the clerk at your local convenience store to give that up for a life as a powerful wizard? Not much. These are the people who are going to go first.

9. Many are the theorists who have proclaimed the death of objectivity and absolutism; that part of it, the theoretical part, is an old story. This is different. It is not a claim, it is an act. Actually it is an uncoordinated series of choices by which all society shifts from one equilibrium/world-view/culture into another. The shift is from an arguably constructed world into a *definitely* constructed world. For while we can claim that the Earth is actually a created thing, and that the map we have of it is the only world we know, that claim, being theoretical, can be contested. Not so the synthetic world. In the synthetic world, it is not necessary at all to claim that the map is the world, because, actually, the map *is* the world. By design, synthetic worlds are designed. There's no Nature there, no History, no Truth; all things there really are what we make them to be. They are inherently a subjective expression, a construct, and there's no need to make claims about it one way or the other. And therefore if we move en mass into synthetic worlds, we resolve the old arguments in favor of the postmodern view, by force. Whatever was the status of things on Earth, we know what they are in cyberspace: Built. From the top to the bottom, it is a construct, a simulacrum. It is as if we have refused to live any other way. If I may express things through a grotesquely inadequate allegory: The Church asked us to believe, but Science said the way to truth was to deny anything unobserved, and so we did. In the end the only truths we discovered were depressing, such as: we cannot observe ourselves sufficiently to keep our studies purged

of our own influence; we will never go anywhere; we don't matter; if we keep ourselves going for a very long time, will just be roasted alive by our own sun and that will be that. Science made us healthier and richer, but it never uncovered anything interesting enough to replace what the Church had offered. We find ourselves alone with our health and our money, but also with the sense of nothingness that Camus identified. Nothingness is dull, so we are now using Science to build a place that better suits our nature. And one of the core features we have built in to this space is that there is no distinction between Science and Faith there; we are allowed to believe in both atoms and angels, in molecules and molochs. I've long thought that the only response proper to deconstruction is construction; not because one has an agenda, but because nothingness is so boring. Just a moment's suspension of disbelief—which really means, to relax and stop resisting the internal and external evidence that myth can be real—and one can live in a world of magic again.

10. From MotherNature.com (see http://www.mothernature.com/Library/bookshelf/Books/50/116.cfm).

11. Observed September 21, 2004, at http://news.bbc.co.uk/2/hi/technology/3235852.stm.

12. Take my home discipline of economics. It is a very hardheaded field, and for that reason I imagine that most economists would be quite skeptical at first about the idea that a video game world can be just as real as our world. But I believe the discipline will eventually have to come to exactly that conclusion. The main reason is the subjective theory of value, which has been one of the core elements of economic theory for more than a century. It holds that individual preferences and costs, expressed in markets, are what determine the value of a thing; its objective characteristics are not important. Consider the diamond-water paradox: diamonds have value because the invisible hand—the collective cost-benefit calculations of everyone—has given them value. That's all there is to it. No one can object; if there is such a thing as "universally shared value," that's what it is. A diamond is worth $100, even if I would be willing to pay only $10 for it, or $1 million; if I have a diamond in my hand, I have $100, whether I think of it that way or not. And therefore, by the same logic, the Staff of Slapping in Sabert's hand is also a $100 thing if the markets say so. And we have learned on eBay that they do. Not only that, but the markets also validate the emotional effects of the Staff of Slapping, such as its propensity to be deployed as a tool for helping me, through Sabert, enjoy the synthetic world I am touring. It declares that the material consequences of all that activity are very real, and therefore any emotional consequences that derive from material effects (such as gain, loss, charity, theft) are quite legitimate. If Sabert gives Ethelbert the Staff, Ethelbert *should* feel grateful and Sabert *should* feel noble and proud and dignified. And therefore, if I am able to experience, through Sabert, moments of nobility and pride and dignity that I only rarely experience on Earth, it is only logical that I would want to spend time as Sabert rather than as Edward. It is a rejection of my role as Edward, but it is an inherently sensible rejection. I would be foolish not to do it. If the environments of play are of sounder construction than the Earth, so be it. Let's go; what are we waiting for? Thus I think the dismal queen of the social sciences will eventually take up a position on the side of the game players and media scholars, viewing synthetic worlds as genuine places that enrich ordinary life in genuine ways.

Appendix

1. This is actually not far from the usage proposed by Heim (1998, pp. 4–6), who tries to get readers to focus on *virtual reality technology* rather than nebulous concepts like "the virtual" and "the real."

REFERENCES

Aarseth, Espen. 1997. *Cybertext: Perspectives on Ergodic Literature*. Baltimore: Johns Hopkins University Press.

Anderson, Craig A., and Brad J. Bushman. 2001. "Effects of Violent Behavior, Aggressive Affect, Physiological Arousal, and Prosocial Behavior: A Meta-Analytic Review of the Scientific Literature." *Psychological Science* 12.5 (September): 353–59.

Atwood, Margaret. 2003. *Oryx and Crake*. New York: Random House.

Balkin, Jack M. 2004. "Virtual Liberty: Freedom to Design and Freedom to Play in Virtual Worlds." *Virginia Law Review* 90.8: 2043–99.

Baron, David, and John Ferejohn. 1989. "Bargaining in Legislatures." *American Political Science Review* 83: 1181–1207.

Bartle, Richard. 2003. *Designing Virtual Worlds*. Indianapolis: New Riders.

———. 2004. *The Pitfalls of Virtual Property*. New York: Themis Group. http://www.themis-group.com/uploads/Pitfalls%20of%20Virtual%20Property.pdf.

Baudrillard, Jean. 1981/1994. *Simulacra and Simulation*. Translated by Sheila Faria Glaser. Ann Arbor: University of Michigan Press.

Baumeister, Roy F., and Mark R. Leary. 1995. "The Need to Belong: Desire for Interpersonal Attachment as a Fundamental Human Motivation." *Psychological Bulletin* 117.3 (May): 497–529.

Bear Stearns. 2004. "Asian Online Gaming: Virtual Worlds, Real Cash." *Asian Equity Research* (mimeo.), January 30.

Beck, John C., and Mitchell Wade. 2004. *Got Game: How the Gamer Generation Is Reshaping Business Forever*. Cambridge, MA: Harvard Business School Press.

Becker, Gary S. 1996. *Accounting for Tastes*. Cambridge, MA: Harvard University Press.

Beezer, John. 1996. "Virtual Currencies and Virtual Worlds." http://adhostnt.adhost.com/beezer/resume/virtec.doc.

Berger, Arthur Asa. 2002. *Video Games: A Popular Culture Phenomenon*. New York: Transaction Publishing.

Bettelheim, Bruno. 1976/1985. *The Uses of Enchantment: The Meaning and Importance of Fairy Tales*. New York: Random House.

Boardman, Anthony E., David H. Greenberg, Aidan R. Vining, and David L. Weimer. 1996. *Cost-Benefit Analysis: Concepts and Practice*. Upper Saddle River, NJ: Prentice Hall.

Book, Betsy. 2004. "These Bodies Are FREE, So Get One NOW! Advertising and Branding in Social Virtual Worlds." http://ssrn.com/abstract=536422.

Borjas, George. 2001. *Heaven's Door: Immigration Policy and the American Economy*. Princeton, NJ: Princeton University Press.

Brickman, Philip. 1978. "Is It Real?" In *New Directions in Attribution Research*, vol. 2, ed. J. H. Harvey, W. Ickes, and R. F. Kidd. New York: Academic Press.

Brickman, Philip, Daniel Coates, and Ronald Janoff-Bulman. 1978. "Lottery Winners and Accident Victims: Is Happiness Relative?" *Journal of Personality and Social Psychology* 37: 917–27.

Brown, John Seely, and Paul Duguid. 2000. *The Social Life of Information*. Cambridge, MA: Harvard Business School Press.

Buchanan, James M. 1965. "An Economic Theory of Clubs." *Economica* 32: 1–14.

Buchanan, James M., and Gordon Tullock. 1962. *The Calculus of Consent*. Ann Arbor: University of Michigan Press.

Burdea, Grigore C., and Philippe Coiffet. 2003. *Virtual Reality Technology*. 2nd ed. Hoboken, NJ: John Wiley–Interscience.

Burke, Timothy. 2002. *Rubicite Breastplate Priced to Move, Cheap: How Virtual Economies Become Real Simulations* (mimeo.), June.

———. 2004. *Play of State: Sovereignty and Governance in MMOGs* (mimeo.), August.

Caillois, Roger. 1961/2001. *Man, Games, and Play*. Urbana: University of Illinois Press.

Calvert, Randall. 1995. "The Rational Choice Theory of Social Institutions: Cooperation, Coordination, and Communication." In *Modern Political Economy: Old Topics, New Directions*, ed. J. Banks and E. Hanushek. Cambridge: Cambridge University Press.

Campbell, Joseph. 1949/1972. *The Hero with a Thousand Faces*. Princeton, NJ: Princeton University Press.

Camus, Albert. 1955/1991. *The Myth of Sisyphus and Other Essays*. Translated by Justin O'Brien. New York: Vintage Books.

Cassell, Justine, and Henry Jenkins, eds. 1998. *From Barbie to Mortal Kombat: Gender in Computer Games*. Cambridge, MA: MIT Press.

Castronova, Edward. 2001. "Virtual Worlds: A First-Hand Account of Market and Society on the Cyberian Frontier." CESifo Working Paper 618, December.

———. 2003a. "On Virtual Economies." *Game Studies* 3.2 (December). http://www.gamestudies.org/0302/castronova/.

———. 2003b. "Theory of the Avatar." CESifo Working Paper 863, February.

———. 2004. "Achievement Bias in the Evolution of Preferences." *Journal of Bioeconomics* 6.2: 195–227.

———. 2005. "The Right to Play." *New York Law School Review* 49.1: 185–211.

Cheok, Adrian David, Siew Wan Fong, Kok Hwee Goh, Xubo Yang, Wei Liu, Farzam Farzbiz. 2003. "Human Pacman: A Sensing-based Mobile Entertainment System with Ubiquitous Computing and Tangible Interaction." Presented at NetGames 2003, Redwood City, California, May 23.

Cooper, Jeffrey R. 2000. "The CyberFrontier and America at the Turn of the 21st Century: Reopening Frederick Jackson Turner's Frontier." *First Monday* 5.7. http://www.firstmonday.dk/issues/issue5_7/cooper/index.html.

Cornes, Richard, and Todd Sandler. 1996. *The Theory of Externalities, Public Goods, and Club Goods*. 2nd ed. Cambridge: Cambridge University Press.

Curtis, Elizabeth, Roy Gardner, and Christopher J. Waller. 2004. "Dollarization in the Ukraine: 1991 to the Present." Prepared for presentation at the Fordham/CEPR New York City Conference "Euro and Dollarization: Forms of Monetary Union in Integrating Unions."

Curtis, Pavel. 1997. "Mudding: Social Phenomena in Text-Based Virtual Reality." In *Culture of the Internet*, ed. Sara Kiesler, 121–42. Mahwah, NJ: Lawrence Erlbaum Associates.

Dahl, Robert A. 1991. *Democracy and Its Critics*. New Haven, CT: Yale University Press.

DFC Intelligence. 2003. *Challenges and Opportunities in the Online Game Market*. San Diego, CA: DFC Intelligence, June.

———. 2004a. *The Online Game Market Heats Up*. San Diego, CA: DFC Intelligence, June.

———. 2004b. *Still Substantial Growth Potential for MMOG Games*. San Diego, CA: DFC Intelligence, August.

Dibbell, Julian. 1999. *My Tiny Life: Crime and Passion in a Virtual World*. New York: Owl Books.

Diener, Ed, and Robert Biswas-Diener. 2002. "Will Money Increase Subjective Well-Being?" *Social Indicators Research* 57.2 (February): 119–69.

Drexler, Eric. 1986. *Engines of Creation*. New York: Anchor.

Ducheneaut, Nicolas, and Robert J. Moore. 2004. "Gaining More Than Experience Points: Learning Behavior in Massively Multiplayer Computer Games." Palo Alto Research Center (PARC).

Duk-kun, Byun. 2003. "Police Say Game Sites Hotbed of Cyber-Crime." *Korea Times*, August 9. http://times.hankooki.com/lpage/nation/200308/kt2003080718330611980.htm.

Easterlin, Richard A. 2001. "Income and Happiness: Towards a Unified Theory." *Economic Journal* 111.473 (July): 465–84.

Folbre, Nancy. 2001. *The Invisible Heart: Economics and Family Values*. New York: New Press.

Fox, Fennec. 2002. "Mother Blames 'EverQuest' for Son's Suicide." *CNN.com*, April 5. http://www.cnn.com/2002/TECH/industry/04/05/everquest.suicide.idg.

Frey, Bruno S., and Alois Stutzer. 2001. *Happiness and Economics: How the Economy and Institutions Affect Human Well-Being*. Princeton, NJ: Princeton University Press.

Fulford, Benjamin. 2003. "Korea's Weird Wired World." *Forbes.com*, July 21. http://www.forbes.com/technology/free_forbes/2003/0721/092.html.

Gee, James Paul. 2003. *What Video Games Have to Teach Us about Learning and Literacy*. New York: Palgrave Macmillan.

Green, C. Shawn, and Daphne Bavelier. 2003. "Action Video Game Modifies Visual Selective Attention." *Nature* 423 (May): 534–37.

Greenfield, David N. 1999. *Virtual Addiction: Help for Netheads, Cyberfreaks, and Those Who Love Them*. New York: New Harbinger Publications.

Griffiths, Mark D. 1998. "Violent Video Games and Aggression: A Review of the Literature." *Aggression and Violent Behavior* 4: 203–12.

Griffiths, Mark D., Mark N. O. Davies, and Darren Chappell. 2003. "Breaking the Stereotype: The Case of Online Gaming." *Cyberpsychology and Behavior* 6.1: 81–91.

———. 2004. "Demographic Factors and Playing Variables in Online Videogames" (mimeo.). Nottingham Trent University.

Grossman, David, and Gloria DeGaetano. 1999. *Stop Teaching Our Kids to Kill: A Call to Action against TV, Movie, and Video Game Violence*. New York: Random House.

Heim, Michael. 1998. *Virtual Realism*. New York: Oxford University Press.

Heins, Marjorie. 2003. "Introduction to Brief *Amici Curiae* of Thirty-Three Media Scholars in St. Louis Videogames Case." *Hofstra Law Review* 31.2: 419–58.

Herz, J. C. 1997. *Joystick Nation: How Videogames Ate Our Quarters, Won Our Hearts, and Rewired Our Minds*. Boston: Little, Brown.

———. 2002. "The Bandwidth Capital of the World." *Wired* 10.08 (August).

Hirschman, Albert O. 1970. *Exit, Voice, and Loyalty: Responses to Decline in Firms, Organizations, and States*. Cambridge, MA: Harvard University Press.

Huizinga, Johan. 1938/1950. *Homo Ludens: A Study of the Play Element of Culture*. Boston: Beacon Press.

Jakobsson, Mikael, and T. L. Taylor. 2003. "The 'Sopranos' Meets 'EverQuest': Social Networking in Massively Multiplayer Online Games." Proceedings of MelbourneDAC, the 5th International Digital Arts and Culture Conference. http://hypertext.rmit.edu.au/dac/papers/Jakobsson.pdf.

Jenkins, Peter S. 2004. "The Virtual World as a Company Town—Freedom of Speech in Massively Multiplayer On-Line Role Playing Games." *Journal of Internet Law* 8.1 (July).

Jones, Gerard. 2002. *Killing Monsters: Why Children Need Fantasy, Super Heroes, and Make-Believe Violence.* New York: Basic Books.

Joy, Bill. 2000. "Why the Future Doesn't Need Us." *Wired* 8.04 (April).

JP Morgan. 2004. "China Internet Sector." Asia Pacific Equity Research (mimeo.). May 24.

Juul, Jesper. 2001. "Games Telling Stories? A Brief Note on Games and Narratives." *Game Studies* 1.1 (July). http://www.gamestudies.org/0101/juul-gts/.

Kahneman, Daniel, Ed Diener, and Norbert Schwarz. 1998. *Well-Being: The Foundations of Hedonic Psychology.* New York: Russell Sage.

Kent, Steven L. 2001. *The Ultimate History of Video Games: From Pong to Pokémon and Beyond—The Story Behind the Craze That Touched Our Lives and Changed the World.* New York: Prima Publishing.

Kerr, Orin S. 2003. "The Problem of Perspective in Internet Law." *Georgetown Law Journal* 91.2: 357–405.

King, Brad, and John Borland. 2003. *Dungeons and Dreamers: The Rise of Computer Game Culture from Geek to Chic.* New York: McGraw-Hill.

Kolbert, Elizabeth. 2001. "Pimps and Dragons." *New Yorker*, May 28.

Kollock, Peter. 1996. "Design Principles for Online Communities." Presented at the Harvard Conference on the Internet and Society. www.sscnet.ucla.edu/soc/faculty/kollock/papers/ design.htm.

———. 1999a. "The Economies of Online Cooperation: Gifts and Public Goods in Cyberspace." In Smith and Kollock 1999, 220–39.

———. 1999b. "The Production of Trust in Online Markets." In *Advances in Group Processes*, vol. 16, ed. E. J. Lawler, M. Macy, S. Thye, and H. A. Walker. Greenwich, CT: JAI Press.

Koster, Raph. N.d. "The Laws of Online World Design." http://www.legendmud.org/raph/gaming/ laws.html.

Kurzweil, Ray. 1999. *The Age of Spiritual Machines: When Computers Exceed Human Intelligence.* New York: Viking Press.

Kushner, David. 2003. *Masters of Doom: How Two Guys Created an Empire and Transformed Pop Culture.* New York: Random House.

Kwan-Min, Lee, and Wei Peng. 2004. "Effects of Playing Computer/Video Games." *Journal of Media Economics and Culture* 2.3: 7–52.

Laird, John E., and Michael Van Lent. 2000. "Human-level AI's Killer Application: Interactive Computer Games." Presented at National Conference on Artificial Intelligence. August 2. http://ai.eecs.umich.edu/ people/laird/papers/AAAI-00.pdf.

Lang, Annie. 2004. *Motivated Cognition (LC4MP): The Influence of Appetitive and Aversive Activation on the Processing of Video Games* (mimeo.). Indiana University.

Lastowka, F. Gregory, and Dan Hunter. 2004. "The Laws of the Virtual Worlds." *California Law Review* 92.1: 1–74.

———. 2005. "Virtual Crime." *New York Law School Review* 49.1: 293–317.

Laurel, Brenda. 1993. *Computers as Theatre.* 2nd ed. New York: Addison-Wesley.

Lenoir, Timothy. 2000. "All but War Is Simulation: The Military Entertainment Complex." *Configurations* 8: 238–335.

Lessig, Lawrence. 1999. *Code and Other Laws of Cyberspace.* New York: Basic Books.

———. 2004. "Insanely Destructive Devices." *Wired* 12.04 (April).

Lévy, Pierre. 1998. *Becoming Virtual: Reality in the Digital Age.* Translated by Robert Bononno. New York: Plenum.

Ludlow, Peter, ed. 2001. *Crypto Anarchy, Cyberstates, and Pirate Utopias.* Cambridge, MA: MIT Press.

MacInnes, Ian. 2002. "Business Models for Interactive Entertainment Communities." International Telecommunications Society Biennial Conference, Seoul, South Korea.

McSwegin, Patricia J., Cynthia Pemberton, and Nancy O'Banion. 1988. "The Effects of Controlled Videogame Playing on the Eye-Hand Coordination and Reaction Time of Children." *Advances in Motor Development Research* 2: 97–102.

Metrick, Andrew. 1995. "A Natural Experiment in Jeopardy!" *American Economic Review* 85.1 (March): 240–53.

Mitchell, Keith, Duncan McCaffery, George Metaxas, and Joe Finney. 2003. "Six in the City: Introducing Real Tournament—A Mobile IPv6 Based Context-Aware Multiplayer Game." Presented at Net-Games 2003, Redwood City, California, May 23.

Mnookin, Jennifer L. 2001. "Virtual(ly) Law: The Emergence of Law in an On-Line Community." In *Crypto Anarchy, Cyberstates, and Pirate Utopias*, ed. Peter Ludlow, 245–302. Cambridge, MA: MIT Press.

Moravec, Hans P. 1999. *Robot: Mere Machine to Transcendent Mind.* New York: Oxford University Press.

Morningstar, Chip, and F. Randall Farmer. 1990. "The Lessons of Lucasfilm's Habitat." In *Cyberspace: First Steps*, ed. Michael Benedikt, 273–301. Cambridge, MA: MIT Press.

Mueller, Milton L. 2002. *Ruling the Root: Internet Governance and the Taming of Cyberspace.* Cambridge, MA: MIT Press.

Mulligan, Jessica, and Bridgette Patrovsky. 2003. *Developing Online Games: An Insider's Guide.* Indianapolis: New Riders.

Murray, Janet. 1997. *Hamlet on the Holodeck.* New York: Free Press.

Nash, John F. 1950. "Equilibrium Points in N-Person Games." *Proceedings of the National Academy of Sciences.*

National Academies. 2002. *Preparing for the Revolution: Information Technology and the Future of the Research University.* Washington, DC: National Academies Press.

Nozick, Robert. 1974. *Anarchy, State, and Utopia.* New York: Basic Books.

Ondrejka, Cory R. 2004. "Living on the Edge: Digital Worlds Which Embrace the Real World." June 5. http://ssrn.com/abstract=555661.

Ostrom, Elinor, Roy Gardner, and James Walker. 1994. *Rules, Games, and Common-Pool Resources.* Ann Arbor: University of Michigan Press.

Owens, Stephanie, and Francis Steen. 2000. "Implicit Pedagogy: From Chase Play to Collaborative Worldmaking." http://www.anth.ucsb.edu/projects/esm/Owens_Steen2000.html.

Pesce, Mark. 2000. *The Playful World: How Technology Is Transforming Our Imagination.* New York: Ballantine Books.

Peterson, Jordan. 1999. *Maps of Meaning: The Architecture of Belief.* New York: Routledge.

Pew Internet and American Life Project. 2003. *Let the Games Begin: Gaming Technology and Entertainment among College Students.* Washington, DC.

Piaget, Jean. 1945/1962. *Play, Dreams, and Imitation in Childhood.* Translated by C. Gattegno and F. M. Hodgson. New York: Norton.

Pierson, Paul. 1994. *Dismantling the Welfare State? Reagan, Thatcher, and the Politics of Retrenchment.* Cambridge: Cambridge University Press.

Poole, Steven. 2000. *Trigger Happy: Videogames and the Entertainment Revolution.* New York: Arcade Publishing.

Posner, Richard A. 2004. *Catastrophe: Risk and Response.* Oxford: Oxford University Press.

Prensky, Marc. 2000. *Digital Game-Based Learning.* New York: McGraw-Hill.

Putnam, Robert. 1995. "Bowling Alone: America's Declining Social Capital." *Journal of Democracy* 6.1 (January): 65–78.

Reeves, Byron, and Clifford Nass. 1996. *The Media Equation: How People Treat Computers, Television, and New Media Like Real People and Places.* Stanford, CA: CSLI Publications.

Reid, Elizabeth. 1999. "Hierarchy and Power: Social Control in Cyberspace." In Smith and Kollock 1999, 107–33.

Reynolds, Ren. 2002. "Playing a 'Good' Game: A Philosophical Approach to Understanding the Morality of Games." http://www.idga.org/articles/rreynolds_ethics.php.

Rheingold, Howard. 1991. *Virtual Reality: The Revolutionary Technology of Computer-Generated Artificial Worlds—And How It Promises to Transform Society.* New York: Simon and Schuster.

———. 1994. *The Virtual Community: Homesteading on the Electronic Frontier.* New York: Perennial.

———. 2002. *Smart Mobs: The Next Social Revolution.* New York: Perseus Books.

Rollings, Andrew, and Ernest Adams. 2003. *On Game Design.* Indianapolis: New Riders.

Rose, Frank. 2004. "The Lost Boys." *Wired* 12.08 (August).

Rushkoff, Douglas. 1996. *Playing the Future: How Kids' Culture Can Teach Us to Thrive in an Age of Chaos.* New York: HarperCollins.

Russell, Stuart J., and Peter Norvig. 2003. *Artificial Intelligence: A Modern Approach.* 2nd ed. Upper Saddle River, NJ: Prentice Hall.

Schelling, Thomas. 1960/1980. *The Strategy of Conflict.* Cambridge, MA: Harvard University Press.

Schumpeter, Joseph A. 1945/1984. *Capitalism, Socialism, and Democracy.* New York: Perennial Press.

Scitovsky, Tibor. 1976. *The Joyless Economy.* Oxford: Oxford University Press.

Searle, John R. 1997. *The Mystery of Consciousness.* New York: New York Review of Books.

Shapiro, Carl, and Hal R. Varian. 1998. *Information Rules: A Strategic Guide to the Network Economy.* Cambridge, MA: Harvard Business School Press.

Sherman, William R., and Alan B. Craig. 2002. *Understanding Virtual Reality: Interface, Application, and Design.* New York: Morgan Kaufman.

Simon, Herbert A., and Jonathan Schaeffer. 1992. "The Game of Chess." In *Handbook of Game Theory with Economic Applications,* ed. Robert J. Aumann and Sergiu Hart, 1–17. Amsterdam: Elsevier.

Simpson, Zachary Booth. 1999. "The In-Game Economics of *Ultima Online.*" www.mine-control.com/zack/uoecon/uoecon.html.

Smith, Anna Duval. 1999. "Problems of Conflict Management in Virtual Communities." In Smith and Kollock 1999, 134–66.

Smith, Marc A., and Peter Kollock, eds. 1999. *Communities in Cyberspace.* New York: Routledge.

Squire, Kurt, and Henry Jenkins. 2004. "Harnessing the Power of Games in Education." *Insight* 3.1: 5–33.

Starr, Paul. 1994. "Seductions of Sim: Policy as a Simulation Game." *American Prospect* 17: 19–29.

Steinkuehler, Constance A. 2004. "Learning in Massively Multiplayer Online Role-Playing Games." In *Proceedings of the Sixth International Conference of the Learning Sciences,* ed. Y. B. Kafai, W. A. Sandoval, N. Enyedy, A. S. Nixon, and F. Herrera, 521–28. Mahwah, NJ: Erlbaum.

Stephenson, Neal. 1992. *Snow Crash.* New York: Bantam.

Sutton-Smith, Brian. 1998. *The Ambiguity of Play.* Cambridge, MA: Harvard University Press.

Taylor, T. L. 2002. "Living Digitally: Embodiment in Virtual Worlds." In *The Social Life of Avatars,* ed. Ralph Schroeder. Berlin: Springer Verlag.

Tiebout, Charles. 1956. "A Pure Theory of Local Expenditure." *Journal of Political Economy* 64: 416–24.

Tolkien, J. R. R. 1939. "On Fairy-Stories." Andrew Lang Lecture, University of St. Andrews, March 8.

Turkle, Sherry. 1995. *Life on the Screen: Identity in the Age of the Internet.* New York: Simon and Schuster.

Turner, Frederick Jackson. 1921. *The Frontier in American History.* New York: Henry Holt.

Vinge, Vernor. 1981/2001. *True Names.* In Vernor Vinge, *True Names and the Opening of the Cyberspace Frontier,* ed. James Frenkel. New York: Tor Books.

Vlahos, Michael. 1998. "Entering the Infosphere." *Journal of International Affairs* 51.2 (Spring): 497–524.

von Neumann, John, and Oskar Morgenstern. 1944/1980. *Theory of Games and Economic Behavior.* Princeton, NJ: Princeton University Press.

Walker, John, 1988. "Through the Looking Glass." http://www.fourmilab.ch/autofile/www/chapter2_69.html.

Webb, Cynthia L. 2003. "The Big Brother Dilemma." *Washington Post*, February 12. http://www.washingtonpost.com/wp-dyn/articles/A61656-2003Feb12.html.

Williams, Dmitri. 2003. "Trouble in River City: The Social Life of Video Games." PhD diss., University of Michigan.

Wolf, Mark J. P., ed. 2002. *The Medium of the Video Game.* Austin: University of Texas Press.

Yee, Nicholas. 2002. *Ariadne—Understanding MMORPG Addiction.* October. http://www.nickyee.com/hub/addiction/home.html.

Young, Kimberly S. 1998. *Caught in the Net: How to Recognize the Signs of Internet Addiction—And a Winning Strategy for Recovery.* New York: Wiley.

I N D E X

Note: The letter *f* following a page number denotes a figure and the letter *t* following a page number denotes a table.

immersion technology, 80, 86–90, 98, 299n8; artificial intelligence in, 95, 96; invention of, 290–92; lifestyle uses of, 255; of traditional virtual reality, 288, 289

imports, 190, 191, 193–94, 195, 199–200, 202, 304n10

income. *See* earnings; wage

inequality. *See* status

inflation, 195–200, 202–3

infosphere, 10

instancing, 119

instant messaging: in culture of gaming, 159; embedded in synthetic worlds, 135; *EverQuest* system of, 91; between players outside of game, 91, 122; virtual reality backdrop for, 54

Institute for Creative Technologies, 254

institutional theory, 100–101, 207

institutions, economic, 174

institutions of synthetic worlds: cooperation in, 107, 115–17, 300n3; designer/user conflicts about, 101–2, 151–56, 300n3; design tools for creation of, 104–7; evolution of, 101–2; governance and, 210–13, 216; interactions with offline world, 100, 102, 121–24; messaging and, 107, 117–18; personalized content and, 107, 118–21; risk and danger in, 107, 114–15, 179, 200–201; status in, 107, 113–14, 115, 119–20, 152; taxonomy of, 103–4. *See also* advancement system; roles; rules

Interactive Digital Software Association, 55

interactivity, 80, 81

Internet access, high-speed: cost of, 52; future population segment without, 260; growth of online gaming and, 53, 66, 68, 86, 131; Korean saturation of, 266

Internet Gaming Entertainment Ltd. (IGE), 164, 165, 171, 250

investment, 174, 188. *See also* avatar capital; human capital; physical capital

invisible hand, 310n12

Jacobs, Mark, 127

Jakobsson, Mikael, 57, 63, 210

Janoff-Bulman, Ronald, 76

Japan, 127, 237

Jenkins, Henry, 57, 296n1

Jenkins, Peter S., 239

Jennings, Scott, 300n3

Jeopardy! 16

Jones, Gerard, 259, 275, 298n10

Joy, Bill, 18, 279

Jung, Carl, 132

Jungian analysis, 109

Juul, Jesper, 57

Kahneman, Daniel, 176

Kantian ethics, 175

karma system, 305n4

Kasavin, Greg, 76, 298n20

Kazaa, 240

Kent, Steven L., 295n6, 297n4

Kerr, Orin S., 156, 236

killing: faction system and, 211, 214, 217; in player versus player combat, 209, 212, 215, 305nn3–4. *See also* death of avatar; hunting of mobs

King, Brad, 56, 290, 291

Kingmaker, 14

KKK (Ku Klux Klan), 228

Kolbert, Elizabeth, 153

Kollock, Peter, 116, 149, 205

Korea: online gaming firms in, 66, 126, 141; PC Baangs in, 159; police intervention in game-related crimes, 237, 238, 296n8; social effects of online gaming in, 265–66, 277–78, 307n8; television coverage of gaming, 123; users of synthetic worlds in, 52–53, 64

Koster, Raph, 127, 157, 176, 182, 216–17, 298n1, 299n12, 300n2, 305n7

Kurzweil, Ray, 9, 17–18, 278–79, 307n7

Kushner, David, 55, 290, 291

Kwan-Min, Lee, 63

labor: marginal product of, 186; migration to synthetic worlds, 260; production function and, 186, 187

labor markets, 150–51, 301n7, 302n8, 304n8; fairness issues and, 153–55, 302n10; production in, 186–88

labor supply, 174; macroing and, 181

Laird, John E., 93, 299n11

LambdaMOO, 156, 217

Lang, Annie, 73

language, influence of games on, 123

Lastowka, F. Gregory, 46, 57, 156, 238, 260, 297n2

Laurel, Brenda, 10, 267, 287, 288, 289, 292, 293

law: absence of, in MMORPGs, 116; blurring of real and virtual, 148, 156–58, 237–38, 253–54, 302nn12–14; in cyberspace, 205, 304n1; diversity in synthetic worlds and, 261; faction systems and, 212; legal scholarship on virtual worlds, 57; licensing agreement and, 30–31, 208; music-sharing technology and, 240; property rights for virtual property, 30, 157, 165, 260–61; value of virtual items and, 46, 171; against video game sales, 64, 277; virtual-item trading and, 157, 163, 165, 166, 261. *See also* crime; governance in synthetic worlds

Law of Demand, 186

Law of Diminishing Marginal Productivity, 187–88